THE JOKER

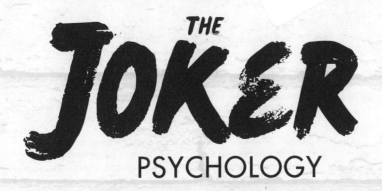

PSYCHOLOGY

EVIL CLOWNS AND THE WOMEN WHO LOVE THEM

EDITED BY TRAVIS LANGLEY

FOREWORD BY MICHAEL USLAN

STERLING

New York

STERLING
New York

An Imprint of Sterling Publishing, Co., Inc.
1166 Avenue of the Americas
New York, NY 10016

ISBN 978-1-4549-3542-1

Distributed in Canada by Sterling Publishing Co., Inc.
c/o Canadian Manda Group, 664 Annette Street
Toronto, Ontario M6S 2C8, Canada
Distributed in the United Kingdom by GMC Distribution Services
Castle Place, 166 High Street, Lewes, East Sussex BN7 1XU, England
Distributed in Australia by NewSouth Books
University of New South Wales, Sydney, NSW 2052, Australia

For information about custom editions, special sales, and premium and
corporate purchases, please contact Sterling Special Sales at 800-805-5489
or specialsales@sterlingpublishing.com.

Manufactured in Canada

2 4 6 8 10 9 7 5 3 1

sterlingpublishing.com

Cover design by David Ter-Avanesyan
Interior design by Nancy Singer

Image Credits:
TCD/Prod.DB/Alamy: 44
Depositphotos.com: ©baavli: throughout (coffee rings); ©goldenshrimp: 56;
©grgroupstock: throughout (jack in the box); ©Tawng: 247; ©vzphoto: 179; ©zzve: 83
Freepik: throughout (brick wall)
Getty Images: DigitalVision Vectors: ©chipstudio: 286; ©CSA-Archive: 163;
©DimaChe: throughout (face cards); iStock/Getty Images Plus: ©ChrisGorgio: 147;
©firc87: 11; ©ihorzigor: 127; ©Naddiya: 197; ©nickylarson974: 106; ©rizal999: 270;
Vetta: ©CSA Images: 220
Courtesy Jens Robinson: 45
Shutterstock.com: AlexandrBognat: throughout
(torn paper); JRMurray76: 28; Sudowoodo: 93
Photos of writers courtesy of authors

Dedication

to Michael Uslan,
Doctor of Comic Books

and in memory of
Jerry Robinson and Adam West

with special thanks
to Jerry, Bill, and Bob for creating the clown

Contents

ACKNOWLEDGMENTS:
Accomplices

TRAVIS LANGLEY

AT THE TIME Michael Uslan volunteered to write this book's foreword, he didn't know I'd always planned to dedicate this book to him. As an educator, historian, author, and filmmaker experienced in taking on one Goliath after another, Michael opened the path that made these books possible. In order to teach the first university-accredited course seriously studying comic books, Uslan as an undergraduate stood before a skeptical dean, who had no intention of approving such a class, and asked the dean to recount the story of Moses and the origin of Superman. The dean described each until the parallel between the two struck him. He stopped in midsentence, stared at young Mike for what felt like an eternity, and said, "Mr. Uslan, your course is accredited."[1] Michael's subsequent accomplishments would include writing the adventures of some of our most enduring heroes (Batman, Archie, the Lone Ranger). No one alive writes *The Shadow* better. He may be best known for bringing Gotham City's hero to the big screen as executive producer of every Batman movie since 1989—originally another giant battle because studio executives then had trouble believing audiences would want a serious Dark Knight. I highly recommend his amazing autobiography, *The Boy Who Loved Batman*.[2] Monmouth University has honored Michael Uslan's body of work by making him the first Doctor of Comic Books. Without him teaching that innovative class once upon a time and without his Batman movie franchise to lead the way for today's motion pictures, I couldn't have written the first book on the psychology of a specific superhero, *Batman and Psychology: A Dark and Stormy Knight*, for which Michael wrote a foreword. Without that first book, my thirteenth—*The Joker Psychology: Evil Clowns and the Women Who Love Them*—would not be here today, bookended by a second Uslan foreword. Without him and Denny O'Neil helping me on that first book, we might not have had people such as Stan Lee, Katy Manning, and John Russo join us later on.

I first met Michael Uslan, along with some other remarkable folks, through the Comics Arts Conference. Held at both San Diego Comic-Con and WonderCon, the CAC is a scholarly conference-within-the-convention which Peter Coogan and Randy Duncan founded, Kathleen McClancy now chairs, and I now help organize. When CAC accepted psychologist Robin Rosenberg's topic for a presentation, she asked if we could enlist other panelists to discuss the Joker's psychopathy. Coogan said to invite Michael Uslan and asked if I'd like to help, "as if I had to ask." I recruited Jerry Robinson, Steve Englehart, and Adam West: (1) Jerry created/co-created the Joker; (2) Steve (who had to join us by phone) wrote "The Laughing Fish," a story cited as evidence that the Joker is genuinely insane; and (3) Adam, of course, played Batman in the 1966–1968 TV series. Skipping a *Family Guy* panel where he could have talked about his then-current work, Adam instead joined us so he could talk about his show's Joker, the late Cesar Romero, and because he wanted to meet Jerry. Adam, Jerry, and Michael each later remarked on what a wonderful experience and historic moment that was. Nina West Tooley and James Tooley helped make that happen. The last time I saw Adam, he greeted me with a surprised smile. "Travis! How the hell are ya, doc?" That's when I had the honor of introducing him to Batman co-creator Bill Finger's only living descendants: Bill's granddaughter Athena and her son Benjamin.

Marc Tyler Nobleman helped the world discover Bill Finger.[3] While Bill's importance had been an open secret in the comic book industry and throughout much of fandom, Marc and many others cultivated the climate that encouraged the powers that be to give Bill his long-overdue official recognition. People who knew Bill personally—such as Charles Sinclair, Irwin Hasen, Murphy Anderson, and Lyn Simmons, all of whom are gone now, plus a few others still with us—helped us learn more. Bob Kane's own biographer, Thomas Andrae,[4] remains a big Bill booster and a treasure trove of information. Playwrights Leonard Schwartz and Roberto Williams helped get the word out through their productions, respectively, *Co-Creator* and *Fathers of the Dark Knight*. It was my privilege and pleasure to assist where I could in the efforts to get Finger co-creator credit,[5] but none of us got Bill his byline. That achievement belongs to Athena Finger who, aided by her sister/copyright attorney Alethia Mariotta, made the request that finally landed Bill his official co-creator credit. No matter how many times you might read that there was a lawsuit, it never reached that point. Athena requested, discussion ensued over details, and Warner granted the request. Learn more about it from the Hulu documentary *Batman & Bill*.[6] Athena's fellow granddaughters of the Golden Age—Christie Marston, Chelle Mayer, Jacque Nodell, and Nicky Wheeler-Nicholson—spread the word about their forebears' roles as comics pioneers, and Jens Robinson still discusses his father Jerry with me.

So many people who bring the fantastic heroes to life have shared their knowledge and experience in our convention panels, interviews, and personal conversations. Comics pros include Neal Adams, Allen Bellman, Greg Capullo, Victor Dandridge Jr., Paul Dini, Steve Englehart, Mark Evanier, Danny Fingeroth, Joe Giella, Mike Gold, Devin Grayson, Dean Haspiel, Phil Jimenez, Chip Kidd, Stan Lee, Paul Levitz, Jonathan Maberry, Molly Mahan, Andy Mangels, Hannah Means-Shannon, Bryan Q. Miller, Dennis O'Neil, Trina Robbins, Jim Salicrup, Bob Schreck, Kevin Smith, J. Michael Straczynski, J. J. Sedelmaier, Brandon Seifert, Gail Simone, Scott Snyder, Gabe Soria, Joe Staton, Maggie Thompson, Peter J. Tomasi, Marguerite Van Cook, Fred Van Lente, Renee Witterstaetter, Marv Wolfman. While all those creators deserve individual spotlights, I must make special mention of now-departed Wolverine/Swamp Thing/ Lucius Fox co-creator Len Wein, who had become my go-to guy at conventions and whom we all greatly miss.

Screenwriters who joined us on convention panels include Christine Boylan, Jonathan Butler, Adam Glass (who also wrote Harley's New 52 origin and interviewed for this book), and Deric A. Hughes, with a nod to *Batman* scripter Sam Hamm for answering an important question. Actors who have discussed heroes and villains with us include Dino Andrade, Lesley-Ann Brandt, Dean Cain, Kevin Conroy, Carmine Downey, Lou Ferrigno, Anthony Michael Hall, Maurice LaMarche, Katrina Law, Loren Lester, Tiny Lister, Jason Marsden, Lee Meriwether, Brandon Routh, Burt Ward. (Thanks again to Adam: Batman introduced me to Robin.) Other panel experts include Will Brooker, Mike Bruen, Eric Bruce, Genese Davis, Cilla Hagle, Alan Kistler, Rick Klaw, Andrea Letamendi, Ryan

Litsey, Mike Madrid, William Patrick Murphy, Jill Pantozzi, Rob Peaslee, Alan J. Porter, Vasilis Pozios, Brad Ricca, Derek Royal, Peter Sanderson, Arlen Schumer, Barrett Tribe, Jamie Walton, Rob Weiner, Marc D. White, Mara Whiteside Wood, Kyle Williamson, E. Paul Zehr. Documentary filmmakers who provided opportunities to express my thoughts on comic book characters include Don Argott, Brett Culp, Scott Devine, Sheena Joyce, J. M. Kenny, Todd Kent, Rick Ramirez, Morgan Spurlock.

Because I met the majority of our contributing writers and most people named in these acknowledgments through conventions, I owe great debts to those who help us at San Diego Comic-Con International (Eddie Ibrahim, Gary Sassaman, Cathy Dalton, Jackie Estrada, Sue Lord, Adam Neese, Amy Ramirez, Chris Sturhann), the Hero Round Table (Matt Langdon), ComiConway (Jimmy Dyer, Kara Rimmer Dyer), and many Wizard World conventions over the years. It was my son Nicholas Langley whose undergraduate comics research under Matt Smith led me to my first Comics Arts Conference. Danny Fingeroth, who has often led or joined convention panels with me, wrote the book *Superman on the Couch* which first inspired me to write this kind of book.

For years, people asked if I would ever do a book on the Joker. We don't know what goes on inside his head or his "real" history, and for storytelling purposes, that's best. For this kind of book, though, that makes analysis so speculative that I felt like something key would be missing. The solution came one day during lunch with Sterling Publishing editor Kate Zimmermann and publicist Blanca Oliviery. When I mentioned my concerns about writing a well-balanced Joker book, Blanca asked, "What if you make it about the Joker and Harley?" And there it was. Even with the greater emphasis on Mister J., Harley Quinn gives us someone we can analyze with greater certainty and guarded optimism. The book's subtitle also occurred to me then. Whereas *The Joker and Harley Quinn Psychology* would have been a mouthful of a main title, the subtitle *Evil Clowns and the Women Who Love Them* could show that it covers her, too. The moral to this story: Good things happen when people buy me lunch.

At Sterling Publishing, a whole team of publicists promote these projects in addition to Blanca, such as Sari Lampert and Lauren Tambini. Editor Kate Zimmermann is wonderful to work with. My original editor, Connie Santisteban, continues to help as consultant and friend. Thanks also to Toula Ballas, Michael Cea, and cover artist David Ter-Avanesyan. My literary agent, Evan Gregory of the Ethan Ellenberg Literary Agency, stays on top of things and fights battles on my behalf. My editorial assistants Jenna Busch and Eric D. Wesselmann have provided a range of support.

For putting up with us when we get lost in the alleys of Gotham and the halls of Arkham Asylum, we thank Josh Apryasz, Adam Griffis, Beverly Hicks, Justin Hinz, Louis Orr, Matt Upholz, Amanda Wesselmann, and more. No words are sufficient to show my appreciation and love for my wife, Rebecca M. Langley, who has been with me since long before these books began. My mother, Lynda M. Langley, read comic books to me when I was little, which motivated me to learn to read, and my dad, Travis Sr., found the baby book page that I mention in this book's introduction. We thank FirstGlance Films' Bill Ostroff and others who took our author photos. For their mentorship and guidance, we thank Ed O'Neal, Carl Auerbach, Chad Brinkley, Rick DeMier, Bob Hanske, Jeff Haun, Aubrey Immelman, Norm Kerbel, Craig Lareau, Ralph McKenna, Mike Miner, Patrick O'Connor, Lea Ann Preston, and Chris Spatz. Educators who have communicated with me about relevant classes include LaDonna Curtis, Kristie DeRuiter, Casey Harris, Jeremy Larance, Steven Leyva, and the late Simon Lopata, Will Grove, and Susan Morrow.

Where I teach at Henderson State University, administrators such as President Glendell Jones, Provost Steve Adkison, and Dean Angela Boswell value creative ways of teaching. Librarian Lea Ann Alexander and staff keep our outstanding graphic novel reading room well stocked. Latrena Beasley, Carolyn Hatley, Sandra D. Johnson, Ermatine Johnson, Salina Smith, and many other staff members keep the place running. Our faculty writers' group (Anji Boswell, Andrew Burt, Matthew Bowman, Jennifer Dawes, Maryjane Dunn, Brian George, Vernon Miles, Deepak Pant, David Sesser, Michael Taylor, Constanze Weise) reviewed the book proposal and portions of this manuscript. Without the students in the earliest Psych in Literature and comics courses that I taught, I would not have chosen to turn my Batman article idea into a book: alumni such as Ashley Bles, Tommy Cash, Carly Cate, Mitchell Cullins, Christine Dickson, Sarah Fuller, Ben Graves, Dillon Hall, Marko Head, Katrina Hill, Alex Langley, Kory Langley, Erica Ash Lemons, Brian Lott, Robert O'Nale, Thomas Sepe, Nicole Smith, Samantha Proffit Taylor, Dylan Weaver, and the one who went on to study Advanced Batman, Sean Shuttleworth. Students in the Comic Arts Club and the Legion of Nerds, the largest organization on campus, keep things nerdy every day. Colten Smith and others have done impressive work growing the Legion's annual NerdCon.

Humor researcher Thomas Ford helped with sources, and he put me in touch with Sibe Doosje to co-author the humor chapter. "Psychopath Whisperer" Kent Kiehl and his assistant Jenica Gallegos sent information on recent research. Eric Bailey helped us access so many old comic book stories. For related assistance, our writers thank Ray Bergner and Cooper Cutting. Countless people online have discussed the Joker and Batman with us. Special thanks go to a handful of the many who provided food for thought while we were working on this book: Bobby Barrett, Joel DiPippa, Jackie Fiest, Eric Ochoa, David Oglesby, Eric O'Sullivan, Deana Kruseman Salazar. For reasons diverse and sometimes hard to explain, we thank Scott Allison, Jenn Bonds-Raacke, Olivia Efthimiou, Kristin Erickson, Cary Friedman, Greg Lemons, Sharon Manning, Matt Munson, Marc Nadel, Buster Ratliff.

Denny O'Neil, Steve Englehart, Alan Moore, Grant Morrison, Frank Miller, and Jim Starlin wrote stories that changed how we see the Joker. Having comic book writers Englehart and Jack C. Harris, along with *Bad Clowns* author Ben Radford, write features for this book is an honor. We cannot thank Gail Simone, Adam Glass, Mark Safarik, Tara Strong, and Denny O'Neil enough for their new interviews, the late and oh-so-great Adam West and Jerry Robinson for interviews they let me save for the day when this book would come along, and Kevin Conroy and the now-departed Len Wein for convention panels quoted herein along with other conversations. Lawrence Brenner rescued one of my Jerry Robinson recordings, and Mike Catron video-recorded the Comic-Con panel with Robinson, Uslan, and West. In this book's foreword, Michael Uslan names great actors who have played the Joker. In addition to revering those he named, I'd like to acknowledge two more: Larry Storch, who voiced the Joker in the earliest Batman cartoons, and Cameron Monaghan, who played proto-Jokers on *Gotham*.

Jerry Robinson, Bill Finger, and Bob Kane gave the world its Joker. In chapter 2, I examine which of them contributed what to the character's creation, and while I make no bones about who deserves the most credit, we have reasons to thank all three. We owe their earliest editors, too: Vincent Sullivan, who put Batman's first stories into print, and Whitney Ellsworth, who edited the Joker's first issue and told the creators not to kill him off at the end. Paul Dini and Bruce Timm added Harley Quinn much later, and actor Arleen Sorkin's performance captivated audiences and elevated Harley to breakout status.

And thank you, readers, for accompanying us on this visit to Gotham's circus. Hang on to your tickets, and please notice the location of your nearest exit. In the event of an emergency, proceed in an orderly fashion—and watch out for the clown.

NOTES

1. Uslan (2011), p. 103.
2. Uslan (2011).
3. Nobleman (2012).
4. Andrae (1989, 2011); Kane (1989).
5. Athena's first convention panels: Finger et al. (2014a, 2014b); Langley et al. (2014a, 2014b, 2014c). See also Langley (2014a).
6. *Batman & Bill* (2017 documentary).

FOREWORD:
That Thin Line

MICHAEL USLAN
originator and executive producer of the Batman movie franchise

IN POLICE JARGON, it's called "the thin blue line" between law enforcement and law-breaking. In psychology, there's always been debate about what sometimes becomes the thin line between sanity and insanity. In comic books from eras past, there was always an easy line of good versus evil, black and white, superhero and supervillain. But in more recent years, that latter line has blurred, becoming gray in the process, as life seems more aptly characterized now as "order versus chaos."

Batman and the Joker tread that comic book thin line. At some ambiguous moment in his life, the Joker descended into madness. Whether portrayed as "the Clown Prince of Crime" or a homicidal maniac or as a modern-day terrorist, he was wrapped in evil. When Bruce Wayne was a boy, he, too, easily could have been driven to the dark side when a gunman slaughtered his parents in front of his eyes on a concrete altar of blood in the streets of a crime-rampant city. Young Bruce, now a traumatized orphan, could conceivably have become the Joker. But, remaining anchored to his humanity by the kindness and commitment of Alfred Pennyworth, Leslie Tompkins, and even Jim Gordon, Bruce Wayne remained true to that vow he made that night over the bodies of his slain parents. Sacrificing his childhood at that moment and making a lifetime commitment to get the guy who killed his mother and father, and all the bad guys, Bruce Wayne became the first major superhero with no superpowers.[1] Perhaps his greatest superpower has been his humanity.

Yet, as the Batman and the Joker do what seems to be their eternal dance, how odd and how stark that this force of great good and hope is cloaked in the guise of a dark, threatening, monstrous bat, while the seething and hideous horror of the Joker is masked by the face of the carnival, evoking Edgar Allan Poe's "The Cask of Amontillado."[2] A "thin blue line," indeed!

Inarguably, the Joker is the greatest supervillain ever created in comic books. Just as over the past 80 years plus, Batman has been widely and wildly interpreted in the pages of comic books, movies, television, and animation, and so has the Joker. Together, they have transcended every fad, style, tone, change in audience tastes, as well as demographics. Their battles, often mind-to-mind rather than fist-to-fist, transcend cultures, not just physical borders.

Created by artist Jerry Robinson and writer Bill Finger, with influences of a playing card and a German silent film (*The Man Who Laughs*, starring Conrad Veidt of *Casablanca* fame), the Joker made his debut in the first issue of Batman comics in spring 1940, in the same issue that introduced Catwoman to the world.[3] Jerry was becoming wary of the litany of thugs, mobsters, and racketeers faced by the Batman month after month. Inspired by the colorful villains featured in the comic strip pages of Chester Gould's *Dick Tracy* and Milton Caniff's *Terry and the Pirates*, Jerry hoped his concept would be a helpful creative contribution to his boss, Bob Kane, as well as Bill Finger.

Almost 50 years later, our first dark and serious *Batman* movie premiered,[4] revolutionizing not merely the way comic book superhero movies were written, directed, and produced, but also revolutionizing Hollywood and the comic book industry itself. Months after my partner, Benjamin Melniker, and I set out to make such Batman films, acquiring the rights from DC Comics, I realized in a pure epiphany that there was only one actor who could play a serious version of the Joker on the big screen. It was Memorial Day weekend 1980. Two big movies were opening: *The Empire Strikes Back* and *The Shining*. In the newspaper, I saw an ad for that horror film. There was this maniacal photo of Jack Nicholson, commonly referred to over the years as the iconic "Here's Johnny" shot. That was it for me! I tore out that part of the newspaper, raced home, and used Wite-Out on Jack's face, a red pen on his lips, and a magic marker on his hair. *Voilà!* Jack Nicholson had to be the Joker!

If the comic book movie world ever decides to build a Mount Rushmore for the Joker, there would be three heads sculpted into that mountain: Jack Nicholson, Heath Ledger, and Mark Hamill, maybe with a space reserved for Joaquin Phoenix. This is not to denigrate in any way other actors who have played the role in keeping with the context of their times, including Cesar Romero, Jared Leto, and more. But Jack Nicholson was the Joker of the late 1980s the same way Heath Ledger was the Joker of the post-9/11 era and Mark Hamill has mastered the voice of the Joker in Batman animation and video games, defining the character for multiple generations of fans.

That leaves this foreword having to address one last joker, Dr. Travis Langley. Let me explain that last remark. The good doctor is not a supervillain, so he cannot be categorized as part of the same class as Dr. Doom, Dr. Sivana, or Dr. Octopus. In fact, the only joke here is that a person with such unapproachable credentials in psychology could also have impeccable credentials as a comic book fanboy and historian. Combining his two areas of expertise, Dr. Langley once again gives us a gift with *The Joker Psychology*. He ventures beyond the surface and probes layer after layer, exactly what a great psychologist—or comic book historian—is expected to do. And he does this with a deep respect for comic books, superheroes, and their creators, something a previous doctor who wrote a popular book about comic books circa 1954 failed to do—to say the least! That previous doctor of psych does, indeed, in my own expert opinion, deserve to be categorized as a supervillain.*

Dr. Langley helps legitimize and add to the work of Batman and the Joker's creators, writers, and artists who, over the decades, have bequeathed us someone we can all aspire to be—a hero—who lives up to an honorable code of ethics and morals that has withstood the test of time. Now, in his latest book, Dr. Langley and his team of experts examine what Two-Face would call "the other side of the coin." If what the great Stan Lee claimed is true—that it's the supervillains who ultimately define the

---

* Psychiatrist (not psychologist!) Frederic Wertham blamed post–World War II juvenile delinquency on comic books in a campaign that damaged the comic book industry and culminated with his 1954 book *Seduction of the Innocent*.

superhero—then this book becomes Dr. Travis Langley's defining work. And that's no joke!

Michael Uslan
Gotham City

Michael Uslan, Doctor of Comic Books, is a comic book historian, author, educator, and filmmaker best known as the executive producer of the Batman motion pictures.

NOTES

1. *Detective Comics* #33 (1939).
2. Poe (1846/1981).
3. *Batman* #1 (1940a—Joker; 1940c—Catwoman).
4. *Batman* (1989 motion picture).

INTRODUCTION:
Who's That Clown?

TRAVIS LANGLEY, PHD
series editor, lead author

INTERVIEWERS OFTEN ASK what my first memory is of comic books or Batman. I tell them it's like asking when I discovered the sun.[1] Soon after *da-da*, *ma-ma*, *bye-bye*, *hi*, and *car* first left my mouth came a point when my new words were *eat*, *pa-pa* (for grandfather), *thank you*, and *Batman*. My baby book shows that I first said "Batman" the month Adam West's *Batman* TV series debuted. I like to think it was the night the show premiered, but we can't know. We do know the three two-part stories which aired that month featured the Riddler, then the Penguin, and then the Clown Prince of Crime.[2] The Joker has been there my whole life. So have other fantastic fiends, but he's the one every Batman fiction needs to feature.[3] The exceptions get lost in the shuffle.[4] No matter how the storytellers deal their cards, the Joker keeps turning face up.[5]

My mom says I'd already loved comic books and Batman before that.[6] Considering the age in question, this would be tough to believe if not for two things: (1) She found a photo of me as a baby nine months old, holding a comic book and looking truly delighted with it.[7] (2) Recently another little boy in our family, also at nine months, expressed his first preference for a specific book by pushing other books out of the way to reach for one, hand it to his mother, and urge her to read *Bedtime for Batman*.[8] It's in our blood. From what I've seen of the popularity of Batman and his colorful foes, we're not alone in our fascination.

In time, *Batman and Psychology: A Dark and Stormy Knight* would be my first published book. In it, I wrote that we cannot fully diagnose Batman's archnemesis, the Joker. Even his obvious psychopathy could be debatable[9] depending on whether he was ever a decent human being

1

(which seems unlikely), and neither psychopathy nor sociopathy is listed as a disorder in the standard psychiatric manuals.[10] His pattern of behavior clearly fits a diagnosis of antisocial personality disorder in many ways, as we'll discuss several times throughout this book, but the term falls far short of distinguishing him from petty crooks.

If "the Joker defies diagnosis" as I've said before,[11] why analyze him here at all?

- Because a *diagnosis* is just a word, a name we slap onto a set of symptoms so we can talk about them whether we understand them or not. Diagnosis is not explanation.

- Because mental disorder is not by any means the only thing psychology examines. There is much, so much more worth trying to understand about any living creature.

- Because we can't give up on trying to understand people whenever it's hardest. Our heroes teach us better.

- Because even if we might never understand the worst of this world's monsters, we hope to grow better at anticipating, tracking, catching, and stopping them, and we need to know how to help those whom they would harm. Don't give the monsters free rein. Don't make it easy for them. Maybe we can even figure out how to keep some from becoming monsters at all.

The Joker is not one of life's real monsters, to be sure. He springs from the essence of nightmares and strange dreams. We spend a third of our lives in sleep and so many waking moments daydreaming as well. Because he is not real, not in the sense that you and I are, he can be versatile enough to entertain all ages—in some of his incarnations anyway. Examining the Joker here might be fun and interesting for fans of the stories, but can it serve any greater purpose? Is there any point in taking a peek into the head of a fictional character, one who is not quite like any real human being? One whose mind may be impenetrable, his memory unreliable, and his motives beyond comprehension? Because while we need to study the worst parts of real humanity as well, some of it can be so brutal that there's nothing to enjoy. The worst thing the Joker has ever done is still fiction, and we want to see heroes rise above him.

He is the nemesis.

Named for the classic wild card in a deck of playing cards, he shakes things up and changes the game. He changes his suit, his face, his position in order to tell a new story, the one that's right for the time. Every story needs its source of conflict, and we want every hero to overcome obstacles great enough to earn that name, *hero*. For us to know that the man in the bat costume is up to the task of defending his city, we need to see him overcome his own challenges, and nobody else challenges him the way the Joker does. Batman represents many things—among them, our desire for mortal human beings to step up to do the best things at the worst of times. We hope—we *wish*—that when things look bleakest and we know no godlike superhuman will fly down from the sky to help, somebody can step out of the darkness to do what's right. When we stand in bright daylight, we don't feel the need for a hero as intensely as we do when we shiver in the night.

What does the Joker represent? How does this character grab our attention at any age? Why does he linger in our thoughts? Let's find out how many Jokers are in our deck.

It's time to deal the cards.

> *"Trust everybody, but cut the cards."*
> —humorist Finley Peter Dunne[12]

"How about a magic trick?"
—The Joker[13]

NOTES

1. e.g., *Legends of the Knight* (2013 documentary).
2. The Riddler—episodes 1–01, "Hi Diddle Diddle," and 1–02, "Smack in the Middle" (January 12–13, 1966); Penguin—1–03, "Fine Feathered Finks," and 1–04, "The Penguin's a Jinx" (January19–20, 1966); Joker—1–05, "The Joker is Wild" and 1–06 "Batman is Riled" (January 26–27, 1966).
3. *Batman* (1943) and *Batman and Robin* (1949) movie serials, which had no Joker, came out long before my time.

4. *Beware the Batman* animated series had no Joker and lasted only one season (2013–2014).

5. *Batman* #1 (1940); *Batman,* episode 1–05, "The Joker is Wild" (January 26, 1966); *The Adventures of Batman,* episode 1–01, "My Crime is Your Crime" (September 14, 1968); *The New Scooby-Doo Movies,* episode 1–02, "The Dynamic Scooby-Doo Affair" (September 16, 1972); *The New Adventures of Batman,* episode 1–01, "The Pest" (February 12, 1977); *Super Friends* (as *The Super Powers Team: Galactic Guardians*), episode 9–05, "The Wild Cards" (October 5, 1985); *Batman* (1989 motion picture); *Batman: The Animated Series,* episode 1–02, "Christmas with the Joker" (November 13, 1992); *Birds of Prey,* episode 1–01, "Pilot" (October 9, 2002); *The Batman,* episode 1–01, "The Bat in the Belfry" (September 11, 2004); *The Dark Knight* (2008 motion picture); *Batman: The Brave and the Bold,* episode 1–13, "Game Over for Owlman!" (March 6, 2009); *Suicide Squad* (2016 motion picture); *Joker* (2019 motion picture); plus direct-to-video films and other appearances along the way. The TV series *Gotham* teases several possible Jokers throughout its run before apparently settling on one (2014–2019).

6. Wolfe (2014).

7. *Green Lantern* #33 (1964).

8. Dahl & Beavers (2017).

9. Shah (2016).

10. American Psychiatric Association (2013); World Health Organization (1992; 2018).

11. Langley (2012), p. 152.

12. Written in a character's dialect as "Thrust ivrybody—but cut th' ca-ards."—Dooley (1900), p. 260.

13. *The Dark Knight* (2008 motion picture).

The Publisher: It's All DC

The Joker originated in publications from Detective Comics, Inc., one of the companies that would merge to become what is now known as DC Comics.

- **National Allied Publications:** In 1934, Major Malcolm Wheeler-Nicholson founded the company that would produce the first American comic books featuring new material instead of reprinting newspaper comic strips.

- **Detective Comics, Inc.:** National Allied's sister company formed in 1937.

- **Superman-DC:** Unofficial rebranding of many National/Detective publications starting in 1940; later simply DC.

- **National Comics Publications:** National Allied Publications and Detective Comics, Inc., merged in 1946, also absorbing All-American Comics into this corporation.

- **National Periodical Publications:** Renamed this in 1961.

- **DC Comics:** Official rebranding of the company in 1977.

Parent Company: Warner Communications; merged with Time to form **Time Warner** in 1989. Time Warner made DC Comics a subsidiary of **DC Entertainment** in 2009.

Location: New York, NY, until 2015. Burbank, CA, since 2015.

Because most comics cited in this book were published by Detective/National/DC Comics, references will identify a comic book's publisher only in the few instances in which an outside company, such as Marvel or Image, published the work.

Starring . . . The Joker

Creators: Officially Bob Kane. Actually Jerry Robinson, Bill Finger, & (probably partial design only—see chapter 2 of this book) Bob Kane.

Debut of Character: *Batman* #1 (1940).

First Television Appearance: *Batman*, episode 1–05, "The Joker is Wild" (January 26, 1966). Played by Cesar Romero.

First Theatrical Appearance: *Batman: The Movie* (1966 motion picture). Played by Cesar Romero.

First Animated Appearance: *The Adventures of Batman*, segments of *The Batman/Superman Hour*, episode 1–01, "My Crime is Your Crime" (September 14, 1968). Voiced by Larry Storch.

Debut of His Own Comic Book Series: *The Joker* #1 (1975).

First Theatrical Appearance with Top Billing: *Batman* (1989 motion picture). Played by Jack Nicholson.

First Eponymous Theatrical Film: *Joker* (2019 motion picture). Played by Joaquin Phoenix.

Longest-Running Performer: Mark Hamill has played the role the longest, voicing the Joker since *Batman: The Animated Series*, episode 1–02, "Christmas with the Joker" (November 13, 1992), the first episode produced with the Joker, or 1–22, "Joker's Favor" (September 11, 1992), which aired earlier. Episode numbers throughout this book's endnotes refer to production order. When discussing the Joker, even numbers misbehave.

Co-Starring . . . Dr. Harleen Quinzel, a.k.a. Harley Quinn

Creators: Paul Dini & Bruce Timm.

Debut of Character: *Batman: The Animated Series*, episode 1–22, "Joker's Favor" (September 11, 1992). Voiced by Arleen Sorkin.

First Comic Book Appearances: Outside DC Universe canon, *The Batman Adventures* #12 (1993); in canon, *Batman: Harley Quinn* (1999).

Debut of Her Own Comic Book Series: *Harley Quinn* #1 (2000).

First Live Action Television Appearance: *Birds of Prey*, episode 1–01, "Pilot" (October 9, 2002). Played by Mia Sara.

First Live Action Motion Picture Appearance: *Suicide Squad* (2016 motion picture). Played by Margot Robbie.

THE ACE OF KNAVES

*"Once again a master criminal stalks the city streets—
a criminal weaving a web of death about him—leaving
stricken victims behind wearing a ghastly clown's grin—the
sign of death from the Joker! Only two dare to oppose him—
Batman and Robin the Boy Wonder! Two to battle the Grim
Jester called—the Joker! A battle of wits—with swift death,
the only compromise!!!"*

—narrative text introducing the first Joker story[1]

*"Their hallmark is a stunning lack of
conscience; their game is self-gratification at
the other person's expense. Many spend
time in prison, but many do not.
All take far more than they give."*

—Psychopathy Checklist developer,
psychologist Robert D. Hare[2]

NOTES

1. *Batman* #1 (1940).
2. Hare (1993/1999), pp. 1–2.

1

Which Joker?

TRAVIS LANGLEY

 THE JOKER IS mischief, he is chaos, and he is evil we don't understand. He is the bright, laughing monster who looks like a clown, created to challenge the dark, brooding hero who looks like a monster.

Few fiends of any kind, whether fictional characters or nonfictional crooks, are so well-known, and no other enemy proves so difficult for Batman to anticipate. The Joker has been called the greatest comic book supervillain, the greatest comic book movie villain, the greatest movie villain, and even the greatest villain of all time.[1] To be sure, not everyone agrees,[2] but just ask those who once ranked the Joker #2 behind Magneto at #1 to consider which of the two they'd find scarier at their door one night. The odds of survival if it's the Joker are beyond prediction, except that they aren't good. Two-Face and Thanos at least give people a 50-50 chance.[3]

Three people—Batman's creators and the earliest ghost artist known to have worked with them—introduced the criminal clown one year after Batman's debut.[4] The fact that they originally plotted for the Joker to die in the issue in which he first appears shows that they had not initially realized the character's potential, but editor Whitney Ellsworth did and he decided killing the villain off would be a waste.[5] In creating the Joker, they gave Batman his archnemesis.[6] When writers and artists develop new adversaries to fight Superman, they must start by considering what will challenge his powers. Because Batman is defined by his psychology—his drives, his personality, and the symbols he adopts—his enemies must challenge him as a person. This gives him a rich rogues' gallery full of foes denoted by their psyches instead of superpowers, and, after all these decades, the Joker remains the most challenging among them all.

But which Joker do we mean?

The Running Joke: Stages of Joker Development

Both Batman and the Joker have proved to be versatile characters, able to adapt to shifts in societal norms and storytelling techniques over the decades since their respective 1939 and 1940 debuts.[7] Their characterizations have fluctuated from nonviolent to brutal, from silly to somber, from fantastic to relatively realistic. Within the fiction, some changes in Batman's personality and personal history have been attributed to differences between alternate universes (with the Golden Age Batman's stories retroactively set on Earth-Two whereas the Silver/Bronze Age Batman inhabits Earth-One)[8] or reality reboots. The Multiverse makeovers—the reality-altering events of storylines such as *Crisis on Infinite Earths*, *Zero Hour*, *Infinite Crisis*, *Flashpoint*, and *Rebirth/Doomsday Clock*[9]—change characters and their lives in much the same way that time travelers' interference keeps altering Marty McFly's family history over the course of the *Back to the Future* films,[10] and so most comic book characters remain as oblivious as Marty's parents to how external forces have rewritten their world and lives.[11] Even within the stories, though, characters know the Joker changes. They remember his original killer phase, his nonlethal kooky clown period, his return to homicide, and other variations along the way—so, in a way, the question of "Which Joker?" may be answered by them all.

Differences in the Joker's depictions have reflected changes in the comic book industry itself. Some of his milestones mark the distinctions between one major age for all comics and the next. The Joker's history has gone through five distinct stages which can be characterized by changes in his personality, his violence, and his impact on other characters' lives.

"The Ace of Knaves" (Sane Killer)

Early Golden Age (1940–1942)[12]

The opening page of the Joker's debut story calls him "the Grim Jester," and narrative text in a panel later in the same story calls Batman "the Dark Knight" for the first time.[13] While a jester might not seem like an opponent fit to face a knight and squire in combat, this incongruity means that the jester is not the kind of adversary that the knight has trained to combat.[14] The medieval jester, the court entertainer who had to be "wise enough to play the fool,"[15] got to insult the high and mighty. His job was often to challenge the nobility and to speak truths that others dared not utter.[16] As the Joker once remarks to Batman, "In the old days, court jesters were held in high esteem! Even the kings envied their freedom to do whatever came into their heads!"[17]

The Joker's earliest nicknames, "the Grim Jester" and "the Killer-Clown,"[18] both suit his role in Batman's stories. A different sobriquet that comes later, though, reflects his place in comic book history as the progenitor of a new breed of superheroes' colorful antagonists: "the Ace of Knaves." The first popular comic book supervillain, the ace who plays first among the knaves,[19] the Joker laughs his way onto the scene as something new—no mere mobster, monster, or mad scientist, though he mixes elements of them all.

One year after Batman debuts in 1939's *Detective Comics* #27, his cast expands to include his crime-fighting partner, Robin; his primary love interest, the Cat (soon renamed Cat-Woman, then Catwoman); and his archfoe, the Joker—all within a month of each other in 1940.[20] As originally depicted, the Joker is a sane, if inscrutable, killer. During his first two years, the clown murders many as the Dark Knight fights this Grim Jester about every other month.[21] Even though the Joker commits his killings in conjunction with other crimes, which would seem to suggest *extrinsic motivation* (drive to achieve external rewards—the pre-Crisis Joker really likes money and jewels), the fact that the murders rarely serve any clear, ulterior purpose indicates *intrinsic motivation* (drive to achieve personal satisfaction—in this case, meaning that he kills for the sheer sake of killing). In his first published crime, for instance, he poisons a man who

The Classic Ages of Comics

Golden Age: Superman bursts onto the scene in 1938's *Action Comics* #1, inaugurating what would become known as the Golden Age of Comic Books.[22] The heyday of the Golden Age passes by the early 1950s as comic book sales wane and superhero series in particular nearly vanish. Plastic Man[23] and the original Captain Marvel[24] are the last to hang on to their own titles until cancellation, and then only the final three (Superman, Batman, Wonder Woman) remain in steady publication.

Silver Age: In 1956, *Showcase* #4 introduces Barry Allen, a new version of the Flash. Following this speedster's success, DC begins introducing new versions of other superheroes, and a new age of superhero comics begins. Marvel Comics will soon take the lead in adding psychological depth to superhero characters and greater complexity to their stories.[25]

Bronze Age: The Silver Age ends and Bronze begins sometime between Green Arrow's discovery that his sidekick has become a drug addict in 1971[26] and the Green Goblin's murder of Spider-Man's girlfriend Gwen Stacy in 1973.[27] Superhero stories begin addressing more mature subject matter and serious social issues. The Punisher arrives in 1974, heralding the emergence of violent and morally complicated villains, heroes, and antiheroes.[28] For DC, this era ends as early as the second Robin's debut in 1983,[29] no later than the conclusion of *Crisis on Infinite Earths* in 1986.[30]

dies one day after the Joker has already stolen his diamond, and therefore the murder itself does not provide external reward. The Joker's choice of targets suggests that he wants to take down the high and mighty, the rich and powerful, but, then again, they might be his targets only because "that's where the money is."[31] The Joker kills for reasons that "make sense to him alone,"[32] if even he understands, and his crimes grow progressively more peculiar.

"The Clown Prince of Crime" (Kooky Crook)

Later Golden Age–Silver Age (1942–1969)[33]

Two years into the Joker's publication history, he stops killing. Editors, concerned about growing public concern over violence in comics, called for the murders to halt. The first major period of the Joker's history abruptly ends and the second begins in one story, "The Joker Walks the Last Mile!"[34] Frustrated over being unable to walk freely in public because he's wanted by the law, the Joker seeks a fresh start. "That's it," he decides. "The Joker must die!" He walks into a police station, confesses to every crime he has ever committed, pleads guilty in court, and dies in the electric chair. His flunkies then snatch the body and revive him with a secret drug. The Joker proclaims, in one of several reminders to readers, "Reclaimed from the dead! All crimes paid for! The slate wiped clean!" Though he soon resumes his status as a thief and a wanted man, he is a killer no more.

Mayhem gives way to mirth as the murderous "Killer-Clown" becomes the madcap "Clown Prince of Crime." The nickname first appears no later than 1947's *Batman* #44 in a story that could have been written by any other ghost writer of the time.[35] Even though "Clown Prince of Crime" or simply "Clown Prince" becomes the most commonly used nickname when referring to him at any point in his publication history, people also use the term to refer to this specific phase of the Joker's career,[36] which can create some confusion.

Instead of committing macabre murders each time he reappears, the Joker now embarks on creative crime sprees that follow zany themes for his own entertainment. "Reborn with a new personality,"[37] he repeatedly goes on crime binges while following a new theme each time, without killing anybody for the next 31 years. He instead resorts "to pulling off astonishing crimes in ludicrous situations, often perpetrated with preposterous gadgets."[38] The 21st-century Joker looks back on this as the stretch when "he constructed outlandish Joker-Mobiles which gently mocked the young Batman's pretensions in the Satire Years before Camp,"[39] drawing distinctions in the degrees and forms of his own absurdity (i.e., satire versus camp) as substages over the course of these years.

While other superhero stories experiment with updating characters and style, Batman stories turn sillier in the late '50s and early '60s when comic book stories see him meeting space aliens,[40] dueling a gorilla,[41] or mutating into one wacky form after another (such as when a scientist's invention accidentally transforms him into Bat-Baby)[42] instead of delving into any deeper concerns. Restrained by DC's in-house decision that the Joker stop killing and then limited further by the Comics Code Authority's guidelines,[43] the Joker gets goofier, too. In one of his earliest stories of this period,[44] a head injury gives him amnesia and a later knock in the noggin cures him of it (a trope popular in 1930s radio programs[45] and 1960s TV situation comedies).[46] His crime sprees follow lighthearted themes designed around such things as giant-sized musical instruments, funny costumes, and historical blunders, his so-called "boner" crimes.[47] One of his last Silver Age stories sees the Joker and frenemy Lex Luthor use a time machine to bring Leonardo Da Vinci and other historical figures to the 20th century just to trick them into committing mundane crimes.[48] Even if the Joker of another era might use a time machine that oddly, serious supergenius Luthor normally shows more sense.

Regardless of his antics, the Joker is considered sane during this time, as one story illustrates when he *fakes insanity* in order to infiltrate an asylum.[49] The impracticality of crimes he commits in order to feign psychosis (stealing worthless items) and the ease with which he gets caught actually demonstrate why a truly insane person would lack the grasp of reality needed to be a masterful supervillain. A deceived doctor diagnoses him with "hebophrenia"—referring to *hebephrenia*, an older name for *disorganized schizophrenia*. (The *hebe*-root refers to youth because this condition tends to start earlier in life, thus interfering with adolescent or young adult personality development.)[50]

The comic book stories become less childish in 1964, but the popularity of the 1966–1968 *Batman* TV series soon spurs the publisher to go backward and make the comic book as campy as the show. The television depiction of the Joker, as played by actor Cesar Romero, stays truer to the pre-1964 wackiness but without the most outlandish (and more expensive to film) sci-fi elements such as travel through space or time. Once the Bat-fad passes and ABC cancels the show, sales plunge so sharply that DC nearly cancels the comic book, too. "When the television show was a success, I was asked to be campy," editor Julius Schwartz said later, "and of course when the show faded, so did the comic books."[51] Fans wanted less camp, more mystery, and darker shadows.[52] In a comic book letter column, one fan explicitly called for the Joker to be "brought back as a murderer" and his laugh "blood-curdling and eerie."[53] When subsequent stories and art darken in order to save Batman, the Joker disappears from publication for four years. His Silver Age is over, and an intermission passes before his Bronze Age begins.

"The King of Arkham Asylum" (Insane Killer)

Bronze Age (1973–1986)[54]

Comic book writer Dennis O'Neil decided to take the Joker back to his deadly roots by making him start killing again in 1973. Artist Neal Adams initially balked at the idea: "I found myself being very uncomfortable with that story, because he was homicidal. I didn't think of the Joker as being homicidal, but Denny did." O'Neil won him over with his view: "Well, Joker's insane. He's a murderer."[55] From that point onward, attributing the Joker's behavior to insanity becomes central to his characterization. The Joker goes no longer to prison when captured but instead to Gotham's asylum for the criminally insane.

Despite the new view that the Joker is insane, writer Steve Englehart felt the character should be even crazier. "If you actually go back and look at Denny's story 'The Joker's Five-Way Revenge,' you will find that he *is* homicidal but he is *not* a maniac. He *says* he is, but he always says he is."[56] Englehart wanted a surrealistic, maniacal Joker. In Steve's assessment, Denny's Joker "*pretended* to be a buffoon, but showed us that he was actually

The Modern Ages of Comics

Called the Modern Age by some,[57] even though such a name by design will grow outdated and will retroactively be dubbed something else when future generations look back on its historical context, the post–Bronze Age period has also been referred to as the *Dark Age*[58] because of its grimmer stories (with a portion that ends in 1991 or 1992 called the *Copper Age* by some). Post-9/11 changes in the world and comics may make *Dark Ages*, plural, a more accurate term. For the Joker, this begins in 1986 or 1987.[59]

Late 20th Century

The success of two alternate-reality deconstructions of superheroes' nature, *Batman: The Dark Knight Returns*[60] and *Watchmen*,[61] inspires the spread of grim and gritty stories throughout mainstream comics and produces a wave of violent antiheroes. Superheroes suffer their greatest defeats (e.g., the death of Superman, the breaking of Batman's back[62]) and disturbing losses (such as the "fridging" of Green Lantern's girlfriend[63] and the Joker's repeated violence against people in Batman's life[64]).

21st Century

In the post-9/11 world, we ache for heroes. The concurrent Internet age, though, swiftly tears heroes down. Stories increasingly examine the superhero's place in a cynical world that still cries out to be saved.[65] Costumes, crimes, and other details become more realistic, maybe to align with superhero movies. Violence turns bloodier and more brutal. Elements of body horror proliferate as gruesome acts such as cannibalism grow more common[66] and an increasing number of characters lose arms, heads, and even a face.[67]

serious about it. My Joker was not particularly serious. I mean he would kill people, but he was a lunatic. The difference is between realism and surrealism. Denny's Joker didn't have conversations about fish."[68] Steve's Joker tried to copyright fish and he could not understand why people wouldn't let him. "I wanted to show that he really was out of his mind."[69] (For more of their views on the Joker, see the interview in Explaining the Joke 3–2: Writer/Editor Dennis O'Neil and a feature that Steve Englehart wrote for us, Explaining the Joke 7–2: The Maniac Who Laughs.)

Much as the Adam West TV series reflected comic book stories from a few years before its time, the post–Bronze Age *Batman* movie directed by Tim Burton tells a story befitting the Bronze with a dash of the early Golden Age Ace of Knaves.[70] This makes some sense, given that the film had been in development since the middle of the Bronze Age and its script was first plotted when only glimmers of the upcoming "revisionist" Dark Ages were on the horizon.[71] The movie's characters view its "homicidal artist" in much the way comic book characters see him, too: They attribute the Joker's inexplicable behavior to insanity. Reporter Vicki Vale and a gangster each call the Joker insane to his face, and Batman refers to him as "psychotic." (Admittedly, Vicki also points out to Batman, "Some people say the same thing about you."[72]) This film replaces the Cesar Romero version's flamboyance with the newer printed version's madness. From it, the world finds out that the Joker is a killer most bizarre. Even so, the film does not present him committing the bloodier acts and making the more personal attacks (killing a Robin, shooting and paralyzing a Batgirl) that had begun to distinguish the comics of the time.

"The Harlequin of Hate" (Personal Killer)

Late 20th Century (1986–2000)[73]

Throughout previous ages, the Joker's attempts to harm Batman and those around him do not succeed. His victims don't debut until the same stories in which he eliminates them. After *Crisis on Infinite Earths* resets DC Universe history, that changes.[74] This timeline, it's personal. The post-Crisis Joker of the Modern Age or Dark Ages of comic books differs from the classic ages in that he becomes a threat in major characters' lives and he becomes more manipulative, constructing progressively more serpentine plots to bring out the worst in them and to make some point about the darker side of human nature—he becomes their devil.

In his first post-Crisis appearance, he shoots Dick Grayson, meaning to kill him. Though Dick survives, this ends his career as Batman's first sidekick, the original Robin, before he then takes on his adult superhero appellation as Nightwing.[75] The Joker's villainy in comics takes a more personal turn when he grows frustrated that others have not come to recognize life as the bleak and cruel joke he considers it to be. He sets out to convince everyone, perhaps even himself.[76] No longer content with harming strangers or merely threatening those in the lives of Batman and Commissioner Gordon, he begins to inflict lasting damage upon those closest to them—crippling Batgirl, killing the second Robin, killing Gordon's second wife.[77] Does he mean to break the Commissioner in order to free the Dark Knight from human ties so he can focus on being Batman, or is the Joker just jealous? These atrocities we will revisit often throughout this book because the pre- and post-Crisis (classic versus modern) division splits his history into the decades before he maims or murders major characters and the decades in which he raises those stakes.

Batman: The Animated Series comes along in the 1990s, drawing material from the best Batman stories throughout his history. There are other animated depictions, including computer games, but this is the gold standard for them all. Again, the dramatization remains truer to previous eras' comics than to those in print at the time. The cartoon in its earliest seasons rarely hints that the Joker would truly commit homicide, much less paralyze or murder important characters. The program introduces a girlfriend of sorts, a psychiatrist-turned-sidekick who will eventually grow stronger as a character whenever she stands apart from him.[78] While the Joker earns his old nickname[79] as the Harlequin of Hate in the comics by making his mayhem more personal, a harlequin in love adds something more personal to the Joker's own characterization whether he wants that or not. She debuts on TV but becomes a popular comic book character on her own.[80]

"An Agent of Chaos" (Terrorist)

21st Century (2001 Onward)

The book *Batman and Psychology: A Dark and Stormy Knight* divided the Joker's history into the aforementioned four main stages. The fifth had started but was not far enough along for anyone to know with certainty that the shift in depiction would endure and broadly redefine the Joker. It's easy to say, "A new era has begun," but more time is needed to see repercussions and judge their lasting impact. The motion picture *The Dark Knight* both epitomizes these changes and solidifies the new pattern of the Joker as terrorist monster, as a long-term planner despite his claims to the contrary. Using order, he sows chaos. Calling the Joker a terrorist may seem too purpose-driven for him, but he does indeed become more purpose-driven. A terrorist kills and destroys in order to instill terror and advance an agenda, however sensible or insensible that agenda may seem.[81]

In the Joker's earliest post-9/11 appearances, he guest-stars in other antagonists' stories[82] until *Infinite Crisis* alters the DC Universe.[83] Then he gets shot in the face.[84] Despite reconstructive surgery and months of recovery, the extreme makeover leaves him gruesomely, ghoulishly scarred. He raises a razor to Harley Quinn's face, meaning to make her look the same, but Batman intervenes.[85] This version of the Joker would inform Heath Ledger and Jared Leto when each played the character on the big screen.[86] Though the facial scars would vanish from the comics, the 21st-century Joker keeps bringing body horror into the stories by having his own face cut off, tricking Batman's allies into believing he has cut off their faces, and chopping off Alfred's hand (discussed at greater length in chapter 3's look at horror).[87]

The Joker, as played by Heath Ledger in the film *The Dark Knight*, "a bleak post-9/11 allegory about how terror . . . breaks down those reassuring moral categories,"[88] exemplifies the Joker at his most diabolical, a master manipulator reaping terror and horror. I've covered this depiction at some length in the past.[89] *The Dark Knight* is about inspiration. Batman's example inspires foolhardy copycat vigilantes (much like the one who shoots the Joker's face in the comics),[90] his threat inspires less fear once the criminals learn he won't kill (which may be why crime goes down in the comic book series when people think it's Batman who shot the Joker), and Harvey Dent inspires the citizens of Gotham City. More than any other villains, the Joker and Two-Face reflect Batman himself as fun-house distortions, converses of who and what he is. This Joker is the Joker, no alter ego. The film's opening bank robbery shows him wearing clown mask over clown makeup. Under the surface there's only more Joker. He gives no history except inconsistent lies. When he considers the impact of his demand that Batman unmask, he retracts the threat and demands that Batman's identity remain undisclosed—unless that was the implausibly complicated plan along, but with the Joker, you cannot know. (In one of the graphic novels upon which Ledger based his performance, the Joker says that Batman's "mask is his real face."[91]) He wants a Batman who has no other self, a Dark Knight whose only deeper layer is further darkness. For the most part, however bizarre he might appear, the film's Joker seems dangerously sane. He understands his actions, develops well-orchestrated plans to foster anarchy, and although the citizens of Gotham will prove themselves better than he expects, he correctly anticipates many actions people will take and he recognizes the reality around him. He has no hallucinations or obvious delusions. When he tells Two-Face he doesn't scheme, "I just do things," either he's lying or he has a view so warped that he fails to recognize his own scheming nature.

The Dark Tetrad: Evil in Four Suits

This book is divided into five sections, loosely (very loosely) related to the Joker's five major eras. From era to era, his evil differs in form and so does his mental state. Four of the five eras differ in terms of how they depict the Joker along the four dimensions of the dark tetrad, with insanity emerging prominently in the other.

Psychologists tend to avoid qualitative personal descriptors, judg-mental labels for people, especially *evil* even though it's one of the most heavily discussed topics in the history of discussing anything. In the 21st century, some researchers examine a malevolent combination of three personality traits (really sets of traits) initially known as *the dark triad*.[92] Associated with exploitative behavior,[93] the dark triad consists of three underlying, inner qualities when combined: psychopathy, narcissism,

Machiavellianism. (This is not to be confused with the well-known *Macdonald triad*,[94] a different set of features regarding three actions—arson, bedwetting, cruelty to animals—supposedly associated with violence and serial offenses,[95] but with such inconsistent empirical support that some forensic experts deem it an urban legend.[96])

Whereas one individual with all dark triad traits elevated may turn criminal, another may instead channel them into legal, nonviolent, socially acceptable outlets such as corporate jobs where exploiting others confers an advantage.[97] The *subclinical* psychopath or narcissist does not let those selfish traits and attitudes interfere with his or her general ability to function in life, and a benevolent Machiavellian (arguably such as Batman) may manipulate others for the sake of the greater good.[98] Even when it reaches unhealthy extremes, the dark triad is insufficient to account for the cruelest of human behavior. Because the callous person who feels indifferent to the distress of others might not take any delight in causing it, researchers added one more trait to the dark triad to describe a *dark tetrad:* sadism.[99] The psychopathic egotist who manipulates others for the sheer fun of hurting them is dangerous indeed.

These qualities loosely relate to the Joker's five major eras:

- **Ace of Knaves**—psychopathy. (Some people argue, "No, he's a sociopath." We'll get to that.)

- **Clown Prince of Crime**—narcissism.

- **King of Arkham Asylum**—insanity, *not* part of the dark tetrad.

- **Harlequin of Hate**—Machiavellianism.

- **Agent of Chaos**—sadism.

The dark triad/tetrad traits are not *orthogonal*, not completely distinct from each other: They overlap. It's easy to see evidence of narcissism throughout the Joker's career. The post-Crisis Joker's elevated cruelty and calculation go together, hurting the heroes deeply while he starts spinning elaborate plans that require foresight and ability to anticipate people's actions and reactions, thus intermingling his increased Machiavellianism and sadism. Because he seems psychopathic at almost any point except perhaps his "Clown Prince" phase, this first section of the book looks more at the character's place in history as the supervillain who changes the course of superhero fiction.

Will the Real Joker Please Stand Up?

After all that, which Joker is this book talking about? Essentially all of them, and yet only one.

Comic book writer Grant Morrison popularized the idea that they're all the same character.[100] "What if all the stories from 1939 until now were true, and they were part of this guy's biography?" Morrison imagined that Batman at one point "was Adam West and the Joker wasn't killing people anymore, he was just trippin' on his own chemicals because everyone in Gotham was trippin'"[101] until the Joker starts killing again, and that all other stages for these characters happen in their history as well. A person can go through changes, some quite extreme, and some of our own world's villains show bizarre flux in their lives. Later stories introduce the idea that the Joker is not one person but three,[102] which might account for the Joker's inconsistencies too well. For storytelling purposes, less clarification on the Joker is better. Previous writers scripted the Joker with a single, chaotic character in mind.

So who is he? What is he? And what's up with that psychiatrist who becomes his harlequin?

NOTES

1. Comics—Dorkly Staff (2013); Thorne (2014). Comic book movies—Bailey (2018); Serafino (2013). Movies—Ranker Community (n.d.). All time—Kenreck (2015); Wizard (2006).
2. IGN (2009); Williams (2016).
3. Two-Face—arguably at his most murderous yet randomly so in *The Dark Knight* (2008 motion picture); Thanos—*Infinity Gauntlet* #1–6 (1991); *Avengers: Infinity War* (2018 motion picture).
4. Respectively, *Batman* #1 (1940) and *Detective Comics* #27 (1939).
5. Cronin (2005); Gold (1988).
6. Coogan (2006); Wallace (2011); Weiner & Peaslee (2015).
7. *Detective Comics* #27 (1939); *Batman* #1 (1940).
8. *The Flash* #123 (1961); *Justice League of America* #21 (1963); *Adventure Comics* #462 (1979).
9. Respectively, starting with *Crisis on Infinite Earths* #1 (1985), *Zero Hour* #4 (1994), *Infinite Crisis* #1 (2005), *Flashpoint* #1 (2011), *DC Rebirth* #1 (2016), *Doomsday Clock* #1 (2018), and associated lead-ins.

10. *Back to the Future, Back to the Future Part II, Back to the Future Part III* (1985, 1989, 1990 motion pictures).

11. Analogy adapted from Langley (2012), p. 28.

12. *Batman* #1 (1940) through the first pages of *Detective Comics* #64 (1942), up until his execution scene.

13. *Batman* #1 (1940).

14. They even have a swordfight in the next issue, *Batman* #2 (1940).

15. Shakespeare (1623/1982b). Written around 1601–1692, its earliest known publication is in *First Folio*.

16. Otto (2001).

17. *Detective Comics* #476 (1978), from a storyline in which writer Steve Englehart took the Joker back to his 1940 roots but with a 1970s perspective.

18. Both come from the Joker's debut stories in *Batman* #1 (1940).

19. And, arguably, the first supervillain regardless of popularity because the Ultra-Humanite, who debuted almost a year earlier in *Action Comics* #13 (1939), originally fell squarely into the mad scientist category.

20. Robin—*Detective Comics* #38 (1940); the Cat and the Joker—*Batman* #1 (1940).

21. *Batman* #1, #2, #4, #5, #7, #8, #9, #11; *Detective Comics* #45, #60, #62. *Detective Comics* #64 ended this "killer-clown" stage in the Joker's career.

22. Dubbed the Golden Age by Lupoff (1960).

23. Until *Plastic Man* #54 (1956).

24. Until *The Marvel Family* #84 (1954).

25. Beginning with *Fantastic Four* #1 (1961).

26. *Green Lantern* #85 (1971).

27. *The Amazing Spider-Man* #121 (1973).

28. *The Amazing Spider-Man* #129 (1974).

29. As Jason Todd, *Batman* #357 (1983); in a Robin costume, *Detective Comics* #526 (1983). See Cloer (2018). This does not yet mark a major change for the Joker.

30. *Crisis on Infinite Earths* #11–12 (1986).

31. Attributed to bank robber Willie Sutton, who denied having said it (Quote Investigator, 2013).

32. *Detective Comics* #475 (1978).

33. Beginning with his post-execution revival in *Detective Comics* #64 (1942). Last Silver Age appearance in a Batman title—*Detective Comics* #388 (1969); last in any title—*Justice League of America* #77 (1969).

34. *Detective Comics* #64 (1942).

35. *Batman* #44 (1947–1948).

36. e.g., Wildman (2014).

37. Wildman (1974), p. 7.

38. Gold (1988), p. 9.

39. *Batman* #663 (2007).

40. *Batman* #128 (1959).

41. *Batman* #130 (1960).

42. *Batman* #147 (1962).

43. Nyberg (1998).

44. *Batman* #16 (1943).

45. Besner (2012). For example, Batman and Superman wonder if Superman has amnesia in *The Adventures of Superman* radio program's 13-part story, "Is There Another Superman?" (January–February 1946).

46. e.g., *The Addams Family*, episode 1–22, "Amnesia in the Addams Family" (February 19, 1965); *Gilligan's Island*, 1–30, "Forget Me Not" (April 24, 1965); and arguably every appearance of King Tut in *Batman*, starting with 1–27, "The Curse of Tut" (April 13, 1966).

47. Respectively, *World's Finest Comics* #48 (1950), *Batman* #64 (1951), *Detective Comics* #193 (1953), and *Batman* #66 (1953).

48. *World's Finest Comics* #177 (1968).

49. *Batman* #74 (1952–1953).
50. American Psychiatric Association (2013).
51. Quoted by Daniels (1999), p. 115.
52. *Batman* #210 (1969), letter by future comic book writer Mark Evanier.
53. Quoted by Weldon (2016), p. 104.
54. From *Batman* #251 (1973) through *Batman* #400 (1986), the last Batman story set on pre-Crisis Earth-One.
55. Quoted by Eury & Kronenberg (2009), p. 145.
56. Mougin (1989), p. 60.
57. Ayres (2016); Overstreet (2005).
58. Ayres (2016); Voger (2006).
59. *Batman: The Dark Knight* #1–4 (1986); *Batman* #408 (1987).
60. *Batman: The Dark Knight* #1–4 (1986).
61. *Watchmen* #1–12 (1986–1987).
62. Respectively, *Superman* #75 (1993) and *Batman* #497 (1993).
63. *Green Lantern* #54 (1994).
64. *Batman: The Killing Joke* (1988); *Batman* #427–428 (1988–1989); *Detective Comics* #741 (2000).
65. e.g., *Civil War* #1–7 (2006–2007).
66. e.g., *52* #39 (2007), *Ultimatum* #3 (2009), and many more. See Staley (2018).
67. e.g., arms—Risk in *Infinite Crisis* #4 (2006), Arsenal in *Justice League: Cry for Justice* #5 (2010); heads—Psycho-Pirate in *Infinite Crisis* #6 (2006), Namor the Sub-Mariner in *Squadron Supreme* #1 (2015); face—the Joker in *Detective Comics* #1 (2011).
68. Mougin (1989), pp. 60–61.
69. Englehart (2012, personal communication).
70. Viewed as Golden Age Joker by Cajun (2016); mix of both by Gould (2015).
71. Hamm (2019); Reed (2014); Uslan (2011); Uslan, personal communication (February 3, 2019).
72. *Batman* (1989 motion picture).
73. Beginning with *Batman: The Dark Knight Returns* (1986, a tale set in Batman's possible future), which foreshadows the death of the second Robin, Jason Todd. The post-Crisis Joker debuts in *Batman* #408 (1987), in which he shoots Dick Grayson, ending Dick's time as the first Robin, in canon. The era's end may be harder to define.
74. *Crisis on Infinite Earths* #11 (1986).
75. *Batman* #408 (1986); *Tales of the Teen Titans* #44 (1986).
76. *Batman: The Killing Joke* (1988).
77. Respectively, Barbara Gordon—*Batman: The Killing Joke* (1988); Jason Todd—*Batman* #427–428 (1988–1989, all released in 1988 despite the cover dates); Sarah Essen—*Detective Comics* #741 (2000). 2000 was the last year of the 20th century, not the first year of the 21st.
78. *Batman: The Animated Series*, episode 1–22, "Joker's Favor" (September 11, 1992); *The Batman Adventures: Mad Love* (1994).
79. First called that in *Detective Comics* #45 (1940).
80. First appearance—*Batman: The Animated Series*, episode 1–07, "Joker's Favor" (September 11, 1992). Enters mainstream DC Universe continuity—*Batman: Harley Quinn* (1999).
81. Langley (2012), p. 111. See also Weiner & Peaslee (2015).
82. Primary opponents: Hush—*Batman* #613–615 (2003); Red Hood—*Batman* #638–642 (2005); Black Mask—*Batman* #643–644; Black Mask and Red Hood—*Batman* #648–650.
83. *Batman* #650 (2006); *Infinite Crisis* #5 (2006).

84. *Batman* #655 (2006).

85. *Batman* #663 (2007).

86. Vineyard (2008), cited by Tapley (2008).

87. Respectively, *Detective Comics* #1 (2011), *Batman* #17 (2013), and *Batman* #39 (2015).

88. Stevens (2008).

89. Remainder of paragraph excerpted from Langley (2012), pp. 21–23.

90. *Batman* #855 (2006).

91. *Arkham Asylum: A Serious House on Serious Earth* (1989).

92. Jakobwitz & Egan (2006); Paulhus & Williams (2002).

93. Jones & Paulhus (2010).

94. Macdonald (1963).

95. Ressler et al. (1988); Singer & Hensley (2004).

96. Franklin (2012); Skrapec & Ryan (2016).

97. Besl (n.d.); O'Boyle et al. (2012); Shpancer (2017).

98. Spencer (2012).

99. Book et al. (2016); Chabrol et al. (2009); Međedović & Petrović (2015).

100. *Arkham Asylum: A Serious House on Serious Earth* (1989); *Batman* #663 (2007).

101. Radish (2013).

102. *Justice League* #48 (2016), #50 (2016); *Batman: Three Jokers* (2019).

2

Who Created the Joker?

TRAVIS LANGLEY

OUR CAST OF CHARACTER CREATORS

Bob Kane, born Robert Kahn (1915–1998): Official creator of Batman and related characters.[1]

Bill Finger, born Milton Finger (1914–1974): Ghost writer behind Batman's defining features, not officially credited as co-creator until 2015.[2]

Jerry Robinson, born Sherrill David Robinson (1922–2011): Earliest ghost artist known to have worked on Batman stories.[3]

WITHIN THE FICTION, the Joker's personal history is unknown, perhaps even to him.[4] He provides wildly conflicting stories of who he is and how he came to be published, and throughout this book we'll address what that means for him in several ways. Within our world, the Joker's creative origin also has conflicting descriptions in terms of who conceived the character and how he came to be. Bob Kane, Bill Finger, and Jerry Robinson gave different, but overlapping, accounts. The biggest discrepancy in their recollections cuts straight to the central issue of who first conceived and named the character. Despite disagreement about *who*, *how*, and *why* they unleashed the Joker on the world, their points of agreement leave behind enough solid pieces that we might fit the puzzle together, perhaps resolving some of those points of disagreement as well.

The puzzle forms a historical picture and reveals a psychological story as well. As we apply critical and analytical reasoning to study, sort, assess, and piece together the available information, we must also consider *credibility* of the sources: believability, based on *expertise* and *trustworthiness*. With so little physical evidence, we must also consider what a terrible, unreliable, and yet utterly essential thing human memory is, with all its biases and other shortcomings. *Critical thinking*, objective analysis of an issue to form a judgment, can go hand in hand with *analytical reasoning*, discerning patterns and figuring out how things fit together.[5] We need to evaluate the witnesses for credibility, the testimonies for consistency and logical alignment, and the available evidence for verification.

Memory (the retention of learning over time) and *motivation* (whatever drives us to initiate and direct behavior) are among the most fundamental topics studied since psychology emerged as a distinct science.[6] Improving our understanding of them is essential as investigators in the field strive to develop better research methods, to learn when to trust our own results and when to question the things we find. The pioneers of *forensic psychology* (a group that includes the psychologist who went on to create Wonder Woman)[7] advanced the science of seeking truth.

As with any long-cold case, from determining whether Shakespeare wrote all of his own plays to identifying Jack the Ripper,[8] a forensic inquiry into the issue of who created the Joker starts with gathering the testimonies left behind and, when possible, whatever evidence remains.

Firsthand Witnesses: Batman's Big Three

The only direct information about the Joker's 1940 creation comes from the three who were there: Bob Kane, Bill Finger, and Jerry Robinson. Regarding his Batman work, Finger only gave a few interviews between a 1965 convention and his 1974 death. Kane and Robinson, though, talked about it in many interviews and wrote about it in autobiographical accounts. My own interview with Robinson on the matter appears at the end of this chapter (Explaining the Joke 2–1: Artist Jerry Robinson).

Batman begins with Bob Kane. Drawing influence from characters such as Zorro and the Shadow, Kane delivered unto National Comics (one of the companies that would merge to form DC) a masked hero he called Bat-Man. A few sources insinuate or frankly indicate that it was Bill

Finger who suggested the bat theme after Kane came to him with an idea for a bird-themed hero. They are wrong. Both Kane and Finger repeatedly and consistently said Kane named the character "Bat-Man" before Finger had anything to do with it.[9]

Whenever I've seen someone claim the bat theme came from Bill Finger, I've asked what their source was, and they've never had one to provide. One author admitted that he should have worded one such description differently in his Eisner Award–winning book, and added, "I was being purposely cagey in that speculative Bob and Bill dialogue. Probably too clever for my own good, since many people have read it as an assertion that Finger came up with the name."[10] While few people who know the history would be surprised if it eventually turned out that Bob Kane swiped "Bat-Man" from somebody else, the name did not come from Bill Finger.

Ghost writer Finger did conceive most of Batman's distinguishing details: Gotham City, the name Bruce Wayne, even the hero's general appearance (dark colors, scalloped cape, bat-shaped cowl). Without Finger's initial contributions, it's not the same character at all. Working for the publisher, other creators made some lasting contributions during that first year, too, such as when Gardner Fox turned Batman's ordinary belt into the utility belt or had the character hurl his first batarang.[11] Fox experimented with giving Batman more imaginative foes, introducing villains such as Doctor Death and the Monk to mix some variety into the line of gangsters and occasional mad scientists, but only when the Joker came along did the creative team start to cultivate the collection of colorful crooks whose themed crime sprees would characterize the most popular Batman stories for decades.

Where did that Joker come from?

Bob Kane, the Name in the Byline

Officially, for more than three-quarters of a century, Bob Kane received sole creator credit for Batman and his distinctive cast. For decades, he insisted that he alone created them. Over the years, though, he revised that a bit, then kept revising. For good reasons, people are less inclined to believe the person whose story keeps changing. Still, the honest person's report might change because that person will reconsider it when evidence indicates that the original information was—or current recollection is—incorrect, while a dishonest person might persuade some people simply by staying stubbornly loyal to a lie.[12] So it's important to consider both the pattern of any inconsistencies and which inconsistencies receive external support.

Seven years after Batman's 1939 debut, *Real Fact Comics* purported to reveal how Kane alone created Batman and company. Presented mostly from Bob Kane's point of view, "The True Story of Batman and Robin!" alleges that Kane was shopping at a novelty store one evening when a friend squirted him with a gag lapel flower. "The prank inspired Bob to invent the most bizarre villain in cartoon history—that prince of pranksters—the Joker!"[13] The five-page story ran with no author credit, but it was surely not written by Bob Kane, who is not known to have ever written a Batman-related story (or much else) on his own. Because the history the story depicts contradicts both external facts and any account later provided by anybody who ever worked on the early stories, there is no reason to consider it as the true story it proclaims to be.

"We needed a villain. I used to play practical jokes on my friends as a kid," Kane said much later in a 1990 television special.[14] "I used to play cards a lot when I was a youngster, and I remembered the joker playing card." That's about as much detail as he ever provided in the version in which he credited himself for the character. By the time of this program in which he talked about creating Batman and the other characters, he'd already spent decades trying to quash fan murmurings that someone else—specifically Bill Finger—had dreamed up most of them, ever since Finger himself said so during a 1965 convention.[15]

"All hogwash! I, Bob Kane, am the sole creator of 'Batman,'" Kane had written in response. "The only proof I need to back my statement is that if Bill co-authored and conceived the idea, either with me or before me, then he would most certainly have a by-line on the strip along with my name, the same as Siegel and Schuster had as creators of Superman."[16] It's a *tautologous* argument (a kind of circular reasoning)[17] to use the byline as evidence for its own accuracy. In the letter, Bob left room for Bill to be misremembering instead of lying: "It's been 25 years now, and truthfully, time sometimes blurs the memory and it is difficult to separate, at times, the myth from the truth, so that I cannot blame Bill too much if at times his memory 'clouds.'" Regarding the Joker, the letter referred to how the then-upcoming ABC-TV series would "have some of the villains that I created, The Joker, The Riddler, Catwoman, etc."[18]

When word got out about Bill Finger, Kane insisted that Bob Kane alone created the characters, including the Joker. After people started hearing that Jerry Robinson created the Joker, though, Kane then sometimes said that "it was actually Bill Finger."[19]

Bill Finger, the Cape Creator

During the 1930s, DeWitt Clinton High School in The Bronx, New York, produced a flood of writers and artists who became critical to Golden Age cartooning: Seymour Reit (co-creator of Casper, the Friendly Ghost); Will Eisner, "father of the modern graphic novel" (*The Spirit, A Contract with God*); Stanley Lieber, a.k.a. Stan Lee (the Marvel Universe); and both Robert Kahn and Milton Finger, before they became Batman's creators Bob Kane and Bill Finger.[20] Even though their time at DeWitt Clinton partly coincided, Kane and Finger did not meet until they later crossed paths at a party. Impressed with Finger, Bob Kane asked him to collaborate by writing adventure stories for Kane to illustrate.[21]

In the wake of Superman's success, writers and artists scrambled to catch that wave. When editor Vin Sullivan gave Bob Kane the chance to come up with something, Kane decided that instead of emulating Superman's nature, he wanted a mystery hero with no superpowers. That weekend, Finger overhauled Kane's Bat-Man to produce the dark hero who would take the world by storm.[22] Finger knew that he would be writing with no byline, as was common in cartooning at the time, because he needed work and because he was agreeable and easygoing—too much so, in some opinions. Irwin Hasen, the last surviving artist from the early Golden Age, drew superhero comics before World War II and co-created the superhero Wildcat with writer Bill Finger.[23] During his last years, I visited Irwin every time I went to New York, initially to introduce him to Bill's granddaughter Athena Finger and her son, but then because Irwin was a hoot. "Bill Finger was a sweetheart of a guy," Hasen told us, "but he didn't stand up for himself."[24] This matches other people's descriptions—"a good guy and a great writer who should have been better known" (artist Murphy Anderson[25]) and "a modest, self-effacing man" (writer E. Nelson Bridwell[26]).

Once Kane finally started saying Bill Finger created the Joker, his description of the character's creation grew much more detailed. "We were looking for super-villains in the first year of Batman. Bill and I were kicking around ideas about a maniacal killer who would play perennial life-and-death jokes on Batman that would test his mettle and ingenuity to outwit him. Then, about a week later, Bill came in with a photograph of Conrad Veidt, a fine German actor, who played in a movie called *The Man Who Laughs*."[27] In another interview, he elaborated, "Bill came to me, I remember this as clearly as 45 years ago, I've a great memory. Bill showed me a photo of Conrad Veidt, the German actor Veidt was in a movie called *The Man Who Laughed*—that's based on a famous novel by Victor Hugo. And that's where we got the Joker from, it was a photograph." Citing his "great memory" but getting the movie title wrong with his next breath does not work in Bob's favor. (Veidt starred in *The Man Who Laughs*,[28] not . . . *Laughed*.) Photos of Veidt as his character Gwynplaine the Laughing Man make it easy to accept Bob's assertion that "it's Conrad Veidt smiling that ghastly smile."[29] Within that same long interview, Kane said both, "The Joker, in fact, was created by Bill Finger" and, maybe out of habit, "I came up with the Riddler and the Joker."[30] (In 1965's *Batman* #169, editor Julius Schwartz named "Bill Finger, who created the Riddler" in print.[31])

In 1974, Bill Finger died broke and alone, two weeks short of his 60th birthday. A decade and a half later, Bob Kane said, "Now that my longtime friend and collaborator is gone, I must admit that Bill never received the fame and recognition he deserved. He was an unsung hero." Kane went as far as to say, "I often tell my wife, if I could go back fifteen years, before he died, I would like to say, 'I'll put your name on it now. You deserve it.'"[32] Saying so doesn't help the man who is long gone. After Bill's son Fred died too, people in the industry commonly (yet erroneously) thought that Bill had no living descendants who would have the legal standing to make the credit request on his behalf.[33]

One of Bill Finger's most vocal proponents was Jerry Robinson, who founded the Bill Finger Award in his honor to recognize comic book

The Swift Death of the
World's Greatest Supervillain

When creating the Joker, they clearly were not trying to develop a villain who would play perennial life-and-death jokes on Batman as Bob Kane sometimes said. Everyone who worked on the issue, including Kane, reported that they originally killed the Joker off in his first appearance. In the second of the issue's two Joker stories, the Joker accidentally stabs himself to death in the course of a fight against Batman. "Bill, are you crazy?" editor Whit Ellsworth said. "We have a great character here."[34] At Ellsworth's suggestion, the last panel was redrawn to include an ambulance scene in which a surprised doctor declares, "He isn't dead! He's still alive— and he's going to live!"[35]

writers whose achievements and body of work have not yet received the recognition they deserve.[36] Robinson said, "Bill Finger, in my opinion, was the best writer in comic books."

Jerry Robinson, Ambassador of Comics

In his introduction to *Jerry Robinson, Ambassador of Comics*, comic book writer/editor Dennis O'Neil proclaimed Jerry to be an exemplification of "the Modern American Artist"[37] for being a skilled and talented artist who cared about producing quality material, a pioneer who worked in a new medium (comics), a self-reliant first-generation American, and a Good Samaritan always willing to help. "He is the most benevolent man I have ever known, in or out of comics, and one of the most decent."[38]

Discovered by Bob Kane at age 17 on a tennis court in the Poconos, Columbia University journalism student Jerry Robinson became the earliest ghost artist known to have assisted on Batman stories during the Dark Knight's first year of publication.[39] Kane once told an interviewer that he had already hired George Roussos as his first art assistant, "then Jerry

Robinson came along and did backgrounds and lettering."[40] Bob's own biography, however, contradicts that: "Shortly after I hired Jerry, I took on a second assistant to draw and ink backgrounds. His name was George Roussos."[41] Jerry, George, and others all confirmed the Jerry-first version.[42]

"At first DC didn't know about us," Robinson explained. "Bob took the finished pages down to the office and pretended he did all the art and the writing. I'm not certain when or how they knew. But at some point they found out." In light of the character's success, Finger and Robinson asked Kane for more money. He refused, so they decided to quit. "When DC heard we were leaving, they got frantic. [Editor] Whitney Ellsworth and [publisher] Jack Liebowitz called us into the office and made us offers not to leave Batman. That was the first meeting Bill and I ever had with anyone at DC."[43] The company gave them substantial raises, greater freedom on stories, opportunities to work on other titles, and direct editorial feedback.

One year after Batman's debut, the character got his own title. *Batman* #1 would be the spring 1940 issue. Suddenly, on top of producing one story per month for *Detective Comics* and another for *World's Finest Comics*, the three men had to put four more stories together quickly. Robinson said the publisher was "going to do one issue to see how well it went. They needed it by a certain date that wasn't far off."[44] In the interview that appears at the end of this chapter, consistent with his many other interviews on this subject,[45] Robinson told us that he was going to write one of the four stories so they could meet that deadline.

For the young Columbia student, the opportunity was exciting. "So I thought of doing a story that would do double duty—that I could write for *Batman* and that would serve as a piece of creative writing for the class," he told Kane's biographer.[46] "That night I went to work on it in my little room. My first thought was to create a villain, a strong villain to oppose Batman. This was before I even tried to write any plot ideas." His private brainstorming session led to his "Eureka!" moment: He would create a sinister clown. "I immediately made an association with the classic joker playing card with that marvelous grinning face," so just past midnight, he went scrambling through his room for a deck of playing cards, one that included the classic joker, for reference. "Everything crystallized then— his name was the Joker, and he would give out joker playing cards as his calling card. Then I made my first concept drawing of the Joker, a playing card with the Joker's face on it." He could not sleep. "I can't tell you how excited I was. I couldn't wait to rush over to Bob's with the idea."[47] Robinson immediately began spinning ideas for the first story.

"Bob liked the idea when I brought in the drawing the next day. He immediately sat down at his drawing board and began to sketch the full figure and round out the concept."[48] Robinson said that Finger soon arrived and loved the idea, too. Seeing the illustration, Finger said, "That's Conrad Veidt!" Neither Robinson nor Kane knew who he meant, so days later Finger brought them a photo from a book about *The Man Who Laughs*. Veidt's likeness provided an additional reference point as they fleshed out the Joker's look and completed the story. The concept was so strong, though, that Kane believed Finger, who was the more experienced writer and who was not also busy with college, should script the story. Robinson recalled, "As it was my very first script, it would have taken me too long, they argued. I worked with Bill, however, to flesh out the concept."[49] The experience hit Robinson hard. "Since my original motivation was to write the story, I was on the verge of tears," he said.[50] "I was heartbroken, but, for the sake of the feature, I had to admit that Bill was far better equipped to write it. I never attempted to write another Batman story. I guess my experience with the Joker story turned me off."[51]

"He did *not*," Bob Kane insisted on the issue of whether Jerry Robinson created the Joker, "and I want to refute this succinctly once and for all, because it's coming straight from the horse's mouth—me. If he did create it, I would have given him credit now, because I'm a very honest person with a lot of integrity."[52] (More than a few people would dispute this self-assertion of honesty and integrity,[53] but he has some defenders.[54]) "He might have brought in a playing card and said, 'Hey, why don't you throw in a playing card here and there.' That, I do not remember."[55] On other occasions, Bob said that Jerry drew the Joker playing card, "but this was after the fact; he did not create the original concept of the Joker. Now, I don't say that Jerry is doing this intentionally, but time has eroded his memory."[56]

Who do we believe? Or in the words of Jack Nicholson's Joker, "Who do you trust?"[57]

Witness Credibility

When we consider *source credibility*, we look at two things: expertise and trustworthiness.[58] A source needs both. For example, one book includes more than half a dozen Bill Finger quotes its author later could not verify.[59] He never met Finger, so those weren't firsthand communications. Where, then, did they come from? Unfortunately, he could not recall when asked and had not retained his research materials, nor could the book's editor help. Despite its author's expertise, the book's trustworthiness becomes uncertain. The quotes may or may not be correct, but Finger gave so few interviews that it would be difficult for comics historians to have missed so many or to have no idea where that author might have found them.

In the case of the Joker's creation, we mostly consider witness credibility because there is very little evidence other than the three individuals' firsthand reports. Only one of the three individuals, Jerry Robinson, spoke with me about this personally, but a few recordings exist in which Bill Finger talked about it and many recordings exist of Bob Kane. Jerry was a versatile artist, Bill established the template for how everyone should write comic book stories, and Bob brought them together. The three of them all had the expertise on how they worked together during that first year, so we have to weigh their trustworthiness. That's not just about honesty. A person can truthfully report things that are wrong, whether because the individual learned them incorrectly in the first place, got misled by someone else, started getting details mixed up with other things that happened over the years, or just can't remember everything.

We couldn't go inside the three men's heads, even if they were alive, to know whether they really believed the claims they made. Bob Kane's biographer Tom Andrae believed the man tried to tell the truth about his life: "I think he was fairly honest but too self-centered to see reality clearly enough and had a bad memory to boot. His ego was always in the way. He primarily remembered what he did on Batman—and that was usually inflated—rather than others' contributions. I constantly had to fact-check what he told me because he had a predisposition to aggrandize his work on Batman."[60]

Setting their truthful intent aside, whether to give them all the benefit of the doubt or to view their conscious intent as unconfirmable, we have to look at human memory and motivation.

Memory

Memory is unreliable. That's a fact. Our overconfidence in our memory and judgment tends to be strong[61] because the alternative would mean mistrusting ourselves and suffering the stress of *cognitive dissonance*.[62] Social psychology's underlying theme is that the world can be a scary, chaotic place, so we do things to convince ourselves that it's less scary and more predictable than it really is.[63] That means we must start by trusting our own memory or judgment before we can use them to trust anything or anyone else. Bob Kane said he had an excellent memory,[64] but his biographer Tom Andrae said that the man did not.[65] Although Andrae as an outside party may offer a more objective view of Kane's memory than Kane could himself, he only dealt with the man late in Kane's life. In younger days, Kane's memory impressed Jerry Robinson: He recalled Kane repeating entire routines he'd heard stand-up comedians perform in clubs.[66]

As Kane said of both Finger and Robinson, time erodes the memory. He acknowledged that the same was true of himself in at least one instance: After saying that Bill Finger created the Penguin and Catwoman, Kane added, "Maybe Penguin was mine—again, time erodes the memory."[67] This pattern of blaming memory erosion suggests a *self-serving bias*, a common human inclination, because Kane asserts that the other two misremembered things when they said they deserved more credit but that his own misremembering might mean he deserved even more credit. In each instance, he interpreted possible memory deficits in his own favor.

The *self-enhancement motive*, to seek out and interpret situations in ways that promote self-esteem, is natural enough, as is the *self-verification motive*, to seek out and interpret situations in ways that confirm one's self-concept.[68] This does not pose much of a problem for people with healthy self-esteem. It's more troublesome for those whose self-esteem is on shakier ground, so they might seek self-enhancing evidence more frantically. Bill Finger was known to have low self-esteem and Bob Kane has been called egotistical or narcissistic many times,[69] whereas

Jerry Robinson was not generally viewed as someone at either extreme. Robinson said of Kane, "Big egos generally hide an inferiority of some kind. That's why they have an ego to protect themselves. Bob was insecure in some ways about the strip. That's why he couldn't share credit and always presented himself as the sole creator of Batman."[70] An inner quality such as *clinical narcissism* is difficult to judge regarding public figures, who may act very differently when speaking publicly and promoting their work. Modern ethical guidelines caution psychologists against diagnosing public figures or anyone else they do not professionally know.[71] Even narcissists act differently in public, which makes their public faces less than ideal foundations for evaluating their inner personas. Grandiose narcissists are more likely to attribute collaborative success to themselves than to their partners, a difference more pronounced when they express their attributions publicly as opposed to how they view things privately, whereas people low in narcissism do not make as many self-serving attributional biases in either instance.[72] Whether Kane was narcissistic or simply gave many people that impression, we might place greater faith in things he said in personal conversations than in public interviews. In addition to interviews for his biography, for example, he also had many personal conversations with Tom Andrae.

Motivation

Motivation colors memory and drives both honesty and dishonesty. Prosecuting attorneys often build cases by proving that defendants had motives to commit crimes or by offering speculation that plausible-sounding motives existed. When investigating the mystery of the Joker's creation, we can look at motivated inaccuracies regardless of whether they were purposeful; to be fair to people who are no longer around to speak up for themselves, there is little reason to treat them as though they consciously meant to mislead. Inaccuracy is inaccuracy either way.

There are many reasons why someone may speak up about a disputed event. An *intrinsically motivated* person does something because the activity is rewarding in and of itself. Many people talk just to hear themselves talk. Some tell the truth because they value truth itself, regardless of consequences. To Bob Kane, "a man known just as much (if not more) for his ego as for his comics,"[73] receiving credit provided inner rewards. Indeed, according to biographer Andrae, Bob Kane loved thinking of himself as the man who created Batman: "Bob confessed that his ego prevented him from giving Bill the credit he deserved."[74] For Finger, known for not standing up for himself enough, the mere act of self-assertion might finally have given him a feeling of reassurance, strength, or power in his own life. Any feelings of resentment he may have harbored might also have motivated him to vent, out of believing or feeling that doing so might provide some relief.

Extrinsic motivation, the impetus to do something in order to get external rewards and fulfill an *ulterior motive*, abounds when we're looking at any dispute over who created some of the most famous, most profitable characters in the history of the world. Kane also confessed to Andrae his fear that giving up any of the credit would mean giving up some of the money.[75] Admiration and attention are other possible external sources that could drive a person to interpret, remember, or report things in certain ways.

It should be easy to see how claiming to have created Batman or the Joker could provide intrinsic or extrinsic reward, but what, then, motivates someone to argue on another person's behalf? How can that be self-serving? Jerry Robinson became one of the most vocal advocates for Bill Finger for years after Bill left this world. Bob Kane, too, argued on Finger's behalf when insisting that Finger, not Robinson, created the Joker. *Altruistic* motives might include concern for truth or empathy for others.[76] *Selfish* or *egoistic* motives for the same behavior, however, could range from some sort of resentment between Kane and Robinson to a desire to be seen championing on someone else's behalf to enhancing self-esteem by feeling like such a champion.[77] Tom Andrae opined that Kane "never gave others, like Shelly Moldoff, who was his ghost artist for 20 years, any credit, nor Jerry Robinson for his creation of the Joker. Bob expressed a lot of anger towards Jerry, stemming, I think, from being jealous of him, of his artistic ability, and of the recognition that he had received."[78]

The Testimonies

We are more inclined to believe claims that show *consistency*. Of the three, Jerry Robinson's account showed the greatest consistency across the different occasions when he described the experience, and Bob Kane's showed the least. Kane switched from saying he alone created the Joker to sometimes saying that Finger did. Once he started saying it had been Bill, his account grew more detailed and showed greater consistency in those new details. Kane shows poor consistency on many other claims, though. At different times, for example, he said he created the Penguin, he said Bill did, and he said he was not sure which of them did.[79]

Admittedly, a person can consistently report a well-established lie. Besides consistency, other things we look for are the kinds of details that people are more likely to include when reporting genuine, vivid memories. Possibly because genuine memories are obtained through perceptual experience, honest reports are more likely to include sensory or emotional details.[80] Jerry mentioned having a craving for a cigarette on the night he came up with the Joker because "I smoked in those days"[81]—sensory detail. He alone described his "Eureka!" moment full of excitement when the idea came to him, the subsequent heartbreak that brought him to the edge of tears when Kane decided Finger should write the story, and the lasting impact which then deterred Robinson from ever trying to write another Batman story—emotional details.

How do their descriptions fit together? When witnesses confirm one another's testimony, they offer some *corroboration*. Other details, though, either fall into dispute (refuted) or lack corroboration (unconfirmed).

- Bob Kane said that he created the Joker, but he also said that Bill Finger created the Joker. Given his history of self-serving embellishment, the less self-serving story seems more likely to indicate what he believed.

- Kane said that Finger came to him with the Conrad Veidt photo first and that Robinson showed them his playing card sketch later, whereas Robinson said it was the other way around.

- Finger agreed with Robinson: The playing card sketch came first. After seeing it, Finger showed them the Conrad Veidt photo.

- Bill Finger did not say that the Joker came from him. Or did he? See the sidebar, "It Came from Coney Island."

It Came from Coney Island

Complicating things are other sources indicating that Bill Finger did indeed say he created the Joker, inspired by the image of a face painted over the Steeplechase entrance at Coney Island. According to Bill's son, Fred Finger, Bill and Bob "were out at Coney Island, just ya-ya-ing around, and Bill said, 'That's the face, that's the face!'—and that's how the Joker's face came." The son, though, was retrieving a child's recollection of a secondhand story about a father he'd admired despite later estrangement. Fred acknowledged that Jerry Robinson's account was "possible, too."[82]

Artists Jim Steranko and Carmine Infantino provided secondhand accounts consistent with Fred's. Steranko said, "According to Bill, it was he who created the Joker, inspired by the imagery he spotted on a Coney Island ride."[83] Infantino reported seeing evidence: "Bill showed me a drawing—Bill used to go to Steeplechase out in Coney Island, Brooklyn. On there was a character that looked like a joker's head . . . . He made a copy of that head."[84] Both artists acknowledged that they'd heard conflicting versions, even from Bill himself, when he mentioned the Conrad Veidt likeness.

- Their secondhand reports leave room for Bill Finger to have mentioned that the Steeplechase face had been *a point of reference*, like the Veidt photo, without his actually having said Coney Island is where it all began.

- Finger was no longer working on Batman stories by the time Steranko interviewed him.

- Both Infantino and Steranko expressed uncertainty as to how the different accounts meshed.

- Both held strong anti-Bob views, arguably biases. Infantino went as far as to say that Bill "made Batman, no one else. Kane had nothing to do with it. Bill did it all."[85] By his own report, Steranko once slapped Bob Kane across the face.[86]

- The Steeplechase anecdote is absent from interviews with and writings by those who worked on Batman in the early days.

In the end, the Coney Island origin does not fit reports by *all three*—Kane, Finger, and Robinson—that the Joker began with the card drawing and the Veidt photo, regardless of their respective order. "That's the face, that's the face!" came later.

The Evidence

Not much physical evidence exists, but there is something. We know Conrad Veidt's photo somehow became an artistic reference during the process. That much was never in dispute. Bob Kane offered a photo of Veidt from *The Man Who Laughs* as evidence that the photo had to come first, comparing it to a clearly similar illustration of the Joker from *Batman* #4.[87] (Notice that came from #4 instead of #1, therefore not the issue in which the Joker first appears.) Kane presented his case to his friend Stan Lee, who co-created countless characters for Marvel Comics and wrote forewords for two books in this Popular Culture Psychology series.[88]

Kane: I had a ghost artist, which I'd like to refute now. His claim to fame was that he created the Joker—Jerry Robinson. And Jerry Robinson created the Joker playing card, which I'll let you look at in a moment. It's over here. Bill Finger, my writer, came to me at the beginning with a picture of Conrad Veidt, who was the actor in a Victor Hugo movie called *The Man Who Laughs*. As you can all see, it's an exact replica of the comic I drew way back in 1939, 1940, and that was my

Conrad Veidt as Gwynplaine in
The Man Who Laughs (1928 motion picture).

creation of the Joker. Jerry Robinson to his dying day will say that
he created. And look, here's my answer to him: Had Jerry come to
me first with the Joker playing card, the Joker would have looked like
this (Conrad Veidt photo) and not like this (splash page from the first
Joker story). . . .

Lee: Well, since this isn't a court of law, I might add one thing, though.

Kane: I did prove my case, right?

Lee: No, you didn't . . . . But whoever created it, the point is—

Kane: No, no, I just proved my case.[89]

Kane then proceeded to repeat his case, which is a point in his favor:
People who do not believe what they're saying more readily welcome a
change of subject and move onto another.[90] In defending Finger, Kane
said, "The only reason I make an issue out of it is that the Joker is the best
villain ever created, outside of Moriarty in Sherlock Holmes."[91]

Jerry Robinson's first Joker sketch.

Jerry Robinson still had the most solid piece of physical evidence—his original Joker playing card sketch. Bill Finger said the sketch came first, and even Bob Kane told Stan Lee that it was Jerry's sketch.

Real Fact

When we're trying to understand what really happened and who deserves recognition for their work, it's important to recognize Bob Kane himself. Downplaying his true importance or distorting it would diminish our credibility and detract from any other point we endeavor to make. Batman begins with Bob. Regardless of where he drew the bat theme from, Bob Kane deserves credit for bringing a costumed mystery-man with no superpowers, Bat-Man (before Finger started writing the name as Batman), to writer Bill Finger to flesh out and then to editor Vincent Sullivan to get published. Had Kane been more forthcoming about his practice of relying on ghost writers and ghost artists, he might be remembered more fondly as a man who had a remarkable eye for talent and an ability to bring people such as Bill Finger and Jerry Robinson together.

On one point, Bob Kane is more likely than Jerry Robinson to be right. Kane said Robinson did not come up with the Joker's background: "But he did *not* create the origin. Bill Finger did, and he should get all the credit for it."[92] Robinson agreed with the first part: He felt strongly that the Joker should never have an origin. According to him though, neither he nor Finger wrote the origin but instead another writer did that later on. Reprint indexes credit Bill Finger with the origin revealed in *Detective Comics* #168's "The Man Behind the Red Hood!" By the time that story came out in 1951, Robinson was no longer working on Batman stories: "I left Batman in 1947."[93] Kane's involvement was minimal by 1951, but he nevertheless had knowledge of what was going on at the time in a way that Robinson did not. Finger apparently wrote the origin.

As for the bigger issue, though, a preponderance of the testimonies and evidence indicates that it was Jerry Robinson who first imagined the Joker. It is worth noting that one DC Comics publication, *The Amazing World of DC Comics* #4, recognized Jerry as such in a headline, "Profile on Jerry Robinson—Creator of the Joker."[94] Perhaps that 1975 article is what prompted Bob Kane to start proclaiming that Bill Finger was the creator, a year after Bill died.

When there's a discrepancy between Bob Kane and anybody else, I'm inclined to believe anybody else.

> *"Still, as Bob Kane recalls Bill Finger as The Joker's creator and Bill told me it was Jerry Robinson's idea, I think we can accept Jerry as having come up with the concept."*
> —comics editor and historian E. Nelson Bridwell[95]

NOTES

1. Beginning in *Detective Comics* #27 (1939).
2. First official co-creator credit on-screen: *Robot Chicken DC Comics Special III* (October 18, 2015). In print: *Batman and Robin Eternal #3* (2015) and *Batman: Arkham Knight Genesis #3* (2015), both published in the same week. See *Batman & Bill* (2017 documentary) for details on how this came about.
3. Beginning sometime during the first year of Batman's appearances in *Detective Comics*. Kane (1989); Rosenberg et al. (2009).

4. *Batman: The Killing Joke* (1988).
5. Levy (1997); Pandey (2009); Smith (2001).
6. Petri (1996); Pink (2009); Schultz & Schultz (2012).
7. Lloyd (2017); Marston (1917, 1928).
8. Shakespeare–McCrea (2005). Jack the Ripper—Louhelainen (2019).
9. e.g., Kane (1989); Porfirio (1972/2011); Steranko (1970); Zimmerman (1986/1989a).
10. G. Jones, email (January 28, 2014).
11. *Detective Comics* #29, #31 (1939).
12. Ford (1996); King (2006); Walters (2000).
13. *Real Fact Comics* #5 (1946).
14. *The Two Masks of the Caped Crusader: An Interview with Bob Kane* (1990), The Family Channel special.
15. Bails (1965).
16. Kane (1967).
17. Levy (1997).
18. Though not published until 1967, the letter was written in 1965.
19. Andrae (1989), p. A–79.
20. Wisnieski (2012). What was in the water there?
21. Nobleman (2012).
22. Kane (1989); Nobleman (2012).
23. *Sensation Comics* #1 (1942).
24. Personal communication (2014).
25. Personal communication (2014).
26. Bridwell (1986), p. 66.
27. Andrae (1989), p. A–79.
28. *The Man Who Laughs* (1928 motion picture).
29. Zimmerman (1986/1989a), p. 16.
30. Zimmerman (1986/1989a), p. 17 (1989a edition).
31. *Batman* #169 (1965), referring to *Detective Comics* #140 (1948).
32. Kane (1989), p. 44.
33. As noted by Nobleman (2012); *Batman & Bill* (2017 documentary).
34. Quoted by Finger Porfirio (1972/2011), p. 83.
35. *Batman* #1 (1940d).
36. Comic-Con International (n.d.).
37. O'Neil (2010), p. 11.
38. O'Neil (2010), p. 13.
39. Andrae (1989, 2011); Gustines (2010); Robinson (2009, 2010, 2017).
40. Andrae (1989), p. A–78.
41. Kane (1989), p. 101; retained in the 1996 revision.
42. Comic-Con International (n.d.).
43. Andrae (2011), p. 99.
44. Andrae (2011), p. 103.
45. e.g., Andrae (2011); Tollin (1975).
46. Andrae (2011), p. 103.
47. Andrae (2011), p. 104.
48. Tollin (1975), p. 3.
49. Robinson (2017), p. 22.
50. Tollin (1975), p. 3.
51. Andrae, p. 104.
52. Zimmerman (1986/1989a), p. 16.
53. Baker (n.d.); Cronin (2008); Feddes (2017); Hanley (2017); Seifert (2014); Sims (2013).
54. e.g., his niece, Bonnie Rosenweig, quoted by Nobleman (2013a).
55. Zimmerman (1986/1989a), p. 16.
56. Andrae (1989), p. A–80.
57. Batman (1989 motion picture).
58. Wiener & Mowen (1986).
59. Daniels (1999)—called into question by Nobleman (2008).
60. Nobleman (2014).
61. Dougherty (2001); Hansson et al. (2008); Hilton et al. (2011).
62. Festinger (1957); McGrath (2017); Levy et al. (2018); Rodriguez & Strange (2015).
63. Baumeister (2010).
64. e.g., Zimmerman (1986/1989a).
65. Nobleman (2014).
66. Ringgenberg (1988/2012); Robinson (2009).
67. Zimmerman (1986/1989a), p. 17.
68. Self-enhancement—Dunning et al. (1995); self-verification—Swann (1997).

69. e.g., Porter (2008); Reed (n.d.).
70. Andrae (2011), pp. 99, 101.
71. American Psychological Association (2003/2017).
72. Selle et al. (2017).
73. Jackson (2013).
74. Nobleman (2014).
75. Andrae (2015).
76. e.g., Batson et al. (1981).
77. e.g., Dovidio et al. (2006).
78. Nobleman (2014).
79. Andrae (1989); Zimmerman (1986/1989a).
80. Gray (2011); Johnson & Raye (1981); Masip et al. (2005).
81. Robinson (2012).
82. Zimmerman (1986/1989b), p. 23.
83. Karlin (2014).
84. Nobleman (2013b).
85. Nobleman (2013b).
86. Infinite Midlives (2014); Jackson (2013).
87. *Batman* #4 (1941).
88. Lee (2016, 2018).
89. *The Comic Book Greats* (1991 documentary series). Online: CrashLanden (2011).
90. Ford (1996); Meyers (2010); Walters (2000).
91. Andrae (1989), p. A–79.
92. Zimmerman (1986/1989a), p. 16.
93. Andrae (2011), p. 111.
94. Tollin (1975).
95. Bridwell (1986), p. 66.

EXPLAINING THE JOKE 2-1

ARTIST JERRY ROBINSON

Travis Langley

Jerry Robinson (1922–2011) was the earliest known ghost artist to work on Batman comics, initially drawing backgrounds but eventually entire stories for which only Bob Kane received credit in print. Weeks before our San Diego Comic-Con convention panel, we had a conversation which Jerry allowed me to record for posterity.

The Character's Creation

Jerry Robinson: I started on Batman at the ripe old age of 17. I was going to Columbia University. I had visions of being a journalist and writer. I just thought of drawing as a way to get into college, and here we are years later. Batman became quite popular by its second or third issue. National Comics decided to add a *Batman* quarterly. Where we only had to add one story a month for *Detective Comics*, suddenly we were producing four stories with a new quarterly. The co-creator—as he should be termed—of Batman was Bill Finger, as you know. He undoubtedly was the best writer, period. He wrote the original story. He outlined the costume, the persona of Batman. He wasn't acknowledged in his own time, unfortunately. He was a close friend and my cultural mentor at the time.

So we got together that day when we found out we had to suddenly produce four stories. Bill, while he was a great writer full of ideas, was a careful craftsman and he wasn't prolific. We immediately saw that he was going to have a tough time doing all those stories at once, so I volunteered to do a story. They knew my writing ambitions. They had read some of my short stories that I had written for my creative writing class, so they readily agreed that I would write one of those stories. I literally went home that night (my home was a little room in The Bronx) terribly excited. It was an opportunity to do work where I would hopefully get paid for writing a Joker story and I was going to hand it into my creative writing class as double duty. That's called creative writing. *[Laughs]*

My first thought was that most all the villains at that time were gangsters, embezzlers, bank robbers. Those were our models for the villains: Pretty Boy Floyd, John Dillinger, Machine Gun Kelly. We had a mad scientist now and then. That was the extent of it. Through my studies, I knew that all the great heroes in literature had an antagonist, and that great characters had some contradiction in terms.[1] I thought for my villain to have a sense of humor would be different.

Names, of course, are very important. It's one of the first things we try to associate with a character. At least I did. Once I started thinking of a villain with a sense of humor, the name "the Joker" immediately came to mind. I immediately associated with the Joker playing card. Playing cards played an important part in my family because one of my brothers was a champion contract bridge player, and my mother was a very good player and I dabbled. So we always had playing cards in the house. And then I think I yelled literally, "Eureka!" because I knew I had the name and the image. I remember searching frantically for a deck of cards in my little room, where I was holed up and did my work. Luckily, I had it and it fortunately had the classic image. I adapted the image, which would be his calling card. Then it was fleshed out—the persona and the things he did. That very night, I drew the first concept sketch, which fortunately I found in the back of a drawer a few years ago. I think it's priceless.

The Adversary

Robinson: As I finished the character sketch of his personality, "The Cask of Amontillado" was an influence on the Joker, his M.O. I was very impressed with the stories of Edgar Allan Poe. Also, I wanted to give Batman a Professor Moriarty, like Sherlock Holmes had. I wanted him to be a master criminal. I didn't think in psychological terms, but he certainly was a psychopath. The first story, I worked with Bill. Bill Finger wrote that finished script from the details we worked out. From the very beginning, he was a murderer; he showed no remorse. He gave Batman a strong antagonist to work against. I didn't think that he was insane. He was clever.

The Joker's Origin Story

Robinson: They've given many origins of the Joker, how he came to be. That doesn't seem to matter. Just how he is now. We didn't give—and I never intended to give—a reason for his appearance. We discussed that, and Bill and I never wanted to give an explanation. I thought—and he agreed—that it takes away some of the essential mystery. It becomes too mundane. He fell in a vat of chemicals—that was one explanation. Well, once you know that, anybody can fall into a vat and they get grotesque scarring, there's another Joker.

We decided deliberately not to explain it, not to write an origin. We thought that would detract from the whole aura, the mystery of the Joker. Where did he come from? How did he get that way? No, we did not explain that, quite deliberately. The origin story was written by a subsequent writer many years later.[2] When you answer the questions, it loses some of its mystery, it becomes too mundane.

Appearance

Robinson: The Joker has a blank face for everybody to etch their own creation on and add wrinkles of their own. It is a character that has grown obviously and can be interpreted and reinterpreted. Certainly in the comics, a visual medium, that's important. I decided to leave his face white simply because I wanted him to resemble the playing card joker. He didn't have green hair. It was just the white of his face and the red of his lips. We did not explain it quite deliberately.

I think the visual is that thread that carries the Joker through all his interpretations and the longevity of it. Why is that? I think one element of it is the fact that he looked like a clown. A clown evokes enormous emotion—you know that. There's a phobia, fear of clowns, *coulrophobia*. Even if you don't have a phobia, when you meet a clown you immediately have a visual reaction.

The story still persists that the look of the Joker came from Conrad Veidt.[3]

Travis Langley: From *The Man Who Laughs*.[4]

Robinson: It's true and not true. Bob and I had never heard of *The Man Who Laughs* before Bill brought it up. Bill was an aficionado of offbeat films, particularly German expressionism. Conrad Veidt was a well-known German actor. In that first meeting when I showed Bill sketches of the Joker, he said that grin reminded him of Conrad Veidt in *The Man Who Laughs*: "That's Conrad Veidt!" That was the first mention of it. He says, "I'll show you." Then he found in his apartment a clip of Conrad Veidt in that role, and he brought it in. I said, "That's astounding. It looks so much like the Joker." That was after the fact. It had nothing to do with the playing card and how I came to that first image. It helped them visualize the character.

Langley: I've heard fans cite Conrad Veidt as evidence when arguing over who deserved credit for creating the Joker.

Robinson: The historian Bridwell interviewed Bill Finger, where he said the Joker was by me.[5] He can be credited, and Bob himself. We all played a role in it. The concept was mine. Bill finished that first script from my outline of the persona and what should happen in the first story. He wrote the first script of that, so he really is the co-creator. And Bob and I did the first visuals, so Bob was also. As Bill said, Bob didn't create any of the other characters except perhaps Two-Face. Bill Finger was really the creative genius on Batman. I think he did more on Two-Face than he admits himself. Sometimes Bill was so self-deprecating that he didn't take credit for things he did do at times. It's a tragedy. He died broke and uncredited. It's why

I started that award [the Bill Finger Award, which recognizes comic book writers and artists who deserve greater acknowledgment for their important contributions to the field] that at San Diego is given in his name every year.[6] Every time I've ever interviewed, I've said it should have been "created by Bob Kane and Bill Finger," like Siegel and Shuster [Superman's creators].

Mercurial Nature

Robinson: In later versions, there are so many nuances to the character that the writers had to focus on one or another. Another element that I thought was best not defined: You didn't know whether he was a criminal psychopath or criminally insane or just weird, or what his motivation was exactly. I thought it was best to let that evolve and let it grow. That's one of the elements of the newspaper strip that I felt should be incorporated into the comics, and I've written about that in the history of comics (*The Comics: An Illustrated History of Comic Strip Art*).[7]

As readers aged and matured and had different viewpoints, so the characters of that time—the good characters—grew and evolved. And so it was with the Joker, who evolved but was essentially the same with many nuances to his character now. So there's room to grow and change. If we had established definitively what he was at the very beginning, that he was criminally insane and so forth and so on, he would have been closed up in a box that you were limited by. I think it was good that we didn't do that because then it was able to grow and different artists have added their own vision to it. Now I don't think we thought, "This is going to be great for future artists," but it was great for the feature and the next issue or two.

All characters that are very memorable will go through changes over time. In some ways it's a tribute to the character that it can grow and evolve but still retain its essential nature. Certainly the Joker is a blank face for everybody to etch their own creation on and add wrinkles of their own. It is a character that has grown on its own, obviously, and can be interpreted and reinterpreted. There are exceptions. I guess you can say James Bond has remained essentially the same. New face, new gimmicks, that's about it. Tarzan has endured. Even Superman has remained essentially the same. I think they would have a harder path because of his invulnerability, so they had to keep inventing new Achilles' heels for him. We had the same publisher. I personally was very good friends with Siegel and Shuster, and we would be in a friendly rivalry. I always thought that Batman was a better concept. Superman's weakness was his invulnerability, and I thought it would never last. Shows how much I knew.

Depictions on Screen

Langley: Have you discussed the Joker with the screenwriters working on the movies or shows?

Robinson: No, I didn't. I was supposed to meet with them in Chicago when they were filming [*The Dark Knight*], but I had a wonderful invitation, which I had accepted some months before, to go to China to give a paper on the comics to a thousand artists from Southeast Asia. I was so anxious to talk to Christian Bale and Heath [Ledger] and the director about it, so I regret missing that, but I knew that I would be back in time to go to London for some of the filming there—which I did.

I did sit in on the story conferences for that first *Batman* serial, which was an experience in itself. I took my first flight ever to California, to Hollywood, in about '42 when they were filming the *Batman* serial. That's the first time I thought Bill could have done a better job of writing that serial. I think they didn't really know the comics at that time.

Langley: Have you ever gotten to discuss the role with the actors who've played it?

Robinson: I did meet Cesar Romero having a drink in a studio meeting room, long before he played the Joker, in about '42 when they were filming a Batman serial.[8] He was a very personable guy.

Langley: Out of the various movies and TV shows and cartoons, is there one that stands out as doing the best job of capturing the character of the Joker?

Robinson: I thought undoubtedly the Nicholson and Ledger performances stand out. They were unique interpretations that were quite different. Nicholson's was a lighter version than Ledger's. I thought he gave a bravura performance for what it was. My biggest objection to that was the script, but Nicholson saved it with his performance. I was very pleased when they told me that Nolan and his brother [filmmakers Christopher and Jonathan Nolan] liked the original concept of the Joker and they wanted to evolve their version from the original, and I think they caught part of that.

Secret to the Success

Robinson: What makes him stand out? You don't know. If I knew the formula, I would have five Jokers by now. No, that combination, I'm afraid, only comes once in a lifetime. So you might analyze it and probe it and give many explanations, but that's after the fact. If we knew before the fact, then we'd have something priceless.

I'm interested in your take on the Joker. You quizzed me enough. *[Laughs]*

And so our conversation continued.

NOTES

1. Up until this point, the material quoting Jerry comes from the Rosenberg et al. (2009) Comic-Con panel. He was repeating things he had previously said in personal conversations before I asked if I could start recording because he was saying such wonderful stuff. The remainder of the interview comes from the recording of one of our pre-panel talks.
2. *Detective Comics* #168 (1951).
3. e.g., Muszalski (2009), shortly before Jerry said that.
4. *The Man Who Laughs* (1928 motion picture).
5. Bridwell (1986).
6. Bill Finger Award (n.d.).
7. Robinson (1974/2011).
8. The movie serial *Batman* debuted its first episode, "The Electric Brain," on June 16, 1943. Cesar Romero was not involved with the project.

3

Horror: A Clown, at Midnight

ERIC D. WESSELMANN, TRAVIS LANGLEY,
& VANESSA HICKS

"Tonight, a precisely twelve o'clock midnight,
I will kill Henry Claridge and steal the Claridge diamond!
Do not try to stop me! The Joker has spoken!"
—The Joker's first words in his debut story[1]

"That, to me, is the essence of true horror—a clown, at midnight."
—horror author Robert Bloch[2]

THE CLOWN ARRIVES, announcing there will be murder at midnight. With those words, the Joker starts a reign of chaos that continues to this day. The Joker never fails to captivate us. Just as Batman will "never get used to the rigored smiles of the Joker's victims,"[3] we remain unsettled by the Joker's seemingly random acts of nihilistic brutality. The strange discomfort goes beyond how a number of people find clowns generally unsettling.[4] Humans have deep-seated psychological needs to understand the actions of others, as well as to reduce uncertainty and find meaning in a seemly chaotic world,[5] but the Joker defies those needs in every way. The threat of death intensifies this need for meaning,[6] and his unpredictable violence always makes the threat of death salient. Even other criminals are terrified of the Joker.[7]

As if to compound the Joker's threat to meaning, we have no real idea what makes him the way he is. Various authors have provided hints of his backstory, but these hints do not satisfy our desire for answers. These hints are simply possibilities. Consistency is scarce in the hints the Joker provides when making claims about his past.[8] The Joker defies predictability by his very nature.

Quoth the Joker

"Take thy beak from out my heart."
—The Joker, quoting Poe's poem "The Raven" to Vicki Vale[9]

"I became insane, with long intervals of horrible sanity."
—author Edgar Allen Poe, describing himself.[10]

We may not have a definitive origin story for the Joker, but we do know his creation has roots in the horror genre. Artist Jerry Robinson told us the works of Edgar Allan Poe influenced the initial conception of the Joker. Credited with creating the mystery genre and the detective story, as well as popularizing gothic horror and arguably defining the American short story,[11] author Edgar Allen Poe (1809–1849) scribed eerie stories that often looked at "madness" from the perspective of the disturbed individual. While psychology per se did not yet exist as a distinct field, only as a topic of discussion within philosophy, and psychiatry struggled to distinguish itself within medicine, Poe tried to describe the human mind in both health and disorder.[12] His writings conveyed detachment from reality, as if at the edge of an altered state such as a dream or intoxication, and temptation to commit evil. The protagonist of "The Black Cat," for example, describes his descent into madness and evil as "the feeble remnants of the good within me succumbed. Evil thoughts became my sole intimates—the darkest and most evil of thoughts. The moodiness of my usual temper increased to hatred of all things and all mankind." while he chooses to rebel against whatever is lawful, orderly, or right.[13] Like many of Poe's evildoers, the Joker does not simply kill his primary targets. Instead, in his earliest stories and then at different times over the years, he issues warnings ahead of time so that his prospective victims might live their final hours filled with fear while dreading what's coming,[14] as surely as the would-be victim in Poe's "The Pit and the Pendulum."[15] Also like some of Poe's later fiends, he commits murder through pranks.[16] Over the past two centuries, many writers, documentarians, and other investigators have attempted to understand how Poe's early experiences, personal losses, historical period, physical environment, and hereditary predispositions may have contributed to his influential talent, emotional instability, addictive behaviors, and preoccupation with morbid subject matter,[17] and to understand his mysterious death.[18]

The Cask of Joker Toxin

Jerry Robinson recalled that Poe's short story "The Cask of Amontillado"[19] helped shape the Joker's *modus operandi* (M.O., mode of operations).[20] Similarities between Poe's malefactor Montresor and the Joker have not gone unnoticed by others over the years.[21] "The Cask of Amontillado" tells of strange and deadly revenge, driven by motives that make sense only to the perpetrator, and perhaps not even to him.[22] The opening sentence offers only a hint as to motivation: "The thousand injuries of Fortunato I had borne as best I could, but when he ventured upon insult I vowed revenge."[23] Who knows what insult he might mean? Montresor may simply have found it insulting that boorish Fortunato has prospered while the fortunes of the once-prosperous Montresors, who "were a great and numerous family,"[24] have come a step down. When the Joker has vengeance in mind, his targets may be no more deserving than that. In the second Joker story, meaning the first of his many returns, he exacts his revenge by killing a police chief who played no part in his previous apprehension[25]—not that the Joker usually needs a personal connection when selecting his victims. The guiding force behind the Joker's choice of targets may be as petty as resenting those who prosper in a cruel joke of a world, because he regularly strikes out against the rich and powerful, the high and mighty.

In "The Cask of Amontillado," it is the villain who wears a cloak and mask of black silk and the victim, dressed in motley with jester hat and bells, whom the Joker resembles later. During the "supreme madness of the carnival season,"[26] these costumes suit both the time and how Montresor thinks of them both. He's delighted to see Fortunato arriving dressed as the fool. It is a tale with no true hero, except perhaps in Montresor's mind, and the Joker has a long history of making his victims look like jokers, starting with the first victim to appear in print.[27]

Montresor's methods suit the Joker's, for he essentially murders Fortunato through an elaborate prank. By playing on Fortunato's ego and drunken state, he tricks his prey into walking into a lengthy trap. Montresor briefly plays the fool, saying he may have been cheated when purchasing a barrel of Amontillado sherry so he must ask Fortunato to taste it for authenticity. Though Montresor offers Fortunato several opportunities to turn back, each time he also offers incentive to continue the trek deep into the catacombs until Montresor chains the churl to a wall. There, he begins laying bricks to build the wall that will imprison the unfortunate Fortunato until he dies of suffocation or thirst. Sobering up enough to comprehend his predicament, Fortunato begins shouting, to which Montresor replies by shouting louder. The trapped man makes several attempts at getting his captor to stop, such as trying to play it off with a laugh at "a very good joke, indeed—an excellent jest." Each attempt entertains Montresor, until Fortunato's stubborn silence sucks away the fun. He covers the wall with a rampart of old bones, and no one ever discovers the remains of the man interred behind them.

According to Montresor, a wrong is "unredressed when the avenger fails to make himself felt as such to him who has done the wrong."[28] And yet despite this, Montresor fails to make himself known as an avenger. As he bricks the man away, he never tells Fortunato why. In the first version of how Batman finally comes face-to-face with his parents' killer, he unmasks himself before Joe Chill,[29] whereas the Joker neither reveals his true identity nor makes his motives fully clear.[30]

The Imp of Gotham

The Joker's uncertainty about his own history, his vagueness of memory, could have come straight out of the stories and poems of Poe, who wrote much on the uncertainty of memory, identity, and how little they were understood.[31] From "among the many incomprehensible anomalies of the science of mind, more thrilling than the fact," Poe wrote that the most exciting might be the frustrating experience of finding oneself on the verge of remembrance without quite managing to retrieve the sought-after recollection.[32] Many of his stories featured unreliable narrators whose delusions, confusions, inability to remember, or refusal to believe their own memories lent the stories a dream-like quality.[33]

Like Montresor tempting Fortunato with Amontillado to start him down the path to his own demise, the Joker often tricks victims into doing the things that will get them killed. In his later depictions, but also a few times early on, the Joker plays the part of Poe's Imp of the Perverse, leading otherwise decent individuals into mischief and those with latent malice to manifest it as murder.[34] In fact, the protagonist in "The Imp of the Perverse" kills by burning a Jokerific candle that emits poison smoke. Playing Gotham's Imp, the Joker recruits several of its pranksters to play practical jokes in an early Golden Age story; baits an eager young psychiatrist by tempting her with his secrets in the late 20th century; and leads a district attorney to lose all hope in the 21st.[35] In these instances, he uses a *foot-in-the-door technique*,[36] getting each to do one lesser act in a step toward escalating their violations: The pranksters' jokes turn from harmless to deadly; the psychiatrist goes from ignoring the Joker's innocuous rule violations at Arkham to helping him escape the asylum and then committing violent crimes at his side; and the district attorney descends from bending rules to pointing a gun at the villainous clown to killing anyone at the flip of a coin, regardless of guilt or innocence. Over the years, the Joker becomes more frequently manipulative, playing on fear and greed to elicit the worst in human behavior. Frustrated that others don't see the world for the cruel joke that he perceives it to be, he wants to show them all that circumstances can turn anyone as bad as he. To his surprise, though, some criminal pranksters will not escalate to murder,[37] Commissioner Gordon fails to break down despite suffering "one bad day,"[38] and two boatloads of people terrified for their lives choose not to blow each other up.[39] The Joker discerns the dark nature of which Poe wrote, but he does not comprehend humanity's better inclinations. In his most melancholy states, Poe had trouble with that, too.

Edgar Allan Poe wrote dark tales of emotionally haunted characters, some with flights from reality. He depicted numerous characters who would lose their grip on reality and, like so many comic book villains that would follow a century later, "go mad" with no specified illness. Time and again, Poe wrote about unnamed madnesses. In his time, early mental health advocates were calling for asylum reform, objecting to the abuse, confinement, and other mistreatment of the mentally ill as prisoners.[40] Poe had concerns about that. His short story "The System of Dr. Tarr and Prof. Fether"[41] spins its tale of lunatics taking over an asylum, wresting control from keepers who have allowed them too much freedom—long before the residents of Gotham's asylum would regularly break out and sometimes take the place over (three times in the same year once).[42]

Poe wrote before 1879 when psychology emerged as a distinct science,[43] and the earliest Batman writers wrote before the American Psychiatric Association published its first *Diagnostic and Statistical Manual of Mental Disorders* (DSM-I) in 1952. At Jack C. Harris's suggestion, writer Dennis O'Neil transplanted the Arkham mental hospital from H. P. Lovecraft's stories into Gotham City where it could house the Joker and Two-Face,[44] several years before the association released the more scientifically based DSM-III in 1980. The asylums that writers such as Poe and Lovecraft depicted may fit gothic horror better than 21st-century mental institutions do, but it's that gothic horror that fits the shadows of Gotham.

Imagine if Edgar Allan Poe, who arguably originated the detective mystery story and wrote tales of madness and murder, could write a tale of mystery and imagination featuring *Detective Comics'* bat-themed hero facing maniacal foes. Imagine Poe's Joker in the shadows of the Gotham asylum.

Arkham Asylum: The American Gothic House of Horrors

"The incessant laughter alone, echoing through dark steel corridors,
is enough to make one doubt the very existence of sanity."
—Jeremiah Arkham, director of Arkham Asylum[45]

"The oldest and strongest emotion of mankind is fear, and
the oldest and strongest kind of fear is fear of the unknown."
—horror author H. P. Lovecraft[46]

The connection between Arkham Asylum and horror goes beyond the topical connection with Lovecraft's fictitious town. The asylum is the topic of several stories, many of which have horror or occult themes. The graphic novel *Arkham Asylum: A Serious House on Serious Earth* depicts a dark nightmare that references the classic Hitchcock horror/suspense film *Psycho* along with depicting infamous occult figure Aleister Crowley as one of founder Amadeus Arkham's correspondents. *Batman: Arkham Reborn* involves a rebuilt asylum designed to psychologically and physically torture the inmates, exacting revenge that might have made Poe proud. *Arkham Asylum: Madness* calls the asylum a "haunted house" and names its story titles after famous horror films (e.g., *House on Haunted Hill; Last House on the Left*). One character who anthropormorphizes the asylum suggests that its very essence could drive someone insane. When villain Savant is incarcerated in the asylum, he muses that "the man who designed Arkham Asylum was as gloriously and deeply unhinged as some of his building's later residents" and then notes a potential resemblance between its structure and the classic Italian poet Dante's conceptual structure of Hell.[47]

Thus, Arkham Asylum is not just terrifying because of the danger presented by its inhabitants, but because people fear its effects on their own sanity. What does it mean to be unable to trust your own mind, your feeling of personal control, your experiential view of the world? Such thoughts are indeed scary. Some psychologists have called this fear of losing one's sense of sanity *phrenophobia* or *anxiety sensitivity*.[48] Although this phenomenon has been studied largely among clinical patients diagnosed with anxiety disorders or depression, it may indeed exist at some level in many people who do not have diagnosable mental health concerns.[49] Part of this fear may involve a belief that mental illness could be contagious.[50] Sabine, a nurse who works at Arkham, laments that the place seems to be overwhelming her and believes that it causes her and her colleagues to express its madness.[51] "Indeed, one wonders if madness might not be infectious in a certain sense, a contagion by virtue of its omnipresent influence," asylum administrator Jeremiah Arkham speculates. "If so, then surely I have been infected by now."[52]

The horrors of Arkham are given shape in the Joker, the asylum's "most notable permanent resident."[53] The Joker is the ideal avatar for Arkham Asylum because he believes insanity is the only realistic way to deal with the randomness and lack of meaning he perceives in the universe.[54] In many ways he is not far off from Lovecraft's own view that human existence and our suffering have little meaning in the grand scheme of the cosmos.[55] Of course, this idea is antithetical to the general human need for meaning, which may be why many of Lovecraft's protagonists are driven mad by this idea just as the Joker is. Indeed, the Joker likely would agree with Lovecraft when he wrote that the "cosmos is a mindless vortex; a seething ocean of blind forces, in which the greatest joy is unconsciousness and the greatest pain realization."[56] Or as the Joker aptly put it, when people are "faced with the inescapable fact that human existence is mad, random, and pointless" they go crazy because "any other response would be crazy!"[57]

The Faceless Joker: Physical Abnormalities and the Evocation of Disgust

> *"I think the Joker will live forever.*
> *I think that he's in some ways the perfect villain. . . .*
> *You may not think so, but he's there,*
> *waiting to chew your bloody face off."*
> —actor Jared Leto[58]

The 21st-century Joker incorporates elements of *body horror* into his mayhem, showcasing graphic, disturbing mutilations, alterations, or other violations of the human body. This horror subgenre with gothic roots[59] has proliferated in the new millennium, even in horror comedy.[60] This type of horror has figured prominently throughout the Joker's history, starting with his first published crime in which his poison gives the victim a hideous rictus grin.[61]

The Joker is not just disturbing in his beliefs and actions, but also by his very appearance. For example, Heath Ledger's version of the Joker—with his facial scars and unkempt look—provides a unique descent into the darker side of human nature.[62] Like many previous comic book iterations, Ledger's Joker exhibits physical abnormalities in addition to being one who ascribes to a *different* type of sanity.[63] This character representation is a double whammy on the fear factor scale. Not only do individuals have a natural propensity toward repulsion toward those who appear physically "offensive" in some way,[64] but also toward those who suffer mental illness. Unlike those with physical abnormalities, however, people with mental disturbances are often perceived to be in control of their behaviors and responsible for causing their own conditions.[65] Individuals believed to be victims of their ailments are met with pity, while those believed to be in control are met with antagonism.[66]

While the Joker has always been portrayed as someone with his own distinctly skewed logic, he is also associated with physical deformities. His original chemical-bleached complexion and frozen smile have given way to facial scars and eventually a rotting, fly-covered, dead-skin mask.[67] The Joker further adopts a two-headed lion cub from the Gotham Zoo for his schemes and fills his run-down carnival hideout with several physically deformed individuals.[68] These various physical deformities associated with the Joker not only evoke fear but also a feeling of *disgust*. In general, *core disgust* is an emotion reliant on the complex notion of "offensiveness," which is predicated on *contamination sensitivity*.[69] The more likely something—or, someone, with respect to *interpersonal contamination*[70]—is to taint another, the more likely that action, or person, is to elicit disgust.

In response to disgust, individuals are most likely to draw a protective line between themselves and the threat, shunning the source of the disgust.[71] Even though the Joker often hires run-of-the-mill criminals, only a select few individuals feel an attraction to him. Harley Quinn is the most obvious person, but other alumni from Arkham Asylum are also drawn to him and his chaotic worldview.[72] However, in instances in which the Joker has threatened contamination or engaged in some sort of physical violation of another, subsequently eliciting disgust in the protagonists, even his closest criminal associates exhibit reluctance to mirror his threats. For instance, the Penguin and Two-Face help the Joker torment Batman in the *Death of the Family* story arc, but they seem unnerved by the Joker's plan to place the supposed skinned faces of Batman's allies on display.[73] Even Harley Quinn expresses discomfort with the Joker's plans during this arc.[74]

The domain of disgust is expanded to include something referred to as *animal-related disgust*, which is thought to be a defense against the distinction between humans and animals.[75] More specifically, sexual deviance, body-envelope violations, poor hygiene, and any interaction with mortality constitute animal-related disgust.[76] While humans and animals share a number of attributes, one of the most chilling to the individual psyche is that of death and decay of the flesh.[77] Thus, in order to guard against unwelcome thoughts of death, prompted by the reminder of the eerie similarities between humans and animals, as aforementioned, individuals attempt to separate themselves from disgust-evoking stimuli. Throughout their storied rivalry, Batman and the Joker have often been considered more alike than different, though Batman is quick to counter any argument of sameness from the Joker. In fact, Batman has evoked disgust-relevant language when he describes the Joker as a "filthy degenerate."[78] Similarly, Batman finds himself questioning the humanity of the Joker on a number of occasions, not always because of the villain's apparent lack of empathy. At times, the Joker's physical body appears to violate biological mandates. Batman comments on the way the Joker's eyes do not contract or expand, depending on emotion, unlike other humans; rather, they remain "fixed, tiny points of blackness."[79]

In addition to violations of *expected* body functions, unrestricted body modification also provokes feelings of inhumanity and, subsequently, disgust.[80] Aside from the involuntary massive body modification the Joker endures following his submersion in the chemical waste,[81] perhaps the most glaring instance of *voluntary* body modification within the Joker's canon comes when he has his face removed by the Dollmaker, and crudely reattaches it to his skull with string[82] only after conducting business in Gotham without a face for more than a year.[83] In addition, at the crescendo of one of his many poetic confrontations with Batman, the Joker goes so far as to make it appear that he has removed the faces of the Bat-Family, to include having the makeshift "faces" laid out on beds of ice in front of the horrified heroes.[84] The domain of disgust expands further, such that revulsion is often elicited when violations of body borders at any point other than the mouth are observed.[85] When describing the process of face removal in grueling detail, the Joker informs Harley Quinn that her world is going to be transformed red as blood drips down over her eyes without the presence of eyelids.[86] Harley Quinn, who refers to Mistah J. as a "tortured soul crying out for love and acceptance,"[87] admits that the faceless Joker is someone she no longer recognizes and appears to be repulsed by him.[88] Other examples of body horror involve the Joker chopping off butler Alfred Pennyworth's hand and removing Batgirl's mother's ring finger (which he subsequently uses to propose to Batgirl).[89]

Unlike fear, disgust involves a spectrum of degradation elevation as well as a connection to notions of purity and sacredness, not readily present in fear.[90] The Joker's actions undoubtedly evoke fear in his victims—even those confronted with the darkest sides of humanity daily at Arkham Asylum where the Joker, on numerous occasions, has converted the facility into his own house of horrors equipped with screaming, bloody towels in wheelbarrows, bodies being thrown down an incinerator chute, and even a "tapestry" made of live humans sewn together.[91] Disgust, however, is an emotion the Joker seems to conjure most when his radical ideals are accompanied by risks of contamination, confrontations of mortality, and/ or body-envelope violations. Taken in conjunction with the fear evoked by one whose system of logic is as erratic and unknown as his origins, the disgust adds to the allure and complexity of the Joker's villainy.

The Terror behind the Painted Smile

"We make up horrors to help us cope with the real ones."
—author Stephen King[92]

"When villains want to scare each other, they tell Joker stories."
—The Trickster[93]

The Joker is one of the most fascinating—and terrifying—villains in Batman's rogues' gallery. Elements of his character have changed over time, from being focused on crimes of profit (albeit with some unpredictable homicidal tendencies) to a 21st-century terrorist who wants to force us to see the dark side of human nature and nihilistically demonstrate that "everything burns."[94] Perhaps the Joker is a mirror that reflects what scares us most, yet we cannot look away because a fictional embodiment of these fears allows us to confront them safely and ultimately gives us power over them.[95] Even though we find him terrifying, we also find him morbidly fascinating. So, like any good villain in a horror film, he will never truly die.

> *"A clown is funny in the circus ring, but what would be the normal reaction to opening a door at midnight and finding the same clown there in the moonlight?"*
>
> —actor Lon Chaney, Sr.[96]

"Have you ever danced with the devil in the pale moonlight?"
—The Joker[97]

NOTES

1. *Batman* #1 (1940d).
2. Bloch (1960/1995), p. 257. Radford (2016), pp. 21–22, deserves credit for bringing these opening quotes to our attention.
3. *Batman* #428 (1988).
4. Radford (2016); Reyes (2017).
5. Baumeister (1991); Lieberman (2013); Proulx & Heine (2006).
6. Vess et al. (2009).
7. *Batman: The Killing Joke* (2016 motion picture); *The Dark Knight* (2008 motion picture).
8. *Arkham Asylum: Madness* (2010); *Batman: The Killing Joke* (1988); *Birds of Prey* #16 (2000); *The Dark Knight* (2008 motion picture).
9. *Batman* (1989 motion picture).
10. Poe (1848/2009).
11. Poe (1846/1984).
12. Laverty (1951).
13. Poe (1843/1981a), p. 385.
14. *Batman* #1 (1940a; 1940d); *Detective Comics* #475–476 (1978).
15. Poe (1843/1981b).
16. Poe (1846/1981; 1849/1981).
17. Giammarco (2013); Kaufhold (2008); Krutch (1926); Meyers (1992).
18. Jones (2015).
19. Poe (1846/1981).
20. Robinson (2011).
21. thatguitarrguy (2012); Uslan, quoted by Langley (2014b); Whitenton (2015).
22. Baraban (2004).

23. Poe (1846/1981), p. 542.

24. Poe (1846/1981), p. 544.

25. *Batman* #1 (1940d).

26. Poe (1846/1981), p. 542.

27. *Batman* #1 (1940a).

28. Poe (1846/1981), p. 542.

29. *Batman* #47 (1948).

30. *Detective Comics* #475 (1976); *Batman: The Killing Joke* (1988); *The Batman Adventures: Mad Love* (1994); *Birds of Prey* #16 (2000); *Countdown* #31 (2007); *Arkham Asylum: Madness* (2010); *The Dark Knight* (2008 motion picture).

31. Examples: Memory— Poe (1838/1981); identity—Poe (1835/1981).

32. Poe (1838/1981), p. 117.

33. Mental Health America (2013).

34. Poe (1845/1981a).

35. Respectively, *Batman* #7 (1941); *The Batman Adventures: Mad Love* (1994); *The Dark Knight* (2008 motion picture).

36. Cialdini (2007).

37. e.g., Donnie, a.k.a. Prank, in *The Batman*, episode 3–11, "The Apprentice" (February 18, 2006).

38. *Batman: The Killing Joke* (1988).

39. *The Dark Knight* (2008 motion picture).

40. Cleman (2001).

41. Poe (1845/1981b).

42. *Batman* #1 (2011).

43. Schultz & Schultz (2012); Wertheimer (2000).

44. Lovecraft (1937); O'Neil (2018); Voger (2006); *Batman* #258 (1974), #326 (1980).

45. *Batman* #491 (1993).

46. Lovecraft (1927/2008), p. 15.

47. *Birds of Prey* #60 (2003).

48. Grand (1959); Schmidt & Joiner (2002); Walen (1982).

49. Bassett et al. (2009); Commons et al. (2016); Paskind (1931); Smári et al. (2003); Taylor et al. (1996).

50. Rachman (2012).

51. *Arkham Asylum: Madness* (2010).

52. *Batman* #491 (1993).

53. *Batman* #294 (1977).

54. *Batman: The Killing Joke* (1988).

55. Lovecraft (1919/1965); (1930/1971); (1932/1976).

56. Lovecraft (1921/1965), p. 156.

57. *Batman: The Killing Joke* (1988).

58. "Joker and Harley: The 'It' Couple of the Underworld," *Suicide Squad* (2016 moyion picture) Blu-ray bonus feature.

59. Gordon (2012); Halberstam (1995).

60. Johnson (2017); Millican (2016).

61. *Batman* #1 (1940a).

62. *The Dark Knight* (2008 motion picture).

63. *Batman and Robin* #14 (2010).

64. Haidt et al. (1997).

65. Weiner et al. (1988).

66. Corrigan et al. (2000); Weiner (2006).

67. *Batman* #17 (2013); *The Dark Knight* (2008 motion picture).

68. *Batman* #13 (2012a); *Batman: The Killing Joke* (1988).

69. Haidt et al. (1997).

70. Rozin et al. (1994).

71. Haidt et al. (1997).

72. *The Dark Knight* (2008 motion picture).

73. *Batman* #16 (2013b).

74. *Batman* #13 (2012a).

75. Haidt et al. (1997).

76. Haidt et al. (1997).

77. Rozin et al. (1999).

78. *Arkham Asylum: A Serious House on Serious Earth* (1989/2004); also "degenerate filth" in *Batman* #15 (2013).

79. *Batman* #15 (2013).

80. Haidt et al. (1997).

81. *Batman: The Killing Joke* (1988).

82. *Batman* #13 (2012a).

83. *Detective Comics* #1 (2011); *Batman* #13 (2012a).

84. *Batman* #17 (2013).

85. Rozin et al. (1994).

86. *Batman* #13 (2012b).

87. *The Batman Adventures: Mad Love* (1994).

88. *Batman* #13 (2012a); *Suicide Squad* #15 (2013).

89. *Batgirl* #14 (2013); *Batman* #39 (2015).

90. Haidt et al. (1997).

91. *Batman* #16 (2013a); *Arkham Asylum: A Serious House on Serious Earth* (1989/2004).

92. Feldberg (2016).

93. *Underworld Unleashed* #1 (1995).

94. *The Dark Knight* (2008 motion picture)

95. Maddrey (2004); Phillips (2005).

96. Barker & Jones (1997), p. 88.

97. *Batman* (1989 motion picture).

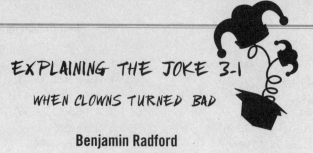

EXPLAINING THE JOKE 3-1

WHEN CLOWNS TURNED BAD

Benjamin Radford

To modern eyes, the evil or scary clown is a relatively common (if not always welcome) sight. From Pennywise in *It* to Twisty in *American Horror Story*, Krusty to Killer Klowns, and Harlequin to the Joker, they're everywhere.[1] But it wasn't always that way.

It's misleading to ask when clowns "turned bad," for they were never really good.[2] Instead, the clown archetype—essentially a trickster figure like Loki or Puck—was ambiguous, either good or bad, depending on their whims. The troubled clown is ancient and universal. The drunken clown in Charles Dickens's 1836 novel *The Pickwick Papers* was one of many that preceded the film *The Man Who Laughs* in 1928 and the Joker's emergence in 1940. But the evil clown figure's influence in America, for better or worse, was largely limited to the printed comics that were alternately dismissed as childish, lowbrow material and elevated as a dire moral threat by crusaders such as Frederic Wertham in the 1950s.[3]

For most of American history, the clowns Americans were most familiar with were the happy, good clowns—the circus clowns whose wacky antics and pratfalls amused audiences, as well as those making balloon animals and corny jokes while doing magic tricks at backyard birthday parties. Other suitably saccharine influences from the middle of the last century included a pair of wildly popular national franchises. The first was Bozo the Clown, who was introduced to television audiences in 1949 and remained popular for decades, peaking in the 1950s and 1960s.[4] Ronald McDonald joined Bozo on the airwaves in 1963, offering an irresistible combination of fast food hamburgers and a family-friendly, clowny atmosphere.[5]

As a result, generations of Americans grew up familiar with mostly happy, good-natured clowns. Non-Westerners didn't necessarily share such cultural assumptions about the default benevolent nature of clowns. European clowns, for example, sometimes wore no makeup and were more morose than merry; early American clowns acted not only as entertainers but as enforcers of social order and morals, punishing or mocking people as they saw fit to keep them in line.

It wasn't until the 1980s that the scary or evil clown really entered pop culture. The emergence of Pennywise in Stephen King's 1986 book *It* (and its 1990 television miniseries adaptation, starring Tim Curry) was a turning point. Two years later, the Chiodo brothers would release *Killer Klowns from Outer Space* (1988), followed the next year by Jack Nicholson as the Joker in *Batman*. By the time Bobcat Goldthwait released his alcohol-and-profanity-laced movie *Shakes the Clown* a few years later in 1991 (Krusty the Clown appeared around the same time), the malicious or malcontent clown was securely cemented in the American psyche.

These scary clowns were not new, and Stephen King hardly created the idea. But what he and others did was to revive, revisit, and reintroduce the original—and in many ways more earthy, less wholesome—side of clowns to an American audience. It was against the distinctly American assumptions of clowns being benevolent that the evil one popped into relief and captured our attention.

The Joker and his ill-intentioned ilk are not a perversion of the clown persona; they are merely the other side of the same coin. Much of the clown's appeal is his contrasting dual nature as the Janus-faced performer whose antics amuse us—until they don't.

NOTES

1. Pennywise—King (1986); Twisty—*American Horror Story*, episode 4–1, "Monsters Among Us" (October 4, 2014); Krusty—*The Tracy Ullman Show*, *The Simpsons* shorts, episode 3–6, "The Krusty the Clown Show" (January 15, 1989); Killer Klowns—*Killer Klowns from Outer Space* (1988 motion picture); Harlequin—a theatrical role traditionally believed to have been introduced in the late 16th century, according to Ducharte (1929) and Senelick (1995); the Joker—*Batman* #1 (1940).

2. Little (2017); Morris (2012); Radford (2016); Stein (2014).

3. Wertham (1954/2004).

4. Brioux (2008).

5. Kroc (1977); Speaight (1980).

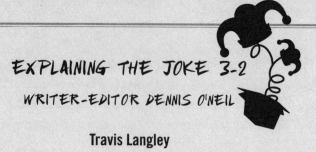

EXPLAINING THE JOKE 3-2

WRITER-EDITOR DENNIS O'NEIL

Travis Langley

Dennis O'Neil wrote the first comic book I remember reading, and he wrote the introduction for the first book I authored.[1] Both were about Batman. Along the way, Denny wrote and edited hundreds of stories for both DC and Marvel, and he has done so much more. In addition to his award-winning work weaving humanity and social consciousness into the adventures of heroes such as Green Lantern, Green Arrow, and Iron Man,[2] he has been one of the most prominent custodians of the legacy that Bob Kane and Bill Finger began. Under editor Julius "Julie" Schwartz, Denny O'Neil and artist Neal Adams brought Batman back to his darker roots after the campy escapades of then-recent years. Thirty-one years after the Joker's last Golden Age murder,[3] Denny defined the Bronze Age Joker both by making the clown kill again and by labeling that killer insane.[4] As editor of the Batman titles, Denny's duties included overseeing the completion of *Batman: The Killing Joke* and the entirety of the story arc in which readers voted for the Joker to kill the second Robin.[5]

Dennis O'Neil: The first time I wrote the Joker, I didn't know what I was doing. I don't think Bob Kane and Bill Finger would have been aware that they were doing an archetype that shows up in mythology constantly.

Travis Langley: When you did your first Joker story, the character had not appeared in the Batman comics for four years. Were you deliberately staying away from some of the classic villains after the Adam West show ended?

O'Neil: That was a conscious decision Julie and I made, not to keep going back to the same well. With the Joker, I could see the melodramatic possibilities of a killer clown. They had made him so wimpy. He wasn't an interesting character anymore because he wasn't allowed to do anything interesting. People wonder if Julie had to get permission for us to change that. I don't think Julie got permission for anything in his life. We just did it, and it worked out pretty well.

Neal Adams didn't like the idea of having the Joker start killing again. What did he want him to do—be silly? I wanted to get back to the killer clown. We owe a great debt to those guys who did the early stories. If Bill Finger hadn't done what he did and Jerry on the art, we wouldn't have Batman and the Joker. I don't take credit for that, and I don't think anybody should who's still alive. I'll get worked up about things like that, then I have to tell myself, "Denny! It's just a comic book!"

Langley: In your introduction to *Batman and Psychology*, you mentioned that people's reactions to the Joker killing a Robin made you reconsider the idea that it's "just a comic book."

O'Neil: It taught me that I wasn't just doing for-hire work, that these things were important to people. I realized that comic-book and some other media characters are all modern folklore, so I should pay some attention to that and not be as cavalier about it as I'd been. Jim Starlin wrote "A Death in the Family"—all credit to him for that.

Langley: Did he have any particular reason for it to be the Joker who killed a Robin?

O'Neil: No, and that was a case where my editorial instincts might not have paid off. The Joker was not whom I would have chosen to serve that plot purpose. Jim wanted to do it and he was the writer on the book. I tried to stay out of their way as much as possible. The movie people are going much more with Jim's idea than mine. I think they did the best Joker: Heath Ledger's Joker in *The Dark Knight*.[6]

Langley: Artist Brian Bolland said you didn't really interfere on *The Killing Joke,* either.[7]

O'Neil: No. That project started under another editor (Len Wein). My job was to get it to the printer on time.

Langley: Speaking of things other editors and creators did with the Joker, would you have ever thought it would make sense to depict him with a girlfriend?

O'Neil: No, I didn't. If I had been the kind of tyrannical, dictatorial editor that is not unheard of in comics, I wouldn't have okayed that. In my private image of the Joker, he does not have girls, he does not masturbate. For him to have a girlfriend, that's way too normal. I think part of what made the character work was the fact that he didn't share anything with anybody and you wouldn't know why. The guy was seriously nuts. But I can't fault Harley Quinn's success. I saw *Suicide Squad* and went, "Yeah, that character works fine on her own terms."[8]

Langley: Frank Miller said that his version of the Joker would not have sexual relations with anybody because that would be too life-affirming. His Joker wouldn't, but Alan Moore's might.[9]

O'Neil: I completely agree with that. Back when these characters were created, nobody gave it that much thought.

Langley: Do you have a general thought on why it's the Joker who is Batman's ultimate enemy? What is it about the character that grabs people?

O'Neil: Here is a writer's answer to your question: He is Batman's exact opposite. Batman is rational and logical and really relentless. The Joker's personality is complementary but different. When I thought about the Joker the first time, I thought, "Okay, clowns are scary. Let's play this like nobody knows what he's going to do. He doesn't know, either." For all those years, the Joker had been such a weak character. I wanted to make him strong and scary.

When the higher-ups insisted on giving him his own book,[10] I quietly and gently said, "You realize he is a villain, and you're making him the protagonist of this series. How are you going to manage that when the Code says he's got to go to jail? To be punished at the end of every story? How do you figure I should handle that?" And I didn't get an answer. But it was a very bad idea.

Langley: That was soon after you established that the Joker was considered insane and started sending him to the asylum. Then eventually they're sending most of Batman's enemies to Arkham Asylum. You wrote the story that introduced Arkham.[11]

O'Neil: Arkham Asylum comes from Jack Harris. When he suggested it, I thought it was a good fit for our continuity. (See Explaining the Joke 7–1: The True Origin of Arkham Asylum, which Jack Harris wrote for this book.)

Langley: But you did add the asylum in your stories. You've made many contributions to the Batman mythos, and you've shaped a lot of other people's contributions, too.

O'Neil: For years, I thought about Batman all the time. Batman has been very good to me. I never expected to get any spotlight on me, but I wish my parents could have seen that I didn't become a dope peddler. Somehow, I became respectable. Go figure.

Though retired from ongoing commitments, Denny never stopped writing. Right before we talked for this book, he wrote something special for *Detective Comics* #1000, a sequel to the classic story in which he introduced Leslie Thompkins to be the voice of pacifism in Batman's life, "There is No Home in Crime Alley!"[12]

NOTES

1. O'Neil (2012).
2. *Green Lantern* #76 (1970); Iron Man #182 (1984)—see Zehr (2011).
3. *Detective Comics* #62 (1942).
4. *Detective Comics* #451 (1973).
5. Respectively, *Batman: The Killing Joke* (1988) and *Batman* #426–429 (1988–1989).
6. *The Dark Knight* (2008 motion picture).
7. Salisbury (2000).
8. *Suicide Squad* (2017 motion picture).
9. Sharrett (1991).
10. *The Joker*, #1–9 (1975–1976).
11. *Batman* #258 (1974).
12. *Detective Comics* #457 (1976).

CASE REPORT I (1940):
RISK MANAGEMENT ASSESSMENT FOR THE PSYCHOPATH

Professionals who treat, guard, or otherwise monitor incarcerated individuals need to develop strategies for working with and around them. Calling some "the dangerous ones" would itself be a dangerous oversimplification. In what specific ways might an individual pose a threat? Which characteristics, events, and other factors in that person's life threaten his or her rehabilitation or therapeutic process, and how might the professional manage those risks? In this series of case reports, forensic psychologist Colt J. Blunt presents risk management assessments that different professionals might have written at different points in the Joker's career.

Diagnostic Summary

The John Doe, true name unknown, alias "the Joker," is a Caucasian man of slim build who was brought to the Gotham City Jail after being apprehended for murder.[1] His age is unknown, though he keeps a certain youthful vigor about him. His appearance is remarkable, as he presents with alabaster skin, bright red lips, and green hair. Despite multiple attempts, the guards here have been unable to return him to a normal appearance. This only serves to bolster the Joker persona he has adopted. Despite my efforts, I cannot crack this aspect of the inmate's psyche. In all my years, I have never met a criminal like him. Other criminals who wore masks got a lot of attention, but those masks came off. At most, this jester's mask has only slipped, revealing the true terror that hides beneath his façade of glibness and jokes.

Diagnostically, he is rather simple. He is not taken with madness, despite his wanton actions. He shows no signs of psychosis, neuroses, or chronic brain syndrome. Rather, he seems to evidence an extreme defect of personality, likely best described as exhibiting both antisocial and dyssocial reactions.[2]

However, I am struck most by his similarities to Cleckley's studies on the psychopath.[3] Inmate appears to be in possession of good intelligence, though his application of this is not for the better good of society. He is adept at using a degree of charm in his interactions, though these should certainly not be trusted. He is free of obvious delusions and neuroses. Indeed, he has not evidenced any degree of obvious affliction of nervousness, including when faced with the jail's more colorful denizens. Though we see flashes of emotion, this appears to be the mask he wears, rather than his true self. I wonder if he experiences emotion at all, or at least any emotion beyond that of a predator stalking its prey in anticipation of a kill. He appears bereft of any form of conscience, never once impressing me as remorseful about his actions. Further, I can discern no reason for certain acts of mayhem he has caused. His accompanying police reports indicate he was responsible for killing a man with poison despite having already robbed the man of a precious gem. I can conceive of only two possibilities in such a case: Either he enjoyed killing the man or the man's life was so insignificant to him that he gave it no second thought. I do not believe that either explanation bodes well for his prognosis.

What strikes me most is that I have no idea who this man actually is. Though he has provided a variety of explanations for who he is, where he came from, and why he did what he did, I take these as nothing more than made-up stories. I know not of this man's relationships, of whether he has ever loved or been loved—or, indeed, if he is capable of such things. I'm equally clueless about whether this man is taken with more carnal pleasures. The one pleasure I am certain he experiences is in misleading those who come to ask him questions. His stories have varied wildly and, upon confrontation, he simply provides a completely different, equally implausible account. I would like nothing more than to get this gentleman on my couch, as I believe that psychoanalysis may be the key to figuring out what truly drives his behavior. I would like to explore his relationship with his family, especially in determining the dynamics with his parents. I would not be surprised to learn he had a limited or nonexistent relationship with his father, combined with extreme enmeshment with his mother, perhaps culminating in a tragic removal of her from his life, ultimately leading to the genesis of his injured psyche. Regardless, further analysis, combined with more than a modicum of reflection, will be necessary.

Recommendations

I was asked to review this inmate's case by personal request of the warden. At this juncture, the utility of this review is unclear. In my opinion, it appears unlikely the parole board would grant him release at any point in the future, given the gravity of the crimes that landed him in our custody. Perhaps the warden is simply looking for better methods of controlling the inmate and preventing him from doing too much damage during his stay. Regardless, there are a few things I can recommend:

- We must learn more about this man. Discovering his history is the secret to unblocking his defenses and treating his underlying personality insults.

- We must not underestimate him. Though his outward presentation is that of sowing chaos, he is highly intelligent and capable of tremendous guile when necessary.

- The guards must be diligent. He is likely to continue his machinations while incarcerated. Random searches should be utilized. We must watch his interactions with others. Judicious use of solitary confinement should be considered, not because we expect him to change his behavior, but rather to ensure the security of the jail and keep the peace.

- If he does secure release at some point in the future, we will need to work closely with the Gotham City Police Department to keep close tabs on his movements.

Respectfully yours,

Consulting Psychologist

Notes

1. The Joker is in a jail cell awaiting trial at the start of his second story in *Batman* #1 (1940) but escapes. He finally goes to prison—specifically, Alcatraz—in his eighth appearance, *Batman* #8 (1942). He does not appear to go to Gotham's own prison until the story that ends his Ace of Knaves period, *Detective Comics* #64 (1942).

2. The American Psychological Association did not release the first edition of its DSM until 1952. When the Joker first appears, sources available included the American Psycho-Medical Association's *Statistical Manual for the Use of Institutions for the Insane* (1918), but it was not universal. Too few psychiatric and psychological professionals agreed on general guidelines for diagnosing mental illness. This lack of diagnostic standards might explain why no one deemed the Joker insane during the Golden Age.

3. Cleckley (1941/1976).

THE CLOWN PRINCE OF CRIME

"Nothing but a bizarre game for life and death can content the Clown Prince of Crime, with Batman and Robin as his opponents in a fantastic— 'Gamble with Doom!'"

—narrative text that gives the Joker this nickname[1]

"Clowns are the pegs on which the circus is hung."

—attributed to showman P. T. Barnum[2]

NOTES

1. *Batman* #4 (1947–1948).
2. Frank (1990), p. 31; Mehr (2016), p. 85.

4

The Spotlight:
The Flamboyant Criminal

SHELLY CLEVENGER & J. SCOTT JORDAN

"And now, people of Gotham City,
the moment you have all been waiting for!"
—The Joker[1]

"It's better to be a flamboyant failure than a benign success."
—punk rocker Malcolm McLaren,
on the best advice he ever received[2]

"WHY BE A disfigured outcast when I can be a notorious crime god!"[3] the Joker thinks to himself as he races from Batman through the halls of Arkham Asylum. To him, he and the Batman are almost god-like, existing in a way that lies beyond the mundane, life-and-death concerns of lowly mortals—a level of narcissism most extreme.

Such grandiose flamboyance has constituted a foundational aspect of the Joker's character ever since he first arrives in comics as a smiling, laughing clown who announces his pending crimes over the radio.[4] He is grandiose and a showman from his first line—an over-the-top statement that provides readers an indication of the journey this villain is going to take us on. Not only does the Joker do horrible things, he needs and wants an audience for them. He is the ultimate flamboyant and ostentatious criminal.

Always a Clown

The Joker's flamboyant behavior is consistent with the diagnostic criteria for *narcissistic personality disorder*,[5] which is in the same group of personality disorders (cluster B—the dramatic, erratic ones) as *antisocial personality disorder*. Indeed, a person can meet the criteria for more than one personality disorder. Considering that his egotistical, attention-seeking behavior has been present throughout every era of his career, even when he was essentially harmless, his narcissism arguably has a more consistent record. Someone with narcissistic personality disorder is not merely egotistical but lives a life dominated by narcissism as a deeply ingrained, maladaptive trait. Diagnostically, this condition is indicated by the presence of five of these nine criteria:

1. Grandiose sense of self-importance. The Joker is full of himself.

2. Preoccupation with fantasies of unlimited success, power, brilliance, beauty, or ideal love. The Joker's fantastic felonies are founded on flights of fancy. Only a person preoccupied with fantasy embarks on crime sprees built around such themes as carrying out slang expressions in literal form,[6] convincing people he's the best comedian in town,[7] making a movie just to humiliate the Dynamic Duo,[8] facing Batman in a surfing competition,[9] and tying his enemies to candles on a gigantic birthday cake.[10]

3. Belief that he or she is special and unique and therefore can only be understood by—or should associate with—other special or high-status people or institutions. For him, that means Batman. Also, he will associate with top supervillains, such as the Penguin and the Riddler, even though he has impulsively killed other villains[11] and many of his own henchmen.[12]

4. A need for excessive admiration. A man who puts his likeness on cars, cards, fish, and anything else he can really wants people to know his face.

5. A sense of entitlement. He takes what he wants.

6. Interpersonally exploitive behavior. He uses others.

7. A lack of empathy. This symptom, the most obvious way in which narcissism overlaps with psychopathy, describes him thoroughly.

8. Envy of others or a belief that others are envious of him or her. Despite remarks such as "Copybat, copybat—suffering from propulsion envy, Batboy?"[13] he does not appear to dwell on thoughts that others envy him. However, perhaps his frustration that others see reasons for hope in the world grows out of some envy that they can feel something he cannot.

9. A demonstration of arrogant and haughty behaviors or attitudes.[14] "I told you not to talk! I don't need you to answer my questions! I can answer my questions myself!"[15]

His narcissism expresses itself in various ways, such as his interpersonally exploitive behavior, his apparent lack of empathy, and his ability to laugh as he commits heinous crimes.

He Commits Criminal Acts with Flair

The Joker has committed some of the most atrocious crimes within the pages of comics, though he also goes three decades without killing anyone at all. During this nonlethal "Clown Prince" period, his narcissism guides his actions more obviously than his psychopathy. The things that all of his acts have in common is that he commits them in a merry manner, hatching elaborate plots for his own amusement at the suffering of others. He does not simply go out and commit a murder or rob a bank in an ordinary or expedient way, but rather he has a plan filled with plot twists and turns and intrigue. He offers commentary before, after, and during the commission of his crimes that involves jokes, often at the victim's expense, which cause him to smile and laugh hysterically. This is one of the hallmark characteristics of the Joker that make his actions so distinct. He is comparable to a stand-up comedian with pre-written jokes and "bits" for each of his crimes. He is constantly performing. The Joker does everything big, from his signature makeup (in some film versions)[16] or makeup-like appearance (in most versions) and attire, to his loud voice and demeanor. Readers are aware of the flashy nature of the Joker instantly and they are not disappointed with each appearance, as he offers something that will be completely shocking and unexpected.

The Joker's most obvious narcissistic trait is his tendency toward grandiosity, such as when he utters such outlandish phrases as "Einstein was wrong! I'm the speed of light. . . ."[17] His first live-action film appearance introduces him to TV viewers in a manner that is literally over the top, when he "springs" himself out of prison while playing softball with fellow inmates. He pitches a smoke bomb instead of a softball. When the batter hits the "ball," it explodes and produces a smoke cloud. Suddenly, we hear the sound of a loud spring, and in the next image, we see a 10-foot spring bouncing as if it has just "sprung" the Joker over the prison wall.[18]

Narcissistic individuals use grandiose statements and behavior as a way to manage their self-esteem, and they have little awareness of the discrepancy between reality and their own expectations. They experience violations of their expectations as revealing something wrong with the world, not something wrong with their own grandiose assumptions.[19]

Real-World Flamboyant Criminals and "Jokers"

There are criminals whose actions in the real world have been so flamboyant and grandiose they seem to mimic the scenes from a comic book, even some who committed their crimes before comic books existed. In fact, the public enemies of the 1920s and 1930s inspired public interest in both flamboyant gangsters and a belief that only larger-than-life heroes could take them down.

Bonnie and Clyde: A Real-World Joker and Harley

The Joker and his paramour Harley Quinn are reminiscent of the real-life criminal couple known as Bonnie and Clyde. Bonnie Park and Clyde Barrow were flamboyant in their crimes, often appearing to be having a great time while committing criminal acts and terrorizing people. They robbed banks with their gang, burglarized establishments, and also committed more than a dozen murders.[20]

Bonnie and Clyde became infamous and internationally known for their crimes, and were seen as outlaws in the 1930s. However, there was also something very appealing about them to the public, just as we see with the Joker and Harley: They are two of the most popular characters in comic book history. Both couples committed large, attention-grabbing crimes—often hurting people—and regularly evaded capture. While the public outwardly detested the acts of Bonnie and Clyde, there was also intrigue surrounding this young couple (as well as the Joker and Harley) who robbed, killed, and shot at the police. People love to hate both of these couples: We know that they are bad, but we can't keep from paying attention to their antics. Bonnie and Clyde became regulars in the media at the time. People followed their exploits and waited to see what they were up to next. While Bonnie and Clyde were committing heinous crimes they became akin to celebrities in the public eye. As their crimes and antics were followed by many at the time, they received substantial media attention, often landing on the front pages of newspapers just as the Joker and Harley received their own share of media attention in fictional Gotham.

Together with their gang, the real-life couple planned and committed large-scale bank robberies that were often very grandiose in nature, later echoed in the fictional Joker and Harley's elaborate and grand heists. Like Harley, Bonnie readily broke her man out of lockup. Bonnie snuck a gun into prison that Clyde ultimately used to escape, which was an act that captured the nation's attention. As a duo, Bonnie and Clyde planned and implemented a prison break when their gang was imprisoned. They hid automatic weapons in a ditch beforehand to use to shoot at guards to free their friends in a large standoff at the prison that gained the attention of the nation.

There was also a great deal of interest in the fact that Bonnie was a female criminal and that she was a willing and eager participant in the crimes. It was almost unheard of in the 1930s for a woman to be a violent leader of a gang. She was boisterous, rough, and it was very clear from her actions, her photographs with Clyde, and her own statements that she was enjoying her life of crime and was not in any way being coerced into that lifestyle. She was the Harley of her time. During their crime spree, Bonnie became a published poet, writing about their experiences, not unlike the way supervillains like Harley taunt superheroes and the authorities. She took to the limelight and relished the attention.

Bonnie's pathology may not have been narcissistic personality disorder but, rather, an underlying *dependent personality disorder*—"an excessive and pervasive need to be taken care of, submissive, clinging, needy behavior due to fear of abandonment."[21] If this is the case, then Bonnie and Clyde's jointly flamboyant criminal behaviors were produced for different underlying reasons. Such an interpretation is consistent with attempts to diagnose Harley Quinn's flamboyance as being driven by yet another cluster-B personality disorder, *histrionic personality disorder*,[22] defined by constant attention-seeking behavior. Regardless of what the true story of Bonnie's involvement with crime is, the enduring narrative associated with Bonnie and Clyde, as well as Harley and the Joker, is that each member of these couples was as interested in committing crime as the other and that being together not only made them more capable of committing these major crimes, but also allowed them to have someone there to fuel their energy and to serve as a receptive audience for their ideas and crimes.

All Clowns Need an Audience: The Socially Dependent Nature of Flamboyance

It is interesting and also somewhat ironic that, despite the different constellations of factors underlying the flamboyant behaviors of the Joker, Harley, Bonnie, and Clyde, all of their different constellations are inherently social in nature. In some versions of the Joker's background,[23] his flamboyant behavior stems from his underlying self-enhancing fantasies and strivings, hyperreactivity, and unfulfilled expectations of others. For Harley Quinn, it's potentially histrionic personality disorder. For Bonnie, the flamboyance seems to be driven by a pathological form of intimate relationship (as happens with dependent personality disorder). As for Clyde, he fit criteria for psychopathy and antisocial personality disorder.[24]

While these diagnoses provide some insight into these four people, who are so excessive that they almost do not seem like plausible people or realistic enough characters, it is important to note that, in both cases, the Joker and Clyde needed an audience and someone to work with them. As narcissists, they need to be the standout or leader, and they need to flaunt their schemes, crimes, and capers with someone who would polish their ego. Harley is unquestionably that person for the Joker, as she often is his cheerleader and partner in crime, and she consoles him when things do not go as planned. This parallels what is known about the relationship between Bonnie and Clyde.

While both of these relationships are seen as partnerships, the fact that the Joker and Clyde were men led others to assume each to be the "real" leader in the relationship. However, there is evidence that the women themselves were just as capable, competent, and motivated to be criminals as the men they were with, but as a result of the society they lived in and the relationships they were in, they could not easily express their competencies or be seen as equal. Arguably, it was the presence of the men that made the difference in the way that Bonnie and Harley expressed themselves and the crimes they committed.

Female-owned flamboyance or grandiosity of crime can be seen in the *DC Bombshells*[25] comic book in which Harley Quinn is absent from the Joker. This series reimagines the characters during a World War II era when Bonnie and Clyde were still fresh in the public mind. The crimes this version of Harley commits are stand-alone or committed alongside her new love interest, Poison Ivy. She is no longer the Joker's moll. She remains rather madcap and violent but now is able to be herself in a new way, arguably because she is without the Joker. She is able to be free and jovial, committing the crimes that *she* wants. She is also able to love the way she wants, with a partner who is loving and kind to her. Free of the Joker, she is still flamboyant and grandiose but on her own terms.

A similar argument can be made for Bonnie as well, but to a lesser extent, as we do not necessarily know how Bonnie would have been without Clyde, because they both died at the same time. The time period in which Bonnie lived (1930s USA) was very patriarchal in nature, women were not viewed as equals, and gender norms concerning what was acceptable or unacceptable for women to do were strict. Before meeting Clyde, Bonnie was working to violate gender norms and was flamboyant in her own way. She was involved with men who were criminals and used guns herself. This made Bonnie flashy in a way that many women were not, even female criminals, as her firearm use, even in the 1930s, violated some norms.[26] It would have been interesting to see what crimes Bonnie might have committed and who she would have become had she become a criminal in her own right, apart from Clyde, as Harley does.

Doing It with Flair

The Joker is the ultimate flamboyant criminal, and his relationship with Harley provides for two outrageous individuals capturing the attention of Gotham. This is very similar to the real-world criminals Bonnie and Clyde, who fascinated America in the 1930s and continue to intrigue people. The fact that these two sets of couples could commit such heinous crimes, but do it with flair is likely why society has remained fascinated with them all.

The Summer of '42: From the Electric Chair to the Limelight

Travis Langley & Eric Bailey

1942 changes how the Joker sees his conflict with Batman. That spring, he realizes he does not want to know Batman's identity. In a position to rip off the mask and end Batman's career, he decides, "It's too simple—unworthy of my intelligence. And I like these battles of wits! The hunt, the chase! That's the breath of life to me!"[27] Keeping Batman alive feeds his own ego. Maybe that epiphany leads to the bigger change unveiled in his next appearance.

That summer's *Detective Comics* #64's "The Joker Walks the Last Mile" is widely cited as the end of the villain's original killer clown phase and the onset of his zany Clown Prince decades. But why, from his point of view, does he change his murderous ways? Getting himself executed, so that he can walk free once henchmen revive him, just ends with him wanted by the law all over again. Why doesn't the Golden Age Joker kill again? Actually, he does. One month later, he kills Robin.

A *Batman* #11 story, which may have been written before "The Joker Walks the Last Mile," confirms that the Joker's stark-white skin color is "my actual face," not makeup. When he has Batman unconscious, the clown tells a henchman not to kill him: "No! Let him live! He is so amusing when he tries to match wits with me!" He views Robin, however, as a nuisance: "You've annoyed me no end with your interferences so I'm going to kill you—simply and quietly!" Cracking a joke about the boy's death, the Joker traps him in a room where poison fumes fill his lungs. By the time Batman arrives, a doctor declares, "The boy's dead!" But Batman uses a pulmotor fan to empty his partner's lungs and bring him back. When he catches up with the Joker, Batman proceeds to "give you the beating of your life!" The story ends with the radio announcing, "Puzzled police found a bruised, battered Joker lying on the court steps. He was taken to a prison hospital for treatment." The news of Batman's violence shocks Dick Grayson (Robin), who asks, "Say, what *did* you do to that guy, anyway?"[28]

The Joker has murdered his first Robin, and the first Batman has brutalized his Joker like never before. The experience may offer a personal reason why the Joker stops killing and starts making his mischief more madcap—maybe fear, maybe respect, maybe satisfaction. He now knows he once pushed Batman to the limit.[29] Or maybe it feels anticlimactic. Expecting fulfillment upon goal achievement (*the arrival fallacy*) can produce post-achievement depression among people who don't readily form new goals.[30]

His bloodthirst sated, for whatever reason, the original Joker now wants laughs and the limelight, grander than ever before.

NOTES

1. *Batman*, episode 1–5, "The Joker is Wild" (January 26, 1966).
2. Fleming (2009).
3. *Batman* #663 (2007).
4. *Batman* #1 (1940).
5. American Psychiatric Association (2013).
6. *Batman* #12 (1942).
7. *Batman* #57 (1950).
8. *Batman* #80 (1953).

9. *Batman*, episode 3–10, "Surf's Up! Joker's Under!" (November 16, 1967).

10. *Batman* #321 (1980).

11. e.g., crime lord Bobby Gazzo—*Batman: Dark Victory* #13 (2000); the Generalissimo—*Batman* #681 (2008); Psimon—*Salvation Run* #2 (2008).

12. *Batman* #251 (1973), #428 (1988); *Detective Comics* #737 (1999).

13. *The Superman/Batman Movie* (1998 animated motion picture).

14. American Psychiatric Association (2013).

15. *Detective Comics* #475 (1978).

16. *The Dark Knight* (2008 motion picture); *Joker* (2019 motion picture).

17. *Batman* #663 (2007).

18. *Batman*, episode 1–5, "The Joker is Wild" (January 26, 1966).

19. Dickson & Pinkus (2003).

20. Knight (2004).

21 Skodol et al. (2011), p. 151

22. Goodfriend (2016).

23. *Batman: The Killing Joke* (1988); *Joker* (2019 motion picture).

24. Leistedt & Linkowski (2014).

25. *DC Comics: Bombshells* #1 (2015).

26. Twine (2013).

27. *Detective Comics* #62 (1942).

28. *Batman* #11 (1942).

29. Anderson (2016); Young (1994).

30. Wilding (2016).

5

Trickster and Shadow: Jungian Archetypes

LARISA A. GARSKI, JUSTINE MASTIN, & ASHLEY MYHRE

"I'd liken him to the Trickster figure of mythology. You just don't know what he's going to do. Instead of killing you, he might actually give you an ice cream—or he might change his mind and kill you!"
—comic book writer/editor Dennis O'Neil[1]

"I'm here now rapping at your window. Looking for you, my Shadow."
—message Harley delivers from the Joker to Batman[2]

THE RIVALRY OF Batman vs. the Joker has captivated readers and audiences since the debuts of the superhero in 1939 and super-villain in 1940.[3] Some argue that one cannot exist without the other,[4] that they need each other.[5] This sentiment has been echoed repeatedly over the years and expressed yet again by Commissioner Gordon when he wonders if Batman's existence may have called the Joker into being: "And you're wearing a mask, jumping off rooftops. Take this guy. Armed robbery, double homicide. Got a taste for the theatrical like you. Leaves a calling card."[6] Joined at the metaphorical hip, the synergy between "Jokes" and "Bats" remains undeniable, but the reason for their complex duality is deeper than a

conflict between rivals. The Joker and Batman are none other than psychoanalyst Carl Gustav Jung's two most infamous archetypes writ large,
battling through the backdrop of a Gotham populated by various motifs
from the collective unconscious, struggling to become healed or whole
or broken all over again.

Enter Arkham Asylum

Though modern mental health professionals may shudder at the depiction of mental illness and psychiatric care in the fictional Gotham City,[7]
there is something eerily familiar in the way the Joker and his confed-
eracy of crooks behave both inside and outside Arkham Asylum.[8] Wild
and unmoored, they career through the streets of Gotham and the halls
of Arkham alike as if these were their own personal playgrounds. Perhaps they are. The Joker, Harley, and many of their costumed criminal
colleagues exemplify the tropes or archetypes of the *collective unconscious*,
a term coined by Jung to denote the shared unconscious of humanity to
which all individuals have access via their individual unconscious. Within
the collective unconscious exist the *archetypes*, inborn tropes of human
feeling and instinct, in their most primal form.[9] The Joker and company
are nothing if not primal.

Jung conceived of the collective unconscious as an internal psychic
repository containing humanity's first myths or primal understandings.[10]
His work later found a champion in mythologist Joseph Campbell, whose
own research into the *monomyth* (the one myth supposedly underlying all
heroic tales throughout the world, better known as the Hero's Journey)[11]
supports the idea of the collective unconscious as a phenomenon universal
throughout the human race. While an individual's personal unconscious
contains repressed chaotic emotions and unresolved conflicts from early
childhood, the collective unconscious contains "the feeling-toned com-
plexes"[12] or emotional blueprints from humanity's past. It is here that we
find the enduring characters, themes, and ideas told in stories from every
era of human existence. they define the central questions of humanity's existence. Over the years, Jung identified many archetypes such as
the Anima/Animus, the Shadow, the Mother, the Child, the Sage, and
the Trickster. Though sometimes confusing to sort out, Jung maintained

that there was a consistent internal logic to the archetypes in particular and to the collective unconscious as a whole, describing them as a series of "inherited possibilities of ideas."[13] The personal unconscious leads to the collective unconscious and an encounter with one often leads to an encounter with the other, with life-changing consequences.

Within Bruce Wayne's personal unconscious, for example, we find the torment of a child who has suffered the violent loss of his parents at a young age. Overwhelmed by the violence he finds both internally and externally, Bruce Wayne crafts a mask out of the *Shadow archetype* (the unconscious representation of all his inner darkness) that allows him to fight Gotham's villains who are themselves personifications of such archetypes of the collective unconscious as *the Anima* (the male's inner representation of feminity, symbolized by characters such as Harley Quinn), *the Trickster* (epitomized by the Joker),[14] and *the Mother* (the infinite maternal goddess, whose Mother Nature aspect manifests in distorted form as Poison Ivy).

The Joker is both symbol and man, a human who has gone so far toward one extreme as to have almost ceased to be a multifaceted individual and to have simply become the Trickster archetype in human form or "an agent of chaos."[15] To be a Trickster is to be both grotesque and refined, smart and stupid, bullish and timid. In Jungian terms, the Trickster was once part of another archetype, the Shadow, but became separated from its original during an earlier phase of human development. Jung described the Trickster as being representative of our "animal beginnings," from which we want both flee and return.[16] This older version of archetypal development both attracts and repels us, showing the depravity with which humanity once lived. Batman and arguably all of Gotham struggle with similar impulses toward the Joker, as they are attracted to his gleeful antics and repelled by his murderous depravities.[17]

The Shadow of My Shadow Is My Trickster

Before Joseph Campbell outlines the Hero's Journey in the format we know today, anthropologist Paul Radin laid out four evolutionary cycles of the hero based on the tribal tradition of the Winnebago. The first cycle was the trial of the Trickster, and it required the hero to reckon with this "figure whose physical appetites dominate his behavior; he has the mentality of an infant. Lacking any purpose beyond the gratification of his primary needs, he is cruel, cynical, and unfeeling."[18] That certainly sounds like Batman's nemesis, but even the Joker has been someone else once.

Before the Joker becomes the Joker, he is just a man who undergoes an accidental transformation, which is in itself symbolic of an initiation rite. During his fall into the vat of chemicals, the man who would become the Joker undergoes a sort of death,[19] in which his identity reunites with the collective unconscious. When he reemerges, he is reborn as someone new—as something new. Just as Bruce Wayne's descent into the collective unconscious allows him to both find and claim the Shadow, the man-who-will-be-known-as-the-Joker finds and claims a powerful archetype, too. The Trickster, archetype of the crude and the grotesque, gives the Joker the power to be both a mastermind and a murderer. He is not just Batman's foil—he embodies Batman's purpose for existing at all.

In ancient tales, the Trickster was a "delight maker,"[20] bringing about joy and feasting and merriment, and prompting more than a little unsavory behavior. This animalistic display, or personification of our baser instincts, is a familiar state of being to which we are instinctively drawn. As the Joker himself observes, "Does every one of these 'Our Town' wannabes feel just as awkward, just as much a gross buffoon as the man in the polka-dot suit?"[21] But the Trickster personified is a formidable opponent because of its powerful nature. While Batman himself is a Shadow, he does not embody Trickster characteristics. Here is where the two differ greatly. Batman lurks in the literal shadows, mostly in solitude with great restraint, while the Joker loves the spotlight and above all chaos. So while the two are "cut from the same cloth,"[22] they differ in fundamental ways. Both being Shadow characters and therefore coming from the unconscious, they are two sides of the same coin.

Yet, the attraction between these two is as undeniable as their general unwillingness to kill one another.[23] Is it only Batman's commitment to justice and the Joker's to chaos that forever unite these two in conflict? If we look below the surface of their aggression, consulting the collective unconscious, the motivations for the Joker and Batman's eternal struggle starts to become clear.

The Joker's Wild

Jung describes the Shadow as the opposite of our ego, the hidden parts of ourselves of which we initially have no conscious awareness.[24] The Shadow is most commonly associated with the dark side of human impulses—rage, lust, selfishness, and greed—that are considered socially unacceptable and that we attempt to repress or deny. The Shadow, the part of oneself hidden in darkness, is not inherently evil, but it can become dangerous when it goes unacknowledged or repressed. Jung thought that the Shadow when ignored can "coalesce into a relatively autonomous 'splinter personality' with contrary tendencies in the unconscious."[25]

On the surface, it is easy to suppose that the Joker himself is a personification of the Shadow archetype: Lustful and aggressive, he is a mass murderer who relishes the macabre. These are impulses that Batman generally rejects for himself.[26] As the Batman matures, he gains more awareness of these Shadow elements within himself, eventually facing the Shadow that lives within his personal unconscious. Alfred drives this point home when he says, "Death and chance stole your parents. But rather than become a victim, you have done everything in your power to control the fates. For what is Batman if not an effort to master the chaos that sweeps our world? An attempt to control death itself."[27] Jungian analysis would take Alfred one step further and observe that an attempt to control death is equivalent to attempting to control both the personal and the collective unconscious. Despite his best efforts, Batman fails repeatedly at joining his conscious ego or the representation of his *Persona* archetype (public mask), Bruce Wayne, with his unconscious Shadow, Batman.[28] Crucial parts of the self reside in the unconscious and thus it is only by facing them within the unconscious and bringing them back to the conscious self that one can become truly whole. Jung held that it is only by the integration of conscious and unconscious components can an individual become a unified self.

The Joker, then, is not simply the embodiment of Batman's Shadow, but the Shadow of his Shadow, embodying the chaos and evil that Batman rejects. Batman often wonders if by simply existing as "the Batman" he has created the villains who taunt and haunt him.[29] From a Jungian perspective, he may have a point: "Every good quality has its bad side, and nothing that is good can come into the world without directly producing a corresponding evil."[30] For Batman to be the hero, there must be a threat to fight. If Batman rejects chaos, then what can the Joker do but "introduce a little anarchy, upset the established order"?[31] Put another way: As every person has a Shadow, every Batman has a Joker.

Harley Quinn & Mister J: A Ghoulish Duo

Jung struggled with his own Batman/Joker dynamic with Sigmund Freud, particularly in their middle years.[32] Freud, father and founder of psychoanalysis, was a bit Batmanesque in his approach to protégés and followers, crafting his own collective of Robins (e.g., psychoanalysts Max Kahane, Rudolf Reitler) and Batgirls (e.g., psychoanalysts Sabrina Spielren, Tatiana Rosenthal). But, like Batman,[33] Freud had a habit of alienating his disciples and colleagues. In Jung, he hoped to find both a collaborator and a confidant, but ultimately sex, repression, and power got the better of them. Like the Joker and Batman, they continued to influence one another's work, even as the bitterness between them grew. While Jung and Freud each grappled with the impact sexual desire and obsession have on the human psyche, Jung criticized Freud for overemphasizing sex as the driving force behind all human endeavors.

Jung's description of the Anima/Animus archetypal relationship has come under fire for its antiquated representation of gender.[34] If the male psyche's collective unconscious includes the feminine Anima and the female psyche's houses the masculine Animus, then what do trans and gender-nonbinary folks find when they follow the Shadow through the doorway into the collective unconscious? The individual's Anima or Animus contains all that human beings find attractive, exciting, spontaneous, and supernatural about life. It is the stuff of life or, as Jung put it, "the Anima is the *archetype of life itself.*"[35] If the Shadow archetype awaits the hero at the threshold to the unconscious, then it is the Anima who meets him and shows him around the place, while the Trickster preens and starts small fires in the background. Abstract though this may sound, this was Jung's concept of the relationship among the Shadow, the Anima, and the Trickster, which is yet again played out beautifully by Shadowy Batman, mercurial Harley, and the king of tricks himself, the Joker. Harley

Quinn, part-time sidekick and sometime villain, causes both Batman and the Joker no end of distress.[36] She attracts and repels, creates and destroys, both of which are a clear indication of her Anima status, because as the emblem of life, the Anima "wants both good and bad."[37] Though at turns Shadow-like, while at others we see the edge of the Trickster, at heart Harley embodies chaotic joy. In her own words, "I've changed a lot, y'know! People look up to me now as a role model. A personification of good will and happiness!"[38]

Here is where things take a turn for the confusing and grotesque, because Harley isn't just the Joker's Anima; he is also her Animus. In Jungian terms, it is possible for a person to channel more than one archetype, switching from one archetype to the next as he or she moves from one human interaction or human relationship to the next. Because he has different relationships to each, the Joker can represent both Batman's Trickster and Harley's Animus. As surely as Harley both attracts and repels Mister J., he wields the same siren power over her, saying whatever feels right in the moment in his effort to manipulate her:

> "I used to be the same way. Powerless against those who wanted to keep me down. 'Til the greatest thing that ever could happen to me did. An impromptu incident of mythic proportions. When my eyes stopped stinging I finally saw the world for the true hypocrisy it is. Once I didn't care about the rules any more, I had all the power. We all have it inside of us. We just got to let it out. And I can show you how."[39]

In reality, of course, Harley and Mister J. are much more than each other's respective archetypal projections. They are flawed and dysfunctional humans who together make one cataclysmically volatile pair. Despite the fact that neither seems to bring the other much joy, they return to one another repeatedly because of the power of *syzygy*, the energizing relationships between the Anima and Animus archetypes. Because this archetypal relationship encompasses "life itself,"[40] the idea of abandoning the person who has come to represent this power is unthinkable for both Harley and the Joker. In fact, when Harley believes that the Joker is dead, she insists on finding the one remaining scrap of his physical form that she can find—his severed face.[41] Taking the enactment of the archetype one step further, Harley puts the face on someone else, Deadshot, in an attempt to reenact her dynamic with Mister J.[42]

Harley is most successful when she has help, often in the form of a new lover or a new mother.[43] Poison Ivy, as a possible emblem of the Mother archetype, becomes the person to whom Harley turns most often when she needs support and refuge from the Joker's violence. In many ways, Ivy is the ideal ally for the beleaguered Harley. Ivy sees herself as the caretaker of the natural world, a Mother Earth of sorts, who wraps Harley in her flowers and encourages her to be good to herself. Rather than ceding her power over to some Trickster, Ivy offers Harley opportunities to use her archetypal power to help achieve her own criminal ends.[44]

The Joker wants Harley to become him. At one point, he forces Harley to dress up and pretend to be the Joker, telling her exactly what to say to lure Batman to a factory where he can be dumped into a vat of chemicals. The Joker's plan is for Harley and Batman to be reborn in this vat. In the Joker's mind, this will bring them together in madness. A Jungian interpretation might view this as the Joker's attempt to assimilate or integrate both his Anima and his Shadow back into himself by returning to where it all began: the vat, that is, the unconscious that made him mad.[45] Joker takes individuation to its gruesome extreme.

Life Really Is a Joke

It may be fitting that at the end of one of their more memorable showdowns, the Joker gets Batman to laugh. In the events leading up to this moment, Batman and the Joker each spend time trying to figure out how to come together as Batman offers to help the Joker seek rehabilitation and the Joker tries to get Batman to see the world his way.[46] This is in line with the Jungian interpretation of the relationship between the Shadow and the Trickster. Cut from the same cloth, the Trickster longs to be reunited with his Shadowed other half. It is in keeping with his character and approach to life that he goes about reuniting with his Batman in the worst possible ways—kidnapping various paramours of Bruce Wayne,[47] poisoning Alfred,[48] paralyzing Batgirl,[49] and bombing Gotham,[50] to name a few. Both Batman and the Joker are driven by an equal yet opposite reaction to the horror they encountered when they first faced the totality of life's possibilities. Batman seeks to control the darkness, whereas the Joker moves to unleash it on himself, Batman, and the world:

Joker: See? Now we can chat. My King and I.

Batman: You're nothing to me but—

Joker: Shhh. Don't do that. Don't pretend. Not here. Not to me. Your faithful court jester. And what does the jester do, if not deliver news to the king? Bad news. Especially. The worst! The fleet has holes. The army's turned pacifist! The children's hands have rotted off and they can't clap for the fairies! Because the jester's the only one he'll hear it from. The only who can make him laugh at it. At himself. And that's what I've tried to do for you, Bats, deliver the worst news of your heart, directly to you.[51]

The great risk of facing the collective unconscious is becoming lost within it, thereby falling prey to neurosis. Both the Joker and, albeit to a lesser extent, Harley struggle with this. Though the Joker's personal origins remain uncertain,[52] it is clear that he deals with what he has found in the collective unconscious by turning toward the extreme of the Trickster Batman does much the same. And so, as Harvey Dent might say,[53] we have two sides of one very Shadowy coin that want to be made whole. Life demands that we balance both sides of the Shadow. As Jung said, "Life is crazy and meaningful at once. And when we do not laugh over the one aspect and speculate about the other, life is exceedingly drab, and everything is reduced to the littlest scale."[54]

But is such a thing possible for Batman and the Joker? They tend to come closest to this idea when they are willing to be vulnerable with one another. Whether it's the Joker asking for a kiss[55] or Batman begging him, finally, to talk to him,[56] their attempts at connection are rarely communicated in a way that the other can understand. So they continue their dance of terror across the streets of Gotham and into the halls of Arkham, occasionally pausing long enough to save their city from total devastation. The only way forward for Batman and the Joker seems to be either mutual annihilation or some kind of coexistence:

Batman: I'm just going to come right out and say it: I hate you, Joker.

Joker: I hate you, too.

Batman: I hate you more.

Joker: I hate you the most.

Batman: I hate you forever.

Admittedly, that exchange of dialogue comes from the comedic film *The Lego Batman Movie*, but parody may be where some greater truth lies. If the Joker and Batman could find a way to come together and admit just how much they mean to each other, what might they achieve? Or, put another way, what might they be able to resolve and finally, at long last, put to rest?

NOTES

1. Quoted by Eury & Kronenberg (2009), p. 149.
2. *Batman* #13 (2012).
3. *Batman* #1 (1940).
4. *Batman: Legends of the Dark Knight* #66 (1994).
5. "Well, I think the Batman needs the Joker more than the Joker needs the Batman." —Jerry Robinson, quoted by Langley (2014).
6. *Batman Begins* (2005 motion picture).
7. Bender et al. (2011); Goodwin & Tajjudin (2016).
8. *Batman* #251 (1973); *Batman: Legends of the Dark Knight* #65 (1994); *Batman* #663 (2007).
9. Jung (1968/1991).
10. Jung (1968).
11. Campbell (1949/2008).
12. Jung (1968/1991), p. 4.
13. Jung (1968/1991), p. 6.
14. *Batman: The Dark Knight* #0 (2010); *Batman: Earth One* (2012).
15. Langley (2012); Weiner & Peaslee (2015).
16. *The Dark Knight* (2008 motion picture).
17. Jung (1968/1991), p. 268.
18. *Batman: The Animated Series*, episode 1–11, "Be a Clown" (September 15, 1992).
19. Henderson (1964), pp. 103–104.
20. *Batman: The Killing Joke* (1988); *Batman: The Man Who Laughs* (2005).
21. Jung (1968/1991), p. 262.
22. *Batman: Legends of the Dark Knight* #65 (1994).
23. *Batman: The Animated Series*, episode 1–11, "Be a Clown" (September 15, 1992).
24. *Batman* #251 (1973); *Batman: The Dark Knight* #3 (1986); *Batman: The Killing Joke* (1988); *Batman: Legends of the Dark Knight* #68 (1995); *Batman: The Man Who Laughs* (2005).
25. Jung (1964).

26. Jung (1964), p. 399.

27. *Detective Comics* #33 (1939)

28. *Batman Begins* (2005 motion picture).

29. *The Dark Knight* (2008 motion picture).

30. *The Dark Knight* (2008 motion picture).

31. Ker (1993).

32. *Batman* #17 (2013).

33. Hollenitsch (2016); McKenzie (2006); Molay (2012; 2017).

34. Jung (1968/1991), p. 32.

35. *Batman: The Animated Series*, episodes 1–46, "The Laughing Fish" (January 10, 1993); 1–47, "Harley and Ivy" (January 18, 1993); 2–07 "Harelquinade" (May 23, 1994).

36. Jung (1968/1991), p. 28.

37. *Batman Annual* #1 (2017).

38. *Suicide Squad* #6 (2012).

39. Jung (1968/1991), p. 32.

40. *Suicide Squad* #6 (2012).

41. *Suicide Squad* #7 (2012).

42. *Suicide Squad* #14 (2013); *Batman: The Animated Series*, episode 1–47, "Harley and Ivy" (January 18, 1993).

43. *Batman: The Animated Series*, episode 1–47, "Harley and Ivy" (January 18, 1993).

44. *Batman* #13 (2012); *Suicide Squad* #14 (2013); *Suicide Squad* #15 (2013).

45. *Batman: The Killing Joke* (1988).

46. *Batman* (1989 motion picture); *The Dark Knight* (2008 motion picture).

47. *Batman: The Animated Series*, episode 1–15, "The Last Laugh" (September 21, 1992).

48. *Batman: The Killing Joke* (1988).

49. *The Dark Knight* (2008 motion picture); *The Lego Batman Movie* (2017 motion picture).

50. *Batman* #14 (2013).

51. *Batman: The Killing Joke* (1988); *Batman: The Man Who Laughs* (2005); *The Dark Knight* (2008 motion picture).

52. *Batman: The Long Halloween* #13 (1997).

53. Jung (1968/1991), p. 31.

54. *Batman: The Long Halloween* #4 (1997).

55. *Batman: The Killing Joke* (1988).

56. *The Lego Batman Movie* (2017 motion picture).

EXPLAINING THE JOKE 5-1

ACTOR KEVIN CONROY AND MYTHOLOGIST JOSEPH CAMPBELL

Travis Langley

Considered by many to present Batman's quintessential portrayal,[1] *Batman: The Animated Series* retold the best of his comic book stories, spun new tales, transformed two-dimensional character Mister Freeze into perhaps the most poignant Bat-villain of them all, and added the Joker's companion Harley Quinn to the mythos. Thanks to this program, many comic book fans now hear one man's voice— or voices—in their heads when reading Batman: actor Kevin Conroy.

During one of the convention panels where I moderated Kevin's question-and-answer sessions, he mentioned Joseph Campbell, whose work is critical to the chapter that leads up to this feature.[2]

Kevin Conroy: One of my favorite philosophers is Joseph Campbell. He wrote *The Hero with a Thousand Faces*. It's about this hero that goes through this arc by being challenged by life, dying and being reborn as catharsis, becoming the hero. It's in the Greek and Roman empires, ancient Indian cultures, African cultures. Anywhere in the world you go there is a story of that hero. That's why he calls it a hero with a thousand faces. It's this subconsciousness throughout human history where this challenged hero rises like a phoenix out of the ashes to become a savior. Batman. That's the Batman story. That's who he is. And I love that about the character. So any of the stories that touch on that aspect of him, I love.

As it turns out, Campbell's original observations about the universal concept of conflict between good and evil address the Joker's role as Batman's adversary, just short of naming the two.

Joseph Campbell: This is a conception inherent in every myth. Universal too is the casting of the antagonist, the representative of evil, in the role of the clown. Devils—both the lusty thick-heads and the sharp, clever deceivers—are always clowns. Though they may triumph in the world of space and time, both they and their work disappear when the perspective shifts to the transcendental. They are the mistakers of shadow for substance; they symbolize the inevitable imperfections of the realm of shadow, and so long as we remain this side of the veil cannot be done away.[3]

For more from the discussion with Kevin Conroy, particularly his thoughts on the Joker's importance for Batman, see Explaining the Joke 14–2: Actor Kevin Conroy, Part 2.

NOTES

1. e.g., Duncan (2016); kaptainkristian (2016); Thill (2016).
2. Conroy & Langley (2017).
3. Campbell (1949/2008), p. 294.

6

Humor: Who's Laughing?

TRAVIS LANGLEY & SIBE DOOSJE

"Humor can be dissected, as a frog can, but the thing dies in the process and the innards are discouraging to any but the pure scientific mind."

—author E. B. White[1]

"Here's another showstopper: A scientist is testing a frog . . ."
—The Joker, trying to find Lex Luthor's sense of humor[2]

THE JOKER LAUGHS and makes others die laughing.[3] A notable facial characteristic is that smile of his, which seems painted or frozen on his face especially as he appeared in Bronze Age comics[4] and in the 1989 *Batman* motion picture. The Joker gets this deformed smile because he falls into a vat of strong acid. Because the smile seems so unchangeable and frozen, it looks as if the Joker is stuck with his sense of humor and, indeed, he must play tricks on others; he cannot do otherwise. Research has suggested that forcing the face into a grin-like position by doing things such as holding a pencil between your teeth might make things seem funnier through *facial feedback*,[5] although this oft-cited finding has been difficult to replicate.[6]

Does the Joker really get the joke, though? "It's all a joke! Everything anybody ever valued or struggled for," he says to Batman. "It's all a monstrous, demented gag! So why can't you see the funny side? Why

An Alliterative Adversary:
What's in a Nickname?

Eric D. Wesselmann

The Chaplain of Chicanery! The Hateful Harlequin! The Clown Prince of Crime![7] These nicknames for the Joker employ a linguistic device called *alliteration*, the repetition of consonants in a phrase. The first prominent psychologist to study alliterations was behaviorist B. F. Skinner, who examined their frequency in 100 of Shakespeare's sonnets. Skinner found that, contrary to popular opinion, Shakespeare did not favor this literary device.[8] Even if the Bard did not use this device commonly, alliterations are found in poetry, prose, and newspapers throughout the world.[9] Alliterations also are common in American superhero comics—especially when they involve the Joker. The Joker has been referred to in both narrative text and in Gotham City newspapers by various names, such as the "Cunning Caliph of Crime" and the "Mirthful Mountebank of Mischief and Menace."[10] Why are these alliterative names for the Joker so catchy? Researchers have found that people pay more attention to alliterations, and may even remember them better, than other word patterns.[11] The preference for alliteration shows up early in life. Infants as young as three months old will listen longer to alliterative sounds than to unrelated (or even rhyming) syllables.[12] Of all Batman's foes, the Joker has the most alliterative nicknames. Furthermore, humor scholars have noted that alliterations can be used for comedy,[13] which may be one reason the Joker (and other characters) use them particularly often in the classic 1960s *Batman* TV show.[14]

aren't you laughing?" The fact that most people don't share his morbid outlook and twisted sense of humor irritates him. But in his frustration over others' failure to see "what a black, awful joke the world was,"[15] he reveals his own failure to comprehend why most people can find hope and joy. When it comes to understanding why others enjoy life, he's the one who doesn't get the joke.

What does it mean to have a good sense of humor? Does it mean that you laugh easily (reacting) or that you make others laugh (enacting)? Can you "get" the joke and understand things others find funny (comprehending) or find things funny regardless of whether anyone else does (idiosyncratic)? Does your humor build people up (constructive) or tear them down (destructive)? These are but a few of the questions humor researchers ask when even considering how they should try to study their subject of interest.[16] Even though humor research is not often seen as a serious, respectable subject for scientific inquiry, humor is ubiquitous in human life. Jokes have inspired people to reach great heights, and they have also incited riots and murder. And when contemplating a criminal who defines his felonious persona by jokes and who conducts entire crime sprees following themes that amuse him or, for that matter, when trying to understand any lawbreaker who's driven by the pursuit of amusement and thrills, it might be wise to identify patterns in how they use humor.

The Joker weaponizes wit.

The Good, the Bad, and the Funny

Whether humor researchers distinguish types of humor in terms of positive or negative, healthy or unhealthy, adaptive or maladaptive, they're somehow investigating if it's good or bad for people. Humor is subjective, quixotic, and tough to pin down. It can be dry or absurd, good-natured or mean. What's funny now won't be funny later. What's hilarious to you might bore us. If you map out comedic formulas, humorists overuse them and they grow less effective. Humor relies on many of the same elements of incongruity and surprise that horror doles out,[17] and maybe that's why the Joker blends them together. Among the many theoretical perspectives that attempt to explain humor, a few prominent ideas have emerged. (See sidebar, "Why So Telic?" on page 111.)

Psychoanalyst Sigmund Freud was one of the earliest professionals to examine the psychology of humor. In his view, people make jokes when the conscious mind allows the expression of thoughts society usually discourages, overcoming repression and social inhibitions to achieve emotional release.[18] He considered this to be essential for mental health. Like E. B. White, quoted at the beginning of this chapter, he noted that scrutinizing a joke's technique diminishes its ability to evoke a natural, hearty laugh. Based on Freud's and their own observations, subsequent psychoanalysts classified humor as one of the *defense mechanisms*, things we do to protect ourselves from anxiety. While they recognized that humor can be inappropriate and that any defense can be overused, they generally considered humor to be one of the healthier, more mature defense mechanisms.[19] Humor in the face of hardship can help people express ideas, feelings, and concerns, and mentally process situations without letting the experiences bring them down.[20] Those whose occupations put them in traumatic situations (*primary traumatic stress*) or make them feel vicariously traumatized through contact with others undergoing trauma (*secondary traumatic stress*) may try to cope by means of *gallows humor*, grim jokes about grave topics, because doing so gives them a sense of control in out-of-control circumstances, elicits social support, and helps them distance themselves from feelings that might interfere with doing their jobs.[21] The person with a nihilistic worldview, such as the Joker, might take that gallows humor to an extreme if all of life seems cruel and bleak.

Modern psychologists, many of whom either reject Freud altogether or accept some of his ideas while disputing his emphasis on unconscious or sexual motives, may interpret the defense mechanism aspect of humor in terms of whether it is *adaptive* (helping the person function—in other words, helping him or her adapt to life) or *maladaptive* (interfering with healthy life functioning). *Adaptive styles of humor* build people up, whether through *affiliative humor*, which enhances how we see others, or *self-enhancing humor*, which promotes the person making the joke. On the other hand, *maladaptive styles of humor* tear people down, whether that means disparaging and harming others (*aggressive humor*) or ourselves (*self-defeating humor*).[22] When Bruce Wayne says of Batman, "A guy that dresses up like a bat clearly has issues," this could seem self-defeating, but he is not really insulting himself. Instead, it's actually self-enhancing because it shows that he's able to joke about himself comfortably, even though only he and Rachel Dawes know it's a joke.[23]

	ADAPTIVE	MALADAPTIVE
REGARDING SELF	SELF-ENHANCING HUMOR "Aren't I just good enough to eat?" —The Joker[24]	SELF-DEFEATING HUMOR "I'm crazy about— Well, hey, I'm just crazy." —Harley Quinn[25]
REGARDING OTHERS	AFFILIATIVE HUMOR "Aw, c'mon, puddin'— don'tcha wanna rev up ya Harley? Vroom! Vroom!" —Harley Quinn, *trying to connect with the Joker*[26]	AGGRESSIVE HUMOR Most of the Joker's humor.

Table with examples along adaptive vs. maladaptive × other vs. self dimensions.

Types of humor have classically been divided into high comedy and low comedy. With greater subtlety and self-conscious sophistication, *high comedy* utilizes clever dialogue and understated characterizations in order to appeal more to thought than to emotion.[27] Criticizing inconsistencies of human nature through satire, logic, and wordplay, high comedy is serious stuff. It could get a response of "Ah, very droll," expressing intellectual appreciation without a loud laugh. *Low comedy*, on the other hand, gets silly. More visually oriented, it employs sight gags and physical comedy such as slapstick, drunkenness, shouting, fighting, boasting, and boisterous jokes. Its verbal expressions lack subtlety. The purpose is simply to make people laugh, without necessarily conveying a contextual message.[28] People don't really have to think about it. They just get to laugh.

The Joker engages in both high comedy and low comedy. His high comedy tends to build himself up, showing off his intellectual superiority and cleverness through wordplay or clues that require his pursuers to "get the joke" before they can get the Joker. His low comedy tears others down, sometimes literally so. He may turn novelty gag items destructive or deadly: the lapel flower that squirts acid, the whoopee cushion or cigar that detonates with high explosive, the pies to the face that poison some people and leave others acid–scarred[29]—his weaponized wit.

Why So Telic?

Eric D. Wesselmann

Reversal theory argues that we have two states of mind, *telic* (serious) and *paratelic* (playful), and that we need to be in the paratelic to appreciate humor.[30] The same joke will be less funny, if at all, when we are in the telic mind-set. A paratelic state can make us find even normally scary or disgusting things funny. The Joker usually seems paratelic while Batman appears telic.[31] They can switch, though: The Joker occasionally gets angry while Batman finds some things funny[32]—and the Joker hates when Batman quips at the clown's expense.[33]

Comprehension-elaboration theory focuses on how easy or hard the joke is to understand, suggesting a curvilinear relationship: Something that takes a little bit of effort to figure out will be optimally funny (neither mundanely obvious nor too hard to grasp).[34] Data, though, suggest that easier is funnier. Empirical evidence supports the Joker's contention that having to explain the joke kills it.[35]

Benign violation theory: A *violation* is anything that "seems threatening, wrong, or negative."[36] This could be anything that threatens someone's worldview. However, for the violation to be funny, a person must reframe it in some way to make it feel *benign*. At some point, the Joker begins to see even the most existential threats as funny, rendering them nonthreatening to him personally.[37]

A Mad Sense of Humor across the Dark Tetrad

The Joker is a comedian of some sort. He is called a crime clown and a trickster. Does the Joker have a sense of humor, and how is this embedded in his personality or personality disorders? The Joker's jokes are bad, but is he also mad? He is often described both ways. It is impossible to assess the insanity of the Joker directly because he is a fictitious character (although chapter 7 has much to say about that). It is possible to describe the Joker through a number of personality descriptions and their relation to a sense of humor, more specifically the humor styles that he employs. Each of the overlapping dark triad/tetrad traits (described throughout this book because they thoroughly fit the Joker) relates to sense of humor in similar, though not identical, ways.

With its indifference to taboos and to the consequences of its own mischief, the Trickster archetype covered in chapter 5 shows some psychopathic qualities.[38] "The notion of the trickster as a character beyond law and morality, driven by impulses, is remarkably similar to modern concepts of the psychopath," psychopathy researchers have noted. "It may be argued that this shared concept of the trickster figure represents a common understanding of a distinct syndrome that overlaps with what we currently know as psychopathy."[39] The Trickster is a subtype of a more encompassing *Jester archetype*[40] which follows the motto, "You only live once." Jester figures live in the moment—also common among psychopaths.[41] The Jester figure's core desire is to live in the moment with full enjoyment. That excessive degree of focus on now could be child-like, immature, irresponsible, or psychopathic. The latter seems true of the Joker, although he enjoys suffering and death more than many other Trickster/Jester figures might. This archetype's goal is to have a great time (true of the Joker) and lighten up the world (partly true in some versions, mainly the "Clown Prince" era). The greatest fear of the characters that symbolize the Jester is that they get bored, and the Joker seems to fit this description, too. There is very little empirical evidence that these archetypes and subtypes exist in the way Jung envisioned them, as hereditary themes inherited through the human collective unconscious, but regardless of where such themes come from, humans are predisposed to perceive patterns and be influenced by them.[42] Themes guide many of our actions and our stories, often without our conscious notice.

The Joker clearly meets the criteria for both antisocial personality disorder (ASPD), as outlined in the American Psychiatric Association's diagnostic manual, and psychopathy, as assessed by the Psychopathy Checklist.[43] This kind of person cannot criticize or joke about himself.[44] The Joker criticizes and jokes about others but rarely about himself, and many a story ends with him frowning as Batman and Robin crack wise at his expense.[45] Because violence and suffering amuse him, he may be described as having an *aggressive humor style*. People strong in this style use humor "as a means of enhancing the self at the expense of others by criticizing or manipulating others. They tease and ridicule others to demonstrate their superiority, without concern for others' well-being."[46] The Joker's behaviors seem to fit this humor style, and indeed, empirical research has shown that psychopathy and Machiavellianism (two elements of the so-called dark triad) are moderately correlated with the aggressive humor style.[47] Natural killers show a caustic sense of humor that relies on cruel wit and biting sarcasm.[48] It is hostile humor that offers relief to the one expressing it, regardless of whether anyone else likes it, and may in fact aim to hurt others to enhance the killer's sense of power.

Both the Joker and Batman are probably low in *self-defeating humor*, a humiliating and personally limiting humor style characterized by "poking fun at their own weaknesses and laughing along when being ridiculed in order to ingratiate themselves to others,"[49] though for different reasons. In the case of the Joker's dark triad traits, this is probably due to his grandiose sense of self-worth. Grandiosity can serve as a coping mechanism to mask feelings of worthlessness. Batman, though, is too bothered by potential shortcomings to laugh at them much because he is afraid to fail.

The Joker's self-absorption and grandiose sense of self-worth indicate that the remaining third of the dark triad, narcissism, or even a narcissistic personality disorder, fits him as well. The narcissist possesses an unreasonable sense of self-importance and lacks empathy, which may suggest psychopathy, but there are egotistic individuals who nonetheless show moral concerns, despite a shortage of empathy. Even though such self-focus may result in aggressive behaviors toward others, the narcissist also needs others to support his self-love system, to affirm his sense of grandiosity in one way or another. The narcissist can only be grandiose in the presence of others. Many narcissists show positive humor styles, especially the *affiliative humor style*, as part of their superficial charm.[50] This humor style uses humor to achieve interpersonal rewards and to enhance social relationships.[51] The Joker neither cares about his team nor indulges in humor that would strengthen their bonds with him. He even casually kills henchmen when the idea springs to his mind, which is deeply antisocial.[52] So it seems unlikely that the Joker uses much affiliative humor. There are strands of narcissism in him, fed by low self-esteem if we're to believe *Batman: The Killing Joke*.[53] This makes it more likely for him to show aggressive humor and a dormant self-defeating humor style.[54]

When the original dark triad model fell short of describing human evil, researchers extended it to include sadism in a *dark tetrad*.[55] The sadist's humor is aggressive. By definition, the sadist takes delight in the suffering of others. For the sexual sadist, that means sexual gratification is largely achieved by inflicting physical and mental pain on others, but for the sadistic personality, hurting others physically or emotionally is a way of life, whether sexual or not.[56] The Joker kills with pranks, often announcing his killing jokes for the sheer fun of making his victims suffer through the worry and for the feeling of power he gets by making fools out of the authorities.[57] Lifting hopes at times makes dashing them hurt more, and that thought makes him laugh.[58] He flaunts his own evil to taunt Batman[59] and pokes at police by naming friends of theirs whom he has killed.[60] Sometimes this goads them into rash actions he can take advantage of,[61] but sometimes he just enjoys taunting them. Psychological cruelty interests him more than the physical. Though he will maim people to amuse himself, make a point, or intimidate others,[62] he usually lacks the patience to relish prolonged physical torture as much as the sadistic villain Black Mask does,[63] because the Joker wants to hit his punchlines faster. He has his own black comedy routine to get through. Between capers, he sometimes manages to devote himself to planning and preparation, but once he starts his set, he wants the hits to keep coming. He likes anticipatory humor and horror.

The Universal Joke: Wise Men of Gotham

When Bill Finger flipped through a phone book until he spotted the name Gotham Jewelers and knew he'd found the name for Batman's hometown, Gotham City,[64] he inadvertently named the place *city of fools*, exactly what the Joker keeps trying to show it to be.

The most universal joke, which seems to be present in every country and culture, makes fun of specific groups of people by treating them as fools. "The stupidity joke picks out a group, typically low status, and makes fun of them for not being smart," says humor researcher Peter McGraw.[65] In the course of gathering support for his benign violation theory, he discovered this insulting form of humor, which is benign to the joke-teller's ingroup while belittling the target outgroup, such as the "dumb blonde" joke or much ethnic humor.[66]

Once upon a time, the "Wise Men of Gotham" were butts of the stupidity joke. Many a joke mocked the intelligence of fools who thought themselves clever in Gotham, Nottinghamshire, England. A nursery rhyme about Gotham's fools dates back to at least 1765:

Three wise men of Gotham,
They went to sea in a bowl,
And if the bowl had been stronger,
My song would have been longer.[67]

Bill Finger took the name Gotham from a jeweler who'd adopted one of New York City's nicknames for the store name. Interestingly enough, author Washington Irving first gave New York City the nickname "Gotham" in order to satirize its residents' foolish ingenuity—in other words, deliberately calling the place a city of fools who outsmart themselves.[68] A few comic book writers who discovered this in recent decades wove that into their stories, indicating that Batman's Gotham City was named after Gotham, Nottinghamshire.[69] In the words of a city forefather, at a time when Gotham City was founded to house the insane, "I even have a name for it. We could call it 'Gotham' after a village in England—where, according to common belief, all are bereft of their wits."[70] Like the Joker and other supposed lunatics of Gotham City, though, the fools of Gotham village were not to be underestimated. By some reports, its people feigned imbecility in order to discourage King John from running a public highway through their village.[71] Despite the cost to their reputation, they succeeded by strategically playing fools.

The Punchline: Wise Fools

The Jester figure that the Joker becomes plays on an ancient idea that the fool who is unfettered by other people's constraints might speak with impunity and challenge assumptions—the so-called "wisdom of the fool."[72] The Fool card in the Tarot deck supposedly represents innocence and the beginning of a quest to gain wisdom.[73] Despite lack of concern for consequences and where that path may go, the Fool is fully engaged in the moment, which can cause careless behavior that ranges from injury to slapstick as the Fool fails to realize that he or she is walking off a cliff. In modern card decks, the Fool became the joker, the wild card that could transmute into any form needed to play the game. Indeed, the Joker character has gone through many transmutations, capable of fitting the needs of any era's stories. As with the classic Fool, people underestimate the Joker at their own peril as he endeavors to reveal what fools others are.

The Joker, with his aggressive style of humor, wants to put the world in its place. Every joke, no matter how cruel, is a benign violation to someone who does not feel the pain of conscience or empathy. Because he does not know how to laugh out of shared joy or weep from suffering, his need to laugh manifests as laughter at cruelty and absurdity of the human condition.

"Except you had to explain it to me!
If you have to explain a joke, there is no joke!"
—The Joker to Harley Quinn[74]

NOTES

1. White (1941/1980), p. xvii.
2. *The Joker* #7 (1976).
3. Starting with his first crime in *Batman* #1 (1940a).
4. Starting with *Batman* #251 (1973).
5. Strack et al. (1988).
6. Skibba (2016); Wagenmakers et al. (2011).
7. *Batman*, episodes 1–05, "The Joker's Wild" (January 25, 1966), 1–06, "Batman is Riled" (January 26, 1966).
8. Skinner (1939).
9. Arya (2015); Boers & Stengers (2008); Smith & Montgomery (1989).
10. *Batman* #28 (1945); Batman #663 (2007).

11. Boers & Lindstromberg (2005); Boers et al. (2014); Lea et al. (2008); Lindstromberg & Boers (2008).

12. Hayes & Slater (2008); Jusczyk et al. (1999).

13. Attardo et al. (1994); Morreall (1982); Triezenberg (2004).

14. *Batman*, episodes 1–05, "The Joker's Wild" (January 25, 1966), 1–06, "Batman is Riled" (January 26, 1966), 1–15, "The Joker Goes to School" (March 1, 1966), 1–25, "The Joker Trumps an Ace" (April 5, 1966), 2–21, "The Impractical Joker" (November 15, 1966).

15. *Batman: The Killing Joke* (1988).

16. Carroll (2014); Martin & Ford (2018); Weems (2014); Wyer & Collins (1992).

17. A portion of this paragraph comes from Langley (2012).

18. Freud (1905/1960, 1928).

19. Vaillant (1977/1998).

20. Freud (1905/1960); Vaillant (1977/1998).

21. Craun & Bourke (2014, 2015); Manning-Jones et al. (2016); Sliter et al. (2014); Thorson (1985); Tracy et al. (2006)—noted in Langley (2012).

22. Kuiper & Leite (2010); Langley (2012).

23. *The Dark Knight* (2008 motion picture).

24. *The Batman Adventures: Mad Love* (1994).

25. *Gotham Girls* (2002 flash animation).

26. *Arkham Asylum: A Serious House on Serious Earth* (1989).

27. Gans (1975).

28. Charney (1978).

29. Flower—too many appearances to list; whoopee cushion—*The Joker* #5 (1976); cigar—*Batman* #251 (1973); poison pie—*The Joker* #7 (1976); acid pie—*The Joker* #1 (1975).

30. Apter (2007).

31. In *Batman Beyond: Return of the Joker* (2000 motion picture), Terry argues to the Joker that Batman has no sense of humor. In *Batman: The Animated Series*, episode 1–04, "The Last Laugh" (September 21, 1992), Alfred makes a similar assertion.

32. *Batman: The Killing Joke* (1988); *The Batman Adventures: Mad Love* (1994).

33. *Batman* #251 (1973). In *The Batman Adventures: Mad Love* (1994), Harley says that when Batman laughs it gives her "the creeps."

34. Wyer & Collins (1992).

35. Martin & Ford (2018); *The Batman Adventures: Mad Love* (1994).

36. Warren & McGraw (2016), p. 409.

37. *Batman: The Killing Joke* (1988).

38. Hyde (1999); Lynley (2016); Sullivan & Kosson (2006).

39. Sullivan & Kosson (2006), p. 439.

40. Hudnall (2015).

41. Hare (1993/1999); Jonason et al. (2010, 2012); Kiehl (2014); McDonald et al. (2012).

42. Hood (2009); Whitson & Galinsky (2008).

43. Goodwin & Tajjudin (2016).

44. Martens (2004).

45. e.g., *Batman* #63 (1951), #73 (1952), #251 (1973); *Batman Kellogg's Special* (1966); *Detective Comics* #332 (1964).

46. Martin & Ford (2018), p. 123.

47. Veselka et al. (2010).

48. Pierson (1999).

49. Martin & Ford (2018), p. 123.

50. Veselka et al. (2010).

51. Martin & Ford (2018); Treger et al. (2013).

52. e.g., *Detective Comics* #475 (1978); *Batman* (1989 motion picture).

53. e.g., *Batman: The Killing Joke* (1988).

54. e.g., Zeigler-Hill & Besser (2011).

55. e.g., Book et al. (2016); Paulhus (2014).

56. American Psychiatric Association (1987, 2013).
57. *Batman #1* (1940a, 1940d); *Detective Comics #475* (1978); *Batman #14* (2012).
58. *Detective Comics #726* (1998).
59. *Batman: The Dark Knight #3* (1986).
60. e.g., *Gotham Central #15* (2004).
61. e.g., *The Dark Knight* (2008 motion picture).
62. e.g., *Batman: The Killing Joke* (1988); *The Dark Knight* (2008 motion picture).
63. *Catwoman #12–16* (2002–2003); *Batman #633* (2004); *Robin #130* (2004).
64. Steranko (1970).
65. Schlender (2014).
66. Davies (1990); McGraw & Warner (2014).
67. Opie & Opie (1951/1997), p. 193.
68. Irving (1807).
69. *Batman: Legends of the Dark Knight #206* (2006); *52 #27* (2007).
70. *Batman Chronicles #6* (1996).
71. Werth (1979).
72. Kaiser (n.d.).
73. Chamizo (2015); Nichols (1980, 2019).
74. *The Batman Adventures: Mad Love* (1994); *Batman: The Animated Series*, episode 3–24, "Mad Love" (January 16, 1999).

EXPLAINING THE JOKE 6-1

ACTOR ADAM WEST

Travis Langley

Adam West played Bruce Wayne/Batman in the 1966–1968 television series *Batman* and its related film *Batman: The Movie*. Throughout the 1970s and 1980s, he reprised the role live in television specials and numerous cartoons. Eventually, he returned to the role for two last animated films, *Batman: Return of the Caped Crusaders* (2016) and the posthumous release *Batman vs. Two-Face* (2017). When Joker co-creator Jerry Robinson and *The Dark Knight* executive producer Michael Uslan first joined us for a San Diego Comic-Con panel analyzing the Joker, Adam sat with us onstage because he wanted to meet them, to hear our analyses of the characters, and to talk about his friend Cesar Romero, who had been the first actor to play the Joker.[1] Before the panel, the two of us met to discuss Cesar and the Clown Prince of Crime.

Travis Langley: On the phone, you mentioned that Cesar Romero would nap before playing the Joker.

Adam West: Yes, he was interesting in that. He'd done so much work, he was really good and a high-energy guy, but he never had any trouble sleeping. I kept watching him like Sinatra watched the back of Tommy Dorsey.

Singer Frank Sinatra said on a number of occasions that watching jazz trombonist Tommy Dorsey from backstage had fascinated him. "I used to watch Tommy's back, his jacket, to see when he would breathe," Sinatra said. "I'd swear the sonofabitch was not breathing. I couldn't even see his jacket move . . . . I thought, 'He's gotta be breathing someplace—through the ears?'"[2]

Adam: I looked at Cesar that way. When we got off the set, he immediately got in his canvas-back chair and fell asleep easily. Give him five seconds, he'd be sound asleep. I wanted to learn to do that. I never fell asleep that easily. But the moment they said, "You're wanted on set," immediately came the energy! The style! The laugh! He was there.

Now Cesar Romero was a marvelous gentleman. Our late executive producer Bill Dozier, was a friend. He cast Cesar. I think that Cesar became kind of a template, a forerunner, of the Joker [for other actors]. With that marvelous laugh. I was fascinated standing toe to toe with that actor in that makeup and that costume. I learned from him—from Cesar Romero, from Burgess Meredith, from a lot of people.

Approaching Batman, I felt obligated to do studies of him and other characters. I did a little backstory in my head for Joker. I had backstories for Batman, too, all the characters. The thing about the Joker was that he was intensely antisocial, but he could dazzle people. He would have made a great insurance salesman. If I were looking at someone like the Joker, if I were trying to play the Joker, I would really want to pick him apart, but you're the psychologist. I'd talk to you. You guys are the ones who can really do that. As an actor, it would be a wonderful opportunity to learn from you, to really dig in to do something truthful and somewhat spectacular.

Travis: Didn't you minor in psychology?

Adam: Long ago . . . . *[Laughs]*

Travis: For you, is there a moment on the show that defines the Joker?

Adam: I just love that scene when Joker springs out of prison, the first you ever see of him. It was theater of the absurd. Absurd in a sense, but *Batman*, it's an island in time. I think that's why the show remains fresh with the homage, comic balloons, zaps, whatever. I was always tongue in cheek, with a little something behind the mask. How could we not have fun with it? Joker with his strange hair—he had green hair, he had red hair, he was like a stoplight, always changing. And they slapped that white makeup right over his mustache. Later in the day, the mustache would pop through. It was insane.

Travis: It was a lot of fun.

Adam: The new ones are so dark. In society now, I worry what kind of role model that is for the inner city kid who needs inspiration. Kids learn from fictional characters. It's not just movies. Comic books, just comic books, have gotten darker. But the graphic novels, oh! The character Parker Robbins, the Hood, sees role models in the supervillains and so he becomes one.

Adam surprised me, I must admit, with his knowledge of this then-recent Marvel Comics character, a 21st-century criminal who rises to become the kingpin of supervillains.[3] Created by writer Brian K. Vaughn with artists Kyle Hotz and Eric Powell, the Hood's background inverts superhero origin tropes.

Travis: There was more going on in your TV show, though. I remember you as Bruce Wayne mentioning the murder of his parents. It's in the first or second line you ever say on the show, and later you say it again to the Joker. The dark thing that drove Batman was in there, too.

Adam: There's room for all these different takes. Batman can be expressed on so many different levels. You know, they have the Dark Knight. I'm the Bright Knight. The typecasting, it's not that binding if you really don't mind having fun about yourself, being a little self-deprecating. It's a very thin, tight wire. You must never lose your dignity. Cesar had that. Cesar never lost his dignity. But I have no dignity to preserve. *[Laughs]*

The next day, during our convention panel, Adam shared an idea that he'd alluded to regarding the Joker's origin, and Jerry Robinson responded.

Adam West: Travis, I did a little backstory in my head for Joker. I reasoned the insanity—the psychopathic quality—I reasoned that he was kidnapped by a perverted clown when he was a youngster.

Jerry Robinson: That would do it.

NOTES

1. Starting with *Batman*, episode 1–05, "The Joker is Wild" (January 26, 1966).
2. Quoted by Akalin (2011).
3. *The Hood* #1–6 (2002).

CASE REPORT II (1966):
RISK MANAGEMENT ASSESSMENT FOR THE NARCISSIST

Consultation Note

I was asked to review the case of the "Joker" upon his readmission to Gotham State Penitentiary, following his apprehension for charges of grand larceny. Prison administration noted concerns regarding the inmate's history of previously expunging his criminal record by allowing himself to be executed, albeit temporarily,[1] as well as malingering (feigning) psychosis in order to be sent for psychiatric treatment.[2] During his current incarceration, guard staff have noted he has been observed laughing to himself at times, leading their untrained minds to assume the inmate must be, indeed, insane. However, based on my years of experience in evaluating criminal minds—both sane and insane—I see no such spark of madness in him. He is not stricken with mania, but rather impresses with megalomania. In diagnostic terms, he evidences a personality trait disturbance, whereby his inflated sense of ego takes center stage. In more mundane terms, he is a classic narcissist. The inmate's behaviors are all designed to draw attention to him. He wishes to overshadow those around him. Through the escalation of the preposterousness of his crimes, he ensures that everyone knows his name and that no one can resist talking about him. However, his ego goes above mere desire for attention; rather, he strives for admiration. He taunts the police and the Batman because he feels himself superior. His inflated sense of self-worth means he sees others as tools to achieve his goals at best, and at worst as nothing worthy of his consideration. It must be noted that his ego is fragile, and he is ever at risk of losing control if there is significant injury to his psyche.

One question has thus far confounded the police and judiciary: Why has the Joker presumably forsaken killing at this point? In my years, I have only rarely seen criminals turn away from killing after such a history, and then it was only in the context of long-term incarceration and a turn to the Good Book. Though it may be tempting to assume this inmate has somehow grown a conscience, I do not think this the case. Rather, it may be that the inmate has realized that, when his

122

primary crimes are those of murder, the acts overshadow the man. That is, his bizarre and ostentatious crimes draw attention to the Joker persona and fulfill a vastly different, though no less basic, psychological need that his murder sprees were never able to.

In my professional opinion, the inmate continues to pose a considerable risk for escape, though I can make this prediction based on history alone. Beyond this, escape serves to prove superiority in the inmate's mind, and leads to more newspaper headlines, more features on the evening news, and more talk. That he would continue his pattern of crime if given the opportunity is equally irrefutable. However, what is perhaps more concerning is the continued existence of the very personality structure that led him to kill in the first place. Barring some sort of head injury that permanently altered his personality, my fear is that he runs the risk of reverting to his old ways, once again returning to killing. This may occur should he suddenly be overshadowed by some other personality or event in Gotham or simply should he become bored and seek to scratch a different psychological itch. Indeed, he may even kill again if it simply seems easier than not killing in a given situation.

It appears exceedingly unlikely the inmate will respond favorably to any sort of conventional therapy modalities, though I have little doubt he would attempt to use therapy sessions to his advantage. I do think extra security will be in the prison's best interests as long as the inmate remains in custody, and make sure you only utilize your most trusted staff. Should he find himself out-of-custody again, I have no doubt he will make his presence known again sooner rather than later.

Please let me know if I can be of further assistance.

Staff Psychologist

Notes

1. *Detective Comics* #64 (1942).
2. *Batman* #74 (1952–1953). Editor's note: The first edition of the American Psychiatric Association's DSM (1952) would have been available then.

III.

KING

THE KING OF ARKHAM ASYLUM

"Ever since I heard the Joker escaped from the state hospital for the criminally insane, I've been expecting him to show up."

—Batman, the first reference to the modern view of the Joker as criminally insane[1]

"Perhaps a lunatic was simply a minority of one."

—author George Orwell[2]

"To whose hands you have sent the lunatic king?"

—Regan in *King Lear*, Act III, Scene VII, by William Shakespeare[3]

NOTES

1. *Batman* #251 (1973).
2. Orwell (1949/2007), p. 159.
3. Shakespeare (1623/1982a), p. 850—first drafted in 1605 or 1606.

7

Insanity: Getting into Arkham (On Being Insane in Insane Places)

MARTIN LLOYD

"I'm not mad at all! I'm just differently sane!"
—The Joker[1]

> *"Insanity is relative. It depends on who*
> *has who locked in what cage."*
> —author Ray Bradbury[2]

ARKHAM ASYLUM IS essentially the Joker's home away from home. In fact, as he likely has no permanent residence, it is arguably his primary home, or at least the place where he spends most of his time. When he is apprehended for a crime, he, along with most of Batman's costumed rogues, is sent to Arkham. Gotham City has an actual prison, Blackgate Penitentiary, but only the less *colorful* criminals are typically sent here. Most of those who spend their time fighting Batman go to Arkham, which is technically a hospital and is therefore designed as much for treatment as for security. With the availability of a prison, why do so many of Gotham's criminals get sent to a hospital?

Presumably, many of those sent to Arkham are there because they have been found *not guilty by reason of insanity* (NGRI). The defense of insanity is based on the idea that those with certain severe mental conditions are not responsible for their actions and are therefore not appropriate targets for retribution or deterrence.[3] Those found NGRI are *not guilty* of the crimes of which they are accused; they cannot be sent to prison or otherwise legally punished. They are, however, potentially subject to involuntary confinement for treatment and the protection of the public. Whether so many of Batman's rogues would realistically be found NGRI and sent to the asylum is debatable. The insanity defense is actually quite uncommon, only attempted in less than one percent of all criminal cases. The number of insanity pleas that are successful appears to have varied considerably over time, but the best figures indicate it is only successful approximately one out of every four times it is attempted. Insanity does not have a single, unifying definition, and the precise standard varies by jurisdiction. The different standards used in the United States will be examined to determine which, if any, can explain the Joker's presence in Arkham, or that of Batman's other rogues.

Right and Wrong

The oldest insanity standard in the United States, and still one of the more commonly used,[4] is the M'Naghten standard, often referred to as the *right and wrong test*.[5] This rule comes from an 1843 British case, in which the defendant, one Daniel M'Naghten, attempted to assassinate the prime minister, Sir Robert Peel, instead fatally shooting Peel's secretary, Edward Drummond. M'Naghten had believed Peel to be involved in a plot against him and that assassination was the only means of protecting himself.[6] M'Naghten was ultimately acquitted on the grounds of insanity, with nine medical witnesses testifying to this insanity.[7]

The controversy generated by the M'Naghten verdict led the House of Lords to take up the matter for the purpose of determining the rules that would govern the defense of insanity from that point forward. They ultimately determined that the rule should be that a defendant could be found insane only if "at the time of the committing of the act, the party accused was laboring under such a defect of reason, from disease of the mind, as not to know either nature and quality of the fact or that it was wrong."[8] This rule has several important components that must be considered in each case. The first concerns the "disease of mind." Although the precise definition of this term is ultimately a matter of law and may vary considerably from one jurisdiction to another, it is generally considered to be roughly equivalent to "mental illness," and therefore to require a diagnosis.[9] It is this diagnosis that justifies the involvement of mental health professionals in the courtroom, though the courts make the final decisions about which diagnoses are acceptable.

The first step in determining whether the Joker, or, indeed, any of the patients housed in Arkham, could successfully be found NGRI is to determine if there is an applicable "disease of mind," or psychiatric diagnosis. As noted before, "The Joker defies diagnosis."[10] Clearly, he meets criteria for psychopathy, a condition marked by criminal versatility, aggression, manipulative behavior, and lack of empathy or remorse.[11] Psychopathy, however, along with other disorders of personality, is generally not accepted as a valid basis for a defense of insanity.[12] A number of jurisdictions also explicitly exclude from the definition of "disease of mind," antisocial personality disorder, a long-term condition defined by disregard for social norms and the rights of others.[13] The Joker would certainly meet criteria for this disorder as well, which is conceptually similar to one of the two main factors of psychopathy, leading the two conditions to overlap frequently. Thus, the Joker's most likely diagnoses would be unlikely to result in a successful insanity plea.

Although they are the most obvious, psychopathy and antisocial personality disorder are not necessarily the only mental diseases for which the Joker might meet criteria, though further diagnosis is complicated at best. While his flamboyant crimes certainly indicate that his mind functions in bizarre ways (e.g., attempting to copyright fish he intentionally disfigured to have clown faces[14]), he does not appear to be classically psychotic. That is, he is not acting under a system of *delusions*, or false beliefs grossly out of touch with reality, held even in light of contradictory evidence; he is not generally depicted as experiencing *hallucinations*, or false sensory experiences abnormally disconnected from reality; and, though odd, his thoughts are coherent. If not overtly psychotic, it is possible his bizarre behavior could be explained by extremes of mood, but he does not really seem to exhibit the extended and distinct periods of euphoria and depression that characterize *bipolar disorder*. One possibility would be *cyclothymic disorder*, in which manic or depressive symptoms are usually present to some degree but never to the extent necessary to qualify as a full-blown mood episode.[15]

Ultimately, it is difficult to identify any existing psychiatric diagnosis that fully captures the Joker's behavioral extremes, though he is quite clearly abnormal in his psychiatric functioning. Given that mental disease is a necessary condition, not only for M'Naghten but for any of the insanity standards discussed in this chapter, it will be assumed from this point on that the Joker has some qualifying mental disease.

Once the presence of a mental disease has been established, the M'Naghten standard offers two paths for a defendant to be found not guilty by reason of insanity. It must be demonstrated that, at the time of the offense, the defendant did not know either the nature of his or her actions or that those actions were wrong.[16] The defendant need only demonstrate one of the two. For a defendant not to know the nature of his or her actions, that individual must have been unaware of the actual physical act being committed.[17] So, as an example, an insane murderer might not have known he or she was dismembering someone, but rather, perhaps due to delusion or hallucination, believed that he or she was chopping down a tree. This prong of the standard is sometimes broadened to encompass a lack of understanding of the consequences of one's actions. That is, the defendant might have been aware of stabbing someone with a knife but, due to some delusion, believed the victim to have been immortal and therefore unable to die.

Regardless of how broadly the nature prong is interpreted in a given jurisdiction, there is little evidence from the character's history to suggest that the Joker is unaware of the nature of his actions. He plans. Though often complicated and bizarre, his plans are specific. In order to carry out these plans, he has to know exactly what he is doing. He is also aware of the consequences of his actions because those consequences, usually death and destruction, are his intended goals. While the Joker would essentially never seem to satisfy M'Naghten's nature prong, this means relatively little because decisions under M'Naghten seldom turn on nature. Rather, most rulings that specific individuals are not guilty by reason of insanity under

M'Naghten make this judgment based on the other prong—the inability to know that their actions were wrong.

M'Naghten's wrongfulness prong essentially requires that defendants believed their actions were morally or (depending on the jurisdiction) legally permissible. Often, this is the result of a delusion. For example, someone may falsely believe the victim to be a threat who must be killed as an act of self-defense. In such instances, the defendants knew what they were doing but erroneously believed that their actions were justified.

Realistically, the Joker always knows, at least on a purely intellectual level, that his actions are wrong. Regardless of any other diagnoses, he is primarily a psychopath. This condition basically entails a lack of interest in moral thinking, not an inability to understand it. He even says to Batman, "You see, their morals, their code, it's a bad joke. Dropped at the first sign of trouble. They're only as good as the world allows them to be. I'll show you. When the chips are down, these—these civilized people, they'll eat each other. See, I'm not a monster. I'm just ahead of the curve."[18] Thus, he is perfectly capable of recognizing that moral codes exist and that his actions are violations of them. He is simply not bothered by that fact. The Joker, therefore, would fail to meet either the nature or the wrongfulness prongs of this standard. Ultimately, the M'Naghten standard cannot explain his presence in Arkham Asylum.

Not Guilty by Reason of Insanity: Silver the Vampire Hunter

It is fairly difficult to identify any member of Batman's rogues' gallery who would realistically be found NGRI under the M'Naghten standard. Even the most clearly psychotic rogue, Maxie Zeus, who has the delusional belief that he is the Greek god Zeus, might fail to meet the stringent M'Naghten standard. He and his conflict with the Joker will be examined in more detail later, but the nature of his delusion does not prevent him from being aware of the actions he carries out or knowing that such actions would violate human laws and moral codes. As it turns out, only a much more obscure character would meet this standard, and this is perhaps unsurprising. The level of disconnection from reality that is required to meet the M'Naghten standard would likely prevent most individuals from having long-term, "successful" careers in supervillainy. In fact, the only character who comes readily to mind as meeting this standard is so obscure, many readers have likely never heard of him.

Atsuo Utchida, a.k.a. Silver, is a self-styled vampire hunter. Unlike the Joker, Silver exhibits clear signs of psychosis. Notably, he has actual hallucinations, whereas the Joker is generally not portrayed as such. When Silver looks at Batgirl or other vigilante heroes, he perceives them as fanged vampires and even believes he sees them feeding on criminals.[19] The fact that Batgirl has returned to action after a long absence (following surgery to repair the injury by which the Joker had paralyzed her[20]) would only reinforce Silver's delusion. He acts under the belief that the world is beset by vampires (which, being the DC Universe, is at least partially true) and he hunts these creatures using stakes and other tools of the vampire hunter's trade. He would likely qualify for a diagnosis of *delusional disorder,* as he has a well-developed delusional system, his hallucinations are completely tied to that delusional system, and he otherwise seems to be able to function normally.[21]

As noted earlier, it is relatively rare for defendants to be found NGRI based on the nature prong, and Silver is no exception. He sets out with stakes and other weapons, which he uses for the purpose of ending life, or at least what he perceives as undeath. He knows exactly what he is doing. The wrongfulness prong, however, is another matter entirely. Silver does not actually believe he is harming any actual human beings. More to the point, he sees himself as protecting humans from a dangerous threat. This is a direct contrast from the Joker, who holds no illusions about the morality of his actions and, indeed, requires no such justification as his actions are often motivated by the desire to do harm. Silver's actions are part of a moral crusade and therefore are morally justified in his view. He very clearly does not know that his actions are wrong, and he would therefore have a valid M'Naghten defense, despite being aware of the nature of his actions. Were Silver to be apprehended, he is one of very few in Gotham who could justifiably be placed in Arkham as NGRI under the M'Naghten standard, giving the Joker a neighbor who actually belongs there.

Getting to Gotham

Insanity standards vary between countries and, within the USA, between states. But which state's laws and legal precedents determine the standards by which Gotham handles its bizarre criminals?

Locating Gotham City within the actual United States can be a tricky matter. The city's location is something of a fluid matter, often changing based on the needs of a story, and is more often just left vague. The closest to an official location that has ever been given has indicated that Gotham is in New Jersey,[22] with later comics showing GPS coordinates also within New Jersey.[23] Other stories, however, have suggested that Gotham lies within the borders of Rhode Island.[24] Regardless, Gotham seems to be located somewhere in the northeastern United States.

There may be another way to pinpoint Gotham's actual location. The only insanity standard that can explain the presence of most of Batman's rogues in Arkham Asylum is the *product test*. At present, only one state uses the product test as its official standard: New Hampshire.[25] This is, at least, in the northeastern United States. Assuming that Gotham must be somewhere that uses the product test, then perhaps New Hampshire is the place you want to go if you want to visit Gotham City (though, really, why would you? The crime rate is atrocious).

Irresistible Impulse

The M'Naghten standard has often drawn criticism for ignoring the class of offenders who fully know what they are doing but lack the ability to control their behavior.[26] M'Naghten addresses purely cognitive problems and is silent on the issue of volitional control. Therefore, individuals driven to illegal acts by command hallucinations or strong compulsions would not have a valid defense under the M'Naghten rule. To address this issue, some jurisdictions have added a supplementary test of *irresistible impulse*. This new standard was often referred to as the "policeman at the elbow" test, as it allowed an NGRI defense for those individuals who would have been unable to stop themselves from committing a crime, even if there was a police officer standing right next to them.[27] This test has never been adopted as a completely separate standard; rather, it is an additional prong added to the M'Naghten standard in some jurisdictions.[28] Currently, four states (Colorado, New Mexico, Texas, and Virginia) use the M'Naghten rule with the addition of the irresistible impulse test.[29]

Allowing for an additional defense of irresistible impulse would likely make little difference for the Joker. True, the Joker would probably continue committing crimes if there were a policeman at his elbow, but only because he would almost certainly kill the policeman. Simply put, it would be difficult to find an example of the Joker ever doing something he did not want to do. He chooses to act in accordance with his plans. There are no rules he is compelled to follow; indeed, he sees himself as an "agent of chaos."[30] Ultimately, he is no more likely to be found NGRI under the irresistible impulse test than he would be under a straight M'Naghten standard.

Not Guilty by Reason of Insanity: Two-Face

Although it would make very little difference for the Joker, allowing for a defense of irresistible impulse would open Arkham's doors to some additional rogues. Chief among these is Two-Face, an attorney who, in a cinematic version of the story, turns to crime because of the Joker's machinations.[31] Long before Arkham Asylum began housing almost every outlandish Gotham criminal, Jack Harris and Dennis O'Neil introduced it into the comics as a place to house two specific villains: the Joker and Two-Face.[32]

Two-Face has received many diagnoses, even having been diagnosed with schizophrenia as a child—though no rationale for the diagnosis is ever given and Harvey Dent does not seem to show signs of psychosis.[33] Yet Dent does appear to suffer from an extreme form of *obsessive-compulsive disorder* (OCD). This condition is marked by recurrent intrusive thoughts (*obsessions*) or behaviors one feels one must perform in response to an obsession or to alleviate tension (*compulsions*).[34] Two-Face demonstrates compulsive behavior in the form of needing to obey the results of a coin toss. With few exceptions, he must go along with the determination of the coin, even if it demands that he sabotage himself.[35] The comic book version shows more signs of obsessions and compulsions than does the version the Joker essentially creates on film.

Under a strict M'Naghten conceptualization, it would be highly unlikely that Two-Face could be found NGRI. As a former attorney, he fully understands the illegality of his actions. He does not appear to experience any hallucinations or delusions, per se, that would obscure his ability to know what he is doing or that it is wrong. In a jurisdiction that allows for a test of irresistible impulse, however, one can see how Two-Face could end up in Arkham Asylum. If he contemplates killing someone, he will flip his coin to make the determination. If the scarred side comes up, it does not matter if there is literally a policeman, or perhaps a costumed vigilante, standing right at his elbow; Two-Face will still have to attempt to kill the intended victim. This is the essence of an irresistible impulse; once the coin has made its decision, he cannot stop himself. There have been rare instances in which it is at least implied that he resists the result of the toss, such as by letting Batman walk out of Arkham Asylum alive, but this notably occurs after he has received substantial therapy to reduce his dependency on the coin.[36] More commonly, the compulsion is so strong that he is unable to act if he cannot see the result of a toss, such as when he loses sight of the coin in a hail of silver dollars.[37] Thus, in most instances, Two-Face cannot resist the impulse to obey.

That the rule governing insanity in Gotham would specifically allow for Two-Face's admission to Arkham is fitting because Arkham Asylum (originally Arkham Hospital) was first introduced in a Two-Face story, during which he lets a coin toss determine that he will not help the Joker escape with him.[38] Thus, Two-Face and the Joker have been tied to Arkham from its inception. The hospital serves as an institution from which they each can escape, as so very, very many criminals would over the years.

While the irresistible impulse test can explain Two-Face's presence in Arkham, it does not explain the Joker's. To explain the presence of both villains in the asylum, Gotham's insanity standard would need to be more permissive than the standards described thus far.

The American Law Institute Test

Even with the addition of the irresistible impulse test, many critics continued to find M'Naghten overly restrictive, while other tests intended to replace it (the *product test*, discussed in detail in the next section) were deemed excessively liberal.[39] In an effort to develop a standard that would allow for greater options, while still providing guidance to juries, the American Law Institute (ALI) proposed a new test:

> A person is not responsible for criminal conduct if at the time of such conduct as a result of mental disease or defect he lacks substantial capacity either to appreciate the criminality (wrongfulness) of his conduct or to conform his conduct to the requirements of the law.[40]

At first glance, this may seem like a simple restatement of M'Naghten with irresistible impulse. Nonetheless, there are subtle differences in wording that have major implications. Perhaps the most significant of these is the change from M'Naghten's insistence that the defendant not "know" the wrongfulness of his or her actions to ALI's requirement that he or she be unable to "appreciate" said wrongfulness. This change allows evaluators and triers of fact to consider the defendant's understanding of his or her actions on an emotional level, as opposed to a purely cognitive one.[41] Also, any lack of understanding need not be absolute, as the defendant need only "lack substantial capacity." This formulation of the insanity defense has proved popular enough that it remains the legal standard in 19 states and the District of Columbia.[42]

Although the ALI test may make a substantial difference in who is ultimately found NGRI, this is still unlikely to help the Joker. First, as written in the Model Penal Code, the ALI test explicitly excludes psychopathy from its definition of "mental disease or defect."[43] Second, even with the more permissive ALI standard, the arguments above regarding why the Joker would not qualify for a M'Naghten defense still apply. He gets the difference between right and wrong; he just does not care. In many cases, doing wrong is probably his goal. Moral indifference is simply not the type of mental abnormality the ALI test was written to cover.

Not Guilty by Reason of Insanity: Maxie Zeus

As mentioned in the section on the M'Naghten standard, Maxie Zeus, perhaps the most overtly delusional of Batman's rogues, would still not meet that stringent standard. Nonetheless, Zeus serves as an excellent illustration of how some defendants who would not qualify for a M'Naghten defense can still be found NGRI under ALI. He suffers from the delusion that he is the Greek god Zeus. As he does not obviously experience other symptoms of schizophrenia, such as hallucinations or disorganized behavior, he, much like Silver, most likely meets criteria for delusional disorder. Thus, the requirement for mental disease or defect is satisfied.

Despite his clear psychosis, Maxie Zeus does not meet the M'Naghten standard because he can understand moral rules, which his behaviors violate. When he kidnaps an Olympic athlete in order to force her to marry him and bear his children, he understands kidnapping and sexual slavery are considered wrong.[44] Thus, he *knows* his actions are wrong. But, does he truly *appreciate* the wrongfulness of those actions? In his mind, he is a god. Rules are for mortals, and mortals exist for gods to do with as they will. Gods, after all, have dominion over humans, as humans do over animals. Thus, Maxie knows of the existence of moral rules, but he does not truly appreciate that they apply to him. He could therefore easily be found NGRI and sent to Arkham under the ALI standard.

Time at Arkham might actually work to Maxie's benefit. He could be free of his delusions while on antipsychotic medication. One such period of lucidity, however, brings him into direct conflict with the Joker. At this time, Maxie decides to sell a diluted form of Joker venom, mixed with

Ecstasy, as a recreational drug, which only serves to invite violent retaliation from the Joker.[45] The fact that Maxie continues to commit crimes while delusion-free should have more consequences than just being the target of the Joker's rage; no matter what standard is used, he would not qualify for an insanity defense for crimes committed during a symptom-free period. Every test of insanity looks only at mental condition *at the time of a given offense*.[46] History of psychosis is irrelevant if there are no symptoms at the time of the crime. Thus, were Maxie to be convicted of his involvement in the drug trade, he should find himself at Blackgate, not Arkham.

Product of Mental Disease or Defect

In 1954, one Judge Bazelon of the District of Columbia federal Court of Appeals decided to adopt a new test of insanity for the District of Columbia.[47] Bazelon was responding to criticisms of the M'Naghten standard and the supplementary irresistible impulse test, both of which could be viewed as relying on an overly narrow and inconsistent with scientific, medical understanding of mental illness.[48] The new standard held, simply, that "an accused is not criminally responsible if his unlawful act was the product of mental disease or defect."[49] This test became popularly known as the *product test*, though, notably, the decision never actually defined "product." Nor, for that matter, did it define "mental disease or defect." The interpretation, generally, is that one must determine if a criminal act somehow resulted from some kind of mental abnormality. It was reportedly Bazelon's intent to both reform and "humanize" the criminal law by allowing mental health experts to address all aspects of a defendant's mental health and overall psychological functioning, as opposed to just those few aspects relevant to the earlier standards.[50]

The product test was never widely adopted in the United States. It was only the official standard of the District of Columbia for less than 20 years, ultimately being replaced by the ALI standard in a later court ruling.[51] Outside of the District of Columbia, only two states, New Hampshire and Maine, ever formally adopted the product test.[52] Though never a popular standard, this test did spur debate among legal and mental health professions about how to devise a fair standard for insanity that avoids some of the perhaps excessive restrictions of the other standards.[53]

Although it may be exceedingly rare, this final test of insanity may be the one that allows the Joker to be sent to Arkham Asylum as NGRI. The Joker knows what he is doing and that his actions are wrong. More than that, he can almost certainly appreciate the wrongfulness of his actions. He does not appear to have any irresistible compulsions that force him to commit crimes. Nonetheless, is his criminal activity the "product" of mental disease or defect? Setting aside the thorny issue of the Joker's precise diagnosis, the answer is most likely *yes*. Returning to the example of his attempt to copyright fish he had poisoned and intentionally disfigured,[54] the Joker engages in planful, carefully considered activity of his own volition, thus not meeting any of the earlier standards. The plan is also completely irrational and makes no logical sense. It is highly unlikely that a mind not operating under some significant mental abnormality could have conceived of this plan. Thus, though the specific nature of the abnormality may be unclear, it indicates a mental disease *of some sort*, and this mental disease was clearly a major contributing factor to the crime, therefore meeting the requirements of the product test. To use a later example, the Joker breaks into a random house, eventually killing the owner, all because he believes it is where he needs to be in order to receive an invitation to the wedding of Batman and Catwoman.[55] Obviously, there is no logical need for him to be at this particular house to accomplish his goal, nor is there any rational reason for him to believe that he would receive a wedding invitation. Again, the fact that his crime was motivated by these illogical connections that could only arise from a mind that is somehow disordered, would seem to satisfy the requirements of the product test.

Even the Joker's less bizarre crimes, those committed for no reason other than malice or convenience, could arguably still meet the requirements of the product test. When the Joker murders Commissioner Gordon's second wife, Sarah Essen, he does so for no bizarre or illogical reason, but seemingly just to facilitate his own escape from justice. He does not even demonstrate his typical amusement at the crime.[56] As previously noted, the Joker shows clear indications of psychopathy. This particular crime, which involves killing just to facilitate a goal, and even purposefully endangering an infant to do so, is consistent with psychopathy, even if it does not suggest any other mental disease. Most often, "mental disease" is defined for insanity standards to exclude psychopathy and, generally, other personality pathology. In at least some of the jurisdictions that used the product test, however, the definition of mental disease was found to include psychopathy.[57] Thus, this would seem to be the only test of insanity that would explain the Joker's presence at Arkham, not to mention that of all the other patients who demonstrate mental abnormality only by wearing colorful costumes and committing somewhat theatrical crimes.

Psychotic but Sane?

Juries may find it hard to understand that a defendant could be psychotic and yet sane. A person might suffer some degree of detachment from reality while nevertheless understanding that certain actions under his or her control would be wrong. If your friend tells you, "Kill Bob," you should know that it's wrong, you shouldn't do it, and you need better friends. If a hallucinatory elephant tells you, "Kill Bob," but you know it's wrong, you shouldn't do it, and you need better elephants, then you could still be sane despite the psychotic symptom.

Though some individuals with psychosis are dangerous, to be sure, the vast majority of sufferers do not pose the degree of danger to others that popular entertainment or isolated examples in the news tend to make people believe.[58] Many individuals find ways to manage their psychosis, take responsibility for themselves, and live productive lives. Mathematician John Nash, a Nobel laureate, learned to reject delusional lines of thinking and to ask others to confirm whether certain things he saw were real.[59] While not every psychosis sufferer has the ability to do that, it doesn't take a supergenius to do it either.[60]

—T. L.

The Final Verdict

If any of the American insanity standards can explain the large population of Arkham Asylum, it can only be the product test, rare though that standard may be. That said, even that standard may not tell the full story. As noted above, successful insanity defenses are rare, and this is largely independent of the standard. The final decisions on insanity are made by the courts, and jurors, at least, seldom appear to understand the legal standards of insanity.[61] Regardless of the standard used, jurors tend to base their verdicts more on whether the defendant intended harm than on any statutory factors. In general, jurors who hold more punitive views (e.g., those who support the death penalty) tend to be less willing to accept the insanity defense,[62] and male jurors, are less likely to accept an insanity defense when a crime has had serious consequences.[63] In a city as dangerous as Gotham, it is hard to imagine the citizens not wanting to see the dangerous costumed criminals, who constantly endanger them, punished to the full extent of the law.

In the end, it is quite possible that the concept of insanity, and the various legal rules that govern it, do not explain the Joker's repeated trips to Arkham. Perhaps in Gotham, other rules determine the population of the asylum. One possibility is an alternative verdict that has been explored in some states, *guilty but mentally ill* (GBMI). This verdict does not typically replace the insanity defense, but gives juries an additional option to consider. Rather than find a defendant guilty, not guilty, or NGRI, juries can return a verdict of GBMI when they believe the defendant is mentally ill but does not meet the applicable insanity standard.[64] While such an option may appeal to Gotham jurors, uncomfortable with letting costumed criminals escape responsibility, GBMI functions essentially the same as a guilty verdict, meaning it would add to the population of Blackgate, not Arkham.[65] In fact, allowing GBMI verdicts tends to result in fewer NGRI findings and harsher penalties for GBMI defendants.[66] Whatever the reason for the Joker's trips to Arkham, the availability of a GBMI verdict is probably not the explanation. This then returns us to the possibility that insanity in Gotham is simply governed by a standard more permissive than those typically found in the United States.

NOTES

1. *Batman and Robin* #13 (2010).
2. World Security Workshop radio program, episode 1–08, "The Meadow" (January 2, 1947).
3. Melton et al. (2018).
4. USLegal (n.d.).
5. Lenzi (1966).
6. Allnutt et al. (2007).
7. Weiner (1985).
8. M'Naghten's Case (1843).
9. Melton et al. (2018).
10. Langley (2012), p. 152.
11. Hare (2003).
12. Melton et al. (2018).
13. American Psychiatric Association (2013); Melton et al. (2018).
14. *Detective Comics* #475 (1978).
15. American Psychiatric Association (2013).
16. M'Naghten's Case (1843).
17. Allnutt et al. (2007).
18. *The Dark Knight* (2008 motion picture).
19. *Batgirl* #28 (2014).
20. *Batman: The Killing Joke* (1988).
21. American Psychiatric Association (2013).
22. *New Adventures of Superboy* #22 (1981).
23. *Batman: Secret Files* #1 (2018).
24. *Swamp Thing* #53 (1986).
25. USLegal (n.d.).
26. Weiner (1985).
27. Melton et al. (2018).
28. Weiner (1985).
29. USLegal (n.d.).
30. *The Dark Knight* (2008 motion picture).
31. *The Dark Knight* (2008 motion picture).
32. *Batman* #258 (1974).
33. *Batman Annual* #14 (1990).
34. American Psychiatric Association (2013).
35. *Batman: Two-Face* (1995).
36. *Arkham Asylum: A Serious House on Serious Earth* (1989).
37. *Batman: The Animated Series,* episode 1–18, "Two-Face, Part II" (September 28, 1992).
38. *Batman* #258 (1974).
39. Melton et al. (2018)
40. Model Penal Code Sec. 4.01 (1985).
41. Weiner (1985).
42. USLegal (n.d.).
43. American Law Institute (1985).
44. *Batman and the Outsiders* #14 (1984).
45. *Batman: Cacophony* #1–3 (2008–2009).
46. Melton et al. (2018).
47. *Durham v. US* (1954).
48. Melton et al. (2018).
49. *Durham v. US* (1954).
50. Melton et al. (2018).
51. *United States v. Brawner* (1972).
52. Weiner (1985).
53. Weiner (1985).
54. *Detective Comics* #475 (1978).
55. *DC Nation* #0 (2018).
56. *Detective Comics* #741 (2000).
57. Melton et al. (2018).
58. Bjørkly (1997); Hampson et al. (2017); Large et al. (2008).
59. Nasar (1998).
60. Bonaduce (2001).
61. Ogloff (1991).
62. Poulson et al. (1997).
63. McGraw & Foley (2000).
64. Melton et al. (2018).
65. Tajjudin & Goodwin (2016) agree.
66. Callahan et al. (1992).

EXPLAINING THE JOKE 7-1

THE TRUE ORIGIN OF ARKHAM ASYLUM

Jack C. Harris

Arkham Asylum has been an integral part of *Batman* since 1974, when it was mentioned in "Threat of the Two-Headed Coin" by Denny O'Neil, Irv Novick, and Dick Giordano in the October edition of *Batman* #258. Some readers might have recognized the institution Arkham, as it was prominently mentioned in the short horror stories by the famed fantasy writer H. P. Lovecraft. Is this where *Batman* writer O'Neil derived his inspiration? Yes, but indirectly!

Earlier that year, as a senior at the Philadelphia College of Art (now the University of the Arts), I and three like-minded friends were teaching the school's first student-created, accredited, liberal arts course, "The History of the American Comic Book." We had been inspired by articles about the first comic book college course, taught by Michael Uslan, at the University of Indiana. (Later, of course, Mike became executive producer of the *Batman* motion pictures.) Part of the curriculum of our course included our guest speakers lecturing on experiences in the comic book industry. Naturally, Denny O'Neil was one of the first people we approached because of his long writing career and his epic handling of *Batman*.

The previous summer, I had spent a great deal of time reading the works of H. P. Lovecraft. His stories of nether gods, such as Cthulhu, Yog-Sothoth, and others who drove men mad, fascinated me. According to Lovecraft, many of these poor souls whose minds had been destroyed ended up in a place called Arkham Sanitarium.[1] What a great place this would be to send such villains as the Joker and Two-Face! No ordinary prison could contain their insanity! At dinner, after Denny spoke at our class, I told him of my thoughts. He agreed, and the very next Two-Face script featured the debut of Arkham Hospital in the Batman universe. And in that story, the villain who aids Two-Face's escape, General John Harris, was named after me!

> *"Arkham Asylum comes from Jack Harris. When he suggested it,*
> *I thought it was a good fit for our continuity."*
> —Dennis O'Neil[2]

NOTES

1. First mentioned by Lovecraft (1937), p. 52. "At first I shall be called a madman—madder than the man I shot in his cell at Arkham Sanitarium."

2. Personal communication to editor Travis Langley (2018, October 27).

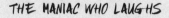

EXPLAINING THE JOKE 7-2

THE MANIAC WHO LAUGHS

Steve Englehart

When I first wrote about the Joker, he was an obscure character in an obscure subgenre, and I got to define him however I wanted—which I did in stories about laughing fish, which really sort of says it. The Joker, even more than the Batcave, is my link to the pulp era, the dark '30s/darker '40s, when the world went to war and pulps roared—as did pulps with pictures, a.k.a. comic books. The early Joker was a homicidal operatic maniac in the days when homicidal operatic maniacs really walked the earth, but that faded after the war ended. The Joker I did had a '70s mind instead of a '40s mind, but he returned to homicidal opera. And then that run got turned into the first adult hero film, *Batman* (Burton/Keaton/Nicholson), and the Joker's homicidal mania drew fans throughout society.

Now, I figured out my Joker in 1976, with Watergate still fresh in everyone's mind. We were well-versed in (possibly) homicidal operatic maniacs, so the mass audience was primed for a Capital-L Lunatic.

> *"What is normal for the spider is chaos for the fly."*
> —commonly attributed to cartoonist Charles Addams[1]

Normalcy (a word I like even though it's "wrong") is like a Venn diagram. Every person on Earth has his or her individuality, but it has to fall somewhere in the Venn or else consequences will ensue. Most of us internalize this as we grow, but some don't. There are many diagnoses for that. Very few are flat-out "sociopath," and only one of those sociopaths is the Joker.

With me, you're dealing with a guy who got his BA in psych but put that frame of mind into writing characters, so I probably have my terms wrong. But I think I have my Joker right. He not only lives outside the Venn, he *laughs* outside the Venn, *at* the Venn. He's no fly, but he's certainly no spider, either. He's not lying quietly in wait; he's out there, out front. . . .

And that led me to think of activists, who have put themselves out front to make the world see them as the people they are. And that led to the idea of a Homicidal Operatic Maniac Activist—a certifiable lunatic demanding his right to be part of society, for all lunatics everywhere.

Then I remembered what year we're living in now.

The Joker Psychology could not be more timely.

NOTE

1. Cartoonist Charles Addams, origin unknown (TV Tropes, n.d.). His character Morticia later uttered a version of the line in *The Addams Family* (2009 musical stage play).

8

Cult of Personality: Personality and Crime

COLT J. BLUNT

"I wondered if sometimes the difference between a psychopath in Broadmoor and a psychopath on Wall Street was the luck of being born into a stable, rich family."

—author Jon Ronson[1]

"There's plenty wrong with me."
—The Joker[2]

AS A GENERAL rule, humans tend to over-estimate the effects of internal factors and disregard potential external factors when considering the actions of others. This is called the *fundamental attribution error*.[3] When looking at those who commit run-of-the-mill crimes, we tend to conclude that they are simply bad people doing bad things. The typical bank robber in Gotham must be nothing more than a bad guy who is too lazy to make an honest living, right? However, we often deviate and make a completely different error when the antisocial act is more extreme. Almost every mass shooting in America is followed by a renewed discussion about the need for greater mental health services, regardless of whether the evidence suggests that the perpetrator had a history of mental illness. For many, it is nigh impossible to believe an abhorrent act could be done out of pure volition; that is, we believe no sane person could commit an act we view as insane. Batman's rogues' gallery frequently gets this treatment, which is reinforced by the fact that so many of them find themselves behind the doors of the Arkham Asylum after being brought to justice for their crimes. However, things are rarely so simple! Is the King of Arkham Asylum psychotic, or simply psychopathic? Was he forged this way through experience or is he simply a slave to his biology?

What Are Personality Disorders and How Do They Differ from Other Mental Disorders?

The practice of mental health diagnosis has some gray areas. When most people think of mental illness, they think of disorders such as schizophrenia and bipolar disorder. Some practitioners refer to these as *severe and persistent mental illness* (SPMI). Such disorders tend to have a significant impact on the lives of those who are diagnosed with them; these disorders often require lifelong treatment with both psychotherapy and medications. The *Diagnostic and Statistical Manual of Mental Disorders* (DSM, or DSM-5)[4] includes a wide range of disorders with various impacts. While someone with a psychotic disorder such as schizophrenia may experience *hallucinations* (perceiving stimuli that do not exist, such as hearing voices) and *delusions* (fixed, false beliefs that persist despite evidence to the contrary), someone with a *specific phobia* may simply experience an intense fear of a specific stimulus, such as the fear of bats (also known as *chiroptophobia*), shared by Bane[5] and a young Bruce Wayne.[6] Though these diagnoses have very different courses, prevalence rates, and impact on day-to-day life, there is no question that they both constitute mental illnesses. However, personality disorders are a different beast altogether.

A personality disorder is an "enduring pattern of inner experience and behavior that deviates markedly from the expectations of the individual's culture."[7] To use an analogy that's sometimes bandied about in criminal hearings, personality disorders are tinted lenses that influence *how* we see the world, whereas psychosis can function like a virtual reality headset that determines *what* is seen. This difference can be seen in the victims of Scare-crow's fear gas: They see things the rest of the citizens of Gotham do not and they perceive them as real. However, the relationship between personality disorders and other mental disorders is difficult to characterize and ever-shifting. In the previous version of the DSM, personality disorders were reported separately from more traditional forms of mental illness and more like developmental disabilities.[8] The idea was that personality disorders, like developmental disabilities, were not acquired, but rather represented a stable trait, unlike more traditional mental illnesses, which were expected to ebb and flow or even remit completely. However, DSM-5 does not differentiate between personality disorders and other disorders in the same way, which is consistent not only with research but also with the original theories behind many personality disorders. For instance, *borderline personality disorder*—which is characterized by unstable and intense interpersonal relationships, mood instability, frantic and at times manipulative attempts to avoid abandonment, identity crises, and self-injurious behavior—was originally characterized as being on the borderline of psychosis and *neurosis* (disorders that involve marked distress but do not impair reality-testing).[9] More recent research has shown that it is closely tied to trauma and shows notable co-morbidity with *posttraumatic stress disorder* (PTSD).[10] We see Harley Quinn evince some behaviors consistent with borderline personality disorder, though not con-sistently a full set. She tends to view the Joker in an idealized manner (even though he has frequently tried to kill her), shows marked *identity disturbance* (altering her entire persona from respected psychiatrist to supervillain to hero), and presents with emotional and behavioral instability, especially in her big-screen debut.[11] Though the way she interprets the Joker's actions may be tainted by her personality structure, she still sees what we see. Fur-thermore, the way she behaves—her criminal acts, including escalation to the point of committing murder—can be seen as her increasingly frantic efforts to maintain the Joker's interests. Her view of the Joker alternates significantly throughout her arc: At times she idolizes him, and at times she works toward his death. Harley's presentation is additionally consistent with aspects of *dependent personality disorder*, which involves submissive and clinging behavior to avoid abandonment, and *histrionic personality disorder*, which is characterized by theatrical presentation, shallow affect, provocative behavior, and a desire to be the center of attention.

Some other personality disorders appear even more closely related to SPMI. *Paranoid personality disorder* involves generally mistrusting others and misreading the intent of others as nefarious, whereas *schizotypal personality disorder* is characterized by discomfort with social relationships, combined with more aberrant experiences, such as *ideas of reference* (seeing strong personal significance in innocuous stimuli), *magical thinking* (holding bizarre beliefs that are inconsistent with societal norms), and odd methods of communication (such as being overly vague or metaphorical). The lesser-known foe Abattoir, who kills his family and believes the life force of others can be absorbed into himself, embodies many of these traits, though he may simply have slid into full-blown psychosis (which could be why he cannot succeed enough to become better known). This is not surprising, however, as these diagnoses are thought to be on the same spectrum as psychotic disorders, such as schizophrenia, and further show the biological basis of some personality disorders.[12]

This brings us to the personality disorder that features criminal behavior among its diagnostic criteria: *antisocial personality disorder* (ASPD), which is a pervasive pattern of disregard for the rights of others and is characterized by criminal behavior, deceitfulness, disregard for the safety of others, impulsivity, irresponsibility, and irritability. On the surface, ASPD seems to be the easiest to understand, as it is embodied by bad people doing bad things. However, things are rarely as simple as they seem. Philosophers have argued for centuries about the nature of humanity, including whether people are born bad or are simply a product of their environment. French philosopher and scientist René Descartes believed in the concept of dualism, which states that the mind and body are distinct yet connected, and that some knowledge and structure is imparted at birth by God.[13] John Locke was critical of Descartes and believed in the concept of *tabula rasa* (roughly translated from Latin as "blank slate"). Locke wrote, "I think I might say that of all the men we meet with, nine parts of ten are what they are, good or evil, useful or not, by their education."[14] Psychological professionals are equally torn, with research pointing to evidence in favor of both arguments when it comes to antisocial behavior. That is, whether one goes on to do evil is affected by both *nature* (our biology) and *nurture* (our environment and experiences). From a nurture standpoint, lack of affection and care during childhood has been associated with the diagnosis of ASPD in adulthood.[15] Jonathan Crane grows up as a bullied child who turns to violence in order to take control of his life and get revenge against those who wrong him. His resulting focus on the fear that he experienced as a child leads to his study of fear as a psychologist, his first acts of violence, and his donning of the mantle of the Scarecrow.[16]

However uncomfortable it may make us, we must also take into account the effect of nature on the development of antisocial proclivities. It's tempting to write off ASPD as simply pathologizing bad behavior, but it is important to consider the research. *Meta-analysis* (an analysis of numerous analyses, comparing multiple studies) has shown that individuals with antisocial personality structures often lack development of structures in the *prefrontal cortex*, the area of the brain most often associated with personality and *executive functioning* (the ability to adapt and make decisions).[17] More important for the study of antisocial behavior, the prefrontal cortex is thought to be responsible for feelings of guilt and remorse; people with underdeveloped prefrontal cortices (plural of *cortex*) show a reduced capacity for such emotions.[18] Similarly, researchers have shown that the *amygdala*, an almond-shaped structure in the brain associated with memory, decision-making, and emotional response, figures in the display of antisocial behavior; specifically, dysfunction in the amygdala can affect emotional processing.[19] Batman's foe Amygdala fittingly lacks this structure, having had it removed in a dramatic attempt to temper his rage; however, this only serves to increase his rage, suggesting perhaps a different origin for his anger.[20] Further research has additionally shown that some people's genetic predisposition involving the neurotransmitter *serotonin*, most commonly associated with positive mood, can impact their likelihood of developing ASPD when paired with adverse childhood experiences, suggesting an interaction between nature and nurture.[21]

Taken in its totality, the research tells us that personality disorders, like more traditional forms of mental disorders, have both biological and environmental bases. Where does this leave the Joker? Is he a product of his environment? Did he become the criminal we have been following since 1940 because of "one bad day," if that story is to be believed?[22] Was the Joker born because the Red Hood experienced an injury to his brain resulting from his fall into a vat of chemicals?[23] Was the man who became the Joker always destined to be evil, a slave to his genetics and neurobiology? Or was it some combination of these things, an interaction between the Joker's nature and nurture? Unfortunately, we may never know for sure, partially because we do not have the ability to scan or dissect the Joker's brain, and partially because any story he tells about his genesis must be taken with a grain of salt. In many ways, the etiology of the Joker's personality is unimportant, and a comprehensive review of his personality structure cannot be complete without first discussing the concept of psychopathy.

Psychopathy: A Not-Quite Diagnosis of Supreme Importance

The concept of psychopathy has been studied for about as long as the Joker has been gracing the pages of comics. In many ways, psychopathy is like ASPD on steroids and incorporates traits of other personality disorders. Psychopathy was first popularized in psychiatrist Hervey Cleckley's book *The Mask of Sanity*.[24] Based on his interviews of individuals within secure institutions, Cleckley developed his theory of psychopathy, which describes a personality profile notable for superficial charm, deceitfulness, antisocial behavior, lack of remorse, restricted emotion, egocentrism, poor insight, lack of long-term plans, and impersonal sex life. Cleckley's book referred to the metaphorical "mask" worn by psychopaths. Spend enough time with a psychopath and you may see that mask "slip," giving you a glimpse at his or her true nature. For a villain like the Joker, the laughs, loud clothes, smiles, and charm hide a stone-cold killer.

Cleckley felt it important to note that psychopathy is distinct from psychosis; that is, psychopaths are not motivated by psychotic symptomatology, such as hallucinations or delusions, though psychopathy and psychosis can co-occur. The Joker could be both psychopathic and psychotic. When these phenomena co-occur in an individual, it is not difficult to see that this has the potential to be a dangerous combination. For instance, whereas a nonpsychopath experiencing a delusional belief that someone was besmirching his or her character may let it slide or take more measured action, the same person with psychopathy may have no qualms about acting violently. A psychopath with the delusion that his or her neighbor was in possession of objects of great value might be inclined to hatch a plot to acquire his or her neighbor's goods, and, with limited regard for human life, may use significant violence to accomplish this. The character Maxie Zeus commits criminal acts when psychotic (believing himself to be the god Zeus) but also when nonpsychotic (selling Ecstasy mixed with Joker toxin).[25] Though professionals differed in their opinions, Jeffrey Dahmer (a serial killer known for dismembering and storing parts from some of his 16 victims for later consumption, as well as injecting their brains with hydrochloric acid) was diagnosed with a psychotic disorder and antisocial personality disorder[26] even though he was declared legally sane. Similarly, the Joker's mental status and indeed the presence of psychosis have varied throughout the character's publication history. He has typically engaged in similar abhorrent behavior; that is, regardless of any potential psychotic motivations, his underlying psychopathy was what allowed him to carry out his despicable acts.

The mantle of psychopathy research has since been taken up by psychologist Robert Hare in modern times. Hare's model of psychopathy[27] is largely based on Cleckley's but has been expanded to consider additional traits. The prototypical is someone who exploits others for his or her own gain and lacks remorse for his or her actions. Such individuals are capable of using deceit and guile, but will often lie when there is no utility to it. They rarely show you who they really are, instead using superficial charm; tend to be similarly superficial and more focused on what they can get out of it, whether it be money, sex, power, or status. Psychopaths often fail to meet their obligations, instead defaulting on commitments or leeching off others. Despite significant research into the construct of psychopathy since its first edition, the DSM does not include psychopathy as a diagnosis. Rather, it is generally considered to be subsumed under the diagnosis of ASPD. However, it is important to note that, while it is likely that all psychopaths meet criteria for ASPD, relatively few who are diagnosed with the personality disorder would qualify as psychopaths. Regarding traits from disorders found in the DSM, psychopathy is best described as existing at the nexus of antisocial and narcissistic personality disorders.

Hare used his model to develop the Psychopathy Checklist (PCL)[28] and later the Psychopathy Checklist–Revised (PCL-R).[29] Though it is popularly referred to as the "psychopath test" at times,[30] the PCL-R is nothing like the type of exam you take in school and differs significantly from the measures most often administered by psychologists. Rather than a pen-and-paper test, which the subject fills out, the PCL-R, as its name implies, is a checklist of features representing the hallmark features of psychopathy. The PCL-R is composed of 20 items that are broadly split between personality characteristics and antisocial acts. Each item is worth up to two points. Though psychopathy is generally viewed as falling along a continuum, a score of 30 is typically used to classify someone as a psychopath. The PCL-R is usually scored based on an interview and a review of records, though it can be scored based on records alone if necessary.

So how does the Joker measure up? Since a clinical interview is not an option, any consideration of whether the Joker is a psychopath is necessarily limited to what we know from the media in which he has appeared. Because we do not know the Joker's true identity, and the background information that he has divulged is of questionable veracity, we lack some key details, such as facts about his childhood. However, the Joker wears much of what we need to score the PCL-R on his sleeve. We know he is a fast-talker with a propensity for untruthfulness. He has the gift of gab and is able to convince henchmen to follow him, despite the fact that he has a reputation for killing them when they have either served their purpose or it would amuse him. Though he shows extreme emotions, it is unlikely that this is a glimpse of his true self, as we quickly see his mask slip when things do not go his way. He clearly cares primarily for himself. He fails to fulfill his obligations to those with whom he associates, frequently abandoning them to fend for themselves. He uses others to get what he wants. He has little regard for the feelings of others and does not appear remorseful for his actions, including multiple murders. Though he is capable of intricate planning, he is often impulsive and loses control of his behavior, resulting in acts of great violence. Though he has plans, they appear short-term and untenable; he is obsessed with corrupting Batman, a task that appears impossible and at which he has failed countless times. He seems to have been habitually unsuccessful while incarcerated or placed within a secure treatment facility; he has escaped from custody on multiple occasions and is returned to secure settings each time for subsequent criminal activity. His criminal history appears most easily described by listing those offenses he has not yet committed as his rap

The ~~Psychopathy~~ Superman Checklist

Just because the Joker claims to be "ahead of the curve"[31] or "just differently sane"[32] does not mean he's right—no more so than the convict who decides he's no psychopath; he's Superman.

In his book *The Psychopath Whisperer*, psychologist and neuroscientist Kent Kiehl reports that an inmate came to him annoyed because "I just got my risk assessment done and the doc told me I was a psychopath. He said it meant I was very high risk to reoffend. I'm no Hannibal Lecter."[33] The inmate's score was high (37 out of 40 in the risk assessment; 39 in Kiehl's own previous assessment), and it is true that convicts who score high on the PCL are four to eight times as likely to reoffend than are inmates who score low. Kiehl explained the test to the inmate item by item, citing the man's own previous statements as examples of each. The inmate grew to understand the score better, but he still did not want to be called a psychopath. He grabbed his copy of his PCL score sheet, crossed out the word *Psychopathy*, and wrote *SUPERMAN* above it. "That's the wrong term for me. I'm renaming this the *Superman Checklist*. And now I'm Superman."[34]

For days after that, the inmate showed others his Superman Checklist score. He told his roommate to call him "Superman" or get beaten up.

—T. L.

sheet is exhaustive. He differs from many psychopaths in that he appears to have a limited history of romantic relationships, having reportedly been married once and being in an on-again-off-again relationship of dubious genuineness with Harley Quinn. The Joker's score of 32.2 (after being prorated to account for items that could not be scored) exceeds the cutoff typically used to classify an offender as a psychopath. This means the Joker experiences a far greater degree of psychopathy than is typically seen in either correctional or forensic mental health populations. So it would not be surprising to see the Joker diagnosed with both antisocial personality disorder and narcissistic personality disorder.

Personality, Crime, and the Law

Courts typically consider the concept of volition heavily in making legal determinations. *Volition*, as the concept is used by psychologists and the legal system, refers to someone's ability to make a decision to engage in an action. Looking at extreme examples, movements resulting from a seizure lack volition, whereas the decision to train for a marathon is volitional. Psychiatric disorders typically vary quite a bit in their effects on volition. Two-Face feels that he *must* obey the results of each coin flip, meaning that his actions show less volition. Personality disorders are a bit more difficult when it comes to volition. For most people with a personality disorder, actions are a choice, though they may be described as being simply more predisposed to carry out those actions. Imagine being in a generally positive mood (referred to as *euthymia* by psychologists) and having someone cut in front of you in a long line at the grocery store. This might make you unhappy. You might consider confronting such a person. You might even fantasize about taking a swing at him or her. However, what is the likelihood of your actually resorting to violence in this situation? Probably not very high. Now, consider the same situation, but you were just on your way home after being fired from your job. Simply put, you are having a rough go of things. Would that affect your mind-set? Would that make you more likely to react to the person in the grocery store? Would your mood put you at higher risk for lashing out? Probably. Now, here is the real question: If you did react aggressively in that situation, would it still have been by choice? Most people would have to grudgingly accept that, while their threshold for action may have been diminished by circumstance, they still made a conscious, albeit poor, choice. Most personality disorders can be seen in a similar light. One Gotham City serial killer, Victor Zsasz, has an absolutely broken moral compass. He sees people as meaningless, yet every stroke of his knife is an individual decision. No force, real or imagined, *makes* him kill. Similarly, Harley's crimes are closely tied to her relationship with the Joker, specifically her conscious attempts to retain him as a fixture in her life. Other personality types may, in some circumstances, be seen as exhibiting less volition. Someone with a paranoid personality disorder may feel less control over his or her decision to eliminate someone he or she sees as a threat, though this is still a decision.

Since psychologists have argued for decades over how to classify personality disorders, it might be tempting to conclude that the legal system has similar beliefs when it comes to criminal cases. However, this is not typically the case. Psychologists operating within the criminal justice system usually learn early in their careers that psychological terms can be meaningless to the courts, where statute (referring to state and federal laws), case law (precedents set forth by court decisions), and legal definitions rule. Courts do not usually make categorical decisions when it comes to concepts like insanity, but rather focus on functional impairments. In other words, courts deal less with what something is called than they do with how it affects someone's thinking and behavior. For this reason, most courts do not have a prohibition against trying to rely on a personality disorder as the basis of an insanity defense. However, because most insanity standards require someone to show that he or she lacked control of his or her behavior or that he or she were so impaired that he or she did not know what he or she was doing or that it was wrong, proving that you meet the criteria of insanity is exceedingly difficult when the sole basis is a personality disorder. But, with a growing body of research suggesting differences in brain structure among people diagnosed with antisocial personality disorder or coded as psychopaths, it is inevitable that there will be ongoing challenges, especially in jurisdictions that recognize diminished capacity, the legal concept that an impairment, while not absolving a defendant of wrongdoing, may render him or her less culpable.

It would be difficult to argue that the Joker's actions are outside of his control. So why does he get sent to the mental hospital? Exactly how does Arkham Asylum fit into the criminal justice system in Gotham?

Diminished Capacity and the Joker's Dream Team

Two TV news anchors react to the Joker's latest arrest:

Man: What do you think, Winona? Will his dream team of attorneys get him off on "diminished capacity" again?

Woman: They always have in the past, Danny. Let's run the tape.

These anchorfolk do not know what they're talking about. Diminished capacity lessens criminal liability but does not eliminate it. The term means that mental faculties were diminished, impaired, due to mental illness or other hindering state. Attorneys will not "get him off" but might instead get him a reduction of charges. In the case of first-degree murder, for example, the defense must cast doubt upon the defendant's capacity for premeditation, deliberation, and specific intent to kill.[35] This seems unlikely when the Joker has repeatedly performed carefully planned, deliberate murders, many of which he announces ahead of time. This is a different issue from insanity. An individual could commit premeditated murder for insane reasons.

This exchange raises a bigger question, though: What "dream team of attorneys" would work for the Joker? He kills his own henchmen.[36]

—T. L.

Getting into Arkham: Or, Being *Sane* in an Insane Place

Arkham Asylum appears to exclusively treat patients involved in the criminal justice system. In most jurisdictions in the United States, government-run psychiatric facilities cater to a wide-ranging clientele, though typically on an involuntary basis. That is, they are sent for treatment by a judge, either under a civil commitment due to inability to care for themselves and/or risk to themselves or others, or under a criminal commitment as a result of being found incompetent to stand trial or not guilty by reason of insanity. Arkham Asylum appears to be somewhat of an anomaly compared to most government psychiatric facilities. Typically, individuals receiving services in psychiatric facilities are referred to as "patients." However, the residents of Arkham are often referred to as "inmates," suggesting that they are serving a criminal sentence. It is unclear if the residents of Arkham are dually committed, that is, primarily found guilty of criminal charges but ultimately sent to Arkham due to Blackgate's inability to treat their underlying psychiatric conditions, or if Gotham exists within a jurisdiction that does not excuse criminal behavior due to a finding of insanity (such as states that utilize a guilty but mentally ill standard, essentially acknowledging that a defendant's behavior was the result of mental illness while simultaneously handing down a guilty verdict and a criminal sentence).

Regardless of whether Arkham Asylum serves primarily as a correctional or a treatment facility, it is not surprising that personality disorders are well-represented among its population. Meta-analysis of studies from 12 Western countries showed that 65 percent of inmates were diagnosed with a personality disorder, including 47 percent with a diagnosis of ASPD.[37] The prevalence of personality disorders in treatment settings is a bit more difficult to pinpoint due to differences in statutes and admission criteria, though studies have estimated that between 30 percent and 50 percent of those in psychiatric clinical populations have a personality disorder, compared to approximately 10 percent in the general population.[38] As such, regardless of Arkham's target population, it is not surprising that so many of its denizens appear to possess significant personality pathology.

The Crux of the Clown

The Joker is a tough nut to crack. While he outwardly appears mad to the layperson, few would argue that it is his personality structure that makes him truly dangerous. Possessing a high number of psychopathic traits, he does not see the world through the same lens as most. The people he comes into contact with have no worth in his eyes beyond what they can do for him; for some, that means their life means nothing. To him, everyone is a potential victim. Not even those he purports to care for are safe from his malevolent machinations.

The Joker's origin largely remains a mystery. Even if the backstory shown in *Batman: The Killing Joke* were true, this likely only tells a portion of the story. Rather, the Joker's true origin may have been a product of genetics, the pairing of two recessive genes that led to a structural difference in his brain that predisposed him to a life of sowing chaos. Regardless of where these traits came from, they are unlikely to remit any time soon.

> *"In my dream, the world had suffered a terrible disaster. A black haze*
> *shut out the sun, and the darkness was alive with the moans and*
> *screams of wounded people. Suddenly, a small light glowed.*
> *A candle flickered into life, symbol of hope for millions. A single*
> *tiny candle, shining in the ugly dark. I laughed and blew it out."*
> —The Joker[39]

Psychopath or Sociopath?

Fans have contemplated whether the Joker is a psychopath or a sociopath, with some heatedly arguing the distinction.[40] One big problem with this debate, though, is that the word *sociopath* has no standard definition. Rather, it has a lot of definitions. Even though clinicians find some of those very useful, a group of experts discussing sociopaths might all be having different conversations from their respective points of view if they're using the same word to mean different things. That's why articles attempting to distinguish *sociopath* from *psychopath* contradict each other in many ways.[41] One popular definition of *sociopath*, the one that may be key when some fans debate whether the Joker is one, identifies the sociopath as a person who was normal until external circumstances shut down that person's conscience or empathy. "Psychopaths are born and sociopaths are made," this views holds. "In essence, their difference reflects the nature versus nurture debate."[42] Flashbacks in *Batman: The Killing Joke*, considered by many[43] (but not all[44]) to be the greatest Joker/Batman story, suggest the Joker is that kind of normal-person-turned-sociopath. In this graphic novel, "one bad day" in which his pregnant wife dies and he falls into a chemical vat turns a failed stand-up comic into a homicidal madman. (Later chapters will examine whether that's even possible.) The argument may hold up for that one example but not for the stories in general, though, because the Joker has been given many origins,[45] and not even he remembers which of the inconsistent accounts might be true.[46] Maybe he was born bad, or maybe he was transformed.

Even though the term *sociopathy* connotes societal causes, the nature/nurture distinction is not among the criteria that classically define psychopathy. When he first appears in comics, the Joker has no origin, and even when he is finally given an explanation for his green hair and bleached skin, his background prior to that remains unknown. Likewise, psychopathy is not defined by information about the person's early life.

—T. L.

NOTES

1. Ronson (2011), p. 262.
2. *Batman: Arkham City* (2011 video game).
3. Ross (1977).
4. American Psychiatric Association (2013).
5. *Batman: Vengeance of Bane* #1.
6. *Batman Begins* (2005 motion picture); *Secret Origins of the World's Greatest Superheroes* (1989).
7. American Psychiatric Association (2013), p. 645.
8. American Psychiatric Association (2000).
9. Stern (1938).
10. Grant et al. (2008).
11. *Suicide Squad* (2017 motion picture).
12. Webb & Levinson (1993).
13. Descartes (1647/1993).
14. Locke (1693/2006), p. 10.
15. Johnson et al. (2006).
16. *Year One: Batman/Scarecrow* #1 (1989).
17. Yang & Raine (2009).
18. Anderson et al. (1999).
19. Blair & Frith (2000).
20. *Batman: Shadow of the Bat* #3 (1992).]
21. Reif et al. (2007).
22. *Batman: The Killing Joke* (1988).
23. *Detective Comics* #168 (1951).
24. Cleckley (1941/1976).
25. *Batman: Cacophony* (2008—2009).
26. Ewing & McCann (2006).
27. Hare (1998).
28. Hare (1980).
29. Hare (2003).
30. Ronson (2011), book title.
31. *The Dark Knight* (2008 motion picture).
32. *Batman and Robin* #13 (2010).
33. Kiehl (2014), p. 119.
34. Kiehl (2014), p. 120.
35. *State v. Shank* (1988).
36. e.g., *Detective Comics* #251 (1973), #475 (1978); *Batman* #663 (2007); and many more.
37. Fazel & Danesh (2002).
38. Sparr (2009).
39. *Batman: Shadow of the Bat* #37 (1995).
40. Duignan (n.d.); Fuller (2019); Likalaruku (2009—see the post comments); Quora (n.d.); Powers (n.d.); Sociopath World (2011—see post comments); Wolf (2016); Yahoo Answers (n.d.).
41. Fansplainer (2018a, 2018b); Grohol (2018); Jewell (2018); Mallett (2015); Pemment (2013); Peterson (n.d.); Purse (2018); Robinson (n.d.); Thomas (2013); Tracy (n.d.); Weiss (2013/2017).
42. Mallett (2015).
43. e.g., Cronin (2015); Marston (2018).
44. e.g., Gilbert (2016).
45. Conley (2017).
46. *Batman: The Killing Joke* (1988).

9

The Brain: Built to Be Bad?

TRAVIS LANGLEY

*"It's one thing to read about how the brain works, and another
to see it in action. Even for a Joker-brain, it's pretty impressive."*
—Ryan Choi (Atom)[1]

*"Frankly, we found some of the brain wave
patterns depicted in the paper very odd.
Those EEGs couldn't have come from real people."*
—an editor skeptical of groundbreaking research on psychopaths' brains[2]

ONE AUGUST DAY in 1966, a well-armed 25-year-old man driven by "unusual and irrational thoughts" (according to the letter he left behind) entered a university tower in Austin, Texas. Attacking people on his way up, killing three, he ascended to the tower's 28th-story observation deck. From there, the former Marine sharpshooter began firing at random people for the next hour and a half, shooting more than 40 people that day before a police officer shot him dead. Ultimately, the sniper killed 17 people.[3] His letter requested that an autopsy "be performed on me to see if there is any visible physical disorder" to account for his brutal headaches and "overwhelming violent impulses."[4] Postmortem examination revealed a pecan-sized tumor in his brain.[5]

Can a change in the brain make someone a menace to society?

Acquiring Evil

Running from Batman, a criminal called the Red Hood plunges into a vat of chemical waste and makes his escape. Upon emerging where the liquid empties into the river, he discovers the chemicals have turned his hair green, his lips rouge-red, and his skin chalk-white. He has become the Joker in appearance.[6] Has the experience changed him internally as well, or was he already the Joker at heart? Character creator Jerry Robinson scoffed at the idea that a single experience could explain the Joker or that falling into a chemical vat would make him anything more than scarred.[7]

It is possible to alter the moral reasoning of a normal person by interfering with that person's brain functioning. One example: *Transcranial magnetic stimulation*, passing a magnetic field through specific regions inside the head to alter electrical activity, may temporarily alter moral judgments when used on an area where the brain's temporal and parietal lobes meet. This area plays a key role in *self-other distinctions* (as it sounds, distinguishing oneself from other people) and a person's *theory of mind* (understanding that other people have their own thoughts, ideas, memories, emotions, and related mental states).[8] In other words, it's crucial to how we think about other people as our fellow sentient beings. When researchers magnetically and momentarily disrupted this area in volunteers' brains, the volunteers had trouble recognizing moral problems, became less likely to consider people's intentions when judging attempted harm, and considered attempted harm to be more morally permissible.[9] Callous indifference to the feelings of others is not at all the same as actively harming them and reveling in their distress. Impeding this area of the brain might not create a Joker, but maybe it could create a Harley Quinn by blinding a person to the degree of someone else's evil.

What about a more permanent change to the brain? Whereas primary psychopathy is a developmental condition present throughout life, not clearly caused by any traumatic event, *pseudopsychopathy* is essentially acquired psychopathy. Damage to the prefrontal cortex, particularly in a brain region necessary for the normal generation and regulation of social emotions, can impair emotional processing in ways that make a person look like a psychopath.[10] Such individuals have already learned basic values, though, and the condition does not turn them into fiends.

Rather, it shuts off emotional considerations, making them callous and cold. Whatever compassion, shame, and guilt remain in them tends to be more thought-driven than emotional.[11] Moral decision-making is utilitarian, practical in nature—a defining quality of Machiavellianism but also associated with other dark triad traits.[12] This kind of damage would not seem sufficient to create a supervillain. But what about the atypical person who only holds himself or herself back from villainous inclinations because of restraints such as those imposed by the prefrontal cortex? What if a brain injury finally let one man's inner beast off its leash?

These are just a couple of examples of how it is conceivable to change a person's moral reasoning to resemble that of a psychopath by changing the brain, whether temporarily or for the long term. Doing so, though, is not known to create supervillains. Even if his chemical bath plays a role, the man who becomes the Joker has to be very different to begin with. So what would we find inside a Joker brain?

Journey to the Center of the Clown

Ryan Choi, one of the superheroes to go by the appellation of "the Atom," shrinks down to microscopic size and journeys into the Joker's brain.[13] Considering that he's traveling through an organ made up of 100 billion cells, which is one of the smaller estimates for the number of stars in the Milky Way galaxy, the amount of brain he explores is limited, a single path to an unspecified location in the brain and then back out. Entering "by way of the nasal mucosal membrane, where the tissue protecting the brain is thinnest" takes him more directly to the more primitive midbrain. "His nose. I'm going in through his nose. This just gets better and better," says Choi. Bypassing the frontal cortex this way, it's a bit like sneaking in through the basement to avoid the guy in charge.

Cerebral Cortex

Numerous researchers and clinicians have reported behavioral similarities between psychopaths and patients who have suffered damage to their brains' frontal lobes, including patterns in attention, emotional responsiveness, persistence, and problem solving.[14] In the brain's cerebral cortex, the wrinkled outer layer where our most advanced functions take place, the frontal lobe is the region at the front of the brain important in self-control, voluntary movement, emotional expression, memory integration, anticipation, and much conscious thought.[15] A master supervillain such as the Joker, who develops elaborate and meticulous plans, needs a healthy frontal lobe. *The Dark Knight* film version of the character is particularly good at anticipating people's actions and planning accordingly. He's only good at foreseeing certain kinds of reactions, though, not those that depend on people's better nature. Other versions of the character show greater impulsivity, such as when the Nicholson Joker casually guns down Bob, the henchman who has been with him through the entire 1989 movie.[16]

Despite the perceived similarity between psychopaths and patients with damaged frontal lobes, though, it turns out that the similarity is greatest among those who show only some psychopathic traits (moderate—maybe Harley Quinn, Poison Ivy, or Maxie Zeus, all of whom have engaged in severely antisocial activities, hurting other people, and yet show capacity to care), not among those who meet most of the clinical criteria for psychopathy (severe—the Joker, the Riddler, Killer Croc).[17] This is an important distinction, an old concern that still matters for researchers because this finding complicates the interpretation of any research on psychopaths' brains. When a study identifies psychopaths as having less gray matter in their frontal and temporal lobes but simply divides participants into psychopaths and nonpsychopaths,[18] it may fail to distinguish between the moderate and severe psychopaths. What if Harley's group shows the brain difference more than the Joker's does?

Other dark triad characteristics present their own differences in the brain. Narcissists, though, have abnormalities very close to the cortical area where the aforementioned magnetic field can interfere with moral judgments.[19] So for people who are narcissistic but not also psychopathic, they might lack empathy for a different reason when their brains do not register other people's distress or intentions normally. An extreme egotist such as the Joker or the Riddler would likely show abnormalities common among both psychopaths and narcissists.

Machiavellianism throws another wrench into the works because people who score high in this trait appear to have *greater* volume in the prefrontal cortex.[20] The manipulative, egotistical psychopath who's highly competent at developing complicated plans and anticipating people's responses seems unlikely to show the kind of frontal cortex deficits that may be visible in less successful criminals. An ongoing problem with research on psychopaths is that so many of those studied come from prison populations. Real-life prison inmates are much more like Joe Chill, the mugger who impulsively kills Bruce Wayne's parents when his dad stands up for his mom and then his mom screams.[21]

Trait sadism, which was added to form a dark tetrad when the dark triad didn't seem dark enough, has not been studied as well as the other three. Most brain research into sadistic behavior focuses on *sexual sadism*, deriving sexual gratification from hurting others. That's not the same as generally enjoying the suffering of others without sexual thrill. Sadists' brains actually indicate heightened sensitivity when observing others' pain, as seen at the junction of the temporal and parietal lobes.[22] Nonsexual sadism has not been so well studied and may be difficult to separate from extreme psychopathy. *Sadistic personality disorder*, though once listed in the DSM as a disorder worthy of further investigation,[23] disappeared from subsequent editions of the diagnostic manual arguably because of such difficulties.[24]

So do psychopaths' brains regularly reveal any particular difference? Researchers discovered abnormal P3 waves (short for P300) in their brains, but initially they could only scratch their heads and wonder what the finding meant. This particular wave is elicited during conscious decision-making and somehow reflects the way in which people evaluate stimuli around them—how they choose and judge. The relationship was surprising but too powerful to ignore: In the study that first revealed this pattern, 40 out of 41 psychopaths (97 percent, including a number with extremely high psychopathy scores) showed a certain kind of abnormal P3, whereas none of the nonpsychopaths did (0 percent).[25] An astounding result, but what did it mean? More advanced brain imaging let them see which of the brain's many parts this odd wave came from: part of the cortex (temporal lobe, not frontal) and parts Ryan Choi might pass near as he heads deeper into the Joker's brain (hippocampus, amygdala).

Limbic System

When Choi journeys through the Joker's brain, he gets bombarded by visions of the Joker's memories—fighting with other kids during childhood, killing his parents in a house fire, committing robberies and murders.[26] Out of all the things that go on in a human brain, why is he getting hit by memories—emotionally laden memories, at that, regardless of whether they're recollections of real events or the Joker's dreams? Maybe Choi is approaching the limbic areas involved in the psychopaths' abnormal P3 wave.

The *limbic system*, the so-called animal brain, generates motivation and emotion.[27] It's a collection of brain parts, including the *hippocampus*, which processes explicit memories for long-term storage; a cluster of parts collectively known as the *hypothalamus*, which governs many basic drives (hunger, thirst, sex drive, responses to danger); and the *amygdala*, which links our motivations and emotions to the stimuli that set them off (actually *amygdalae*, plural, because there's one on each side of the brain). Electrical or chemical stimulation to hypothalamus or amygdala can make an animal leap to attack[28] or, with only a slight difference in target location, cower in fear,[29] and the Scarecrow's fear gas would likely need to operate on these in order to induce fright in people exposed to it.[30]

Memories of different kinds are stored throughout the brain, but Choi doesn't just access any random bit of knowledge. He does not abruptly experience the sensation of juggling—a *procedural memory*, remembering how to perform a skill that the Joker has been able to perform.[31] Nor is suddenly awash in the Joker's knowledge of chemical terms—*semantic memory*, remembering what things means. No, he encounters some of the Joker's *episodic memories*, recollections of events whether real or imagined, the kind of memory the hippocampus will process. The fact that each amygdala is at an end of the hippocampus may figure into why we can form such strong associations between emotions and particular memories, and why strong emotion makes an event more memorable,[32] though not necessarily more accurate. Passing close to where amygdala meets hippocampus might be why Choi encounters episodic memories so violent.

The role of the amygdala in producing antisocial behavior is not so simple. In addition to evoking violent responses, it's also important in evoking empathy. The aforementioned problem with sexual sadists also applies to this part of the brain: Sexual sadists show greater activation here in response to other people's pain—elevated sensitivity, not reduced.[33] Psychopathic indifference or lack of empathy to others may mean that

The Amygdala and Consequences

Janina Scarlet, Travis Adams, & Jenna Busch

Though the Joker can anticipate consequences, they do not worry him.

Typically, the fear of an adverse outcome is processed in the amygdala. However, individuals low in emotional affect may demonstrate lower amygdala activity, which can in turn make them less fearful of negative consequences.[34] Psychopathic individuals appear to have lower amygdala function compared to healthy controls and nonpsychopathic yet antisocial individuals.[35]

Some research studies point to the involvement of limbic structures, such as the amygdala and the hippocampus, in prompting violent and criminal behaviors. Much as surgical removal of the anterior temporal lobe has been shown to reduce violent and criminal behavior in some individuals, as well as to increase social warmth and empathic responses toward others, surgical lesioning of the amygdala may reduce violence and criminal behaviors in individuals with severe aggressive tendencies by helping the individual to regain emotional control.[36]

Could a change to something like the amygdala turn an ordinary person into a villain? The amygdala has been found to be impacted by tumors and vascular malformations or birthmarks/growths, possibly causing abnormal behavior in individuals that resulted in a mass shooting, and its role has been questioned in other types of attacks as well.[37]

the severe psychopath's violence is less amygdala-driven than is the mild or moderate psychopath's. Poison Ivy is capable of much greater anger than the Joker is.

Remember that tower sniper whose autopsy found a pecan-sized tumor in his brain? It was located by his amygdala. To this day, experts

Psychosis: The Insane Brain

Eric D. Wesselmann & Travis Langley

"He's psychotic," Batman tells Vicky Vale of the Joker.[38]

Psychologists consider someone *psychotic* if he or she exhibits delusions, hallucinations, or abnormal patterns of thoughts, speech, or other behavior indicating severe detachment from reality. The most common disorder in this category is schizophrenia, although there are others (e.g., schizoaffective disorder and extreme forms of bipolar disorder).[39] *If* the Joker is psychotic (whether or not that's in addition to being psychopathic, a separate thing), why would that be? He may have inherited a genetic predisposition to psychosis. Doctors might focus on a neurotransmitter imbalance—either too much or too little of a particular chemical may be associated with mental health issues. Excessive *dopamine* is a culprit in many cases of schizophrenia.[40] A neurotransmitter-focused

disagree on whether a tumor pressing against the amygdala could have produced such meticulous, well-planned violence.[41]

Trouble on the Brain

What's the worst thing you've ever done in a dream? What if, one day, only that part of you woke up to face the world? Perhaps a psychotic state such as schizophrenia or a form of dementia might remove restraints holding you back from doing this. Could that piece of you, if unleashed, rain terror on the world? The Joker has argued that he acts as he does because he became truly awake—one interpretation of the vague "super sanity" term that an Arkham Asylum therapist suggested might fit him.[42]

The Brain: Built to Be Bad? 171

treatment involves providing medication that will stabilize the chemical(s) involved. In the noncanon story *Batman: White Knight*, an experimental drug temporarily cures the Joker of his various psychotic tendencies.[43] (Admittedly, it also changes his skin color, something real antipsychotic meds are not known to do.)

What if structural issues in the Joker's brain make him insane? For example, research has found that some individuals diagnosed with schizophrenia have enlarged *ventricles* (fluid-filled gaps in the brains). Medication won't make the brain regrow lost tissue and fill those gaps.[44] If the Joker has received a traumatic brain injury or if the chemicals he falls into make him start losing specific brain tissue, that may contribute to his transformation into the Joker.[45] However, it would not explain such an abrupt change. Furthermore, psychosis caused by brain injury should be cured when the Lazarus Pit heals him, but it only makes him temporarily seem sane for the amount of time it makes other people lose their minds.[46]

NOTES

1. *The Brave and the Bold* #31 (2010).
2. Quoted by Hare (1993/1999), p. 1.
3. Hight (2001/2016); Lavergne (1997). Total includes the shooter's mother and wife, whom he killed the previous night; an unborn child killed during the sniper event; and one man whose injury killed him 35 years later.
4. Whitman (1966).
5. Lavergne (1997).
6. *Detective Comics* #168 (1951).
7. Rosenberg et al. (2009).
8. Koster-Hale & Saxe (2013); Saxe & Kanwisher (2003).
9. Young et al. (2010).
10. Koenigs et al. (2007).
11. Koenigs et al. (2007, 2012).
12. Bartels & Pizarro (2011).
13. *The Brave and the Bold* #31 (2010).
14. Elliott (1978); Gorenstein (1982); Schalling (1978).
15. Goldberg (2001).
16. *Batman* (1989 motion picture).
17. Damasio (1979); Hare (1978, 1984).
18. Müller et al. (2008).

19. Schulze et al. (2013).
20. Verbeke et al. (2011).
21. *Detective Comics* #33 (1939).
22. Harenski et al. (2012).
23. American Psychiatric Association (1987).
24. As of American Psychiatric Association (2000).
25. Kiehl (2014); Kiehl et al. (2006).
26. *The Brave and the Bold* #31 (2010).
27. Czerner (2002).
28. Siegel (2005); Siegel et al. (2007).
29. Davis & Whalen (2001); Roberts & Nagel (1996).
30. Gas introduced in *Batman* #189 (1967). See Langley (2012), Case File 5–1, "The Scarecrow," for analysis.
31. *Batman: Legends of the Dark Knight* #65 (1994).
32. Levine & Burgess (1997); Nairne et al. (2007).
33. Harenski et al. (2012).
34. Kiehl (2006).
35. Gao & Raine (2010); Glenn (2011); Kiehl (2006).
36. Kiehl (2006).
37. Kluger (2013a, 2013b).
38. *Batman* (1989 motion picture).
39. Glahn et al. (2006); Heckers et al. (2013).
41. Frederick (2016).
42. *Arkham Asylum: A Serious House on Serious Earth* (1989); *Batman* #663 (2007).
42. Carlsson et al. (1999).
43. *Batman: White Knight* #1–8 (2017–2018).
44. e.g., Davis et al. (1998); Weinberger et al. (1980).
45. Poca et al. (2005); Reveley et al. (1984).
46. *Batman: Legends of the Dark Knight* #145 (2001).

CASE REPORT III (1974):
RISK MANAGEMENT ASSESSMENT
FOR THE LEGALLY INSANE

This marks patient's fifteenth admission to Arkham Hospital, having successfully escaped on several prior occasions.[1] Patient's history is significant for violence, including multiple incidents of homicide. Diagnostic formulation comes by way of the court-appointed psychiatrist, who diagnosed him with Schizophrenic Disorder, Undifferentiated Type; Antisocial Personality Disorder; and Narcissistic Personality Disorder. I am a bit skeptical of his primary diagnosis of Schizophrenic Disorder.[2] First, it is rare for Schizophrenia to first surface outside of late adolescence and early adulthood. Certainly, it is possible he has experienced undiagnosed Schizophrenia for years, though this appears unlikely given his significant history of residence within secure facilities where such symptoms would presumably have been witnessed firsthand. I suppose it is additionally possible he has experienced an extended prodromal phase without obvious psychosis, but, again, this would be exceedingly rare. Second, there is limited evidence of many hallmark features of Schizophrenia, including hallucinations and delusions. There is, perhaps, some evidence of disorganization of thought and behavior. His affect is bizarre, taking on an almost "silly," juvenile quality. He presents with oddities of behavior, including frequent, maniacal laughter and facial expressions which are inconsistent with topics of conversation, such as smiling while being questioned about objectively heinous acts. Regardless, his diagnoses have led to a legal finding of insanity and court-ordered treatment at Arkham.

Of further concern is that any psychosis he may experience is superimposed over a personality structure characterized by antisocial and narcissistic traits. Though this results in current diagnoses of Antisocial and Narcissistic Personality Disorders, he is perhaps best characterized as a psychopath or a malignant narcissist. Though a personality such as his might be capable of restraint when necessary, active psychosis may only serve to erode his impulse control, especially given his apparent proclivity toward disorganization and

173

behavioral disinhibition. Furthermore, should he experience hallucinations or delusions, especially those in which he perceives himself to be in danger, interprets others to be working against him, or hears specific orders to commit violence—whether directly through voices or indirectly by inferring messages from other sources—his personality structure is of such configuration that he would have significantly decreased compunction about lashing out violently.

I have little faith in our ability to treat his personality, though he may benefit from processing the potential motivations behind his acts. Further, the process of therapy may help further clarify his diagnosis and determine the degree to which his behavior can be attributed to his personality structure versus psychosis, as well as assist in development of future plans to manage his risk. Further, I would certainly urge that he comply with any recommendations for treatment with psychotropic medications, as well as any other plans developed by psychiatry. Treatment of any potential underlying psychosis could reduce the danger he poses to society to some degree, or at least bring us to a situation where he is less unpredictable. At worst, perhaps the medications will have a sedating effect, rendering him less inclined to expend his energy in violent endeavors.

As far as milieu goes, I recommend that he reside on a smaller unit in a single-occupancy room, both to limit potential noxious stimuli as well as to reduce the likelihood of injury to his peers.

Given his history of violence both in the community and within secure settings, I would recommend against any form of independent privileges. Rather, I believe he will require significant supervision at all times to ensure the safety of Arkham staff, patients, and the public at large.

Thank you for referring this case to me.

Regards,

Senior Staff Psychologist

Notes

1. *Detective Comics* #251 (1973) makes the first mention of the Joker having "escaped from the state hospital for the criminally insane," which is then referred to as Arkham Hospital for the first time in *Batman* #258 (1974).

2. The American Psychiatric Association's DSM-II (1968) was available at the beginning of this period, and major revisions soon followed in the 6th printing (1974).

IV.
HARLEQUIN

THE HARLEQUIN OF HATE

"Harlequin of Hate"
—title of scene in which Harley learns
the Joker plans to kill her[1]

"Repent, Harlequin!" said the Ticktockman.
"Get stuffed!" the Harlequin replied, sneering.
—from a short story by author Harlan Ellison[2]

"Inside. He's laughing red and black and red and
black till there's nothing left to laugh."
—actor Heath Ledger, from his Joker diary[3]

NOTES

1. *Batman* #663 (2007).
2. Ellison (1965/2016), p. 498.
3. Broadview Pictures (2014); Hooten (2015).

10

Lies: Why Lie on the Couch?

BILLY SAN JUAN & TRAVIS LANGLEY

"One who deceives will always find those
who allow themselves to be deceived."
—author/diplomat Niccolò Machiavelli,[1]
for whom Machiavellianism is named[2]

THE JOKER LIES. He is so bold in his deceptions, so frank with his opinions, and so skilled at using truths to cut deep that he manages to convince some people he's just being brutally honest. Some characters and even real people who have witnessed the Joker spouting obvious falsehoods may nonetheless buy into the notion that "The Joker is the only one who will never lie to you because he is consistent about his philosophy."[3] The film composer who said that was referring to the same film in which the Joker tricks his own henchmen into killing each other, gives conflicting explanations for his facial scars, switches addresses to mislead Batman and the police, and asks Harvey Dent, "Do I really look like a guy with a plan?" right while he's in the middle of executing an intricately woven plan.[4]

Why does anybody ever believe him? Shouldn't people see through somebody like that? Shouldn't a therapist? The Joker charms Dr. Harleen Quinzel by tempting her with secrets, flattering her intelligence, and making her feel special when he seemingly opens up to her about his childhood with one of many lies about his past.[5] Why does he mislead everyone, including his therapists, and why does any therapist fall for it? This is a real issue that clinicians must face. Clients lie to therapists for many reasons and in many ways—a problem compounded when the client is psychopathic.

Content: What

Admittedly, Arkham Asylum's residents have not chosen to go there for the sake of their mental well-being. Clients who enter therapy *involuntarily*, whether under court order or simply to appease the people in their lives, lack insight and motivation to change. Within the legal system, they may acknowledge mental disorders only long enough to say they weren't responsible before but they're all better now and should therefore go free. Outside the legal system, involuntary clients lack that incentive to admit anything's wrong: "All of these patients have in common their claim that there is nothing really wrong with them."[6] Even among those who actively seek therapy, voluntarily spending time and money in hopes of improving their lives, most admit to having lied in therapy[7] and the few who say they have not could be lying about that. Why mislead the professionals hired to help?

And what are the clients lying about?

Lies about Symptoms

Misreporting one's condition or misrepresenting it in nonverbal ways can serve the function of *malingering* (feigning symptoms that do not exist—false positive) and *underreporting* (hiding symptoms that do exist—false negative).[8] Does the Joker feign his symptoms or does he hide them? Yes.

In different eras, he has both feigned insanity to get himself into a mental hospital and feigned recovery to get out of one.[9] Unconcerned about truth, he expresses or conceals whatever information serves him at the moment. In the film *The Dark Knight*, for example, he both feigns a generalized impulsivity and hides the complexity of his horrifying plans in order to make others underestimate him and doubt their own convictions. Surely a man wearing a nurse costume and sloppy clown paint can't be a mastermind, they might think. In the pivotal interrogation room scene, he may underreport his pain when he laughs and taunts, "You have nothing! Nothing to threaten me with. Nothing to do with all your strength." Admittedly, he might be showing the indifference to pain common among many psychopaths, but it is also possible that the laughter is helping him hide his experience of physical pain in order to cast doubt on the masked vigilante's otherwise steadfast resolve. Displaying a contradictory emotion, whether in the interrogation room or in a clinical setting, may help the individual hide a feeling and maybe even help that individual believe that the feigned emotion is the real one.

Lies about Life

Therapy is a process of vulnerability. In order for the therapist to help, the client must be (or become) willing to discuss intimate parts of his or her life. The process can be uncomfortable, if not painful. If proper rapport is not carefully constructed, clients may be tempted to be dishonest in reporting their symptoms. They may construct false narratives for various purposes. The client who's trying to make life sound worse than it really is may deemphasize whatever is good in life (such as available social support and resources) while sensationalizing whatever is bad (such as medical conditions or psychosocial and environmental stressors), whereas the one trying to make life sound better can do the opposite. The deceptive client may do so through omission, exaggeration, juxtaposition, distortion, utter fabrication, denial, or some mix thereof.

The most common lies in therapy may be *lies of omission*, deliberately leaving out key information in order to mislead the other people and sketching a selectively imprecise picture of the facts.[10] The client who complains about Mom's nagging may give the therapist an inaccurate impression by failing to mention the client's broken promises or all the times the mother tolerated such passive aggression without complaint. When the Joker bemoans how Batman beats him up, but refrains from telling Harley that it was to stop Mister J. from shooting more people, the villain has committed a lie of omission. Because the purpose is to mislead, it's still deception.

Lying through exaggeration amplifies a truth by adding lies to it or overstating details. When the Joker tells Harley that his father abused him, he might base this claim on facts while exaggerating the severity of mistreatment. Whoever the Joker is, early in life he would have been a little boy born to human parents. An exaggeration of actual memory can be easier to keep track of than total fiction would, and might be more believable because the liar draws on genuine feelings, fleshes the description out with real details, or answers questions without pausing to make up every facet on the spot.

Lying through juxtaposition and lying through distortion, like exaggeration, includes accurate details but in incorrect combinations or with distorted details. Each part is correct in and of itself but, arranged in a certain way, they mislead. When the Joker gives Batman and the police the addresses where they can find Rachel and Harvey and tells them they can only save one of them, he switches the addresses. By saying each person is in the other one's location, he tricks Batman into rescuing the wrong person and thus dooming whomever he most wanted to save.[11]

The baldfaced lie brazenly, blatantly, and unashamedly presents a falsehood regardless of whether it reflects reality or not.[12] Insisting he's no schemer to someone who should know that he definitely is one would make the Joker either a baldfaced liar or deluded about himself.[13] It could go either way.

"Now I can be theatrical and maybe even a little rough, but one thing I am not is a killer," the Joker tells Gotham City on TV, right after mentioning a gang boss he'd killed. Then he uses another lie, unabashedly pretending that he isn't wearing flesh-colored makeup to hide his white skin, in order to boast that he's more honest than Batman: "I have taken off my makeup. Let's see if you can take off yours." To citizens lured by his promise of free money that night, he proclaims himself to be the person they should trust, right before he releases deadly gas and starts killing them.[14]

A lie common in therapeutic situations is false agreement, a.k.a. positive resistance. Adolescents are particularly prone to saying, "Yes," to ideas they disagree with or to requests they do not intend to follow through on.[15] Falsely agreeing can feel like a way to avoid criticism or debate, and when it comes to things they don't want to do, they may claim they forgot or did not get the opportunity. Growing up, Harley witnesses many examples of her father's false agreement as he repeatedly fails to keep promises, and yet she keeps clinging to hope that he might come through. Seeing through this behavior of his takes her a long time, and this may have predisposed her to look for the best in the worst of people.[16]

In cases of *self-deception*, people may not realize they're misleading others, because they're already lying to themselves. People may unconsciously mislead themselves or creatively interpret events to the point of *distortion* in order to protect their self-esteem.[17] When the Joker yells at Harley for his own decision to turn the Jokermobile down the wrong street despite her attempt to warn him,[18] blaming her lets him avoid seeing that he has chosen poorly. Some degree of self-deception is normal and possibly necessary for mental health. Sometimes you mislead yourself, accepting *positive illusions* or favorable misperceptions, especially about your ability to control events around you, in order to keep harsh reality from crushing your soul. You have to make yourself get out of bed in the morning.[19] During Harley's time with the Joker, she engages in a great deal of self-deception to manage her *cognitive dissonance*, the disharmony over holding conflicting ideas.[20]

The Benefits

One of the things that can stump Batman about the Joker is that the clown's motives at times seem unfathomable. Chapter 2 touched on intrinsic and extrinsic motivators for either lying about or misremembering personal history unrelated to mental health treatment or criminal activity, both of which matter when looking at those deemed legally insane. Psychopaths, in particular, may lie for reasons even they may not know.

Intrinsic Motivation: Inner Benefits

A person may lie for *intrinsic reasons,* in that the lie itself satisfies inner motivation through feelings such as comfort, relief, satisfaction, amusement, or power.

People who lie compulsively (a symptom called *mythomania*) may feel so uncomfortable about the truth that a lie feels safer. If someone dislikes the lie, the liar doesn't feel personally judged, but if someone dislikes that person's truth, that can be unpleasant and detrimental to self-esteem. A lie can relieve emotional suffering in the moment, even if it creates greater problems in the long run.[21]

However, psychopaths don't have that problem. They're indifferent to the value of truth. They might lie habitually but not compulsively because they simply say whatever suits the moment, regardless of whether it's true or not. Many times, though, the lie is rewarding, maybe even entertaining, when it gives the liar a feeling of power over someone or a sense of achievement for pulling one over on him or her. Regular liars of any type overestimate the frequency with which others believe them, failing to realize that many people choose not to expend the time or energy to call them on it. Unfortunately for those who do choose to call them on it, thinking they can throw the psychopath off his or her game as seen in so many movies and TV shows, they're still playing the game, and that alone is a win for the psychopath. It would be difficult to have any conversation with the Joker without him feeling like he has already drawn the other person into his web.

The psychopath, unconcerned about truth and untruth, is rarely fazed by being caught in a lie. The psychopath tends to view any social exchange as a "feeding opportunity," a contest of wills that will have only one winner. "Their motives are to manipulate and take, ruthlessly and without remorse."[22] Regardless of any external gain they might take from the exchange, the motivation is intrinsic because it's about taking for the sheer sake of taking. The Joker, in particular, would derive amusement from any reaction he might elicit.

Extrinsic Motivation: External Gain

Clients may also be dishonest in therapy sessions for the sake of secondary gain—*extrinsic motivation*. In other words, they have ulterior motives. Instead of lying for its own sake, they're out to get something. Specific settings, such as forensic or custody assessments, may offer a secondary gain for skewing the truth. Such a secondary gain may involve reducing a sentence, obtaining custody, or razing Gotham to the ground. The Penguin enjoys greater success than the Joker when it comes to sometimes fooling authorities into believing that he has reformed, prompting the authorities to release him back into society.[23]

Some external gains are more abstract and may offer inner benefits as well: Intrinsic and extrinsic rewards may be intertwined. In trying to make an analogy about the nature of the Joker, Alfred Pennyworth tells Bruce Wayne about bandits who stole precious stones only to discard them. The bandits' motivation appears to be intrinsic satisfaction over the achievement, as though they were unconcerned about the gems' extrinsic worth. Then again, by misdirecting outsiders by stealing objects not of interest to themselves personally, they may get an extrinsic reward in terms of the impact they made upon those outsiders.[24] When similarly "only burning my half" of a mound of money and acting unconcerned about its value, why does the Joker bother making a production out of its destruction? Deception is executed through more than words.

A Clinician's Concerns

The success of therapy relies on a genuine, open, and trusting relationship between the provider and the patient. However, there are many reasons that a patient may not fully be honest when speaking with the therapist. Purposeful deception is not uncommon. Even in therapeutic relationships where a strong and supportive rapport is established, complete honesty is rare, due to perceived taboos in areas such as sexuality. Dishonesty can serve the intrinsic purpose of simply making the client feel more comfortable. In the case of someone such as the Joker, it's all part of the fun.

There are many instances in which lying to a therapist may provide a positive or beneficial result. This may occur via the feigning of an illness, the intentional misconstruing of fact, deliberately omitting certain facts, or in other ways. The gain to be had via intentionally feigning illness varies depending on the situation. In certain cases, clients risk incarceration, loss of custody of their children, or some other punishment. Therapists have several tools at their disposal to identify when secondary gain is a variable during therapy or assessment. In therapy, clinicians are trained in gently addressing the existence of possible secondary gain as well as mitigating a client's reports related to his or her attainment of that gain. Validation of the gain, and the emotional motivations behind it, are key in letting someone know that it is understandable to lie, though that may not be the best course of action. In assessment, various assessments have particular methods and measures to identify malingering. Effectiveness varies, and no method is perfect. Though the specifics of these measures must remain confidential to protect the integrity of these assessments, they exist to raise a red flag about possible lying for the purpose of secondary gain. It's too easy to grow overconfident in one's own ability to spot such red flags. People overestimate their ability to know when others are telling the truth, just as young Dr. Harleen Quinzel enters Arkham certain that she can handle herself but the Joker sells one lie to her after another.[25]

A prominent personality psychologist asserted that, out of the many psychological needs that drive human behavior, three shape the majority of human behavior: *need for affiliation* (NAffil), *need for power* (NPow), and *need for achievement* (NAch[26]). A client high in need for affiliation, the need to belong with others, or the personality trait of *agreeableness*, motivated to get along with others, may give the therapist answers that seem socially acceptable or that might otherwise earn the therapist's approval. The affiliation-motivated therapist might believe lies for the same reason that an affiliation-motivated client dispenses them. Even one as intelligent as Harley Quinn will more readily trust others, respond to flattery, and believe lies from people whose acceptance they want.[27] Needs for power and achievement, especially power, motivate those like the Joker to take advantage of that. Harley functions better when she gains some acceptance from strong individuals, such as Poison Ivy and Power Girl, who befriend her for other reasons.[28] *Social desirability* motivates most people, but especially those high in need for affiliation, to present themselves in socially acceptable ways and to want others to like them. This is especially true when those others actively evaluate them and get to know them on a personal level. The person who says something to be shocking rather than likable, as the Joker so frequently does, is motivated more by desire for *interpersonal power*—in this case, the power to manipulate someone else's reactions. The Joker says at times that he wants to make people laugh[29] but, except during his Clown Prince period, his actions say that he's mainly out to evoke fear.

Dishonesty serves a purpose, usually several purposes at the same time. It can be a protective measure, ensuring that we are safe from shame within ourselves or judgment by others. It can be a safeguard, an act of caution against someone we do not quite trust yet. It may even be an unconscious act, a lie we are unaware of to ourselves or others. Dishonesty can be a subversive tool to serve a need or desire, which may sometimes be chaotic or harmful.

Fear and Shame

Fear and shame may be the most common reasons clients lie to their therapists.[30]

Fear is a survival mechanism present from the beginning of life, a feeling of alarm that prepares us for possible danger, whereas *shame* is learned, a feeling of humiliation or distress stemming from awareness of wrong or foolish behavior.[31] They may go together when the person is afraid of entering a situation that can cause shame. Either may cause a person to mislead a therapist. The client might fear being caught, exposed, or judged. Also, knowledge that the therapist works for the penal system may make the client fear potential consequences for whatever he or she might reveal. Psychopathic inmates lack shame, but nonpsychopaths may feel great embarrassment about what they've done or about being seen in lockup. The Joker exhibits a response different from fear when placed in a dangerous situation. His reaction is in line with research that those with antisocial behavior do not experience a cognitive deficit when experiencing fear,[32] and the man has no shame.

Therapy clients may experience shame if they believe that the therapist will judge them for their thoughts, actions, or emotions. To avoid this negative experience, these clients may underreport their symptoms, deny problems, and misrepresent facts. The Joker does not feel shame because he lacks the empathic response to care about other people's judgments. If anything, he takes pleasure in knowing that other people are beholden to the socio-emotional constructs that cause shame because it is a tool of manipulation he can use for his own chaotic purposes. Harley, however, is capable of feeling shame at times because of her criminal actions, which may be why she criticizes therapy and the concept of trauma so harshly during a therapeutic session: She's trying to avoid the truth about her deeds and needs.[33]

Lack of Trust

The quality of the relationship between therapist and client, known as *rapport,* is an important aspect of the therapeutic process. Therapists build rapport by actively listening to the client with sensitivity and empathy. However, this process takes time to develop. In some cases, it may not develop at all, due to variables outside the control of either therapist or client. Some examples may include a patient's previous trauma, a therapist's personal countertransference, and pragmatic concerns such as inability to schedule consistent sessions. In cases where rapport is not established, patients may not trust the therapist enough to reveal deeper-rooted issues. This does not necessarily mean that they dislike the therapist, but rather that they do not feel comfortable with that level of vulnerability.

An examination of the Joker's relationship to others, and trust itself, would be fascinating to explore. However, it is an impossible discussion to hold because we simply do not understand the Joker's motivations. His cognitive mechanisms are an enigma. Even though we can't examine his thoughts, we can examine his behaviors. The Joker is able to establish a false sense of rapport with Dr. Quinzel, and uses this as a tool of exploitation. It can be argued that he uses this tool to recruit his henchmen as well. Such actions are indicative of a Machiavellian mastery of manipulation.

Symptoms of antisocial personality disorder, characterized by a "pervasive pattern of disregard for, and violation of, the rights of others,"[34] may include interpersonal manipulativeness as a way to hurt others or simply to get what the person wants. The Joker repeatedly demonstrates the full range of antisocial personality disorder symptoms, including "aggression to people and animals, destruction of property, deceitfulness or theft, or serious violation of rules."[35] Whereas psychopathy is classically defined in terms of how a person feels about morality and other people, this personality disorder is more about what the antisocial individual actively does. One view of the Psychopathy Checklist is that half of it assesses traditional, underlying psychopathy and the other half looks at antisocial actions.

Psychopathic Fun

The Joker's most obvious motives for lying are to manipulate others and to entertain himself. To derive enjoyment from purposely deceiving people must surely indicate a lack of remorse toward and empathy for those he is deceiving. Each of the dark triad traits[36] indicates a predisposition for exploitive, hostile, or ill-intentioned behaviors, similar to those exhibited by the Joker.[37] For some modern depictions of the Joker, whose intentions lie in sending an anarchistic message,[38] there is an added factor of enjoyment in their deception exposing hypocrisy and weakness in others.

Lack of Insight

Therapy patients may provide misinformation unknowingly when they are unaware of their thoughts/actions, or unaware of the ramifications of those thoughts/actions. For example, some perpetrators of domestic violence may truly believe that they are "disciplining" their significant other, and furthermore that their aggressive acts are not harmful. In cases like this, the language that a therapist uses is very important to help distinguish outright dishonesty from a skewed perception of reality. For example, a therapist may use words such as "punish" or "lay hands on" instead of "punch" or "choke," because in the patient's perception there was no punching or choking. If this is true, some of the Joker's dishonesty may be unintentional because he truly does not grasp the level of harm in his anarchic behaviors.

Stages of Change

When a client lacks insight, a framework known as the *transtheoretical model*, a.k.a. *stages of change*, can be helpful for progression toward a positive prognosis. Psychotherapy patients move through a series of stages in the course of modifying an unwanted behavior or thought process. Though fluid, each stage has a ballpark range of length. Movement toward the subsequent stage relies on a number of factors, including the therapeutic relationship, situational factors, and other variables.

- **Precontemplation:** Patients in *precontemplation* (not yet contemplating) do not intend to change their thoughts or behaviors, and they may not even be fully aware of the effect of their choices on psychosocial functioning. Many patients in this stage include those mandated to therapy (for example, through a court order), patients who enter therapy in response to a recommendation of a friend/family member, and patients who

A Clinical Counter: Spotting a Lie

Batman is the world's greatest detective. Like a detective, clinicians and evaluators must harness a wide variety of skills, tools, and experiences to spot when a client may be omitting or fabricating information. Had Dr. Quinzel utilized these skills and tools, she may have been able to identify the lies and half-truths that the Joker has used to manipulate her.

Consultation: One misconception about clinical psychology is that the therapist works alone as a solitary purveyor of talk therapy. Despite media depictions, clinicians regularly seek consultation and supervision, especially in cases where they feel a strong countertransference toward a patient. This consultation allows the therapist to process his or her thoughts and feelings, which may be interfering with treatment. It offers the therapist an objective view of his or her treatment approaches, to see if they are actually working. Consultation serves as an ethical safety net to catch any possible boundary violations. Were Dr. Quinzel to have properly consulted others regarding the Joker's clinical case, a supervisor or colleague may have helped her recognize the emotional manipulation taking place.

Collateral Information: The Joker's criminal file is an extensive index of various crimes. Properly assessing his case file should have helped Dr. Quinzel foresee the dangers of falling for his charming ways and would have revealed lies he'd told to others. This step allows for a well-rounded understanding of the client's issues and the way those issues affect his or her psychosocial functioning.

Psychological Testing: Psychological testing is commonly misconstrued as "a way to read people's thoughts." This is not the case. Instead, psychological testing is a method of objectively measuring symptomology, the impact of that symptomology, or a person's way of observing/interpreting the world around him or her. A battery of psychological tests may have helped Dr. Quinzel understand the Joker's worldview, and in doing so could have provided several warnings about his devious motives.

feel like "something is off" but cannot identify what is occurring. Patients in this stage may be resistant to treatment, or dismiss it completely. The Joker may lie in the precontemplation stage, wherein he does not intend to take action and is unaware that his behaviors are problematic.

- **Contemplation:** Patients who are contemplative recognize the issue at hand, and furthermore are beginning to be motivated to change. They may weigh the pros and cons of behavior change and begin to comprehend that the benefits of change outweigh the discomfort of the process. Some patients may begin to procrastinate during this stage or miss appointments altogether due to the discomfort at recognizing that their current method of psychosocial functioning is maladaptive. When the Joker tempts Dr. Quinzel with the idea that he might be open to a therapeutic dialogue, he is signaling that he is in this stage, even though he really is not.

- **Preparation:** Patients move forward when they are ready, motivated, and willing to take action in the near future. They may have already taken small steps in modifying their behaviors or thoughts, and they are open to solidifying these plans with the therapist to create a short-term goal. These goals include observable and measurable achievements, such as exercising on a schedule, reaching out to social supports, reduction in drug use, or practicing anger management techniques. Here, the Joker reverses therapeutic roles, as is demonstrated visually when he's taking notes while Dr. Harleen Quinzel now sits on the couch. She is getting prepared to make a transformation.

- **Action:** The action stage occurs in a span of months, during which the goals set in the preparation stage are being met. Dr. Quinzel takes action by becoming Harley Quinn, but the Joker does not take action toward become a better human being. At other times in her life, though, Harley takes action by rejecting the Joker and trying to become a better person.

- **Maintenance:** The maintenance stage of change happens after a lifestyle modification has occurred and the patient is working to prevent reversion to his or her previous functioning. As Harley mentions to her mother, though, this can be difficult.[39]

Lying on the Couch

The Joker would be a terrible therapy patient. He would tell the truth when it benefits him, lie when it entertains him, and speak in half-truths as though it were his fluent language. Furthermore, the remorselessness he has displayed throughout his career indicates that addressing the deception itself as a symptom would not be a productive avenue. Arguably, deception is part of the Joker's persona. He may even argue that it is one of the things that bind him and Batman in their eternal dance of justice and crime. And though Batman may use deception to protect those he loves and strike fear into criminals, the Joker uses deception for one very singular reason: It's fun.

NOTES

1. Machiavelli (1532/1903), p. 70.
2. Christie & Geis (1970); Paulhus & Williams (2002).
3. Composer Hans Zimmer, from Bentley (2009) radio transcript.
4. *The Dark Knight* (2008 motion picture).
5. *The Batman Adventures: Mad Love* (1994).
6. Karson (2016).
7. Howes (2016).
8. Malingering—Berlin (2007); Rogers (2008). Underreporting—Franco et al. (2016).
9. *Batman* #74 (1952–1953); *Batman: The Dark Knight* #3 (1986).
10. Kleiman (2013).
11. *The Dark Knight* (2008 motion picture).
12. Kolvachik (2014).
13. *The Dark Knight* (2008 motion picture). "Supervillains are the dreamers and schemers of the fictional realm."— Fingeroth (2004), p. 162.

14. *Batman* (1989 motion picture).
15. Pickhardt (2015).
16. *Gotham City Sirens* #7 (2010).
17. Monts et al. (1977).
18. *Batman: The Animated Series*, episode 1–47, "Harley & Ivy" (January 18, 1993).
19. Collard et al. (2016); Goleman (1989); Kaufman et al. (2018); Makridakis & Moleskis (2015); Taylor (1989).
20. Festinger (1957).
21. Linehan (2014).
22. Hare (1993/1999), p. 145.
23. e.g., *Batman Annual* #11 (1987).
24. *The Dark Knight* (2008 motion picture).
25. *The Batman Adventures: Mad Love* (1994); *Batman: Harley Quinn* (1999); *Suicide Squad* #6–7 (2012).
26. McClelland (1978).
27. Costa & McCrae (1991).
28. *Batman: Harley Quinn* (1999); *Harley Quinn and Power Girl* #1–6 (2015–2016).
29. *Detective Comics* #62 (1942); *Batman* #57 (1950); *Batman: The Killing Joke* (1988).
30. DePaulo & Kashy (1998); Howes (2016); Kolod (2019).
31. Barrett (2018).
32. Hoppenbrouwers & Bulten (2016).
33. *Heroes in Crisis* #1 (2018), #5–6 (2019).
34. American Psychiatric Association (2013), p. 659.
35. American Psychiatric Association (2013), p. 659.
36. Jonason et al. (2014)
37. Jones & Paulhus (2017)
38. *The Dark Knight* (2008 motion picture).
39. *Harley Quinn* #51 (2018).

EXPLAINING THE JOKE 10-1:
PROFILER MARK E. SAFARIK, PART 1

Travis Langley

Mark Safarik's law enforcement career spans more than 30 years, including 23 years in the Federal Bureau of Investigation, where he became one of the most respected members of the Bureau's Behavioral Analysis Unit (BAU) as a criminal profiler. An internationally recognized expert in the analysis and interpretation of criminal behavior, Safarik led the consultation efforts on many high-profile national and international violent crime cases and has lectured numerous police forces around the world, sharing his expertise in the analysis of homicide and complex crime scene behavior. He has reviewed and consulted on thousands of violent crime investigations.[1]

He has also analyzed the criminals of Gotham City on convention panels at WonderCon and San Diego Comic-Con International, applying his knowledge of offender motivation and behavior to the fictional examples.[2] Since 2008, he has been a consultant on popular TV series, such as *CSI: Las Vegas*, *Criminal Minds*, and *Bones*. The Biography Channel's series *Killer Instinct* featured Safarik revisiting challenging cases he'd faced in the BAU, sharing insight into the science of behavioral analysis.[3]

During our interview for this book, our discussion about the adversarial relationship between the Joker and Batman veered into consideration of how the Joker sees Harley Quinn. Safarik stressed that the investigator does not romanticize the perpetrator.

Mark E. Safarik: It doesn't mean that when I interview them I'm not friendly or trying to build a level of rapport, because I'm trying to get information. And a lot of times they are, too. You get a psychopath, and he's pumping you for information as much as you are from him. It's being aware of that dynamic—that would be really key.

Travis Langley: That's an important part of the Joker stories, when they show him manipulating Batman or Harley Quinn. Especially in the post-9/11 stories, stories depict him manipulating everybody around him.

Safarik: I would say that's true, because the Joker is really a pure psychopath. So, in his universe, the way that he looks at the world is basically "What's mine is mine, and what's yours is mine. I will act friendly with you and I will do things for you, but everything has an ulterior motive and that ulterior motive is for the benefit of me, and I don't really care about you. And when you're not of any more use to me, then I will discard you." But they're very careful about it. They're great mimics. They can read the notes, but they can't hear the music. So they know when people are really crying, emotional, and really distraught. They see that, they can mimic that, but they can't really feel it. The Joker is great at that. He's great at manipulating his enemies and the people around him like Harley Quinn, not because he has any care or concern for them but because they serve a purpose for him. He'll be like that as long as he's getting what he wants. Once that's over with, he can kill the person and not have any qualms about it, because once they've served their usefulness, they're just an object to be used. You don't have any emotional attachment to an object. You can kill the object and your affect can completely remain flat. And that's what people have a hard time believing. They want to see the Joker through the eyes that they have—that they have friends and people that they care about, and that the Joker is in that position. With Harley Quinn, they want to see that he cares about her, not as a friend but in sort of a romantic way because she's a woman. But that's not the way he thinks about life at all. That's not the way the Joker perceives life. It's all about what's best for him: "What does it get me to do that?" and "I'm happy to do it, as long as it advances my position."

Langley: There are people, especially young ones, who see the film *Suicide Squad* and, from that, romanticize the Joker/Harley Quinn relationship. Part of it is because, at the very end, the Joker breaks Harley out of jail.[4] The only way that scene works for a character, a pure psychopath like the Joker that you were talking about, is if he's just doing that to use her for something else. Then it makes sense.

Safarik: Exactly. That's right. There's no altruistic motive for doing that. But see the problem: For most people, they don't think like that. Most people aren't psychopaths. *[Laughs]* They want to ascribe those kinds of personalities and motives and altruistic thought processes like they have to these characters, and you can't.

Interview continues in Explaining the Joke 13–1: Profiler Mark E. Safarik, Part 2 on page 259.

NOTES

1. Forensic Behavior Services (n.d.).
2. e.g., Bender et al. (2012).
3. Starting with episode 1–01, "A Killer Among Us" (September 17, 2011).
4. *Suicide Squad* (2017 motion picture).

11

Relationship Abuse:
When the Joker Isn't Funny

WIND GOODFRIEND & RYAN HARDER

"With stars in her eyes and beliefs about love in her heart, a woman can fall in love with a man and a dream."

—clinical social worker Karen Rosen[1]

"Love can overlook a traffic ticket, but can it forgive a robbery? A murder? What is the worst thing a person can do and still be loved?"

—Harley Quinn[2]

RELATIONSHIP VIOLENCE IS not the victim's fault. No child dreams of growing up, falling in love, and getting belittled and beaten by his or her partner. Yet this situation applies to about one in four women and one in seven men.[3] Attractive, intelligent women and men of every social class, ethnicity, and sexual orientation find themselves in love with people who abuse them—just as the Joker abuses Harley Quinn. Understanding the psychology of victim perceptions and experiences may be the key that unlocks the mystery of how so many people find themselves trapped by abusive love. What are the cognitive processes relevant to falling in love with the wrong person—and of escaping the trap? Why does Harley love the Joker despite everything, and how does she eventually get out?

Created by writer Paul Dini and artist Bruce W. Timm as a sidekick for the Joker in *Batman: The Animated Series*, Harley quickly became a rich and compelling character in her own right. Details of Harley and the Joker's tempestuous and problematic relationship—and the psychological forces behind it—have varied slightly during decades of adaptations, reboots, and retellings. However, the basic story has remained the same since its initial depiction in the award-winning comic *The Batman Adventures: Mad Love*. Its flashback shows Harleen Quinzel as a staff member at Arkham Asylum who falls in love with the Joker, entering into a romantic, criminal, and abusive relationship with the Clown Prince of Crime. The evolution of this relationship reflects several phenomena discovered in psychological research on how and why such contentious dynamics occur.

The Foundation of Childhood

Our individual psychological experiences are rooted in our childhood. *Intergenerational transmission* of behavioral patterns occurs when what we observe and learn from our family of origin becomes repeated in our adult life.[4] In essence, many psychologists believe that our childhood patterns become implicit templates for what we expect and respond to later in life. One of several contradictory accounts of her background depicts Harleen as a little girl with younger brothers to look after, a mother who earned an MD and gave up her medical practice to support her husband, and a father who is a good-hearted criminal. She is told by her parents that any unhappiness she feels will be rewarded if she learns to "be patient, be a good girl and help out."[5] Harleen's ability to sacrifice her own needs for those she loves, her perception that criminals can be good guys who are misunderstood by the world, and the idea that she will be most loved if she serves a silent and supportive role are thus embedded deep in her psyche. Make sacrifices, stay in a servile role, and don't ask for much—that's how you earn love.

For Harleen, her mother and father frequently engage in shouting matches during conflicts. By observing this, she learns that arguments are an expected part of love—but she also learns that the conflict is supposed to be temporary. "It was like they both had built up a lot of pressure inside and when they shouted, a safety valve opened to let it out. Then they could find their way back to okay."[6] The arguments were always followed by apologies and promises, giving Harleen an enduring and optimistic view that love eventually conquers all.

Harleen learns that if you can make people laugh, they let their guard down, allowing you to trick and manipulate them. A related lesson from her childhood is that people will underestimate her if she takes on a "ditzy" characterization of her true self, including a blank facial expression, high voice, and exaggerated Brooklyn accent. As a girl, she also realizes that "when you made people laugh, they felt good and they liked you—they didn't want to hurt you."[7] All these lessons become relevant when Harleen Quinzel becomes Harley Quinn, the seemingly flaky sidekick of the Joker. But they become particularly poignant when she uses them to suppress her inner brilliance and self-esteem simply to avoid the Joker's abuse.

Seduction: Beauty and the Beast

How do intelligent, relatively well-adjusted people fall into abusers' hands? This question has been addressed in several psychological studies, but one of the most intriguing is an analysis of interviews with 22 women who either were currently in abusive heterosexual relationships or had successfully escaped.[8] The women were young—between 16 and 32 years old, a range that would include Harley (because a psychiatric resident who went directly from high school to college to medical school would be in her mid- to late 20s). One of the central questions in the interview asked why they were initially attracted to the person who eventually became their abuser.

The researcher then identified themes in their answers that she called the *process of seduction*, "forces that initially pulled these women into their relationships making them dependent and more likely to tolerate abuse once it began."[9] While several of these processes were identified, one in particular is relevant to Harley Quinn: the *Beauty and the Beast romantic fantasy*. Based on the children's fairy tale, this fantasy centers on the idea that patient, true love can "cure" people who appear to be angry and abusive, eventually healing them and allowing their inner "Prince Charming" to emerge. In Harley's case, she wasn't just hoping for any prince—she was hoping for the Clown Prince.

According to these findings, it is the semblance of vulnerability and pain that draws some people toward abusive men. Some victims hold the illusion that only they can heal his pain because they are "the only person who truly understands him." One of the study's participants explained, "There was a part of me inside that just really saw this little boy who was frightened, and afraid, and didn't like himself. And I was like a mother in a sense. I was going to make it better. Fix it for him."[10] Another woman noted in her interview, "He was a bully that I was willing to tame . . . I thought that if I gave him everything that I had that we could live in bliss forever."[11]

Everyone around Harley seems to realize that her attraction to the Joker is unhealthy—but Harley sees it as reasonable and romantic. To her, the Joker is a vulnerable child-like soul, the product of misunderstanding and a victim of abuse himself. He makes sure this is her impression in one of their early therapy sessions, surprising her with a (likely fabricated) story of physical abuse by his father. Her analysis shows her empathy toward him when she reflects, "It soon became clear to me that the Joker, so often described as a raving, homicidal madman, was nothing more than a tortured soul crying out for love and acceptance."[12] The Joker plays up this story, purposely manipulating her and making her feel special. He tells her, "A woman like you only comes along once in a lifetime."[13] His compliment feeds into the romantic fantasy that they are each special, as is their love. Unfortunately, as the participants of the interview study discovered, early patterns of violence often remain unchanged, or even escalate. There is usually no magical cure for relationship abuse: Sometimes a Beast is just a beast.

Misogynistic Power over Women: "Mistah J."

Throughout the Joker's abuse of Harley, an enduring aspect of their relationship is the uneven power dynamic. Harley consistently tells herself that they are in love and that she is more than his employee or henchgirl. But over and over again, both she and we are reminded that he is not interested in any kind of egalitarian or even symbiotic relationship. Typical of relationships in which a man abuses a woman,[14] he only wants one in which he controls her, utterly. This desire is made salient in the fact that even though they are theoretically in a "boyfriend/girlfriend" situation, she will call him "Sir," "Mistah J.," or even "Boss." This blatant power differential would be unacceptable for the vast majority of people in dating relationships and emphasizes his lack of respect for her.

The Cycle of Violence

When young Harleen's parents fight, she sees how it always ends with sincere-seeming apologies and expressions of love. To her, an apology *means* something. Unfortunately, her implicit confidence in the authenticity of apologies is another reason the Joker can target her as his victim and continue to manipulate her as their relationship progresses. False apologies are a central part of what is called the *cycle of violence* in abusive relationships.[15] The cycle of violence is a common pattern, made up of three phases that repeat themselves over and over:

- Phase 1: *Tension building.* The perpetrator becomes moody, insulting, verbally abusive, and critical. He or she withdraws affection and becomes increasingly volatile.

- Phase 2: *Battering.* The perpetrator becomes physically abusive.

- Phase 3: *Contrition.* The perpetrator apologizes and begs forgiveness, while declaring love and devotion.

The cycle of violence is seen repeatedly in the relationship between Harley and the Joker. Frequently, as they are planning a scheme or debriefing afterward, the Joker's anger or frustration is targeted toward Harley. In the *tension-building phase*, he often performs physical behaviors that are insulting and demeaning. He physically pushes her aside,[16] shoves fish in her mouth even though she hates the taste,[17] and belittles her; at one point he tells the other members of his gang that she is only good for "running and fetching."[18] He frequently insults her with comments such as, "You presume to tell me what I should think is funny? In fact, when have you ever contributed a worthwhile idea?"[19]

Their stories depict many examples of the *battering phase.* Here is where the relationship is the most horrific, when we see the Joker's complete disregard for Harley's feelings or safety. The battering phase is when an abuser explodes with the anger that rose in the tension-building phase, when he or she attempts to have complete control over the victim. He strangles her and throws her across the room.[20] He throws a gun at her head.[21] He backhands her on multiple occasions.[22] He locks her in a small closet.[23] On several occasions, he tries to murder her, either by killing everyone and failing to rescue her or by directly attempting to end her life.[24]

The most tragic part of the unhealthy relationship dynamic between Harley and the Joker comes in the third and final phase of the cycle of violence, *contrition*. Unlike Harley's parents, when the Joker apologizes, he is not sincere. Instead, his words are simply a manipulation tactic for him to either win her back as a useful sidekick or to keep her from getting any kind of revenge on him when she appears to have the upper hand. The Joker often apologizes after engaging in violence, or at least provides some kind of token gesture. In one example, after throwing her across the room, he tenderly touches her cheek and smiles at her.[25] In another, after failing to kill her, the Joker smiles at Harley and tells her she's great.[26] At one point when his abuse seems to have really upset her, he simply asks, "Would it help if I said I was sorry?"[27]

In each instance, Harley returns to the Joker, convinced that he really is penitent. Harley is so motivated to believe that he is sincere that she may see apologetic gestures when there are none. A powerful example of this occurs in the final pages of *Mad Love*, when she survives the Joker throwing her out of a tall building's window (intending to kill her).[28] She is bandaged, arrested, and sent to Arkham Asylum, where she seems to be coming out from under his control. She thinks, "No more obsession. No more craziness. No more Joker." But she then sees a flower and a note reading: "Feel better soon. J." She is convinced that the note is from the Joker, as his apology—when it may have come from the supervising psychiatrist at Arkham, Joan Leland. All is forgiven, and Harley will return to the Joker again and again.

The cycle of abuse traps victims in a roller coaster of emotion, in which they live for the brief moments of tenderness and love from their partners. But abusers often apologize out of convenience, knowing that they are going to go back to their old ways whenever it suits them. The cycle results in victims repeatedly telling themselves that "this is the last time," but then returning to the abusers when the contrition seems genuine. Research shows that, on average, victims return to their abusers *seven times* before finally escaping permanently.[29] It's unknown how many times Harley returns to the Joker, but we know it's a lot. Batman, Poison Ivy, and others all ask her why she keeps going back. A sample response shows the hope she maintains for most of their time together: "Don't get me wrong. My puddin's a little rough sometimes—but he loves me, really."[30]

The Catharsis Hypothesis and Domestic Violence

The cycle of violence includes a phase of explosive anger in which physical abuse occurs. Some psychologists once believed that an effective anger management technique would be to avoid such explosions by letting small amounts of aggression out. The idea, called the catharsis hypothesis,[31] was that anger is like a pressure cooker: Blowing off a little steam prevents the pressure from continuing to build. Unfortunately, catharsis didn't hold up in empirical tests. Study participants were first made angry, then given the chance to "vent" their anger in small doses to see if it would calm them down. Surprisingly to the people who liked the theory, these participants' anger actually increased. Perhaps this is why the Joker's anger is never abated, and why he continually lashes out at both Harley and the rest of the world. "Letting off steam" with small acts of aggression doesn't help; it can actually make things a lot worse.

Cognitive Reframing

The cycle of violence is one reason why some victims stay, at least temporarily. Another powerful reason for their endurance is *cognitive reframing*,[32] which occurs when we shift our perceptions in biased ways. Cognitive reframing is like mind games we play on ourselves, resulting from lessons we've learned in childhood, from our culture, or from the influence of other people in our lives. There are several specific types of cognitive reframing that have been identified in research studies, and we see these emerge in Harley's experience with the Joker.

Because of intergenerational transmission, people who were exposed to conflicted relationships in their childhood are both more likely to see relationship violence as "typical" and to have higher thresholds for what they believe "counts" as aggression, violence, or abuse. In short, this version of cognitive reframing leads people to build up a tolerance to relationship violence, as if they've been desensitized to it.[33] Harley reflects this perception when she tells people, "Sure, my relationship's a little temperamental. But what relationship doesn't have its ups and downs?"[34]

In addition, people exposed to consistent violence in several of their relationships may develop a cognitive reframing experience called *self-blame*, in which they believe they are the cause of the violence (instead of their partner, the one who is really to blame). Self-blame is also more likely to occur when the perpetrator of abuse brainwashes his or her victim by emphasizing that the violence wouldn't happen if the victim would just "behave" by giving in to all demands and remaining servile. When the Joker kicks Harley out of a moving van, she responds by thinking, "He's right! And I could use some alone time on my way home to think upon what I've done."[35] One of the most poignant examples of self-blame in Harley's life is after the Joker tries to kill her when she successfully pulls off his scheme, "The Death of a Hundred Smiles." He is enraged that she figured out how to carry out the plan when he couldn't, and thus he tries to murder her. As she lies on the pavement, broken, instead of seeing his abuse for what it is, all she can think is, "My fault. I didn't get the joke."[36]

While there are other forms of cognitive reframing, one is particularly relevant to the heartbreaking dynamic between Harley Quinn and the Joker. A researcher asked women to identify whether their partner had ever engaged in several violent behaviors, such as kicking, burning them, and beating them up.[37] Some of the women admitted that these things had occurred, but wouldn't say that the behaviors were because of conflict— instead, the women reframed the actions as what the researcher behind the study called *joking violence*. In other words, the women in this study denied that the behaviors from their partner were abusive and instead interpreted them as "joking" that had, unfortunately, sometimes gotten out of hand.

Harley is desperate for a world full of lighthearted humor. This is one of the reasons she's drawn to the Joker in the first place, and why she takes on the character of the harlequin clown. She actually tells Batman, "Clowns are the only folks who see the world for what it really is: a joke."[38] So, it makes sense that "joking violence" would be a way for her to cognitively reframe the violence in her relationship when she is not yet ready to face the reality of how abusive the Joker is to her. When Batman challenges her to really examine the Joker's violence by asking, "You think it's funny when he hurts people?" she simply responds, "It's just a joke."[39] But relationship violence is never funny. How does Harley eventually see through her cognitive reframing, to escape the trap the Joker has used to snare her?

Stages of Escape

While it is hard for many victims to leave their abusers, thousands of people do successfully escape violent relationships each year. Escape is difficult and complicated. One research team called this process *disentanglement* from abuse, using the metaphor of an insect caught in the abuser's web.[40] When these researchers interviewed women who had left their abusers, they found similarities across individual experiences such that they could identify several separate stages in the disentanglement process. Harley Quinn could have been included as a participant in their study, as she also appears to have gone through each stage.

The first stage of disentanglement is *seeds of doubt*, when the victim first starts to question what is happening to him or her. Participants in the study said it was like "a small voice somewhere inside me saying, 'you don't deserve this.'"[41] While victims aren't psychologically ready to label their experience as abuse at this stage, they do decrease their patterns of cognitive reframing and start to question their abusers' motives. When Harley realizes that the Joker has attempted to kill everyone in Gotham City with a bomb—including herself—she tells Batman that she is starting to doubt whether the Joker is really the man she thought he was.[42] When she notices that the Joker gives all of his attention to Batman, and none to her, she similarly reflects, "Maybe I'm better off without him."[43] The seeds of doubt appear to have been planted.

After seeds of doubt have had time to start growing, the second phase of disentanglement is *turning points*, which are usually accompanied by *objective reappraisals*. Here, an event (the turning point) occurs in the victim's life when he or she has a cognitive paradigm shift. Whereas abuse in the past was downplayed or denied, now it is seen for what it really is. The victim stops making excuses for the abuser and realizes the nature of their unhealthy dynamic. Perhaps the best evidence that Harley goes through objective reappraisal is a song she sings to a gang of criminals in which she describes her time with the Joker. She lists several examples of the terrible things he's done, such as poisoning her, breaking bottles on her head, and pushing her off a roof. In the lyrics, she notes that she originally tried to laugh these behaviors off—but now, looking back, she sees them for the abuse they were.[44]

For many victims, once objective reappraisal has happened, their tolerance for abuse decreases dramatically. While they may not leave immediately, they begin to defend themselves more and demand better treatment. A powerful example of this in Harley's evolution comes when she finally admits that the Joker treats her badly and she confronts him: "You say 'jump' and expect me to say 'how high?' And there was a time that was okay—'cause I thought that's what I deserved. But I seen a lot and done a lot and changed a lot since then. I'm still crazy for you, puddin', but if we're gonna have a future together, things've gotta be different."[45]

Next, victims in violent relationships often experience *self-reclaiming actions*. Here, they initiate new behaviors or relationships with other people that serve to bolster their confidence and self-esteem, which will eventually empower them to escape. When Harley forms a friendship with Poison Ivy, she sees what a healthy (although criminal) relationship can be. Ivy consistently defends her, supports her, and treats her with love, explicitly helping Harley work on her self-esteem and ability to stand up to men in general.[46] During one period when she has left the Joker (at least, temporarily), Harley lives in a women's shelter focused on female strength, finding peace, and psychological empowerment.[47] Harley slowly comes to terms with her unhealthy obsession with the Joker, admits to herself that he is abusive, and tries to leave him for good.

The final stage of disentanglement is *last straw events*, where the abuser does something so terrible that the victim finally resolves to leave the relationship permanently. Last straw events may be when the abuser becomes violent toward other people beyond the victim him- or herself (e.g., toward children), a particularly violent episode, or an event with significant psychological or emotional meaning. While it's difficult to establish a particular "last straw" for Harley because of the various character timelines and reboots, an example of a significant psychological moment for her occurs when she is in Arkham waiting for the Joker to rescue her, but she learns that he has simply replaced her instead.[48] Her anger toward him and how he's treated her finally reaches the tipping point. The replacement Harley is a sign that he doesn't care for her, personally, at all. This time when she escapes the asylum, instead of finding him to reunite, she waits for him to be arrested and takes her revenge by physically beating him with a club. While this kind of revenge is still abuse, it shows that, for Harley, the power dynamics in the relationship and in her own mind have changed. Psychologists call this type of response *violent resistance*, a tactic often used as a last resort when victims are finally trying to escape for good.[49]

From Victim to Survivor

Harley's journey is a hard one, but it reflects the path that millions of women and men have traveled. Relationship violence offers one of the most ironic psychological experiences in existence: Instead of love, kindness, and support, your partner offers physical and mental pain. The person who should be the most comforting in the entire world is the person who is the most hurtful instead. But the fact that Harley goes through this pain is one of the reasons that she is a relatable, popular character: She experiences something that makes her vulnerable and human.

The hope for Harley Quinn is that she does eventually leave the Joker and establishes her own, independent identity. There are several versions of this outcome, including her becoming a member of the Suicide Squad,[50] partners and friends with Poison Ivy,[51] a professional psychiatrist,[52] a landlord of apartments on Coney Island,[53] or even—temporarily—Wonder Woman's sidekick.[54] These outcomes vary, just as the outcomes of real men and women who are survivors vary. What matters for Harley is that she experiences an evolution of character that ends with her escape from the Joker's abuse and her slow but steady process of healing. It is what we hope all victims of relationship abuse can achieve: the ability to move past the role of victim and into the one of survivor.

NOTES

1. Rosen (1996), p. 151.
2. *Harley Quinn* #7 (2001).
3. National Domestic Violence Hotline (2019).
4. Dunlap et al. (2002); Rivera & Fincham (2015).

5. Dini & Cadigan (2018), p. 3.

6. *Harley and Ivy: Love on the Lam* (2001).

7. Dini & Cadigan (2018), p. 25.

8. Rosen (1996).

9. Rosen (1996), p. 158.

10. Rosen (1996), p. 162.

11. Rosen (1996), p. 163.

12. *The Batman Adventures: Mad Love* (1994).

13. *Harley Quinn* #5 (2001).

14. Johnson (1995).

15 Walker (1979).

16. *Batman: The Animated Series*, episode 1–22, "Joker's Favor" (September 11, 1992).

17. *Batman: The Animated Series*, episode 1–34, "The Laughing Fish" (January 10, 1993).

18. *Harley Quinn* #1 (2000).

19. *Batman: The Animated Series*, episode 1–56, "Harley and Ivy" (January 18, 1993).

20. *Batman: The Animated Series*, episode 1–51, "The Man Who Killed Batman" (February 1, 1993).

21. *Batman: The Animated Series*, episode 1–56, "Harley and Ivy" (January 18, 1993).

22. *The Batman Adventures: Mad Love* (1994); *Justice League*, episodes 2–21 and 2–22, "Wild Cards" (December 6, 2003).

23. *Batman Adventures Holiday Special* #1 (1995).

24. e.g., *Batman: The Animated Series*, episode 2–07, "Harlequinade" (May 23, 1994); *Batman: Harley Quinn* #1 (1999); *Harley Quinn* #1 (2000); *Batman* #663 (2007).

25. *Batman: The Animated Series*, episode 1–51, "The Man Who Killed Batman" (February 1, 1993).

26. *Batman: The Animated Series*, episode 2–07, "Harlequinade" (May 23, 1994).

27. *Batman: Harley Quinn* #1 (1999).

28. *The Batman Adventures: Mad Love* (1994).

29. National Voice of Domestic Violence (2018).

30. *Batman: The Animated Series*, episode 1–56, "Harley and Ivy" (January 18, 1993).

31. Bushman (2002); Hornberger (1959).

32. Goodfriend & Arriaga (2018).

33. Arriaga et al. (2016).

34. *Batman: The Animated Series*, episode 2–07, "Harlequinade" (May 23, 1994).

35. *Harley & Ivy: Love on the Lam* (2001).

36. *The Batman Adventures: Mad Love* (1994).

37. Arriaga (2002).

38. *Legends of the Dark Knight 100-Page Super Spectacular* (2014).

39. *Batman: The Animated Series*, episode 2–07, "Harlequinade" (May 23, 1994).

40. Rosen & Stith (1997).

41. Rosen & Stith (1997), p. 175.

42. *Batman: The Animated Series*, episode 2–07, "Harlequinade" (May 23, 1994).

43. *Batman: The Brave and the Bold*, episode 2–19, "Emperor Joker!" (Oct. 22, 2010).

44. *Batman: The Animated Series*, episode 2–07, "Harlequinade" (May 23, 1994).

45. *Harley Quinn* #25 (2002).

46. *Batman: The Animated Series*, episode 1–56, "Harley and Ivy" (January 18, 1993).

47. *Detective Comics* #837 (2007).

48. *The New Batman Adventures*, episode 1–07, "Joker's Millions" (February 21, 1998).

49. Johnson (2007).

50. *Suicide Squad* #7 (2012).

51. *Batman: The Animated Series*, episode 2–07, "Harlequinade" (May 23, 1994).

52. *Harley Quinn* #29 (2003).

53. *Harley Quinn* #2 (2014).

54. *Harley's Little Black Book* #1 (2015).

EXPLAINING THE JOKE II-1
WRITER GAIL SIMONE

Aaron Sagers & Travis Langley

Gail Simone has become one of the top writers in the comic book industry today. Titles she has written include *Wonder Woman*, *Deadpool*, *Red Sonja*, *Secret Six*, and many stories starring Barbara Gordon, first as Oracle in *Birds of Prey* and then as Batgirl in her own title.[1] Simone took on the challenge of writing about Barbara's life after physically recovering from the paralysis the Joker inflicted on her many years earlier in *Batman: The Killing Joke*.

Q: What does the Joker mean to you personally?

Gail Simone: The Joker is interesting because at one point, like Wolverine, he was one of my favorite characters. And I lost interest in him for the same reason I lost interest in Wolverine: At one time, they were both unpredictable, you weren't sure which way any encounter was going to go. Wolverine often turned on his allies. The Joker, too. But at some point, I feel like their very popularity put them on a bit of a treadmill and a lot of their behaviors were repeated just often enough to make me lose a lot of interest.

 The Joker can only kill so many of his own goons, he can only commit so many horrific atrocities, before it becomes a little rote and hard to explain why it's appealing at all. That said, in the hands of someone truly creative, he still has the capacity to scare and charm. When Scott Snyder writes him, just as an example, it doesn't feel like just another tick of the torture porn box; it feels like that unpredictability is back and I remember why I liked him so much. For me, the sweet spot with the Joker is when you don't know what's coming.

Q: Separately from him, how do you view Harley?

Simone: Harley, for me, exists in two states: the classic version that is very much Timm/Dini's version, and then the more complicated version that exists now in comics and film. I have tremendous fondness in my heart for the classic version and was actually quite resistant to the newer, ostensibly saucier one. But she's grown on me, and now I quite like both. I love that she's someone who has, unlike many popular characters, been given an actual character arc that has stuck: She went from educated therapist to obsessive gun moll to a sociopath to someone who has learned to love herself and respect herself. She's shown actual character growth. That's pretty unusual.

I've only gotten to write her a very little bit, but I genuinely enjoyed the way she tells the world to go to hell. She's going to do what she wants, and I think a lot of readers find that tremendously uplifting.

Q: The Joker puts Barbara Gordon through the greatest trauma of her life. Does it matter that the Joker, in particular, was the one who did that to her?

Simone: Well, it did for the writer of the book, I'm sure. *The Killing Joke* is magnificently told and beautifully illustrated, but Barbara is little more than an afterthought in it. It's from a time when the female characters were thought to have little value and it shows. After she's hurt, she's barely in the story at all. It's a Joker story, not a Batgirl story—which would be fine, but it always felt like a tremendous waste to me, throwing away a great character to put another notch in the Joker's "I'm so dark" ledger.

It's fine to have a great Joker story. I just always thought it missed the character of Barbara and didn't place any importance on her. Which gets a bit disturbing, if you follow it down the rabbit hole deep enough.

Q: Does Batgirl reconsider her own views on killing? Why doesn't Batman or Batgirl kill that clown?

Simone: I don't think so. Batgirl is, I feel, the smartest member of the Bat-family. She had grief, she had rage. I don't think, given the chance, she'd kill the Joker for revenge. That's just not who she's ever been in canon, really, although it's been flirted with a few times. Lots of crime victims don't necessarily want their attacker dead, even if they want them punished or incarcerated. I see Barbara in that group.

And Batman doesn't kill the Joker because he doesn't kill anyone.

Q: How do Barbara and Harley relate to each other? When Barbara has done things with Harley, most writers skip over the fact that Harley fell in love with the monster who shot and paralyzed Barbara just to try to make a point.

Simone: I think it matters where on the timeline. You're right, it's sometimes ignored. But Harley *today* doesn't idolize the Joker in the same way. And I think Batgirl sees Harley in general as more troubled than evil.

Sometimes things happen that don't fit my versions of the characters. I didn't create either of them, and a hundred writers have written them, so we're not going to agree on everything. But one of the reasons I love Batgirl and Batman is that they *aren't* the Punisher. They don't see themselves with a gun mowing down poor people and the mentally ill. They're protectors, not executioners. We don't want cops executing people in the streets. I think it's okay to still want heroes who don't kill on a whim.

Q: When you write Harley, what's your take on why she fell in love with him and how she sees him now?

Simone: I don't believe I have written her talking about the Joker much. But if I was writing classic Harley, it would be for the same reason a sweet, law-abiding woman might fall in love with a man on Death Row. They're lonely, and something in the relationship makes them feel alive. People are drawn to abusive relationships all the time. It's common as dirt, sadly.

Q: As a writer, how do you perceive the romanticization of the abusive Harley/Joker relationship within some corners of pop culture, and how do you push back on that?

Simone: It's important to remember that the semi-heroic version of Harley is a fairly recent commodity. The Harley that exists now has outgrown the Joker for the most part. Also, characters don't have to be perfect to try to improve themselves. I find some of the Harley/Joker stuff that some people are very invested in to be weird, certainly. I don't really claim to understand it, but almost every human on Earth knows someone in a relationship they don't personally understand. If you present Harley as a hero, then, yes, it's not great to have her obsess over a mass murderer who clearly has contempt for her.

Q: Can Harley become truly mentally healthy?

Simone: Oh, sure. I have to believe that there's a path for almost anyone. I don't want to believe anyone is never going to be able to function more fully and happily. In that way, I find Harley kind of hopeful.

Q: How much of Harleen Quinzel is still within Harley, and do you see her as a separate self from Harley?

Simone: I think Harley has unleashed the beast, but Harleen's education, Harleen's smarts, Harleen's intuition, they're always there—which, again, is hopeful.

NOTE
1. Respectively, starting with
   Black Canary/Oracle: Birds of Prey #1 (2003)
   and *Batgirl* #1 (2011).

EXPLAINING THE JOKE 11-2
WRITER ADAM GLASS

Travis Langley

Adam Glass is a screenwriter, television producer, and comic book writer. His television work has included *Supernatural*, *Cold Case*, and *Criminal Minds: Beyond Borders*. For Marvel Comics, he wrote such titles as *Deadpool* and *Luke Cage*.[1] During his run on DC Comics' *Suicide Squad* title,[2] he provided the New 52 version of Harley Quinn's origin,[3] which is mostly the version depicted on-screen in the 2017 motion picture when Margot Robbie played the role. I asked him about how that story deviated from the first version, the Eisner Award–winning story *Mad Love* by Paul Dini and Bruce Timm.

Adam Glass: I got asked to do a bunch of books. I was pushing for *Suicide Squad* because I was a big fan of John Ostrander's work.[4] Also at the time, my son was little and we were watching a lot of *Batman: The Animated Series*. I had gotten it on DVD for him. I had watched it when it had originally come out, so obviously there was a ton of Harley in there. I always loved Harley, but I wanted to see who Harley could be outside of the Joker. What if she went on her own, solo? You could see when she'd team up with Poison Ivy away from him, that was truly Harley. Who is Harley Quinn outside of Joker? Who is she as an independent woman out there making her own choices without the Joker relationship?

You always want to be respectful of who comes before you, so what I wanted to do in my origin story was stay true to their story. What is familiar? What is fresh? I wanted to give a fresh take on it. I loved what Bruce [Timm] and Paul Dini had done with Harley, so I kept that in mind, but I was trying to do Harley for this generation. I don't think I changed much.

Right away, before the book even comes out, fans were angry at her new design. I had nothing to do with the design.

I'm just the writer. I think my big change in the origin story was two things. I gave Joker a way that he got to her. Remember, the Joker's a genius. Evil genius he may be, but a genius. Also, Harley comes off as sort of a *[laughs like Harley]* ditzy girl, but the truth is, she's a doctor. She's very smart, too. She's got intelligence. So there's a bit of a dance going on between them, and a psychological chess match. As they're sitting there talking, they're going back and forth. He does his research, learns Harley has daddy issues and what happened to Harley's father. He presents her with her dad's killer's ring and finger to show her: "See, I know something about you." I tried to go [to] a little deeper level in that psychological warfare, but also [kept] him trying to get to something, for us to learn something new about her. Right? But play within the realms that were set up by Paul and Bruce.

The next thing, which had its own controversy, too, was him pushing her into the same chemicals at ACME that he had been pushed into. He's trying to re-create a version of himself, but he can't. Everyone is different. Everyone is going to come out of that thing differently. And the Joker—he's such a narcissist. He thinks, "If I do this, I'll just create another version of me, and everything will be fine." But what ends up happening is that Harley's her own person. He comes out the way he does, and Harley is going to come out the way she does. There are similarities, but in the end, he can't completely control her and she becomes her own person. And I think a lot of this comes from my own psychology. I look for stronger women. Women of strength. I want the home in my life to have strength. I saw Harley a little bit as a victim and wanted her to have a little more strength. I started to write it from that place. This is pre-"Me Too," and everyone has a different take on the Joker and her relationship, but I did see it as *abuse*. I also thought it was real. I thought, at the end of the day, the Joker probably would have an abusive relationship. It would be hard to justify, but love comes in all different shapes and sizes and forms. There was a part of Harley that needed the Joker, and that's the thing

I tried to write in there. The Joker, in his sick, twisted way, cares about her. And in her own sick, twisted way, she loves him.

When she's telling her backstory, she has this moment when she goes back to one of her hideouts, where they lived their normal, everyday life, and she talks about it. She says, "Everyone only saw this side of him. I saw another side of him. The times when he wasn't being a criminal and we were lying in bed, lounging." He's not the Joker 24/7. He really isn't. There are moments when he has to go to the bathroom, he has to take a shower, he has to sleep, he makes love, whatever he's doing. Who is he in those moments? I'm sure a large amount of him still is the Joker, but there are also parts of him that Harley saw that no one else saw. There's this intimate side to him, which might identify their relationship a little more and why she would put up with this guy. And as crazy as he is, power is intoxicating and he is powerful. So there is no justification about what their relationship is, on the abuse side of it, but I tried to have Harley claim her own stake and stand as an equal to him. So if there ever was a future for them, it would have to be very different than the past.

Travis Langley: You wrote the *Suicide Squad* part of the big "Death of the Family" crossover.[5]

Glass: Yes. Something I did in that was a little controversial. I remember people being upset when he locks her in a room with other Harley Quinn costumes and skeletons. And the hint is, "Oh, I've made others like you before. You're not my first creation." It's sort of like playing a little with the Frankenstein myth, right? "I play God and I create all this stuff." I was really trying to hear the harlequin, the costume, the original costume girls–fans, not just girls, the fans overall. Men and women who felt like their Harley had sort of been pushed out. That this Harley in the New 52, they didn't recognize. And I did hear that. I wanted to sort of pay homage to them and have them feel like that their original Harley has not been completely forgotten. I was playing with that like, "What if your Harley was a different Harley?" Not anything concrete about it, but just possibilities. Maybe he's just playing head games with her, but it's whatever you want it to be. It's like a song. I don't have to have a concrete answer for you. Even if my answer is this, you might see it completely differently. That's what's great about art. It's how you interpret it. And your interpretation might be completely different. I want to write in a way where I leave it open: Is it real? Is it not? Is he playing head games? Have there been other Harley Quinns? I don't want to give a firm answer on that. It's whatever you want it to be.

Langley: Grant Morrison has some wild ideas, but his idea that somehow, regardless of the reason, they're all the same Joker over the years has grown popular. Now you're talking about Harley: Maybe these are all different versions or different pieces of the same archetype?

Glass: Yes, exactly. Take the Earth-Two Joker [the original character who debuted in 1940]. You have the older Joker and he's very different. More of a killer, more deadly.

Langley: Yeah, he killed about 30 people in those first two years.

Glass: With gas. Laughing gas. And I just remember those stories where people were dying with the death grin. It's really dark and really sort of scary and creepy, and I remember being a kid and reading those and just being like, "Oh my God, the Joker is a really scary dude."

Langley: We've got a chapter on the psychology of horror in the first section of the book, the one that corresponds more to the Joker's first two years. Comedy has more to do with the "Clown Prince" period. When he throws Harley in the chemical vat, it hearkens back to the first full page of that first story in 1940, where the guy is dead in the last panel and has that rictus grin in that the Joker has a history of remaking other people and cars and fish in his own image.

Glass: I tried to sort of reach back to the roots and be true to the artists that came before me. Sometimes it's accepted, sometimes it's not. I can't guess what people's reactions will be. I can only do my best work and try to do something interesting and different. I'm always trying to bring something to it. So for me, that's all it was. I wasn't trying to have a definitive answer about "Is it Harley?" but if you were looking for that, here's a possible portal into that sort of explanation of how that could be.

Langley: There is an interesting moment, late in your first set of *Suicide Squad* stories, that raises the question: How crazy is Harley? When she puts the Joker's face on Deadshot and climbs on top of him, talking like he's the Joker, are you playing it like she's psychotic and she's thinking of talking to the Joker or for her it's just a mental exercise?

Glass: I think it's both. It's like, "I can't have this conversation with you because now I think you're dead." [Characters thought the Joker dead at the time.] "So I'm going to have this conversation and it's going to be cathartic for me. It's the conversation I need to have that I can never have with you." So that's really where it was coming from. I saw that people could see this as crazy. At the same time I pitched it, it was bananas.

Langley: And people definitely know some things about your take on her origin, because the *Suicide Squad* movie shows pretty much your version of her origin, tweaked a little.

Glass: It's really nice. David Ayer, the director, put out a tweet of the script and my book right next to each other, which was really sweet of him. Met him at the premiere and he gave me a big hug and said, "Thank you." It was an evolution of what everyone who came before me did. I was sort of on the shoulders of these giants who came before me and just adding to what was already there.

Langley: The Harley that we think of as a psychiatrist wasn't even referred to for a long time. She initially is a background character, like the old school Adam West show where there's always a girl hanging out with the gang.

Glass: I agree. And she evolved, which is amazing.

Langley: Is there anything you didn't get to do with Harley that you wish you had?

Glass: I didn't have a chance to explore her connection with Deadshot more. Not that I think she would end up with Deadshot, but they both went through a lot together. There is a part of him that actually started to like her and care about her, too, and you're going on these missions, and you're barely surviving them, and everyone else around you is dying, so I wanted that bond to grow and be stronger. A friendship of sorts.

Langley: Do you see Harley as somebody who can be a healthy person?

Glass: We live in a world where a lot of people have lived messed-up lives or come from bad pasts. Everyone deserves a second chance. Harley is who she is. Would it be your stereotypical healthy life? Probably not. But could Harley turn around? I think she already does do some good. She has a conscience and struggles and a way of doing things that are unconventional by society's rules. But who's to say what's sane anymore? I think we live in a world where a lot of the rules have gone out the window. If you would have told me 20 years ago that today we'd be celebrating Transgender Day—which is amazing and a beautiful thing and awesome, and I have nothing but love for my transgender friends and brothers and sisters out there—I would have told you you're crazy, the world would never accept that and be that. So there's room for everybody in this world, and there's definitely room for Harley.

I think Harley speaks to the audiences right now, and she speaks to a lot of kids out there who are struggling with being different and might not sort of fit the norm, might be labeled nuts or crazy. I think she loves who she loves. We've seen that. She doesn't care. There are no boundaries to her. I think Harley is, in some ways, the truest of all the characters in DC because she's true to herself.

NOTES

1. e.g., *Deadpool: Pulp* #1–4 (2010); *Luke Cage Noir* #1–4 (2009–2010).
2. *Suicide Squad* #1–19 (2011–2013).
3. *Suicide Squad* #6–7 (2012).
4. Ostrander wrote many *Suicide Squad* stories, starting with *Suicide Squad* #1 (1987).
5. *Suicide Squad* #14–15 (2013).

12

The Allure:
The Therapist Who Falls

**LEANDRA PARRIS, ERIC D. WESSELMANN,
SHELLY CLEVENGER, & AMANDA VICARY**

"The heart wants what it wants—or else it does not care."
—author Emily Dickinson[1]

*"Have you ever been in the
presence of true greatness?. . .
It's to die for."*
—Harley Quinn, describing the Joker[2]

WHY WOULD ANYONE fall in love with a psychopathic, physically deformed murderer like the Joker?
Even if there was some initial seductive excitement about
his twisted charisma and the challenge of taming a monster, why didn't the scales fall from Harley's eyes once the
"honeymoon" was over and the Joker showed his true,
Carnivalesque colors? Psychologists have often been vexed by
human thoughts, feelings, and behaviors that seem counterintuitive—is it
something about the person, the situation, or some complex interaction
between the two?[3] Many individuals in the real world find themselves in

circumstances like Harley's (albeit without the supervillain trappings), and psychologists have long tried to understand the complicated dynamics that lead to these situations.

Falling for the Fallen: Countertransference in Therapy
Leandra Parris & Eric D. Wesselmann

"Yes, I admit it, as unprofessional as it sounds,
I had fallen in love with my patient."
—Harley Quinn[4]

> *"The excitement felt in the countertransference may prove to be so intrusive as to seriously tax the therapist's ability to think."*
> —psychotherapist Alberto Stefana[5]

Dr. Harleen Quinzel joins the Arkham Asylum staff and falls in love with the Joker while she is treating him.[6] How did that happen? Shouldn't the good doctor have known better—been trained to recognize and avoid this situation? Unfortunately, this situation can happen in therapeutic contexts. In fact, studies indicate that between 13 percent and 29 percent of therapists reported having sexual and romantic fantasies about their clients.[7] These feelings do not arise spontaneously, but rather can occur as a natural by-product of some of the key processes that facilitate helpful therapy.

Psychologists strive to create a sense of trust and openness with clients. The therapist is trained to demonstrate empathy toward the client with unconditional positive regard to create an effective therapeutic relationship.[8] The therapist empathizes with the client genuinely, without judgment and regardless of his or her behaviors, even if criminal. This allows the therapist to be a trusted source of support and serve as a guiding force toward healing and recovery. In theory, Harleen shows the Joker unconditional positive regard by not judging or chastising him when he asks her for a machine gun;[9] obtaining one for him, however, would be beyond the pale for a therapist, no matter how much unconditional positive regard he or she has for the client!

Unfortunately, these clinical strategies can result in either the patient, the therapist, or both developing feelings that go beyond the therapeutic relationship. As the relationship grows, some clients and therapists find it hard to draw the line between what is a healthy, strong therapeutic alliance and what is becoming a relationship built on emotions, rather than the goals of therapy. The depictions of the relationship between Harley and the Joker vary from being one-sided[10] to mutual.[11] However, the classic depiction focuses on Harley's feelings being more intense for the Joker than vice versa. Psychologists would consider Dr. Quinzel's burgeoning feelings for the Joker *countertransference*—a process in which the therapist attributes feelings or behaviors (positive or negative) to the client that are associated with other aspects of the therapist's life.[12] For example, therapists may find commonalities between the client and the therapist's friends, family, or past lovers. Harleen sees a similarity between the Joker and her criminal father.[13]

Of course, countertransference involving something negative can interfere with the therapists' ability to empathize and effectively work with their clients.[14] Given her history of abuse, Harleen could develop negative feelings toward the Joker, disrupting her ability to provide therapy with an effective, nonjudgmental approach. However, Harleen's empathy does not appear to be diminished. In fact, it increases after she hears of the Joker's past abuses and witnesses him being brought back to the asylum after a run-in with Batman.[15] This could result from her self-admitted attraction to those with "extreme personalities."[16]

Countertransference that involves sexual feelings is more common among male therapists,[17] with female therapists often being more resistant because of the increased stigma for them, as well as general gender-role socialization for women and their feelings—especially their sexuality.[18] It is possible that Harleen does not experience this type of gender-role socialization within her.[19] However, she is vulnerable to countertransference as a young, psychodynamic-driven therapist. Younger therapists like Harleen also are more likely to recognize and acknowledge their sexual fantasies and attraction for clients, compared with older therapists.[20] Reasons for this difference are unclear, but perhaps less experience in the clinical setting, as well as factors related to generational shifts in what is appropriate to discuss, may increase the visibility of sexualized countertransference among younger therapists. That is, because Harleen is

The Purpose and the Hare

Travis Langley

Why does anyone fall for a killer? In the overall picture of the devotee's life, what purpose does that serve? Psychologist Robert Hare studied hundreds of psychopaths, along with more than a few people who entered their lives.

"It is difficult for most of us to understand how some people can disregard the monstrous crimes committed by the killers they so admire. What is clear, however, is that these devoted admirers are often victims of their own psychological hang-ups. Some participate because of a romantic need for unrequited love, others because of the notoriety, titillation, or vicarious danger they experience, and still others because they see a cause worth fighting for, such as abolition of the death penalty, a soul to be saved, or the firm belief that the crimes were an inevitable result of physical or emotional abuse in childhood."[21]

—*Psychology Checklist (PCL) developer Robert Hare*

less experienced, perhaps not as well trained as she believes she is, and is in the process of developing her own identity as a person, she may be at increased risk of developing romantic feelings toward her clients.

Romantic countertransference can create a dual relationship between the therapist and the client, interfering with the therapist's ability to be objective and act in the best interest of the client.[22] In the case of Harleen, the outcome of her countertransference is a failure to adequately help the Joker while also exposing herself to violence and crime. In this way, neither the client nor the therapist benefits from the therapeutic relationship. However, there are some ways that such an outcome can be avoided. Clinicians participate in training programs increasingly focused on helping them recognize and adequately address feelings of counter-transference, regardless of their romantic nature.[23] When therapists begin to feel that countertransference is occurring, they are ethically obligated to discuss and process these feelings with a supervisor. Such discussion helps the therapist understand his or her reactions and develop strategies for keeping them from disrupting the therapeutic relationship. If these feelings are too strong or cannot be addressed, the therapist is then obligated to refer his or her client to another clinician. For Harleen, it would have been best practice for her to avoid pursuing such high-profile cases with serial killers, given her attraction to them and her desire for fame, rather than the therapeutic success of her client.[24] Furthermore, once she started to have feelings for the Joker, she should have protected herself and the Joker by referring him to another clinician and processing those feelings with her supervisor. Had she done so, it is possible she would have been able to avoid her transformation into Harley Quinn.

Victims Who Fall for Victimizers: The False Glamour of Abusers
Shelly Clevenger & Eric D. Wesselmann

"Have you ever loved someone you knew was wrong for you? Someone who hurt you over and over again and hurt those around you but you could forgive them because losing them would hurt even more?"
—Harley Quinn[25]

"A person whose survival is threatened perceives kindness differently from a person whose survival is not threatened."
—psychologist and women's studies scholar Dee L. R. Graham[26]

Harley Quinn has been a fan favorite since her introduction in 1992.[27] Her most recent role in the 2016 film, *Suicide Squad*, has inspired a whole new generation of fans. There has even been the hashtag #relationshipgoals, used in social media posts, which references (and potentially romanticizes) the relationship between the Joker and Harley Quinn.[28] However, their relationship often is characterized by intimate partner violence (IPV): a wide range of behaviors (e.g., extortion, physical violence, rape, stalking) meant to inflict harm, that occur within a relationship. IPV has resulted in 2 million injuries and 1,300 deaths annually for women in the United States.[29] Research suggests that IPV is common, with one in three US women and one in four US men having experienced it at some point in their lifetime.[30] These behaviors often occur in a repetitive pattern, with multiple types of abuse occurring at once. Unfortunately, art imitates life in the context of Joker and Harley's relationship, as Joker regularly abuses Harley in various ways.[31]

Poison Ivy asks Harley why she tolerates the Joker's abuse.[32] Many women who experience IPV face this same question. There are many reasons why victims stay with abusive partners, including financial and psychological dependence.[33] Sometimes they stay simply because they love the person and have a strong emotional attachment to that individual, downplaying or reinterpreting the abuse whenever possible to see it as somehow normal.[34] Harley's response to Ivy illustrates this last point: "Don't get me wrong. My puddin's a little rough sometimes, but he loves me, really."[35] Eventually, while separated from the Joker, Harley realizes that she may have been suffering from Stockholm syndrome because of "those insane rationalizations, those desperate denials" that she used to make.[36]

Falling in Love with the Wrong Person

Harley has had several opportunities to leave the Joker, yet she continues to remain emotionally attached to him despite the repeated abuse. In one version of Harley's origin story, she pursues the Joker after he escapes from Arkham Asylum. Her previous torture at his hands has not decreased her attraction to him; rather her attraction intensifies.[37] Another story shows Harley admitting she still has romantic feelings for the Joker, even after he has cut her cheek with a razor, strung her up with a chain by the neck, and bitten off a piece of her ear.[38] Psychologists might label this phenomenon *traumatic bonding* or *Stockholm syndrome*. The media coined the phrase to refer to situations in which hostages bond with their captors, but this specific phenomenon has been largely unstudied.[39] Some psychologists and other researchers interested in IPV have expanded this concept to cover bonding that occurs in abusive relationships.[40]

Individuals are likely to experience this type of traumatic bonding

Harley Nightingale Goes to Stockholm

Owen Farrington (Owen Likes Comics on YouTube) offered some insightful analysis on whether Stockholm syndrome really fits Harley Quinn, shared here with his permission:

This traumatic bonding with the Joker is argued by many to be reminiscent of Stockholm syndrome. Coined after the 1973 Norrmalstorg robbery, *Stockholm syndrome* is described as when hostages begin to express empathy and sympathy and overall positive feelings toward their captors, to the point of defending and identifying with them.[41] However, one of the most vital parts about Harley's character is that she, in fact, was never kidnapped by the Joker (not as part of her origin) and instead chose to become Harley seemingly all on her own, donning the iconic costume in *Mad Love* to break the Joker out of Arkham Asylum.[42] I think because of this key difference, Harley isn't necessarily an example of Stockholm syndrome. While she does display some similarities to those suffering from Stockholm syndrome, her condition is inverted *Florence Nightingale syndrome*,[43] in which a caregiver develops romantic or sexual feelings for the patient—however, this with the added twist that Harley is being manipulated by her patient. So it's some sort of quasi-Stockholm syndrome/Florence Nightingale syndrome.[44]

—T. L.

when there are four key dynamics in their relationship. First, they perceive a threat to their survival. Harley is well-aware of the Joker's unpredictable and violent temperament, flinches when he is angry at her, and even has nightmares about him.[45] Second, individuals may experience traumatic bonding when the abuser isolates them from other people's perspectives. The Joker does not like Harley having relationships outside of his gang, such as her relationship with Ivy or the Suicide Squad.[46] Third, individuals may develop this kind of traumatic bond as a coping mechanism if they perceive their situation as inescapable. Given the Joker's penchant for stalking Harley and showing up unexpectedly (and violently), she likely develops a sense that she cannot escape him completely.[47]

Fourth and finally, individuals in this situation often perceive intermittent small acts of kindness from their partner as rays of hope that their relationship can get better. These momentary respites can cause the increase in emotional attachment.[48] For example, some survivors have noted that during these break periods they would "just fall in love all over again" and be "so happy that I thought to myself, 'See, he is a good man.' I would just love him more and more."[49] This pattern also occurs in Harley; as she convalesces in Arkham Asylum after the Joker throws her out a window, she is determined that she is done with their relationship. However, she sees a flower from him and falls in love all over again.[50] Of course, just as in real life, this honeymoon period ends and the cycle beings anew. The constant ebb and flow of hope and terror ultimately can lead to feelings of depression, low self-worth, learned helplessness, and posttraumatic stress—symptoms that we sometimes see in Harley.[51]

Women Who Fall for Serial Killers
Amanda M. Vicary

"I've always had this attraction for extreme personalities. They're more exciting, more challenging. . . . You can't deny there's an element of glamour to these super-criminals."
—Dr. Harleen Quinzel[52]

> *"Evidence supports the key evolutionary expectation that women have evolved a preference for men who show signs of the ability to acquire resources and a disdain for men who lack ambition."*
> —evolutionary psychologist David M. Buss[53]

From the first moment that Dr. Harleen Quinzel sees the Joker in Arkham Asylum, she finds him fascinating.[54] Is the psychiatrist who becomes Harley Quinn fascinated just because she is interested in high-profile cases or is there something she finds irresistibly attractive in the Joker himself? Harleen would certainly not be the first woman to fall head over heels in love with a violent killer. For example, infamous serial killer Ted Bundy proposed marriage to his former co-worker Carole Ann Boone while she was on the witness stand, and even though he was suspected in the violent deaths of over 30 young women, Boone accepted his proposal and later bore his child.[55] Charles Manson, the Menendez brothers, and even recent mass shooters have received love letters from adoring women.[56] Although researchers have known for many years that women enjoy reading and learning about crime more than men do,[57] less is known about why. Despite their violent and aggressive acts, the murderers themselves hold appeal for some women. Why would anyone be romantically attracted to a convicted serial killer? What is it about Harleen (and these other women) that would make them find such a man enticing?

Fame and Fortune

Psychologists studying Harleen's attraction to the Joker may focus on her *motivation* for pursuing him as a relationship partner. What does she feel she is lacking in her life, and how does she think the Joker can satisfy those needs? Evolutionary psychologists argue that humans seek romantic partners who have specific qualities that would help them solve adaptive problems faced by their ancestors.[58] In other words, human mate preferences have been influenced by the pressures experienced in our hunter-gatherer past. For women, who are generally physically weaker than men, one of these pressures would have been finding the resources (such as food and shelter) to help ensure survival for themselves and their children. Thus, women should focus on finding romantic partners who would have the best chances of providing these resources and protection. Although it is unlikely that modern women think, "I need to find a man to hunt and kill an antelope for me so I can eat tonight," evolutionary psychologists posit that these thought patterns are still with us today.[59] In other words, they say heterosexual women are still attracted to the characteristics in men that would have been appealing in the ancient past. Indeed, Harley fantasizes about spending the rest of her life "with her lovin' sweetheart," having children and living to a ripe old age with him.[60] Harley is even willing to tolerate the Joker torturing and brainwashing Robin in order to make him into a mini-Joker that they might raise as their own child.[61]

What characteristics do serial killers like the Joker have that would be appealing evolutionarily? Serial killers are famous, and famous individuals often have high status in society. Before Harleen encounters the Joker for the first time during her stint as a psychiatric intern at Arkham Asylum, she already knows who he is.[62] Indeed, likely all of Gotham City is aware of the Joker's antics, given the numerous catchy nicknames he has been afforded both by the press and by the police (e.g., the Harlequin of Hate). In short, he has achieved a high level of fame.

In general, high status leads to greater access to resources in modern times (e.g., fancy cars, designer clothes).[63] Think about celebrities: Movie and music stars are often portrayed on television and in tabloids as having an excess of money and being given special treatment over the average person. Even though a serial killer comes to his celebrity status by rather nefarious means (i.e., killing people), according to evolutionary psychology, it might not matter to an admirer who perceives this person as someone who can still provide for his or her needs.

In a study designed to investigate whether the appeal of fame would apply to serial killers, female college students were presented with a video clip about an alleged killer. The purported news clip contained images of his mug shot and stated that he had killed multiple women. Students were asked to rate both how famous and how attractive they found the killer. Results showed that the more famous they thought he was, the more attractive they found him. In other words, the fact that he had murdered women did not keep his fame from still being appealing.[64] And in Gotham, perhaps in that entire world, is any supervillain more famous than the Joker?

It seems likely that the high level of notoriety the Joker has achieved is something that Harleen finds attractive, even if on a subconscious level. Indeed, a survey of thousands of women from around the world found that, on average, women rank characteristics indicative of status as being more important than "good looks" in a romantic partner,[65] perhaps also explaining why Harleen is not disturbed by the Joker's rather unsightly appearance.

The Thrill of the Kill(er)

Not every woman in Gotham is attracted to the Joker, however, so an evolutionary psychological account cannot fully explain Harley's unusual attraction to him. The Joker holds something else beyond status that appeals to Harley specifically: the promise of excitement. When she first goes into psychiatry, she doesn't anticipate that many of her patients would seem "just plain boring" to her.[66] The Joker represents a taste of the unpredictable, exciting, and challenging. Their sessions are filled with witty banter, sexual chemistry, and a hint of danger, none of which are present in her sessions with her other, boring patients.[67] She begins to crave that excitement.

This craving for excitement has a technical name in psychology: sensation seeking. *Sensation seeking* is a trait distinguished by the desire for "varied, novel, complex, and intense sensations and experiences and the willingness to take . . . risks for the sake of such experiences."[68] Researchers suspect there may be a biological component to sensation seeking, in that those high in sensation seeking tend to experience less physical arousal when faced with aversive events, and therefore are not as likely to avoid them.[69] In other words, for some people, riding a roller coaster may be terrifying, but for others, the physical anxiety isn't as extreme, leading them to be more willing to go for another ride. Considering Harleen's adventurous past (e.g., outwitting several goons on Coney Island as a small child, flying through the air during her gymnastics routines as a young adult),[70] it would not be surprising if she were higher than average on this personality trait. Indeed, Harley notes to Batman that she actually enjoys some of their conflicts.[71]

In the previously described study regarding fame, women who tended to agree with items such as "I sometimes like to do things that are a little frightening" and "I'll try anything once" were more likely to say they would be willing to write to the killer and also be more interested in going to meet him while he was in prison.[72]

At first glance it seems counterintuitive that anyone would fall in love with a serial killer like the Joker. What greater threat to one's own survival could there be than falling in love and spending time with someone who is known to kill? However, research suggests that these killers may hold appeal for a variety of reasons, including their celebrity status. Of course, not all women will fall in love with a killer. Indeed, given the likelihood of Harleen being high in the trait of sensation seeking, it is perhaps not surprising that she found love with the person who could give her continual excitement in a way few other men could—the killer she affectionately calls her "puddin'."

Breaking the Cycle

Regardless of the reasons why Harley became emotionally involved with the Joker, she ultimately recognizes that it is not a healthy relationship. Many individuals who are in abusive relationships eventually realize that something needs to change, and unfortunately the abuser often will not stop being violent.

These individuals recognize that they need to leave their abuser when they reach their perceived breaking point.[73] Some survivors note that their breaking point was when the violence was directed against someone they loved (e.g., a child or pet); they felt that the violence against them was acceptable or "not a big deal," but it became a different story when it happened to someone else. Another survivor noted that after the abuser hurt her dog, "It was like the spell he had me under broke."[74] This real-world example mirrors one of Harley's final straws: when the Joker allows her pet hyenas to become rabid and she is forced to kill them.

Many survivors also had someone in their life to provide the social support necessary to help them find the strength to break free.[75] This is often a friend who does not give up on the survivor, who just keeps "coming back no matter how much I justified what he did to me."[76] This, too, can be seen with Harley and one of her closest friends, Poison Ivy. Ivy often takes Harley in after the Joker kicks her out (or tries to kill her).[77] Ivy also brings Harley with her to Sanctuary, a treatment facility for traumatized superheroes. While there, Harley receives individual therapy in the computerized confessionals and Ivy assures her that she will always be there to provide emotional support.[78]

The best way to assist someone in an abusive relationship is to support him or her and realize that it is often not as simple for him or her as just walking out the door and not looking back. Psychological treatment and social support are paramount for successfully helping IPV survivors break free from the cycle of violence. Part of this process is helping survivors come to terms with the fact that an emotional bond with their abuser may still exist, but that bond is not a reason to stay in an abusive relationship. As one survivor said, "I loved him so much. I don't think I will love anyone more ever again, but I realized love doesn't have to be physically painful."[79] Or, as Harley notes during a fight with the Joker, "Because I love you doesn't mean I belong with you. So I think we should break up."[80]

"He will choose you, disarm you with his words,
and control you with his presence.
He will delight you with his wit and his plans.
He will show you a good time,
but you will always get the bill."

—a psychopath in prison[81]

NOTES

1. Dickinson (1862/1998).
2. *Suicide Squad* #15 (2013).
3. Kenrick & Funder (1988); Kihlstrom (2013).
4. *The Batman Adventures: Mad Love* (1994).
5. Stefana (2017).
6. *The Batman Adventures: Mad Love* (1994); *Suicide Squad: Extended Cut* (2016 motion picture).
7. Sonne & Jochai (2014).
8. Farber & Doolin (2011); Rogers (1956).
9. *Suicide Squad: Extended Cut* (2016 motion picture).
10. *The New Batman Adventures: Mad Love* (1994).
11. *Suicide Squad: Extended Cut* (2016 motion picture).
12. Carveth (2012).
13. *Detective Comics* #23.2 (2013).
14. Carveth (2012).
15. *The Batman Adventures: Mad Love* (1994).
16. *The Batman Adventures: Mad Love* (1994).
17. Sonne & Jochai (2014).
18. Bordini & Sperb (2013); Kelly (2014); Kreager & Staff (2009).
19. *The Batman Adventures: Mad Love* (1994).
20. Sonne & Jochai (2014).
21. Hare (1993/1999), p. 150.
22. Carveth (2012); Sonne & Jochai (2014).
23. Sonne & Jochai (2014).
24. *The Batman Adventures: Mad Love* (1994).
25. *Injustice: Gods Among Us* #2 (2013).
26. Graham et al. (1994), p. 34–35.
27. *Batman: The Animated Series*, episode 1–22, "Joker's Favor" (September 10, 1992).
28. Helle (2016); Lopez (2016).
29. National Coalition Against Domestic Violence (2017).
30. Black et al. (2011).
31. e.g., physical abuse and attempted murder, *The Batman Adventures: Mad Love* (1994); theft and stalking, *Batman: The Animated Series*, episode 2–28, "Harley and Ivy" (January 17, 1993).
32. *Batman: The Animated Series*, episode 2–28, "Harley and Ivy" (January 17, 1993).
33. Arriaga & Capezza (2005).
34. Arriaga (2002); Arriaga et al. (2016); Clevenger (2019); Clevenger et al. (2018); DeKeseredy et al. (2018); Navarro et al. (2016).

35. *Batman: The Animated Series,* episode 2–28, "Harley and Ivy" (January 17, 1993).

36. *Detective Comics* #831 (2007).

37. *Suicide Squad: Extended Cut* (2016 motion picture).

38. *Suicide Squad* #15 (2013).

39. Namnyak et al. (2008).

40. Cantor & Price (2007); Clevenger (2019); Graham & Rawlings (1998).

41. Fuselier (1999).

42. *The Batman Adventures: Mad Love* (1994); *Secret Origins* #4 (2014).

43. AMRI Staff (n.d.); Jason et al. (2002). Really a trope, rather than clinical syndrome, despite popular vernacular.

44. Sidebar excerpted from Farrington (2016), with permission. Parenthetical note added by editor.

44 Cantor & Price (2007); Clevenger (2019); Graham & Rawlings (1998).

45. *Batman: The Animated Series*, episode 2–28, "Harley and Ivy" (January 17, 1993); *Batman: Harley Quinn* #1 (1999).

46. *Batman: The Animated Series*, episode 2–28, "Harley and Ivy" (January 17, 1993); Suicide Squad #14–15 (2013).

47. *Batman: The Animated Series*, episode 2–28, "Harley and Ivy" (January 17, 1993); *Suicide Squad* #14 (2013).

48. Dutton & Painter (1993); Graham & Rawlings (1998).

49. e.g., Clevenger (2019).

50. *The Batman Adventures: Mad Love* (1994).

51. Graham et al (1995); Walker (1984); for examples of Harley's mental health outcomes, see *Batman: The Animated Series*, episode 2–28, "Harley and Ivy" (January 17, 1993); *Heroes in Crisis* #1 (2018); *Heroes in Crisis* #6 (2019).

52. *The Batman Adventures: Mad Love* (1994).

53. Buss (1994), p. 31.

54. *The Batman Adventures: Mad Love* (1994).

55. Rule (1980).

56. Christensen & Wallman (2018).

57. Vicary & Fraley (2010).

58. Buss & Schmitt (1993).

59. Buss & Schmitt (1993).

60. *The Batman Adventures: Mad Love* (1994). Also, in *Suicide Squad* (2016 motion picture), Enchantress shows Harley her deepest desire, in which the Joker and Harleen have a life of marital bliss raising children.

61. *Batman Beyond: Return of the Joker* (2000 motion picture).

62. Dini & Cadigan (2018).

63. Henrich & Gil-White (2001).

64. Vicary (2011).

65. Buss (1994).

66. Dini & Cadigan (2018), p. 125

67. *The Batman Adventures: Mad Love* (1994); *Suicide Squad* (2016 motion picture); Dini & Cadigan (2018).

68. Zuckerman (1994), p. 27.

69. Lissek et al. (2005).

70. Dini & Cadigan (2018), p. 125

71. *The New Batman Adventures: Mad Love* (1994).

72. Vicary (2011).

73. Clevenger (2019); Rosen & Stith (1997).

74. Clevenger (2019).

75. Clevenger (2019); Rose & Campbell (2000); but see Strube & Barbour (1984).

76. Clevenger (2019).

77. *Batman: The Animated Series*, episode 2–28, "Harley and Ivy" (January 17, 1993); *Batman: Harley Quinn* #1 (1999).

78. *Heroes in Crisis* #1 (2018), #5—6 (2019).

79. Clevenger (2019).

80. *Suicide Squad* #15 (2013).

81. Hare (1993/1999), p. 21.

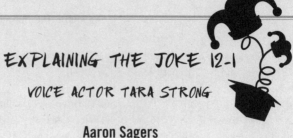

EXPLAINING THE JOKE 12-1

VOICE ACTOR TARA STRONG

Aaron Sagers

Tara Strong is a voice of chaos and a voice of justice. And while the characters the actor gives life to extend far beyond Gotham City, it is her work as a one-woman dynamic duo (or is it quarreling quartet?) of Harley Quinn/Dr. Harleen Quinzel, and Batgirl/Barbara Gordon, that makes her an intriguing voice to provide perspective on Mister J.

Though Harley was originally voiced by Arleen Sorkin when introduced in *Batman: The Animated Series* in 1992, the erstwhile Arkham Asylum psychiatrist (who becomes the Joker's sidekick/victim and eventual supervillain and antihero in her own right) has been portrayed by Strong in numerous works beginning with 2011's *Batman: Arkham City* video game.

Strong has similarly performed as Batgirl. Her Barbara Gordon was first heard in 2000, in the animated series *Gotham Girls* (where she performed opposite Sorkin's Harley) and later in the 2016 adaptation of *Batman: The Killing Joke*.

As someone who has provided voice to two females significantly affected by the Joker, Tara Strong has spent a lot of time in her characters' heads. In the following interview, she discusses how she views the psychology of the fabulously emancipated Harley, and the brave, bold Batgirl.

Aaron Sagers: As far as assuming the mantle of Harley Quinn following Arleen, what did you set out to do differently?

Tara Strong: When they brought me in, they said they did not want an audition. That made me a little bit nervous just because Arleen's version was so well known, so highly revered, so beloved, and so uniquely hers. There aren't many voices that you hear in animation that really stand out as unique in terms of how they pronounce things and the highs and lows and manic love, insanity behind what she created. So, initially, I was nervous when they said they don't want it to be a sound-alike. Of course, I was doing Batgirl alongside her when I first moved to Los Angeles. I held her in such high regard and didn't want to disappoint her in taking what she had created to a different level. So there was a tremendous amount of pressure to come up with something that honored her but still made it my own in a way that fans would be able to relate [to] and embrace her. Those are some pretty big shoes to fill.

When I first came in, they said, "We don't want you to do a match. We want you to make it your own, but based in her essence." We just started playing around and came up with the version of Harley that I did for *Arkham City*. It was terrifying. I think until it was released, and even on the day it was released, I was terrified. I think it was when I received positive feedback from the Internet that made me feel really special. Then that sort of solidified when someone else would do it, I sort of became the new quintessential Harley voice. That's been rewarding in my career when fans are like, That's not Harley— Tara's Harley—because for me, when I first came to town, Arleen was Harley. I think that will always be true. The fact that most people equate both of us as the Harleys is, in my opinion, an honor and something I take very seriously and hold in high regard. I'm so grateful that people like my version.

Sagers: What's fascinating to me is that it's essentially not one Harley because you have the video games, you have the animated appearances, and then even the *DC Super Hero Girls*, which is a depiction of Harley all on its own. How do you approach the different Harley personalities? How does your work vary when you're tackling the different iterations of her?

Strong: It's really so dependent on the world that we're entering and the vibe that we're entering. The previous *DC Girls* was geared toward the younger audience. This new version of *DC Super Hero Girls* expands that audience. We have been doing video game or serious shorts or dark sorts of movies. Those dictate a different voice because of the world that that particular Harley is living in. I can't even count at this point how many different versions of Harley I've done, but I can tell you that within those versions, I'm always highly conscientious of putting her in whatever world has been envisioned by the creative team.

Sagers: *DC Super Hero Girls* is for a younger audience and hardly has a complicated backstory. How do you keep Harley's moral ambiguity in mind while also keeping her accessible to this younger audience?

Strong: I put her in that world. She is an actual person that lives within me and that I then share from my brain with the world. So when she's in high school, she's in high school. She's not yet been tarnished by this insanity of her love life. She has not yet been faced with basically the origin story of who she becomes in this darker version of her. Who would this person be in high school? That's who I become and it's almost not a challenge because in my mind I become her and so I know how she'll answer a question. I know how she'll laugh, I know how she'll respond to a cute guy or her best friend. That becomes a 100 percent authentic truth in that world.

Sagers: As an actor, you're having to explore the psychology of these characters. Did you study psychology?

Strong: No. I mean I've been acting professionally since I was 13. I've taken classes in acting and scene study and character breakdown since I was very young. In terms of psychological training, I actually love reading books on the human psyche and what makes people tick. I myself have been in therapy and I think it's completely closed-minded to think we've learned all we've needed to learn while we're here. I think it's important to explore new therapies and new kinds of therapies and learn all different parts of your own psyche. Those come into play in my acting and my world. I was going through something emotionally at a stage in my life when I was actually doing something with Harley. Harley has become a sort of therapy for me, especially in the video game world, where she gets to really take out all of her frustrations and, oddly enough, it seems to mirror similarities in my own life. And she's grown within the video game world, as I have.

Sagers: You also voice Barbara Gordon. Do you think that there's a kinship or an understanding between those two characters, considering their relationship as enemies connected to Batman but also impacted by the Joker?

Strong: Absolutely. It's funny. If I wasn't such a good little Jew girl, I'd get a Batgirl tattoo on one shoulder blade and a Harley on the other. Like my angel and my devil. I always get really excited when I get that opportunity because they're both in the same world, in the same city, in the same crime-fighting or crime-committing relationships and they're so intertwined. I feel so fortunate to be able to encapsulate and become both of these people because both of them are so heavily in my psyche.

Sagers: After voicing Barbara in *The Killing Joke*, how would you imagine a scenario of Barbara and Harley meeting? Obviously they have, but do you think Barbara kind of looks at Harley like, "I get why you might be a little screwed up based on the history with this guy"?

Strong: Of course. I'm sure she has an understanding. Especially *The Killing Joke* where we're tapping into some sort of sexuality with Batgirl, but everybody understands at some point in their life feeling like they would do crazy things for love or stepping outside of their own comfort zone or their own personality to do something unlike them because of a relationship. You could take it down to something as basic as listening to a new kind of music to acting in a way that's not particularly something that feels innate to your personality. So I'm sure she, as a human, as an intelligent creature, would empathize with Harley, even if she may be disgusted by something she does. They're both very deep characters, so it's not like one might think the other is just a complete idiot. I think they both would appreciate the intricacies of each other's personality.

Sagers: What is it about the Joker that appeals to Harley?

Strong: Part of it is, of course, the familiarity. They've been together a really long time, right? Joker, no question, in the past has been abusive and I think Harley is coming into her own, being her own strength that we see right now in all areas of the entertainment business. She's her own entity, separate of the Joker. She was just sort of doing his bidding and now she is her own powerhouse.

Sagers: I'm curious about your reaction when you see people romanticizing that relationship between Harley and the Joker. Clearly, it is an abusive relationship.

Strong: People can relate to that. We've all been in relationships that aren't great for us. We've all been in relationships with acceptance behavior that didn't feel authentic to our higher selves or of the highest frequency that we're in. I think people recognize parts of themselves in that. No one that I've met in my travels at cons—which has been many, many, many thousands of people cosplaying as that couple— celebrates the abuse so much as the crazy love. It's the people dressed as Harley and people finding their power and their strength in this crazy love and allowing themselves to be nutty, unafraid of what they look like, unafraid to say who they love, regardless of what other people think. But I don't think that they currently celebrate the abuse. I think that's taken a back seat. It's certain open for discussion as to whether or not there's anything in that history that's appealing.

I don't think the original iteration of Harley and Joker's relationship would work today in any way.

Sagers: When you're getting a script and you're taking her on, do you think that she largely processed the abuse that she suffered and those horrors that she took part in?

Strong: I would say if you're going to be committing horrific crimes, bashing people's skulls in, I'd say for the more violent video game versions of Harley, she's a sociopath. She's not really internalizing the pain that she causes people and probably she puts the abuse somewhere in there, too. I would say the similar thing, like when you see someone hurting an animal, it's so shocking to me that somebody could physically hurt an animal. Often those people are people that commit crimes against humans. I don't think that's a normal brain. I don't think she, as a conscious thinking person, looks at her crimes and feels remorse. I think that's part of the sociopathic side.

Sagers: How do you approach Dr. Harleen Quinzel versus Harley with the Joker versus post-Joker Harley. Do you view them as independent characters and how do you bring that to life?

Strong: It's based on what's happening, where the scenario is, what the story is. It's all completely dictated to me from the perspective of the creative team. So whatever they've written, whatever the scenario is, wherever they are, I as the actor put myself in that scenario. I become Harley in that scenario. I don't think, "Oh, I'm going to act nicer now as the psychiatrist" or "I'm going to hack left crazy because I'm in a good place with Joker or whatever." I become that Harley in that iteration. So it's not even a conscious thing.

Every single voice actor at my level has had extensive acting, training, and performances. You'll never watch a voice-over session with an actor just standing there or sitting there. They're moving their arms, there's a physicality to them, and we become these characters. So when I'm Harleen as the psychiatrist, that's who I am. That's who I believe I am in that moment. I found that it's strictly from an actor's perspective of becoming that character.

Sagers: But do you view her, these different versions—Harleen, Harley with Joker and without—do you view them as almost independent characters?

Strong: I don't know about independent characters because there's always that essence to her. I don't know that I could even verbalize to you what I do. I just put her in those scenarios and they're not completely separate entities or I would be a different character, but there's always some sort of bloodline of Harley that translates through every version that I do.

Sagers: Do you think she was a good therapist?

Strong: If I'm evaluating therapists, no, I don't think she was! I think if you're going to fall in love with your patient, you should not be a therapist.

Sagers: How much of Harleen is still inside of Harley?

Strong: It depends on the scenario, depends on the script and the story and where we're at. But when she's completely crazy and killing people, she's certainly not a therapist. Not one I'd like to see.

Sagers: In *Mad Love*, she breaks the Joker out of Arkham Asylum and turns herself into Harley Quinn. But in the *Suicide Squad* iteration, the Joker drops her into an acid bath and he turns her into Harley. Is there a preferred origin that you happen to like of hers?

Strong: I'd prefer to do it on her own and be her own strong woman making choices just based on "who I am as a woman."

Sagers: Do you think that she could ever become an outright hero?

Strong: Sure. I mean there are versions of her being a hero and she's certainly a hero to certain people, but an all-out hero? Yeah, I think she could.

Sagers: How would you see that happening with her? How would you imagine that would look if she was actually part of those teams, part of the Justice League? How would she fit in?

Strong: I guess she would have to do something pretty extraordinary to prove her loyalty. It would have to be some sort of brilliant storyline where she proves that she pledges allegiance to the good guys, and then would continue to prove herself in that world. It would probably be a struggle for some time and then hopefully she would use her powers and her brains for good.

CASE REPORT IV (2000):
RISK MANAGEMENT ASSESSMENT
FOR THE MACHIAVELLIAN

To whom it may concern,

I write to you, the members of the Arkham Asylum release board, to urge against any possible future release of the patient known as the "Joker." As you well know, I spent a long career within Arkham and have had a chance to personally evaluate many of her most sordid residents. Coming from a position of some authority, I can tell you, without reservation, that the Joker is the one that continues to haunt me the most, and this is no small feat. Though I first became personally acquainted with him following a finding of insanity by the courts, it soon became my firm opinion that this man maintained his full faculties. He is not driven by psychosis, no matter what image he tries to portray.[1] He is a much better manipulator than we originally believed. He embodies the persona that Machiavelli wrote about in *The Prince*: He cares not for the virtuous man's concept for morality, for morality only makes one weak in his eyes.[2] The Joker wields his lies and half-truths as a skilled fencer thrusts his épée, though the Joker has proven much more lethal than even the best swordsman. I need not remind you of the full roster of deaths the Joker has caused, either by direct or indirect actions. I am certain Commissioner Gordon has not forgotten.[3]

I write to you not as a psychologist—necessarily constrained by my oaths of practice—but rather as a man who, in the twilight of his life, has the wisdom to recognize and speak truths that do not come easy to a man of youth and optimism. There is no hope for the Joker. He will not be rehabilitated. He will never not pose a danger to society, much less become a functioning member of it. We have seen the results of our attempts at using therapy to make a whole man of him. When given the opportunity, the Joker was able to turn the promising Dr. Quinzel to his own desires, making her simultaneously his plaything and key to freedom;[4] further, I believe he did this, at least in part, to injure us and to remind us that none are safe.

I urge you to keep these words in mind should the Joker ever petition for release. Listen not to his words, for they are poison. And should you, for some reason, believe that he may yet deserve a chance to prove himself through treatment, then I offer my final recommendation: electroconvulsive therapy at high amperage, until all bodily functions cease. Only then will he be cured of his evil.

Most respectfully yours,

Retired

NOTES

1. Editor's note: By the time of *Batman: The Killing Joke* (1988), DSM-III and DSM-III-R (American Psychiatric Association, 1980; 1987) were available as diagnostic tools. DSM-IV (1994) precedes Harley's first appearance in DC Universe canon, *Batman: Harley Quinn* (1999).
2. Machiavelli (1532/1903).
3. *Batman: The Killing Joke* (1988).
4. *The Batman Adventures: Mad Love* (1994).

V.

WILD CARD

AN AGENT OF CHAOS

"I'm an agent of chaos. And you know the thing about chaos?"
—The Joker[1]

"In all chaos, there is cosmos, and in all disorder a secret order."
—psychiatrist Carl Jung[2]

NOTES
1. *The Dark Knight* (2008 motion picture).
2. Jung (1968/1991), p. 31.

13

The Rivalry: These Two Guys

TRAVIS LANGLEY

"See, there were these two guys in a lunatic asylum . . ."
—The Joker, telling a Batman a joke[1]

"Insecurity is at the heart of every rivalry."
—author Beth Moore[2]

MUCH OF THE research on rivalry focuses on sports rivalries (mostly at the group level between teams or between their fans).[3] Efforts to study rivalry between individuals tend to concentrate on sibling rivalry[4] or competition for mates.[5] An effort to understand other forms of real-world rivalry between individuals, such as a feud between two heavyweight boxers[6] or a cat-and-mouse pursuit between FBI investigator and con artist,[7] benefits from a review of the specific individuals' lives and the details of all their past interactions. That can be difficult when we're talking about fictional characters who have gone through multiple versions and revisions across all forms of media, characters whose tales have been told by many, many creators working under various conditions and with various, even conflicting, points of view.

As long as Batman feels to us like someone who *could* exist, we suspend our disbelief. I've said before that "we don't scoff at the accumulated effects and logical impossibility of one man having thousands of adventures as long as we can accept him as the man in the adventure he's having right now and as the boy in the tragedy where it all began."[8] The Joker dances all over that line of disbelief. Performing his magic tricks, he teases us under the implicit acceptance that, even though the tricks look impossible at face value, the magician can perform them under real-world conditions whether we can guess the trick behind each illusion or not. Even when he looks impossible, he's at the edge of "maybe." His ongoing conflict with Batman is such a magic trick: We accept it in the moment, in the story at hand, even though we know it cannot exist overall. For us to care about the characters and go along with the most fantastic elements of science fiction or fantasy without dismissing them as frivolous or infantile, speculative fiction must ring even truer to human nature than most other fictional forms do.[9] Suspending our disbelief regarding their impossible history may require us to get even pickier about whether their interactions ring true, especially on Batman's side, because we can never fully know the Joker. The more bizarrely the clown behaves and the more difficult his choices are for us to comprehend, the more human Batman's reactions should be.

It's Simple—We Kill the Bad Man

In recent decades, especially in light of how the Joker started killing characters who matter to Batman and Commissioner Gordon after *Crisis on Infinite Earths*,[10] every angle in considering how Batman and the Joker relate to each other turns toward one question: Why doesn't he kill that clown? That long publication history has made it harder to justify why the Joker continues to live. Films or other depictions that show Batman killing anybody at all cannot explain why he would let the Joker live.

On Batman's end, he keeps citing two main reasons why he will not kill: because he values all life and because he fears that if he kills once, even to stop the Joker, he will not stop. Philosophical and logical reasons why he should consider killing the clown abound. Philosopher and author Mark D. White does an impressive job of reviewing arguments for and against it in his co-edited book, *Batman and Philosophy: Dark Knight of the Soul*.[11] Psychologically, though, what motivates Batman to let the Joker keep breathing? As a child, Bruce Wayne's life is shattered by a killer. He

The Bat's One Rule

No matter how many times you might read that Batman gunned down more people than the Shadow when he first appeared in print, it is not true. He's okay with knocking a criminal to his death in his first story, but that was not yet a Batman story; it was a plagiarized *The Shadow* story.[12] The creators took a few months to figure the character out. The one time Batman fires at a human being prompted editor Whitney Ellsworth to call Bob Kane and Bill Finger in and tell them that Batman must never kill, adding, "Never let us have Batman carry a gun again." Finger agreed. "I goofed," he told artist and comics historian Jim Steranko,[13] and gave artist Jack Burnley a strong reason: "Batman shouldn't have ever had to kill people."[14]

Later stories show Batman seemingly bend or break his no-kill rule when he leaves villains Ra's al-Ghul and KGBeast to perish in death traps,[15] but subsequent authors establish that he'd known each could survive—and, indeed, he's right.[16] Batman leaves the Joker in many predicaments where the crook's demise looks likely, and yet the clown keeps coming back. Most of the Joker's earliest appearances end with him seemingly dying, often by falling into the ocean, only to reappear within a month or two every time.[17]

"He'll be back. He always comes back—and when he does, he'll find us ready and waiting!"
—Batman[18]

wants to stop killers, not become one. Bruce Wayne grows up dedicated to stopping crime. He becomes Batman through a lifetime of deeply ingrained self-discipline, exerting steely self-control to channel his anger and pain into outlets that would help others.

Killing is not as easy as a lot of people think it might be. Police officers who are authorized to use deadly force when necessary are supposed to avoid using it if any alternative is possible, and being Batman requires being able to find an alternative in any situation. Killing the Joker would mean the end of Batman's mission: Police do not maintain a relationship with the Punisher. Do we really want unlicensed, unauthorized killers running about taking it upon themselves to murder the right people, with no one to hold them accountable? Batman's mission is bigger than his own efforts to take down one criminal at a time. He wants to inspire others to do the right thing, not to inspire gun-toting vigilantes to take to the streets. Still, as he tells Jason Todd, he knows the arguments for ending the Joker and struggles with them every day.[19]

Beyond Batman's general aversion to killing, though, might there be something about the Joker himself that makes the Caped Crusader keep him around? And why doesn't the Joker kill him? What are these guys to each other?

Cat and Mouse, Bat and Clown

In most cases, the pursuit of a criminal is not a *rivalry*, not a competition to beat each other to the same goal or to achieve superiority within the same field. Arguably, investigator and suspect both share one prize for which they compete: control of the suspect's freedom. Most criminals do not know who, if anyone, is after them. Some find out. For one thing, news reports might mention who heads an investigation. For another, there are criminals such as numerous serial arsonists who like to watch their fires from out in the crowd. Although, this may become less common now that many of them know that authorities therefore photograph such crowds.[20] Some serial criminals avoid drawing attention to themselves, so much so that authorities may not spot a pattern for some time in order to realize that a series is in progress, a problem that helped the Green River Killer evade capture for many years.[21] That's not a comic book supervillain. Serial offenders who are more heavily ego-driven, though, want spectacle.

Ego-Serving Fantasy

Unlike the murderer at Green River, the one who dubbed himself BTK sent letters to taunt journalists and police, along with photographic evidence, puzzles, and poems. Years after he last killed, his itch for attention finally led to his arrest. Police tracked him down through a disk he sent as part of a new round of messages when he wanted fresh attention.[22] Batman's recurring enemies do not simply commit crimes. They commit them with flair. They seek sensation and attention, and they do not wait for lesser mortals to assign them their criminal identities. The most outlandish ones name themselves when they debut: "Now I flaunt my two sides like a flag—the flag of Two-Face!"[23] and "The Joker has spoken!"[24] (Of course, in the print versions, most superheroes name themselves, too.) Even those who adopt childhood taunts for their criminal personas— most notably the Penguin and the Scarecrow—embrace those names, choosing what they'll go by in the crime game instead of leaving that up to others.[25] They, too, get themselves arrested as a result of their clues and taunts. As the Penguin puts it, "Where's the thrill in committing the perfect crime if no one knows it was you?"[26]

The offenders eager to see their pseudonyms make headlines want to be seen as special. BTK sent authorities a chapter list for a proposed book he wanted anyone to write titled *The BTK Story*. Many who send messages to authorities not only want to outsmart others but also want people to feel outsmarted. The occasional serial offender who communicates directly to a specific investigator may want something else, a nemesis, and to be seen as a nemesis as part of whatever fantasy the individual is playing out. BTK once sent a death threat poem that named the lead investigator. Interrogators must approach each suspect differently, feeding or provoking those egos in different ways, if they're to elicit confessions. While even some of the most egotistical never confess, plenty of the egotists want to regale an audience with sordid details.

Psychological Needs

The earliest reason the Joker gives for letting Batman live (a reason he repeats many times throughout the years, often to no one other than himself [27]) is that he loves the challenge, but there are different reasons for loving a challenge. Is it about the thrill of the chase, the greater achievement in taking on a more difficult task, or the effort to push oneself to become better? Whereas the Joker argues that he pushes Batman in ways that make him a better superhero,[28] the clown mainly seems to enjoy the chase. Why else would he keep committing crime sprees when they keep ending with him defeated? Each spree is its own joyride. Most of his criminal activities are about entertaining himself, although after *Crisis on Infinite Earths*, he finds it harder to amuse himself than he used to. Thrill-driven serial criminals tend to escalate the dangerousness and possibly the heinousness of their activities as they search for new delights, having habituated to some of the old ones,[29] and so the Joker starts making his attacks more personal. His former sidekick, Gaggy, says he has turned into a sullen jerk during his "Agent of Chaos" era.[30] The reason the Joker grows crueler and more manipulative post-Crisis may be that he is raising the stakes, increasing the level of difficulty because he wants a more entertaining challenge.

The kinds of challenges that the Joker finds entertaining and the extreme behaviors he so often engages in suggest that he rates high in another psychological need, *sensation seeking*, "the need for varied, novel, and complex sensations and experiences, and the willingness to take physical and social risks for the sake of such experiences."[31] Socially acceptable exploits (*nonimpulsive socialized sensation seeking*) won't cut it for him. He doesn't just want to walk on the wild side; he aches to run its length in socially unacceptable ways (*impulsive unsocialized sensation seeking*). By itself, that does not necessarily mean lawbreaking, but, for him, the sensation-seeking need together with psychopathy will drive him to break all restraints, including any law. Having Batman to challenge him makes the thrill even greater. "Without Batman," the Joker has said, "crime has no punchline."[32]

Having Batman as his opponent also feeds his ego. On a number of occasions when he muses over why he does not eliminate his foe, he links his sense of self-worth to the excitement of their conflict, as in the first occasion when the Golden Age Joker calls killing Batman "too simple— unworthy of my intelligence! And I like this battle of wits! The hunt, the chase! That's the breath of life to me!"[33] The Bronze Age Joker similarly muses to himself that killing an unconscious Batman would be a hollow victory: "I've always envisioned my winning as a result of cunning, at the end of a bitter struggle between the Batman and myself, him using his detective skills and me employing the divine gift men call madness. No! Without the game that the Batman and I have played for so many years, winning is nothing! He shall live, until I can destroy him properly!"[34]

The Bromance

Some fans perceive a "bromance" or friendship of sorts between the Joker and Batman,[35] which some consider fraught with sexual tension.[36] Within the limits to which we can ever compare this to real-world connections between criminals and their pursuers, it would be at most a one-sided feeling. As far as he's capable of having any such feeling, the Joker might feel a bond like that to Batman, but real investigators do not become buddies with serial killers, spree killers, and mass murderers, much less with a serial/spree/mass murderer. Because these are fictional characters, after all, some writers may approach it otherwise, but it is unrealistic to think that a crime-fighter haunted by the Joker's murders, someone who has seen the bodies and even known some of the victims well, would see their connection as friendly or romantic (as retired FBI profiler Mark Safarik notes in his interview, which follows this chapter).

That is not to say that Batman could never befriend some other former criminal, one who'd committed crimes not so heinous and who'd truly turned a new leaf. He hangs onto hope that criminals can reform. He is certainly capable of falling for a felon. In fact, the two most consistent love interests in his life have been outlaws: Selina Kyle (Catwoman) and Talia al-Ghul. In Catwoman's earliest appearances, he keeps "accidentally" letting the sexy thief escape.[37] In every main DC reality from the Golden Age through today, at some point he reveals his identity to Selina. His feelings toward Talia begin long before she turns terrorist in his eyes and cool when her crimes grow more malevolent.

There are indeed detectives and other investigators who befriend criminals they've hunted. The FBI agent in charge of impostor/con artist Frank Abagnale Jr.'s case became the man's friend for 30 years after Abagnale got out of prison. The conman was no murderer, though, and as part of his conditions for early release, he gave the authorities unpaid assistance investigating fraud and scam artists. Eventually, he went on to build his own business as a top security consultant, teaching classes at the FBI Academy and continuing to refuse payment for his government services for over 40 years.[38] Regardless of whether his motives for reforming were noble or practical, Abagnale turned from criminal to crime-fighter.[39]

None of this is to say that the Joker himself might not romanticize or "bromanticize" the relationship. When Batman plans to marry Catwoman, the party-crashing Joker asks in earnest during a moment when he and Batman sit: "Am I your best man?"[40] Like the serial criminals who want to think their pursuers have more personal feelings for them than they really do, the Joker likes to think of himself as the bro most important to Batman.

At times the Joker hints at sexualizing their relationship, such as when he gooses Batman or says, "Quick question: When the clock strikes twelve, do I get a little kiss?"[41] With him, who knows? These could easily be things he says or does in his endless attempts to get under Batman's skin, like Bugs Bunny planting kisses on Elmer Fudd to show him who's in charge—an exertion of dominance.[42] Writer Frank Miller, whose graphic novel *Batman: The Dark Knight* had the Joker call Batman, "Darling," saw nothing sexual about the Joker. Miller felt the Joker would not have sex "because sex is death to him. Put more accurately, death is sex." Regarding gay signifiers, such as "Darling," he said in a 1991 interview, "I know we live in very rough times in terms of persecution of gays and gay stereotyping, but I wasn't trying to address this," while adding that "the homophobic nightmare is very much part of the Batman/Joker mythos.[43]

"Now Get Me Santa Claus!"

After telling a room full of gangsters, "It's simple: We kill the Batman," and offering to make it so, the Joker later tells the Batman that "I won't kill you because you're just too much fun."[44] Yet he has tried to kill Batman. Because he normally expects Batman to overcome deadly obstacles, it could be argued that these are no more attempts at murder than occasions when Batman seemingly leaves him to die. Each expects the other to survive—most of the time.

After beating a Batsuit-clad man with a crowbar, the Joker howls delightedly, "I did it! I finally killed Batman! In front of a bunch of vulnerable, disabled kids! Now get me Santa Claus!"[45] Okay, the man dressed like Batman instead turns out to be an impostor, who rolls over and shoots the Joker in the face (which leaves Gotham's citizens thinking Batman finally tried to kill the clown). Nevertheless, the Joker thinks for a moment that he has killed Batman, and that delights him. This is the Joker we're talking about, after all, so don't expect consistency from him. When he finally returns to action after getting shot that time, the Joker tells Batman, "I could never kill you. Where would the act be without my straight man?"[46]

There is no simple explanation for how the Joker relates to Batman because there is no simple explanation for the Joker. Key aspects of his personality and experience remain unknown and unknowable, as is the case with a number of real-life serial offenders. They don't all want attention and, even among those who do, the ones who rattle off one confession after another (whether for the attention or to keep their executions postponed) are not reliable sources into their own psyches. Their words are valuable, and yet they are often no more than clues.

Psychological Reasons Why We Like the Joker

Lucia Grosaru

Superheroes are only as powerful as the supervillains they face and defeat. It is the magnitude of evil embodied by a fiend that shows the true social relevancy of a hero. The Joker knows this. He is certain that he and Batman complete each other.[47] And we like him when he unwillingly ends up proving over and over again that the Dark Knight is both the solution and the hope Gotham City needs when dealing with crime.

A charismatic sociopath, the Harlequin of Hate demands attention from both fellow characters and real-life audiences. But why do we like him as a character when everything he seems to bring about is terror, deceit, and chaos?

- *Passion.* He is passionate about his "work." Whatever the Joker plans to do next, he fully commits to it. We admire determined people with a mission, and passion can be exciting to witness.[48]

- *Brilliance.* He is extremely intelligent.[49] It is his knowledge of science, chemistry in particular, that makes him such an effective sadistic mastermind. His complex plans may be crazy, but they work because he can set all the required elements in motion.[50] From Smylex to ferries rigged with explosives to various puzzles and social conundrums, the Joker is using his *cognitive abilities* and knowledge to make Gotham City fear him and take his bright red smile seriously.

- *Insight.* He reveals the nature of things.[51] Taking others out of their *comfort* zone, testing their limits and making them show their real face while he himself continues to hide his own, is part of the Joker's job description.[52] Whether his plans play on basic human flaws such as greed, on an individual's moral compass, or whether he tests Batman's strength to obey his one rule of not killing, the Clown Prince's chaos-inducing actions deliver answers about the underlying principles that govern individuals and communities.[53]

- *Self-awareness.* He is self-aware and authentic. The Joker is definitely not *legally insane* (see chapter 7), even though his depiction often references his supposed insanity.[54] The truth is that he knows what he does is wrong, understands his own inner workings, and will let his potential victims know beforehand what they are about to experience. Unlike other villains, the Joker does not try to justify his actions through some principle or moral code.[55] He calls himself "the world's first fully functioning homicidal artist"[56] and lets you deal with that.

- *Power.* He is powerful, and power is appealing.[57] Citizens and authorities of Gotham fear him, crime bosses want to do business with him, and Batman has the toughest time when he has to solve the intricate mess he creates. This, together with his role in turning other people into criminals[58] and in the first film version of Batman's own origin story,[59] makes the Joker one of the most powerful supervillains ever depicted in popular culture.

When paired with traits and abilities that we value, evil becomes more palatable. The Joker's complexity as a character is mirrored in our reactions to him. We are shocked and terrified by what the world could look like if Jokers made up the majority of the global population, but at the same time cannot help but be mesmerized by his masterful use of rather basic, available-to-all human skills and resources.

Whether he is our *Shadow*[60] (the dark, unconscious part of our psyche—see chapter 5) or just an extreme external challenge that we must overcome, he Joker's best act may be to make us discover what we each hide behind the mask and, most importantly, decide how to use the weakness or the strength that we find there.

NOTES

1. *Batman: The Killing Joke* (1988).
2. *Esther: It's Tough Being a Woman* (2008 DVD program). Trivia: Moore grew up in what later became my house.
3. e.g., Berendt & Uhrich (2016); Botzung et al. (2010); Hoogland et al. (2015); Wenger & Brown (2014).
4. Levy (2010).
5. Ainsworth & Maner (2014); Bleske & Shackelford (2001); Brewer & Abel (2015); Stone (2017); Wade & Fowler (2006).
6. Kram (2001).
7. Abagnale & Redding (1980).
8. Langley (2012), p. 55.
9. Chester (2016); King (1981/1983); Kress (2005).
10. *Crisis on Infinite Earths* #12 (1986).
11. White (2008).
12. Kane & Andrae (1989).
13. Steranko (1970), p. 47.
14. As Burnley recounted to Kistler (2019).
15. Respectively, Batman Annual #8 (1982); Batman #420 (1988).
16. Batman #400 (1986), #439 (1989). See also Kistler (2019).
17. e.g., Batman #5 (1941).

18. *Detective Comics* #60 (1942).
19. *Batman* #650 (2006).20. Douglas (2007).
20. Sasser & Sasser.
21. Reichert (2004).
22. Douglas (2007).
23. *Detective Comics* #66 (1941).
24. *Batman* #1 (1940a).
25. Penguin—*Detective Comics* #58 (1941); *The Best of DC* #10 (1981). Scarecrow—*World's Finest Comics* #3 (1941).
26. *Detective Comics* #611 (1990).
27. e.g., *Batman* #11 (1942), #251 (1973), #663 (2007); *Detective Comics* #62 (1942), #570 (1987).
28. *Batman* #17 (2013).
29. Zuckerman (1971, 1979, 1994).
30. *Gotham City Sirens* #6 (2010).
31. Zuckerman (1979), p. 27.
32. *Batman: The Animated Series*, episode 1–51, "The Man Who Killed Batman" (February 1, 1993).
33. *Detective Comics* #62 (1942).
34. *Batman* #251 (1973).
35. Ide (2017); Twelftree (2015).
36. Klock (2002); Zambrano (2018).
37. e.g., *Batman* #1 (1940c), #2–3 (1940), #10 (1942).
38. Abagnale & Associates (n.d.).
39. Abagnale & Redding (1980).
40. *Batman* #48 (2018).
41. Respectively, *Arkham Asylum: A Serious House on Serious Earth* (1989) and *Batman: The Long Halloween* #4 (1997).
42. Starting with director Tex Avery's *A Wild Hare* (1940 cartoon).
43. Sharrett (1991), p. 37.
44. *The Dark Knight* (2008 motion picture).
45. *Batman* #655 (2006).
46. *Batman* #663 (2007).
47. *The Dark Knight (2008 motion picture)*.
48. *Algoe & Haidt (*2009); Chapais (2015); Curran et al. (2015); Schindler et al. (2013); Sweetman et al. (2013).
49. Kaufman et al. (2016); Prokosh et al. (2009).
50. Beaussart et al. (2012).
51. Ogle & Bushnell (2014); Śmieja & Stolarski (2016).
52. Lange & Boecker (2018).
53. Barden et al. (2005); Laurent et al.(2014); Powell & Smith (2013).
54. Beginning with *Batman* #251 (1973).
55. Jauk et al. (2016); Kottler (2010).
56. *Batman* (1989 motion picture).
57. Connell (1971); Meier & Dionne (2009); Sinfield (2004).
58. *Batman* #7 (1941); *The Batman Adventures: Mad Love* (1994); *The Dark Knight* (2008 motion picture).
59. *Batman* (1989 motion picture).
60. Jung (1964).

EXPLAINING THE JOKE 13-1
PROFILER MARK E. SAFARIK, PART 2

Travis Langley

Travis Langley: You spent 20 years with the FBI, and for much of that time, you investigated serial criminals. I see a lot of public misconceptions about serial criminals. For one thing, a lot of people assume they're all evil geniuses.

Mark Safarik: That's something I always try to dispel when I lecture about it. Human nature is diverse. All serial killers aren't all white males in their mid-20s who hate their mothers. They're a diverse population. Some of them have mental health problems. Some of them are psychotic. Some of them are quite organized and have significantly above-average intelligence. Some are real planners. Some are individuals who commit the murders to do other things after the murders, and some individuals are guys who want to torture. They want a living victim alive so they can torture. Other serial offenders are exactly the opposite: They don't want a living victim. They're not interested in that interaction. In fact, that interaction is uncomfortable for them. So that's what's so important about understanding the type of offender that you're dealing with. You can't make gross generalizations about serial killers or serial rapists. You have to look at their crime scenes. You have to look at the crime and all the dynamics in the crime to understand basically the type of person you're dealing with—the personality, how they would interact with family, friends, co-workers, if they have a job. If you can assess if there are mental health issues within the crime scene, how they select their victims, whether they're careful and do a lot of planning, or whether they're very haphazard.

    Albert DeSalvo is not the Boston Strangler. He's way too organized. He doesn't fit any of the parameters of that sort of serial killer. It all comes down to what they do and how they do it, who they do it to, and once you start looking at those dynamics, that starts to help you form the picture of who you're looking for, what type of offender you're looking for. People make really gross generalizations. But these criminals are human beings, and their behaviors and motivations can be diverse. And then you throw in drugs and alcohol and mental health problems, and what comes out of that, you know, really could be anything.

You could be like Jerome Brudos and have a real fascination with women's feet and their shoes. He was a serial killer who collected women's shoes. He had hundreds of pairs of women's shoes, and he would kill his victims, cut their feet off, put them in different shoes and take pictures of it. That's a unique kind of guy, sort of a one-in-a-million type of serial killer. Most aren't going to engage in that. You have a guy like Ricky Giles who killed his victims and engaged with them for weeks afterwards, sexually, when they were dead and decomposing. Again, really very unusual type of serial killer. You won't find that in most serial killers. So you just have to really look at each case or series of cases to figure out what you're dealing with.

I've never romanticized that relationship between the offender and me as investigator. My job is to stand in the shoes of the victim. Because, honestly, by the time cases would get to us in the behavioral unit, they've already been worked significantly, by the police and homicide investigators who got the case. And generally it's when the case goes cold or they run out of leads, they don't really know where they should be looking next that we would get those kinds of cases. My job is to have a real analytical approach to the investigation, to take my emotions out of the case. I don't need to be emotionally involved. In fact, I would do a disservice to the case to be concerned or emotionally involved. Sometimes cops or investigators get really frustrated or really angry about what somebody would do. But I look at it like, "But that's what this guys does, right? So that's who he is, and that's what drives him." So I'm not getting angry with them. So I talk to these guys, and they've done really heinous things. I'm curious because my job is to figure out why. What is going on in their head that makes them make these different choices?

I was asking them questions that are not typical of crime shows. I really wanted to know: What were you thinking when you made this decision, and how did you make this decision about this victim? Why not some other victim? And about the approach and about the weapon. These are all conscious decisions that these guys make. So what was it about how you were thinking about this crime? Were you concerned about the police, were you concerned about evidence, were you concerned about witnesses? Those kind of things to understand the thinking pattern.

But, really, remaining emotionally attached—that's really the sort of antithesis of what a lot of people think of, this sort of romanticized relationships between Hannibal Lecter and Will Graham or Batman and the Joker. I really try to keep emotions out of it because all it can do is create problems when I'm doing analysis of the facts and dynamics and behavior and evidence, because my job is to get these guys identified in a situation where law enforcement can arrest them.

Langley: Looking at the Joker's interest in Batman, fans think about and argue over why he keeps pursuing Batman, and I see some discuss what that has to do with real life. There are serial criminals who taunt police officers and maybe even focus on specific investigators, aren't there?

Safarik: Oh, yeah, absolutely. Some are quite intelligent—they're psychopaths, but quite intelligent, and for them, it's the challenge . . . of dealing with law enforcement. Who's smarter—me or you? Well, of course, they think they're always smarter. Because they're a serial killer, they've already had success in the killings and they've gotten away with it, and the fact that police are working the cases and can't solve them reinforces for them that they are smarter and that they can continue to do this. And actually their M.O.s do improve with each crime, for something about how to do the crime. Sometimes they get close to being identified or caught or seen, and they make an effort to change that, to fix that flaw in the next crime. So the fact that you have a serial offender means that you have somebody who has essentially reached a level where everything is working for them in their M.O. You got guys like the BTK Strangler who . . . really enjoyed the back and forth with the police. And when it was waning, he actually initiated contact. The other thing that goes along with that is, because they have pride in their crimes, they don't want other people taking credit for it. Because there are, as odd as it seems, people who will take credit for crimes they never committed, for whatever reason, the mental health issues—but when guys get arrested for a crime like one that Dennis Rader committed as BTK, it's like, "Wait a minute. Nobody's taking credit for what I did." So they'll release information that basically says, "You've got the wrong guy because I'm still out here."

And I think that's essentially the dynamic that exists between Batman and the Joker. The Joker sees Batman as a worthy adversary. And he needs that. He needs that because he's not challenged by the local cops, right? He just thinks the local cops are stupid, not worthy of his time or effort. So he seeks out somebody like Batman, who is, as he sees it, on his level but the opposite. So that's the challenge, and he needs that challenge. He needs that stimulation, as psychopaths often do. They get bored and that's oftentimes why they start taking more risks in their crimes. Because what they're doing isn't enough. "I need more thrill, more risk, more challenge." Not all offenders. Not all are like that. Some aren't interested in the media. Some aren't interested in the attention. But guys like Rader and [John Wayne] Gacy are very smart guys—smart not only in their communities but in how they plan their crimes. They just happen to think that they are smarter than all the investigators, and for them it's a game.

Langley: Well, that pops up all over with Batman and his enemies, whether we're talking about the Joker, the Riddler, the Penguin, others. Their egos and their desire for attention define them. Serial criminals in real life might not be wearing the costume, but Rader and others, they want a supervillain name essentially, like BTK.

Safarik: Right, part of psychopathy has a narcissistic component to it. They see themselves as the center of the universe, and that everything revolves around them. And they require that adulation and that media attention and they want to be known. They like reading about themselves. And, of course, not all criminals are like that. Not all serial killers are like that. But there are those like Gacy [and] Rader, where that is really a challenge. That dynamic that exists between them and the police, that's very powerful. It's intoxicating when you've got a task force of 30 or 40 detectives, that task force information is in the news every day, and you sit there knowing that you're the person responsible for that. You're the person manipulating that investigation and they still haven't caught you and you're getting away with these crimes. And you can still commit another murder under their noses, and they're stuck with another unsolved crime that they're trying to piece together. It's intoxicating to essentially have that much power or control.

Langley: When you said that the Joker, in his perspective, needs Batman, it reminded me of a number of people I've heard say that Batman needs the Joker more than the Joker needs Batman. With your experience with criminals and with investigators of many kinds, does that sound realistic?

Safarik: I don't think so. Not from my perspective, because for me, there will always be another Joker. There are a lot of Jokers out there. . . . People ask me, "Well, what's the toughest case you've ever worked on?" and I can't even tell them that because tough cases come in all different forms. Tough which way? In the analysis? In the offender? The fact that I know exactly what's going on but I can't solve it, or we can't identify the guy? I think, from my perspective, there's just always another Joker out there. There's always another smart, organized, planning guy. Sexual sadists—those really dangerous guys. We arrest one, I know there's another one just around the corner. And I don't need to keep that relationship. I want these guys off the street and I want them in custody. But for those guys, on the reverse side, they need that. They need that attention. Now, there have been some cops who've been in that same position. I think of the Zodiac murder case. There was a San Francisco cop, when the case was going cold and there wasn't much attention, he actually started writing notes [bogus messages supposedly from the Zodiac Killer]. He had a lot of attention on him for a long time, and all of a sudden, that went away. He didn't want it to go away. So he actually was ginning up information, but that's pretty rare. It's more often that the bad guy needs that attention from the law enforcement investigators who are working that case or the media, not the other way around.

Langley: From Batman's view, yeah, there's the Joker now, but there's a Riddler or there's a Penguin after that. There's an endless line of them.

Safarik: And there's a lot of other, lesser characters, you know, the Onomatopoeias of the world.

Langley: Oh, you know that one.

Safarik: They don't really rise to the level of the Joker. That's like a lot of cases that we work. But then you get guys like the Joker, who are kind of like the BTKs, the John Wayne Gacys, the Ted Bundys, the Ed Kempers of the world.

Langley: Those guys weren't found insane.

Safarik: No. I think most people think of insanity of being related to mental health, but insanity is a legal definition. What makes these guys really successful is that they're not. They're not psychotic. If you're a psychopath, you clearly understand the difference between what's right and what's wrong, but you choose to do wrong because that's what makes you feel good. That's what you want, and you don't have any compunction about not doing wrong because there isn't any moral equivalency for you. You're not like, "Oh gosh, I shouldn't do that because it's not right." They don't think like that at all. It's basically, "Do I want it? Do I have to break the law to do it? Yeah. Do I care? No, I don't. Will I hurt people when I'm doing this? In some way, emotionally, financially, physically? Yeah. Do I care? No. It's what I want."

Langley: I point out that the Joker knows what he does is wrong, but for a character like him, that's what's fun about it.

Safarik: Exactly. He may derive some emotional satisfaction from inflicting that kind of pain. I think that romanticizing an offender/investigator relationship works from the offender's perspective but not from Batman's perspective. Because, like you say, there's always another Joker, another Penguin or Riddler, some other semi-worthy opponent. And then there's a lot of guys who aren't that worthy.

These kinds of traits that we see in the comic book characters, we really see those in real life. Do they translate over? Can you be a serial killer, or in a mass murder, do we really see those kinds of guys? Or spree killers or serial killers.

Langley: Or we'll see a character like the Joker, who's all three.

Safarik: Yeah, he's all three. Exactly. Occasionally you might find a guy who goes from one to the other, but they don't keep going back and forth and changing around. It's just a dynamic that doesn't really exist in human nature.

EXPLAINING THE JOKE 13-2:
STORYBOARDING THE DARK KNIGHT

Jeffrey Henderson

Years ago, while working on another project, I was asked to contribute some preliminary concept art and storyboards for *The Dark Knight*, before Heath Ledger was officially cast.

The producer shared that Christopher Nolan very much wanted the film to be grounded in reality—even more than his previous installment, *Batman Begins*. They wanted the film to be more akin to a heist/crime thriller than a "superhero film" . . . and that also extended to the character of the Joker.

They wanted their version to very much be its own thing, honoring all the previous versions of the "Clown Prince of Crime" while completely reinterpreting the character and keeping him faithful to the "real world" vision of Gotham that Nolan had established in *Begins*. They wanted this version of the character to be iconic on its own, and I was given kind of a "broad strokes" list of visual and stylistic references: Stanley Kubrick's *A Clockwork Orange*; the Sex Pistols—particularly Sid Vicious; "Thin-White-Duke"-era David Bowie; and a specific note to check out Jerry Robinson's version of the Joker from *Batman* #1 from 1940.

Without giving anything away about the actual script or story, they told me that what they hoped would made their version of the Joker so compelling—and dangerous—was that he had an uncanny ability to always be ten steps ahead of everyone; but had no real sense of what was true of his own past. That he was more like a brilliant wild animal than a rational human being: more visceral than cerebral. They explained that one of the defining characteristics of this version of the Joker would be that he was an "unreliable narrator": so psychologically damaged that he was unable—or unwilling—to distinguish between reality and his own mythology.

When I finally saw the finished film (which, to this day, is one of my absolute favorites), I was astonished at how far they had taken and expanded those concepts they had shared with me. The script was brilliant, but Heath Ledger's performance was—and is—indelible and I believe will remain the gold standard that all future versions will be compared to.

Of all those amazing, iconic scenes with Ledger's Joker, the ones that always resonate with me the most are when he shares the multiple, emotionally charged, and conflicting accounts of his own "origin story." He doesn't seem to know which one is true anymore ... but even more terrifying: the prospect that he actually does, and just doesn't care anymore.

An "agent of chaos" indeed.

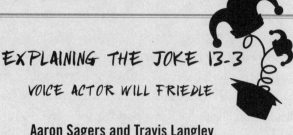

EXPLAINING THE JOKE 13-3
VOICE ACTOR WILL FRIEDLE

Aaron Sagers and Travis Langley

Batman Beyond carries the stories that start in *Batman: The Animated Series* into the future. The show features Terry McGinnis as a thief-turned-hero, a new Batman who is mentored by an old and disheartened Bruce Wayne.[1] The Joker's specter hangs over the series, first in the form of gang members who emulate him, truly toxic fans called the Jokerz, and then as a figure who seems to be the Joker, back from the dead, in the animated film *Batman Beyond: Return of the Joker*.[2] Actor Will Friedle, who voiced Terry McGinnis, the younger Batman, interviewed with us about *Batman Forever* and the Joker's lasting impact.

Will Friedle: Batman is forever. He is eternal, and *Batman Beyond* seemed to resonate. I think it's because it is one of the first times Batman was young. Terry McGinnis was in high school, so kids got to see themselves. They could think, "Wait, I could grow up to be Batman." I think that resonated. The idea of *Batman Beyond* was so popular and still resonates. None of us expected that.

Aaron Sagers: Why does the Joker have his own popular culture legacy?

Friedle: It is a good question. I think he has been brought to life by so many amazing actors. So you get to see a bunch of different versions of insanity. That connects with people. There is this taboo craziness. Everyone sees the Joker, and might look at him like, "That's me if I was unhinged." There is something about that.

Sagers: And why does the Joker matter to Batman?

Friedle: In the world of Batman, there is something about the Joker and Batman being more related than either wants to admit. A lot of people, myself included, look at the Joker as if Batman didn't have a moral compass: He could easily have gone the other way, and they are two sides of the same coin.

Sagers: How do you think Terry viewed the Batman/Joker relationship?

Friedle: What I thought was interesting is everyone said, "Oh, Terry was able to beat him his first time, and Bruce kept fighting him and fighting him." So why was Terry able to do it? One of the reasons is he had no background on the Joker. He had to go to Commissioner Barbara Gordon, and say, "[Bruce] never talks about him, so he was one of the worst." There wasn't that history in any way. To Terry, the Joker was just another villain he had to knock down, whereas Batman/Bruce Wayne and the Joker had this backstory. Terry had none of that. He just walked in, said this is the guy I've got to beat, and got to take him down. There was none of that baggage.

Sagers: Without that baggage, you can be a better hero against the Joker?

Friedle: Yeah! As opposed to somebody from Terry's rogues' gallery, who he had a history with. That's going to be a tougher fight than some guy dressed as a clown he has to take out.

Sagers: In *Return of the Joker*, the Joker is treated almost as an infection inside of Tim Drake, and essentially larger than a human character. He can get to anyone.

Friedle: I like the way that's handled and how they did it in the *Batman Beyond* world. When the Joker was gone, his legacy resonated into the gang of Jokerz. He lasted. Everyone can see themselves in the Joker a little bit. We love to see ourselves in Batman, but can also see ourselves in him a tad. It is true, they did treat him like an infection. When he is in the bloodstream, he doesn't go away.

NOTES

1. Beginning with *Batman Beyond*, episodes 1–01 and 1–02, "Rebirth" (January 10, 1999—both parts).

2. *Batman Beyond: Return of the Joker* (2000 animated motion picture).

14

Trauma: More Than One Bad Day

LEANDRA PARRIS & ERIC D. WESSELMANN

"That's how far the world is from where I am.
Just one bad day."
—The Joker[1]

"Traumatic experiences do leave traces, whether on a large scale . . .
or close to home, on our families, with dark secrets being imperceptibly
passed down through generations."
—psychiatrist Bessel van der Kolk[2]

 TRAUMA IS NOT necessary for someone to decide to become a hero or villain, but it often plays an important role in fictional characters' origin stories. The Joker argues that simply "one bad day" full of enough trauma can drive a sane person mad[3]—and presumably to crime. However, some characters emerge from their trauma as heroes while others turn to villainy. What makes the difference between one man becoming the Agent of Chaos and the other the Dark Knight? Why does one wounded woman become Oracle while another transforms into Harley Quinn? The answer may come from understanding the nature of one's trauma and what happens in the crucial moments following the event.

The Nature of Trauma

Psychologists typically view *trauma* as exposure to an event that poses life-threatening (or at least serious) injury or involves violence—events that are overwhelmingly distressing.[4] Someone who is abused by his or her significant other, as is the case for Harley Quinn,[5] often experiences trauma. Individuals may be traumatized simply by witnessing an event, such as when Bruce Wayne witnesses his parents murdered in front of him.[6] Furthermore, one need not be present at the event to experience trauma; simply witnessing the aftermath firsthand may be traumatic, which is why first responders can develop posttraumatic stress symptoms.[7] Thus, the Joker has the ability to traumatize Batman by forcing him to find his friends and family dead, dying, or tortured, despite Batman not actually seeing the Joker commit these atrocities.[8]

Given that trauma can be vicarious, it is no surprise then that roughly 89 percent of the population experiences at least one traumatic event in their lifetimes.[9] Yet despite the high rate of exposure to trauma, only 9–10 percent of the population develops a posttraumatic stress disorder as a result.[10] This is because experiencing trauma has the potential for both negative and positive outcomes, with a wide range of other reactions that do not qualify as extreme. More extreme outcomes are often termed posttraumatic *stress,* as opposed to posttraumatic *growth.*[10] These differential outcomes are most apparent between Batman and the Joker, one turning his grief into motivation for helping others while the other works to bring others down to his tragic state. Another strong example is comparing Barbara Gordon to Harley Quinn, who both are victimized by the same man. Barbara, after being shot and paralyzed by the Joker, goes on to fight crime as Oracle.[11] By contrast, Harley takes on the role of queen of crime.[12] Even when she separates from the Joker, she still engages in criminal and maladaptive behaviors.[13]

Some explanation for these characters' disparate reactions may come from the type of trauma they experience. There are two main trauma forms: acute and complex. *Acute* trauma results from an event that has a distinct beginning and end,[14] such as Barbara getting shot, photographed, and left for dead by the Joker.[15] While the consequences of such an event may last for quite a long time, the actual event is time-limited. While Barbara's subsequent paralysis causes long-lasting distress,[16] the traumatic event itself begins when she opens her door to see the Joker with his gun and ends when she is stabilized at the hospital. By contrast, *complex* trauma is more recursive, repeating over time.[17] The abuse Harley experiences at the hands of the Joker falls into this category. The Joker hits Harley regularly, and she can never really be sure when it is over, as he can lash out unexpectedly and without warning.[18] Complex trauma is also typically associated with ongoing childhood abuse,[19] such as the kind experienced by both the Joker and Harley.[20]

Of the people who undergo these two types of trauma, those experiencing acute trauma demonstrate fewer symptoms of traumatic stress and are more often able to reach positive outcomes despite their experience,[21] such as how Batman and Oracle start fighting crime. Complex trauma, due to the ongoing and recursive nature of causal events, may not allow the victim time to heal or address the trauma, as exposure is continuous or soon repeated. This increases the severity of the symptoms and risk of maladaptive behaviors.[22] While trauma can indeed result from one bad day, more often extreme negative outcomes, such as psychopathology or villainy are the result of a series of bad days that exceed the individual's capacity to cope adequately. Even though the Joker insists it's only one day that was his undoing, the reality is that he was already experiencing what he perceived to be a bad life. Prior to becoming the Joker in *The Killing Joke* version of his background, he is unsuccessful in his job, feels judged by others to be inferior and incapable, and struggles to support his family. The climax of his woes involves his wife and unborn child dying in a freak accident, and then he almost dies by falling into a pit of chemicals that turns his physical features clown-like.[23] Although the Joker gives varied accounts of his background, he has indicated on multiple occasions he also may have been abused as a child.[24] Thus, his transformation into the Joker likely is the result of more than one, albeit horrible, day.

Symptoms and Outcomes of Trauma

Traumatic experiences can have a lasting impact on the body in several ways. In an attempt to react to danger and avoid further risk, the body can become *hypervigilant*.[25] A person may startle at the slightest change in the environment or constantly look around to ensure that he or she is safe. Other physical impacts may include anxiety and panic attacks, which increase the heart rate, make it hard to breathe, and, in the case of panic attacks, leave the person feeling as if he or she were in very real danger of dying. These physical symptoms appear to come from the prolonged *flight-flight-freeze response* the body has when responding to threats of injury or death.[26] While these instincts and physical responses may be key to surviving a traumatic event, the body typically cannot withstand the ongoing activation of these systems. This can lead to, among other things, heart disease, numbness of certain body parts, sleep disturbances, ulcers, and difficulties with learning and cognition. During the time leading up to his back-breaking defeat by Bane, Batman is constantly on the brink of exhaustion, recognizing that his constant exposure to trauma is destroying him physically and mentally.[27] When other characters, such as Alfred, Robin, and Detective Harvey Bullock, note that he looks spent, they are picking up on these bodily side effects of traumatic stress.[28]

Not only does trauma impact the body, it can change the way the mind works and processes information. Those suffering from symptoms of trauma may find they cannot stop themselves from thinking about the event, the memories and thoughts becoming invasive,[29] such as Barbara remembering what the Joker did to her "every time I open the door."[30] Those suffering from trauma may find they cannot escape even when they sleep, as nightmares and night terrors replay the horrors of their experience.[31] This can be seen through Barbara Gordon as well, as she has recurring dreams in which she relives being shot with variations on the night.[32]

It's common for those who have experienced trauma to develop distortions in how they think about themselves, the traumatic event, or others.[33] Victims of trauma may forget certain elements of the event or come to believe, mistakenly, that it was completely their fault or that they deserved what happened to them. Barbara Gordon becomes angry with herself following her victimization,[34] while Harley regularly takes responsibility for the Joker's abuse of her.[35] (Both internalize it but in different ways.) In addition to alterations in how they view themselves, victims of trauma may change the ways they perceive others. They may develop distortions that cause them to think that no one can be trusted, that everyone blames them, or that the only way to protect others is always to keep them nearby.[36] One such distortion can be seen through Barbara's comments about Batman judging her as weak,[37] which may not reflect his actual feelings toward her but instead reflect the expectations she projects onto others.

In addition to changing the way people think about the world, trauma can change the way a person feels and behaves. Emotions such as guilt, shame, sadness, worry, and anger are common among trauma survivors. While these feelings can be normal responses to abnormal situations, if the person does not address them adequately, they can grow into more severe states such as major depression, anxiety disorders, and difficulties with emotion regulation.[38] Batman has difficulty dealing with the tragic murder of Jason Todd (the second Robin) at the hands of the Joker. Afterward, Batman becomes withdrawn and harbors guilt over Jason's death.[39] At the point of exhaustion, he even refers to a child that he saves as "Jason."[40] Behavioral changes are also common, such as avoiding certain people or areas associated with the trauma.[41] Increased substance use, difficulties with making or maintaining relationships, poor self-control, more aggressive responding, and withdrawal from social events can occur. In dealing with Jason's particularly brutal death, several characters note that Batman has become more aggressive. Despite Batman's previous assertions that heroes are "not brutalizers," the newspaper headlines describe him as "on the rampage" and indicate that he "batters bandits."[42]

Finally, trauma can have generational effects—from parents to children. For example, one study found that children experiencing psychological concerns were less likely to respond to treatment if their mothers had experienced trauma through abuse or neglect.[43] Batman continues to harbor guilt and fear over the horrors the Joker has inflicted on Barbara and Jason, and this likely contributes to his continual relationship difficulties with Dick Grayson (the first Robin and later Nightwing) and Tim Drake (the third Robin, later Red Robin).[44]

Historical trauma among marginalized populations, such as Native and African-American populations,[45] greatly impact individuals as well as the group. Historical trauma occurs when a group of people are collectively traumatized (e.g., through internment, colonization, denial of civil rights), often occurring to more than one generation.[46] For example, women have a shared historical trauma associated with the increased risk of sexual violence, abuse, and oppression that can be seen through characters such as Barbara Gordon and Harley Quinn. Both have been victimized by the Joker.[47] Their shared frustration extends beyond the Joker to Batman as well: At one point, the two engage in a fight and Barbara outlines the way a man, Batman, may come to view the two women negatively, and they end the struggle with a comforting hug.[48]

Risk and Protective Factors

People respond differently to trauma—sometimes with severe psychological consequences called *posttraumatic stress* (like the Joker and Harley Quinn), and other times with positive psychological outcomes called *posttraumatic growth* (like Batman and Barbara Gordon). One factor that predicts the ultimate outcome is the nature of the traumatic event itself. The more intense the event, the longer it lasts, and the more severe the consequences, the greater the risk of trauma symptoms.[49] It is key to note that intensity is based on the person's perception of the event. This means that two people can experience the exact same event, with similar consequences, but perceive the situation differently in terms of severity and intensity. These perceptions influence the narrative the person holds regarding his or her experiences. For example, Harley Quinn states that she doesn't "believe in trauma"[50] (an unusual view for a psychiatrist) while Barbara Gordon swears to never be a victim "again,"[51] indicating she accepts that she was victimized. This may be one reason why Harley continues to vacillate between doing heroic and criminal actions, whereas Barbara responds to her paralysis by the Joker by ultimately becoming the hero Oracle, the leader of the team Birds of Prey, and an intelligence expert for Batman and other heroes.

Following a traumatic event, several crucial characteristics can influence whether a person recovers in a positive way. The first is a feeling of safety, both physically and psychologically.[52] Following a traumatic event, it is important for survivors to feel that their basic physical and safety needs are being met. In the case of Barbara Gordon, she is provided medical attention, stabilized in a secure hospital, and supported by those close to her.[53] Similarly, after the murder of his parents, Bruce Wayne is comforted by multiple people (Officer Jim Gordon, butler Alfred Pennyworth, Dr. Leslie Thompkins).[54] Harley Quinn, however, is never truly safe, because she often remains in the presence of her primary abuser as one of his criminal accomplices. Returning to some routine or semblance or normality is also important.[55] Doing so can help reestablish feelings of safety and connect the individual back to social connections that are necessary for recovery. Harley and the Joker both leave their previous lives behind, never to return to their previous jobs or pursue their initial goals. Barbara and Batman, on the other hand, return to their lives to the best of their ability. Although, it is worth noting that even Harley can never resume her original career path, she does grow more heroic once she goes to work counseling residents of the Free Spirit Assisted Living Home.[56]

Another factor is whether the person can identify and use adaptive coping strategies. There are many ways in which people try to make themselves feel better when faced with trauma. Not all of these methods are truly helpful. For example, increased use of psychoactive substances may offer a form of escape or tension reduction, but such methods of coping are rarely, if ever, effective in leading to positive outcomes.[57] We see this on one occasion when Batman is traumatized by his inability to save a young girl, so he experiments with an addictive super-steroid called Venom in order to make himself more powerful.[58] This example highlights the need for trauma survivors to find ways to process and directly deal with their symptoms and/or negative emotions. It is possible that previously useful ways of coping (e.g., listening to music, talking to friends) may no longer work or be enough for the person to deal with trauma. Trauma survivors must then find new, but still adaptive, ways to cope. Batman struggles with his brief dependence on Venom but eventually finds ways to overcome his need for the drug as he learns to accept that he cannot save everyone, no matter how hard he tries.[59]

Perhaps the most crucial component of recovering from trauma is social support. Those with positive social support are more likely to experience posttraumatic growth and recovery. Bruce is taken care of by friends and family after his parents' murder, and Alfred continues to be a strong and positive guiding force throughout his life. Barbara finds support from her father as well as a family and circle of superheroes (e.g., Dick Grayson and the entire Birds of Prey team). However, if the individual does not receive positive social support, he or she is more likely to develop symptoms of posttraumatic stress. The Joker continually surrounds himself with criminals after his "one bad day"; Harley struggles, depending on whom she is around. When she leaves the Joker and is with someone who treats her as an equal relationship partner, such as Poison Ivy, she begins to process what she has been through and cultivate a more positive self-image.[60] Sometimes she even helps superheroes to combat social ills.[61] When she returns to the Joker, however, she falls back into a routine of criminal behavior and unhealthy co-dependence. As this book's editor has noted elsewhere, she is a bit of a *social chameleon* who, at times, "molds her personality to suit Ivy, then snaps into ruthlessness around [the Joker] and betrays her best friend when she's in Joker moll mode."[62]

The need for positive social support comes from the validation that one gets from others. Validating how victims of trauma feel and are experiencing the event is important for creating psychological safety and disrupting the potential for cognitive distortions. Finding sources of support from people who have had similar experiences can be a source of validation and empathy that is not always possible from other people in their lives. Through her relationships with Poison Ivy and Barbara Gordon, Harley Quinn finds these sources of support. This is also why the creation of Sanctuary—a retreat for traumatized metahumans—is so important, and its eventual loss is so devastating.[63] If a victim lacks validation and empathy from others, that increases the risk that he or she will develop distortions and engage in maladaptive coping. A clear example of this is the Joker, who even before his transformation perceived others as judging or doubting him.[64] Furthermore, after his transformation he appears to doubt or dismiss empathy or validation from Harley, suggesting that his traumatic symptoms have caused him to no longer trust these assertions or feel they are necessary. Yet he spends a great deal of time trying to get people to be like him, such as his desire to cause Commissioner Gordon to lose his sanity and his anger at Batman for not appreciating the apparent randomness of the universe, as he does.[65] This suggests that, in some ways, the Joker does in fact want someone who can be like him to prove that anyone can turn out the way he has. The fact that he is often unsuccessful in these attempts is further invalidating. Even Harley eventually leaves him and builds a life beyond their relationship.

For social support to be positive, it must also include relationships that the victim finds trustworthy and safe. Trust is hard for victims of trauma, particularly when their trauma resulted from abuse or negligence by someone else.[66] In the case of Harley Quinn, when the Joker is her only source of support, her behaviors and functioning worsen. This is because, despite her feelings for him, Harley can't fully trust him, as she can't predict how he will react or respond to her. However, when Harley befriends Poison Ivy, she not only finds a validating source of support but a friend she is able to depend on. While Harley's criminal behavior doesn't stop, she does appear more self-assured and happier than when she is with the Joker.

The positive influence of Harley's friendship with Poison Ivy can also be attributed to the sense of empowerment that comes from the relationship. Empowering victims of trauma is one way to offset the loss of control that is often experienced during traumatic events. This can also be seen through the example of Barbara Gordon when she becomes Oracle. Despite her paralysis and the trauma of her experience with the Joker, she continues fighting crime and helps other heroes through advanced computer and network systems. The ability to contribute to missions and save others has an empowering influence on Barbara, further helping her address her own traumatic past. The same can be said of Batman, who is empowered by the support of his family and allies in Gotham. Further, Batman indicates that he protects others in order to make a difference in their life, the way his parents would have made a difference in his.[67] The Joker, however, is rarely empowered by others in any healthy way. His original trauma is allegedly built on being abandoned and having power taken from him by criminals.[68] He continues to try to regain this sense of power by taking it, forcibly, or by trying to reduce others to the same state. This is not sustainable and ultimately does not work for the Joker.

Addressing Trauma

Though not always necessary, treatment can be crucial. While most trauma survivors are able to adapt and cope on their own with minimal treatment,[69] it is important that those who continue to suffer from traumatic symptoms for longer than a month seek professional help. Such help is often provided through a trauma-informed lens, which requires the clinician or agency to realize the impact of trauma, recognize symptoms of traumatic stress, respond effectively to those symptoms, and resist revictimizing the individual by creating a safe and supportive climate that does not unnecessarily expose victims to more stress or trauma.[70] This is why the creation of Sanctuary seems so important. Sanctuary is a superhero mental health facility, offering Batman, Barbara, and even Harley's best friend Poison Ivy a chance to heal and recover from their traumatic experiences so that they can better serve others. Had the Joker been able and willing to access similar trauma-informed services, perhaps he would not have ended up, as he says, certified and mad.[71] Trauma alone does not turn him into the person he is, but it might release whatever few restraints previously keep him from becoming something so extreme. For Harley, who starts out as a better human being, her journey toward a healthier lifestyle is no less complex than her trauma because, whether trauma is ongoing or results from just one bad day, it takes more than one good or even great day to overcome it.

NOTES

1. *Batman: The Killing Joke* (1988).
2. Van der Kolk (2014), p. 1.
3. *Batman: The Killing Joke* (1988).
4. *American Psychiatric Association* (2013); Brock et al. (2016).
5. *The Batman Adventures: Mad Love* (1994).
6. *Detective Comics* #33 (1939); *The Untold Legend of the Batman* #1 (1980).
7. American Psychiatric Association (2013); Haugen et al. (2012); Marmar et al. (2006).
8. *Batman: The Killing Joke* (1988); *Batman* #428 (1988).
9. Kilpatrick et al. (2013).
10. Ozer et al. (2003); Tedeschi & Calhoun (2004).
11. *Black Canary/Oracle: Birds of Prey* #1 (1996).
12. *Suicide Squad* (2016 motion picture).
13. *Batman: The Animated Series*, episode 2–28, "Harley and Ivy" (January 17, 1993); *The New Batman Adventures*, episode 1–20, "Girls' Nite Out" (October 17, 1998).

14. Mahoney & Markel (2016).
15. *Batman: The Killing Joke* (1988).
16. *Suicide Squad* #48 (1990); *Suicide Squad* #49 (1991).
17. Mahoney & Markel (2016).
18. e.g., *Batman: The Animated Series*, episode 3–16, "Harlequinade" (May 23, 1994); *Batman* #663 (2007); *The Batman Adventures: Mad Love* (1994); *Harley Quinn* #1 (2000); *Suicide Squad* #14–15 (2013); and many more. See also Alonsagay (2018); Canfield (2017); Helle (2016); Karbank (2017); Levine (2014); Lopez (2016).
19. Mahoney & Markel (2016).
20. *The Batman Adventures: Mad Love* (1994); *Detective Comics* #23.2 (2013).
21. Brock et al. (2016); Mahoney & Markel (2016).
22. Brock et al. (2016); Mahoney & Markel (2016).
23. *Batman: The Killing Joke* (1988).
24. e.g., *The Batman Adventures: Mad Love* (1994); *Birds of Prey* #16 (2000); *The Dark Knight* (2008 motion picture).
25. American Psychiatric Association (2013).
26. Sapolsky (1994); Van der Kolk (2014).
27. *Batman* #484–485, #487 (1992), #493, #497 (1993).
28. *Batman* #486 (1992), #494–495 (1993); *Detective Comics* #660 (1993).
29. American Psychiatric Association (2013); van der Kolk (2014).
30. *Birds of Prey* #8 (1999).
31. American Psychiatric Association (2013).
32. *Suicide Squad* #48 (1990).
33. American Psychiatric Association (2013).
34. *Suicide Squad* #48 (1990).
35. e.g., *The Batman Adventures: Mad Love* (1994).
36. Brock et al. (2016); van der Kolk (2014).
37. *Heroes in Crisis* #4 (2019).
38. American Psychiatric Association (2013); Brock et al. (2016); van der Kolk (2014).
39. *Batman* #440 (1989); *Batman* #441 (1989); *Detective Comics* #606 (1989).
40. *Batman* #441 (1989).
41. American Psychiatric Association (2013).
42. *Batman* #440 (1989).
43. Swartz et al. (2018).
44. *Batman* #493–494, 496 (1993), #614, 618 (2003); *Detective Comics* #606 (1989); *Robin* #13 (1995) .
45. Evans & Davis (2018); Williams-Washington & Mills (2018).
46. Evans & Davis (2018); Nutton & Fast (2015); Williams-Washington & Mills (2018).
47. *Batman: The Killing Joke* (1988); *The Batman Adventures: Mad Love* (1994); *Suicide Squad: Extended Cut* (2016 motion picture).
48. *Heroes in Crisis* #4 (2019).
49. Brock et al. (2016).
50. *Heroes in Crisis* #1 (2018).
51. *Suicide Squad* #49 (1991).
52. Brock et al. (2016).
53. *Batman: The Killing Joke* (1988).
54. *Batman Begins* (2005 motion picture); *Detective Comics* #457 (1976); *Gotham*, episode 1–01, "Pilot" (2014, September 22); *The Untold Legend of the Batman* #1 (1980).
55. Brock et al. (2016).
56. *Harley Quinn* #3 (2014).
57. Brown et al. (1995).
58. *Batman: Venom* (1991).
59. *Batman: Venom* (1991).
60. e.g., *Batman: The Animated Series*, episode 2–28, "Harley and Ivy" (January 17, 1993); *Heroes in Crisis* #6 (2019).

61. *Batman: The Animated Series*, episode
    3–16, "Harlequinade" (May 23, 1994);
    Batman and Harley Quinn (2017
    motion picture).
62. Langley (2012), p. 148, citing *Gotham
    City Sirens* #24 (2011).
63. *Heroes in Crisis* #1–6 (2018–2019).
64. *Batman: The Killing Joke* (1988).
65. *Batman: The Killing Joke* (1988).
66. Gobin & Freyd (2014).
67. *Batman* #615 (2003).
68. *Batman: The Killing Joke* (1988).
69. Brock et al. (2016)
70. Substance Abuse and Mental Health
    Services Administration (2014).
71. *Batman: The Killing Joke* (1988).

EXPLAINING THE JOKE 14-1:
WRITER/EDITOR LEN WEIN

Travis Langley

Len Wein "edited and wrote Batman for many years, and wrote a whole batch of Joker stories," as he put it.[1] Co-creator of characters such as Swamp Thing and prominent X-Men including Storm and Wolverine,[2] Len made lasting contributions to Batman's history, in terms of the guidance he gave to authors whose work he edited, the tales that he told on his own, and creations such as Wayne Foundation executive Lucius Fox.[3] Even though he once told an interviewer that "Lucius Fox has earned me a great deal more money than Wolverine ever has,"[4] he said during our last conversation that this had changed and that "Marvel's treating me well."[5]

In the course of our various discussions and convention panels together, Len shared some thoughts on the Joker.[6]

The Greatest Villain

Len Wein: He's the only villain who knows he's the villain and embraces it. He adores being evil. There's a moment in *The Dark Knight* when he says essentially, "You know, if I kill you, I win. If you kill me, I win." How do you beat something like that?

The Greatest Joker Actor

Wein: I think for me it's a tie. It's [Heath] Ledger (*The Dark Knight*), who's brilliant in the role and has the moment when I realize he is fully identified, when he still has the fire engine and he's driving with his head out the window and his tongue lolling. He's a mad dog! And the other one is Mark Hamill (*Batman: The Animated Series*).

Does Batman Need the Joker?

Wein: Basically, they're the only ones who can provide a real challenge [for each other]. Batman needs somebody as good as he is to fight. It's embarrassing to pit him against Bugsy Malone in a suit. There's no competition. So he needs someone as off as he is.

The Joker's Origin

Wein: When Alan [Moore] first proposed this story to me and turned in the original outline [for the graphic novel *Batman: The Killing Joke*], it was to be the definitive origin of the Joker, he said. I said, "That's wonderful, but I don't think anyone has the right to do that." I think there are many characters in comics that are better served the less you know about them. So I said, "You can't make it definitive. It's a great story. You gotta fix that." And so he adds [to the Joker's dialogue], "Sometimes I remember it one way, sometimes another," just to clear the air. It's a great story, but maybe it's all in his head. You never know."

NOTES

1. Weiner et al. (2016).
2. Swamp Thing—*House of Secrets* #92 (1971); Storm—*Giant-Size X-Men* #1 (1975); Wolverine—*The Incredible Hulk* #180–181 (1974).
3. *Batman* #307 (1979).
4. Quoted by Burlingame (2013).
5. Wein (2015, September 11), personal communication.
6. Langley et al. (2012); Letamendi et al. (2011); and especially Weiner et al. (2016).

EXPLAINING THE JOKE 14-2:
ACTOR KEVIN CONROY, PART 2

Travis Langley

Continued from Explaining the Joke 5–1: Actor Kevin Conroy, Part 1 (page 107).

Favorite Scene

Kevin Conroy: *The Killing Joke* at the end, playing that last scene with Mark [Hamill] was really challenging for me, and I loved it. That laugh, getting into that crazy laugh, I was really proud of that.

Travis Langley: What did you see as the reason why Batman is laughing at the end of *The Killing Joke*?

Conroy: I've always seen Batman and Joker defining one another, the ying and the yang. I wouldn't be the Batman I am without Joker, and Joker without Batman. I see the laugh at the end as taking the Joker inside me and that laugh is the Joker's sigh to me. *[Does some of the laugh]* As it grew, it got crazier and crazier. I wanted it to be the Joker laugh because it was the element of Joker in Batman.

Favorite Villain

Conroy: Joker, because of my relationship with Mark. The whole cast is crazy, and Batman doesn't kill so he puts them away at Arkham Asylum. Everybody is there. So trapping Batman there, having to find his way out was a brilliant idea. All the villains are fantastic, part of the secret sauce of the show is this crazy tribe of villains.

　　The wonderful thing about working with Mark, the process of making the show, the actors get the scripts first. So nothing has been tainted. When we first started to do the show, all we had were sketches. We were really working from scripts and our imagination. The interaction is like a radio play. I always equate it to kids playing ball when we were little, and the more generous the other kid, the better the volley of the ball. Mark and I really volleyed the ball back and forth together, we loved to play catch, we loved to watch each other act. When you can see it *[Slips into Mark Hamill as Joker impression]* Eww, Batty *[Slips out of impression]* and then he's gonna eat the microphone! He becomes Joker. You know Jim Carrey's rubber face? Mark does that, he transforms and becomes the character. So you're in this small room with this madman, it's a little scary. *[Audience laughs]* Who knew that was going to come out of him! I only knew him as Luke Skywalker, like Luke Skywalker is doing Joker—are you kidding? He's such a nice young man. Then he comes in to this performance like an alien coming out of his throat.

So early on, it's just us! Then six months in, around '92 or even '91, well before it came on the air, the first artwork came back. This stuff would go to Korea—South Korea, not North—and get painted. We'd do ADR [automated dialog replacement] and sync audio with visual. So they'd show us animation with the soundtrack, and there'd always be mistakes; it was all done by hand. There's lots of little line changes, the fight sounds and stuff. Mark and I are in there together doing the first ADR of the show of the first frames that have come back. *[Performances Woosh]* The sound comes up, the Shirley Walker score, and those colors go across the screen, the characters come up on the screen. I look at Mark and I say, "Did you know this is going to be like this?" *[Audience laughs]* He says, "I didn't have a clue!" We were grown actors that felt like we were 12 years old. It was so beautiful and we both realized it was something very special.

15

Therapy: Can Counseling Cure the Clown?

TRAVIS LANGLEY, APRYL A. ALEXANDER,
VANESSA HICKS, WILLIAM SHARP,
JUSTINE MASTIN, YONI SOBIN,
JENNA BUSCH, ASHER JOHNSON,
ERIN CURRIE, & KATHLEEN LA FORGIA

*"Maybe this is our last chance to sort this bloody mess out.
If you don't take it, then we're locked onto a suicide course."*
—Batman to the Joker[1]

THE GRAPHIC NOVEL *Batman: The Killing Joke* begins and ends with Batman trying to reach out to the Joker, to offer him a chance to change course before it kills either of them. "I just wanted to know that I'd made a genuine attempt to talk things over and avert that outcome. Just once," Batman says, and so he offers his time and resources toward helping the Joker become a better human being. "We could work together. I could rehabilitate you. You needn't be out there on the edge anymore." The Joker turns him down, though, saying, "No. It's too late for that. Far too late."[2]

But what if he'd said, Yes?

The therapist who's married to this chapter's first author says that the psychopathic Joker would just be lying. "He seems like the type to pretend to go along with treatment so he can manipulate the situation, and it ends in a big mess."When dealing with criminal psychopaths, "you might get some of them to improve for selfish reasons if they'll start to recognize the negative consequences their actions cause themselves, but he hasn't really suffered those."[3] True, pain and incarceration do not even bother the Joker. He escapes confinement seemingly whenever he pleases. Sometimes, though, he does suffer other unpleasant consequences—in particular, depression and frustration. When injuries hinder him from promptly committing his next crime, he broods over his failures.[4] Because the Joker secludes himself during these spells, Batman and the stories' readers rarely glimpse these episodes. Therapists could try to help the Joker recognize those depressive periods as aversive consequences of crime, but they might only find that the Joker instead interprets them as consequences of failure. That, in turn, might only motivate him to get better at being bad.

No matter how grim the client's prognosis might seem, not all therapists have the liberty to dismiss the remorseless recalcitrant as a hopeless case. To keep a person locked up under involuntary confinement, forensic psychiatric hospitals must adhere to strict guidelines. They may have to follow laws that require them to develop treatment plans unless they want the person to walk free (*absolute discharge*) or, when a *guilty but mentally ill* verdict permits, be deemed sane enough to go to prison to serve the remainder of a criminal sentence.[5] Once authorities start sending the Joker to the asylum instead of prison,[6] this becomes an issue for the hospital administrators and clinicians who are required to develop a treatment plan, even for someone so *treatment-resistant.*

Psychiatric hospitalization for the criminally insane generally includes medication and plenty of it.[7] Arkham Asylum shows not a complete absence of medication to reduce the inmates' immediate dangerousness, but a puzzling shortage of meds or signs that the residents are receiving any. Why is that every time security falls apart and a mass breakout occurs, all the supervillains are unsedated and ready to spring into action?

When criminal behavior results from a client's mood state, judgment impairment, hallucinations, or delusions, prescribing medication makes sense, but how does the hospital handle the criminal whose personality produces the malice? Medications treat states, not traits. A pill cannot give someone a personality—not even a whole bottle's worth forced down the Joker's throat (though it did make a great alternate-reality story).[8] When morphine, mood stabilizers, and antipsychotic meds calm the Joker enough to converse more rationally than usual, he's still a cruel crook who'd love to commit murder.[9] Incidents in which telepathic manipulation or a resurrection pit makes the Joker seem more lucid[10] provide no hint as to what he's really like. A sci-fi burst of apparent sanity suggests nothing about real-world human nature or how the Joker might respond to any actual treatment. In fact, after the divinely powered Spectre momentarily enters the Joker's soul and makes him suffer the horror of all his sins, the Spectre concludes that the Joker truly has no conscience.[11] Medication alone cannot remake a monster.

Without medications, what can a therapist do? Mostly, Arkham's therapists talk. These psychiatrists and psychologists encourage patients to discuss their lives, thoughts, and desires, usually following no obvious therapeutic model.[12] Stories about Arkham therapists show them working alone, occasionally sharing a thought with a colleague or supervisor, but otherwise nobody knows what they're up to without reading their notes. That is unrealistic. We don't see evidence of weekly staffings of the entire treatment team, which would include people such as a psychiatrist, psychologist, neuropsychologist, physician, social worker, head nurse, occupational therapist, rehabilitation therapist, substance abuse counselor, and other specialists.[13] Such meetings would not only provide the primary clinician with input and support, but they might also help lower the frequency with which Arkham staffers turn into supervillains or join the long list of victims.

Now let's hold our staff meeting and find out what our professionals, who do follow established therapeutic models, think about the potential psychotherapies.

I. Him

Travis Langley

Among the psychologists and other professionals who have written for this Popular Culture Psychology series and who weighed in on this issue, the nontherapists among us expressed greater pessimism as to whether anything could ever make the Joker better. One of our forensic psychologists agreed with the Punisher, who raises his gun to the Joker during a Marvel/DC crossover and tells him, "I've got all the therapy you need right here, comedian."[14] Others, though, must at least consider whether therapy is possible in the course of their clinical and counseling occupations. None of us said definitely, "Yes, the Joker will respond well to treatment," and it's even possible that therapy could teach him new tricks for manipulating others, but some gave him a tentative, wary "maybe."

Empathy Training for Psychopaths

Apryl A. Alexander

Given psychopaths' high likelihood of recidivism and the harm they cause society, mental health professionals have been trying to identify treatment approaches for individuals with high psychopathic traits. Although there is pessimism surrounding amenability to treatment for psychopathy, there is little scientific evidence to suggest psychopathy is untreatable.[15]

It is no surprise that the Joker has been characterized as a psychopath.[16] One of the hallmark features of psychopathy is lack of empathy. Lack of empathy is consistently included in different conceptualizations of psychopathy.[17] However, there is little consensus on how *empathy* is operationally defined. In recent conceptualizations, six elements comprise empathy: emotional recognition; victim harm recognition; assuming responsibility; perspective-taking; guilt response; and emotional expression.[18]

- *Emotional recognition* is the ability to recognize one's own emotions and emotions of others or identifying feelings.

- *Victim harm recognition* is the ability to identify and recognize the harm inflicted upon the victim through the offender's transgression or acknowledging the violation of the victim.

- *Assuming responsibility* simply means the offender accepts full responsibility for his or her actions without distortions.

- *Perspective-taking* is identifying with one's victim(s) and developing a compassionate understanding of the victim(s).

- *Guilt response* is feeling bad for violating the victim and experiencing the victim's emotional state.

- *Emotional expression* means the victim's pain and hurt is experienced by the offender as he or she struggles through victim impact issues.

One does not have to venture far to find examples of how the Joker exhibits each of these elements. He repeatedly maims, harms, kills, and manipulates others with little to no recognition of their harm unless he is making a joke of it. The infamous "pencil trick" in the film *The Dark Knight* further elucidates his lack of emotional expression and guilt response when he harms others. Given these examples, it's reasonable for a mental health professional to consider indicators of increased empathy as a treatment goal for the Joker.

Many correctional treatment programs incorporate empathy interventions in an effort to enhance and promote empathy toward victims. These interventions often involve improving perspective-taking skills through role playing/taking, attribution retraining, writing hypothetical apology letters to the victim(s), and learning to better decode facial expressions to enhance emotional recognition.[19] Researchers and treatment providers have remarked that highly antisocial or psychopathic offenders cannot learn empathy if they do not have any.[20] Those with psychopathic traits are often skilled in manipulation and impression management.[21] Individuals who lack empathy may be motivated to simulate empathy.[22] Further, individuals who are high in psychopathic traits can be adept at identifying vulnerable staff, forging alliances with them, and may attempt to manipulate staff to provide special favors, break institutional rules, violate boundaries, and/or even develop personal or sexual relationships with them.[23] The Joker engages in many of these behaviors in his many hospitalizations at Arkham Asylum. Mental health professionals have been fooled by his narratives, superficial charm, and manipulations. The Joker coaxes psychiatrist Dr. Harleen Quinzel into falling in love with him and helping him escape from Arkham Asylum, which violates her professional ethics.[24] Research is unclear as to whether current victim empathy interventions focusing on developing empathy for past victims generalizes to future situations, nor does empirical research consistently support this idea.[25]

Is there hope that the Joker can be treated and desist from crime? It's unclear, especially since Arkham Asylum cannot hold him long" enough to undergo intensive assessment and treatment. In the graphic novel *Batman: The Killing Joke*, dialogue between Batman and the Joker suggests that the Joker himself does not believe he can successfully rehabilitate.[26] Though it is recognized that he has psychopathic traits warranting treatment, approaches to reducing victim empathy should be avoided.

Existential-Phenomenological Therapy
Vanessa Hicks

Unlike other schools of psychological theory, *existential-phenomenological psychology* relies less on expert interpretations of behavior and more on existence as it is humanly experienced.[27] In essence, "it is less important *what* we believe than the *manner* in which we believe."[28] *Existential-phenomenological therapy* with Harley Quinn and the Joker would focus on my employing a nonpathologizing way of being and actively avoiding the position of an expert dispensing interpretations:[29] Don't treat them like they're sick, and don't act coldly clinical. The purpose of this therapy is not to "cure" or "fix," but rather to authentically *understand*.

Adopting an existential approach to psychotherapy requires that an emphasis be placed on the individual's concrete lived experience.[30] Investigation into one's lived experience is achieved through the *phenomenological method*, which requires the therapist to stay "open to the details of thought, feeling, imagination, and behaviour precisely as they occur."[31] This investigative style involves three steps: (1) setting aside preliminary biases to focus primarily on the immediate data of experience; (2) focusing on description, rather than explanation; and (3) avoiding placing hierarchies of significance upon descriptions and instead treating each as having equal value.[32]

The Joker is often portrayed as somewhat of an anarchist. He urges others to "introduce a little anarchy," while going on to describe himself as an "agent of chaos."[33] The Joker appears to utilize aspects of the phenomenological method, himself, adopting a state of being ("chaos") that is outwardly devoid of any hierarchy of values. Following an exclamation such as this in therapy, I would first *set aside* whatever biases I have concerning "chaos" and its subsequent value. Second, I would ask a series of questions to extrapolate what the Joker understands to be "chaos." Examples might include "Describe a situation you would categorize as chaotic," or "What do you mean by chaos being 'fair'?" Thus, my primary purpose remains exploring the Joker's understandings of the world through *description*.

The Joker provides context for what he considers to be chaotic, as he describes the difference between "sane men" and "lunacy" as "just one bad day." He claims that the realization of "what a black, awful joke the world was" caused him to go "crazy as a coot."[34] Similarly, Harley Quinn says she and the Joker are bound by lunacy, as she loves him "for the way his demons dance with mine."[35] Both the Joker and Harley continue to reject any sort of hierarchy of values, such that they do not view "lunacy" as any less valuable than sanity. Quite the contrary, the Joker is fond of describing himself as "differently sane."[36]

As a therapist, I serve as a representative of all others in the Joker's and Harley's worlds, and I must challenge their beliefs and assumptions regarding others, along with the impact on their ways of being.[37] While the Joker purports to abandon traditional systems of values, he indirectly constructs a new hierarchy of significance, one that denounces order and rationality. Thus, from an existential standpoint, the Joker has not yet fully gained awareness of the freedom he has to mold his perspectives as he sees fit, as his ways of being seem somewhat reactionary to those he deems as unworthy. Conversely, Harley exhibits instances of heightened awareness of the freedom of thought, belief, and behavior that she possesses, most notably in her assertions that the Joker's opinions of her are "only a ghost of time."[38] Moving forward in therapy, my primary aim would be to help the Joker gain awareness and change those things within his control to change, while acknowledging and accepting those aspects of his legacy he cannot change.[39] Somewhat similarly, Harley is apt to continue to gain further insight into her individual freedom and power to make meaning in her life as she so chooses through the unfolding dialogue between her and the therapist.[40]

Psychoanalysis

William Sharp

The Joker as sociopath wouldn't respond well to classical psychoanalysis. Freud wouldn't trust that any Oedipal transference could be garnered in the service of fusing the life and death drives differently, as he is so gratified with carnage and killing. Could other contemporary psychoanalytic approaches help the Joker? Perhaps.

Many since Kernberg, Kohut, and Spotnitz considered pre-Oedipal transferences. Some might be able to keep the Joker in therapy, but, again, between the narcissism and getting the Joker interested in any other option when he gets so much gratification with his current behaviors, I doubt it. Case in point: He gets Harley to come to him as opposed to him coming to the side of "civilization." I think to be successful, one would really have to remember that any character or personality, when charged with a relationship, puts up resistances. We all have resistances. Any of us coming to therapy will resist; we can't help it. Our personality is our way of dealing with certain feelings. If someone could remember and not pathologize the Joker, get curious about why he is the way he is—more from some feeling induced, maybe even some feeling he never got in critical windows of development—then he or she might be able to help. But he is likely to kill you first, so what's there to do? Pass him on to some intern studying primitive mental states and hope she doesn't get killed?

As for Harley—totally able to bring her back. She has shown a capacity in her former life so it's in there. Maybe think of her case as more a *folie à deux*? She does well with the band of crazies in the Suicide Squad. She is not the sociopath that the Joker is. Her antisocial behavior comes later in life, so I wouldn't think of it as core to her character. Not that I am saying it would be easy, but she would be interesting and a challenging case—with some hope. I think along the lines of a Sybil[41] or *Three Faces of Eve*[42] (not their multiple personality diagnosis, but as a major undertaking). Both Harley and the Joker remind us of what happens when drives are fused in ways that destruction (*tension reduction*) is the gratification and how working with early mental states is taxing on the therapist (if not downright deadly).

Narrative Couples Therapy

Justine Mastin

Within the psychotherapy community, professionals debate about the use of couples counseling when violence is present in a relationship.[43] Many therapists consider it necessary for the perpetrator to attend "pro-feminist-based"[44] treatment before even beginning couples counseling. There is evidence that couples counseling—even in couples where violence is present—has benefits and can be performed safely.[45] There are also some jurisdictional provisions surrounding the use of couples counseling when violence is present,[46] but it's unlikely that Gotham City has these.

While there are myriad types of couples counseling available—assuming that Harley is able to get her mischievous companion to agree to such a thing—the best option would be *narrative couples therapy*. An advantage of this modality is the stance of the therapist as a collaborator for the couple, rather than an expert. The Joker does not respond well to others trying to exert power over him.[47] He does a bit better when others have power *with* him[48] (such as a few occasions when he works with Lex Luthor[49]). Harley could benefit greatly from this collaborative approach in her own right, after being accustomed to having power held over her. Being seen as the expert on her own life—and her own relationship—might be the most healing part of this therapy for Harley, regardless of what happens within the tricksters' relationship.

Finding healing for the Joker—and for the relationship—will be trickier.[50] In *narrative couples therapy*, the skill of "externalizing"[51] is of extreme import. In this paradigm, the couple is not seen as a problem, but rather the problem is seen as the problem. This nonpathological languaging might appeal to both the Joker and—as Dr. Quinzel has clearly turned her back on clinical interpretations—Harley as well. Externalizing gives the couple the opportunity to name their problem. Might they name this problem Batman? Narrative couples therapy explores clients' *problem-saturated story*,[52] meaning the story where the problem is dominant. The dominant narrative for the Joker and Harley is certainly centered around Batman. For Harley, she resents that her partner would rather pursue his vendetta against the Dark Knight, either solo or with her playing a supporting role, than spend quality time scheming with her and seeing her as an equal partner.[53] As for the Joker, he gets infuriated when Harley tries to be an equal partner, rather than accepting her lower-status role as just another one of his lackeys, so that he can continue his tête-à-tête with Batman.

This question of where the two see each other in their lives calls upon another narrative therapy technique, *re-membering*,[54] which asks the question: Who are the members in our "club" of life and what is their status there? At times when Harley is submissive to the Joker, she accepts him as her superior, though she longs for more. And for the Joker, Harley is a subordinate who continues to try to rise above her station, much to his chagrin.[55] This disagreement about who the Joker and Harley are to one another generates tension in their relationship.

In order to move clients away from the problem-saturated story, a narrative couples therapist looks for unique outcomes,[56] times when the narrative deviates from the problem-saturated story. In this case, when was a time that the two engaged with each other as if they were equal teammates? There are a few occasions that we can point to as unique outcomes: the Joker keeping a photo of Harley on his desk,[57] expressing momentary concern for Harley's repeated disdain of fish,[58] and indicating that his reason for sending Harley away on a rocket (problem) is because time with her reminds him of what it's like "to care for someone who cares for me" and is "the first time in recent memory I've had those feelings" (deviation).[59] The narrative couples therapist might attempt to treat these as indications of a side of the Joker that has the ability to feel and even care about Harley, as one would do with a partner instead of a subordinate. When Harley uses her preferred term of affection for the Joker, *puddin'*, instead of the more formal *Mister J.* or *Boss*, it indicates times when she feels a more equal power differential.

By exploring the problem-saturated story, externalizing the problem, re-membering, and finding unique outcomes, a new *re-authored* narrative begins to form. With skillful re-authoring of the couple's narrative, these two might just find a conclusion to their (bad) love story in which they both survive.

II. Her
Travis Langley

Because so many of this book's writers hold little hope that therapy could make the Joker a better person and because it might make him worse, most stayed out of this chapter because they had little to add beyond a flat no. But like those who give the Joker a very tentative maybe, those who vote no on him nevertheless agree that there is hope for the former psychiatrist now known as Harley Quinn.

Acceptance and Commitment Therapy
Yoni Sobin & Jenna Busch

Acceptance and Commitment Therapy (ACT) assumes that psychological distress results from trying to avoid the unavoidable in our thoughts and emotions and from engaging in actions inconsistent with our core values. ACT's goal is to help slow down the process, take a step back, check perspective, and experience life, including the good and bad equally.[60]

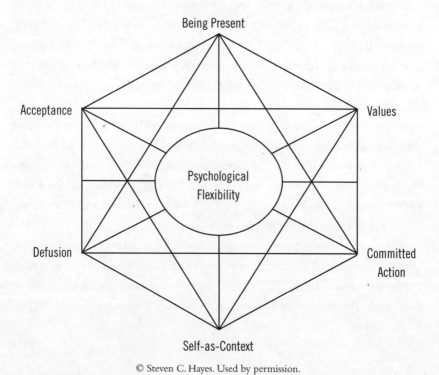

© Steven C. Hayes. Used by permission.

ACT has been used to treat unhealthy interpersonal problems.[61] ACT-based treatment might help Harley to (1) recognize the toxicity of her relationship with the Joker, (2) see the futility of pursuing the Joker's affections, (3) regain agency in forming healthy validating relationships, and, importantly, (4) rediscover herself.

The first sessions would introduce Harley to the ACT model. Harley and her therapist would practice mindfulness, focusing on becoming an observer of—rather than a believer in—thoughts such as "I can't handle this without Mistah J." or "Joker knows best." The therapist would help Harley become like a member of the audience who sees the Joker's manipulations, rather than being an actor whose lines are scripted for her by the Joker. For instance, he knows that a small gesture will turn Harley's attentions back to him. When he sends her flowers after pushing her out a window, her response is that his abuse "feels like a kiss" rather than scorning him, as she does moments before she sees the flowers.[62] Harley would come to see her thoughts of (co)dependency and self-degradation are essentially no different from "The sky is blue" or "Batman fights crime in Gotham."

If successful, Harley would learn to notice herself (literally and fig-uratively) and pause before acting. The Joker reduces Harley's awareness of her emotions and internal experiences. When Harley is abused by the Joker, he sometimes makes small, seemingly conciliatory (but actually manipulative) gestures, such as leaving a rose with a note. Despite his actions, such as putting her in the hospital, she has repeatedly pushed aside her anger and hurt, then gone back to him.

ACT would take Harley through a series of steps toward healthier functioning.

- *Defusion* (stepping back and observing her thoughts and emotions objectively) helps her identify emotions and thoughts, giving them less power over her decision-making, reducing her autopilot tendencies.

- This leads to *acceptance* (allowing her thoughts and emotions to exist without judgment) and gives her freedom even if she con-tinues to associate with the Joker. Harley might learn to accept,

"I am experiencing pain, betrayal, and hurt because Joker hit me."
Harley would learn to identify the internal experiences of shame
and guilt holding her back from leaving the Joker.

- Identifying her true *values*, Harley would likely discover how
  highly she values relationships and helping others (she is a psychiatrist, after all), feeling connected, and enjoying adventure.
  Understanding that targeting Batman does not represent her
  values, she would discover how she has become *fused* with the
  Joker's values of superiority and chaos and lost her own direction
  and identity.

- Finding ways to take *committed action*, Harley may seek
  appropriate ways to help others. For instance, when Harley
  realizes the Joker is going to kill Jason Todd in one story,
  she alerts Batman to prevent it from happening.[63] With
  encouragement, Harley may develop a persona focused on
  something positive in her life. She already likes helping residents
  at the Free Spirit Assisted Living Home.[64]

Over time, Harley would step back and recognize that her thoughts
and emotions toward the Joker are not inherently dangerous, and are
only holding her back from building health, reciprocal relationships. She
would be able to view herself as the player rather than the chess piece. As
Harley distances herself from the Joker's manipulations, a strong support
network of friends and allies would be crucial. Most notably, she forms a
healthier relationship with the infamous Poison Ivy, who builds Harley
up instead of beating her down: "Cheer up, kid. You just need some
lessons in good ole female self-esteem."[65]

Schema Therapy

Asher Johnson with Travis Langley

A *schema*, a.k.a. *scheme*, is an underlying mental pattern of interrelated
ideas connected in the structure of how a person perceives things and
thinks about them.[66] Your schema of the concept "clown" might include
costumes, makeup, tiny cars, humor, slapstick, pies in the face, monkeys,

circuses, tears, sad clowns, friendly clowns, scary clowns, sewer openings, movies or cartoons featuring clowns, locations where you saw clowns, and anything at all that reminds you of clowns and associated concepts. A toddler who says, "Clown," upon seeing a bald man who has frizzy hair on the side has done so because of a clown schema barely beginning to develop.[67] Some sets of associations can become pervasive, rigid, and dysfunctional to the point that they are *maladaptive*: They interfere with the person's ability to function, to adapt to life,[68] such as when a phobia generalizes so severely that the person afraid of a white rat then feels anxiety at the mere sight of fur or other small animals.[69]

Schema therapy identifies maladaptive schema modes to help the client to develop more functional associations and ways of viewing the situation at hand. For instance, Harley Quinn's first crush is a high school boy named Bernie Bash, the first person who ever seems to understand her, even though he does not fulfill her emotional needs.Because this sense of feeling understood by someone becomes a strong part of her schema for people she finds attractive, a person who activates that part of the pattern (in this case, seeming to understand her) may also activate the associated attraction. She says that she falls for the Joker because of "the way he spoke to me, as if he knew me my whole life."[70]

If Harley operates from an early age on a maladaptive schema of emotional deprivation, she learns to expect that most people will not know how to fulfill her emotional needs, and therefore this expectation prepares her to accept this from intimate partners.[71] It is common for an individual who operates on an expectation of emotional deprivation to select emotionally unavailable partners, such as the Joker, while also dealing with the consistent frustration that her partner will not meet all her needs.[72]

A key part of schema therapy, *schema mode work*, consists of seven steps to help her work through her schema mode of emotional deprivation:

1. Identify and label Harley's relevant schemas.

2. Explore the origin and adaptive value of each schema.

3. Link her maladaptive associations to her current problems.

4. Demonstrate the advantages of modifying or giving up an association if it interferes with access to a healthier one.

5. Access Harley's emotionally deprived childhood through imagery.

6. Conduct dialogue among the modes, with the therapist initially modeling the healthy adult.

7. Assist Harley with generalizing her healthier schemas to life situations outside therapy sessions.

Not everyone can be helped. Sometimes an individual's maladaptive schema is *ego-syntonic*, which means the individual remains in agreement with his or her thought processes and the individual continues to believe that some of the maladaptive behaviors are working.

Feminist Therapy
Erin Currie

Many feminists who were therapists during the civil rights area saw the negative impacts that social and political systems had on their female clients' mental health, but the traditional therapies didn't provide tools for their treatment. They created feminist therapy to address the negative impacts: society's self-fulfilling prophecy associating masculinity with power and success, and femininity with weakness and dependence; the assumption that gendered behavior is natural and that deviation is unnatural and shameful; and the traumas created by misogyny, such as domestic violence, sexual assault, and denial of reproductive autonomy.[73] *Feminist therapy* was originally designed to treat women, so it is an obvious fit for Harley Quinn. However, it has been expanded to address the ways that men are also negatively impacted by gender socialization, of which the Joker has been the victim as well.[74]

The foundation of feminist therapy is an egalitarian relationship between therapist and client in which the therapist models an alternative to society's devaluation of the perspectives of the less powerful. Therapy is seen as the meeting of two experts: the therapist with expertise in mental health, and the client with expertise in his or her own thoughts, feelings, and lived experiences.[75] Although Harley has evolved beyond being the Joker's love-struck lackey and abused girlfriend, she still has a tendency to submit to more dominant others.[76] Using an egalitarian approach, a therapist can help clients identify their own needs and goals. For clients like Harley, who are used to following orders, this can be a lengthy process. Working with the Joker from an egalitarian approach could challenge his perception of the world as being made up of those with power and those without, a view he uses to justify his criminal behavior.[77]

Feminist therapists work with clients to explore the social construction(s) of gender. Doing a gender analysis with the Joker, a therapist would look for the impacts of the rules of masculinity. The root of his life of crime can be traced back to the pressure to live up to the masculine ideal of being a financially successful provider for his family. In *The Killing Joke*'s version of his history, he joins a criminal group when his comedian career won't support his growing family. The death of his pregnant wife and the physical transformation he experiences during that first criminal act are significant traumas.[78] The traditional rules of masculinity that prohibit seeking support and expressing emotions associated with weakness, such as sadness and fear, prevented him from using healthy methods for dealing with his trauma.[79] The Joker adheres to the methods prescribed to men who have been hurt: lashing out in violence, dissociation from emotion, and distancing from intimate relationships.[80] The therapist's job would be to introduce him to healthier, more effective ways to deal with his trauma.[81]

In addition to addressing gender directly, the impacts of a wide range of power inequalities are addressed in feminist therapy.[82] Harley is an excellent example of the ways in which unequal access to power can impact one's mental health. If Dr. Harleen Quinzel had been exposed to feminist therapy as part of her training as a psychiatrist, she might have been able to change Gotham's corrupt power structures through community organizing instead of joining the Joker in violence that harms Gotham's powerful and powerless alike.

The ultimate goal of feminist therapy is client empowerment. Clinical interventions emphasize identifying and promoting the client's strengths, especially those who have been shamed during gender socialization. The client and therapist work together to develop the client's skills and identify social connections to overcome the client's limitations.[83] Although the Joker may think he has freedom through his actions, he has denied himself a quality emotional and relational life.[84] A feminist therapist would attempt to help him understand his losses and find ways to create those connections. For Harley, therapy would focus on identifying the internal resources and relationships that support her in promoting healthy growth.

Ecosystemic Structural Family Therapy

Kathleen La Forgia

When Harley finally moves into her own comic series, she has come to realize that her relationship with Mister J is not healthy. She has changed from being in love with him to vehemently loathing him. Harley at different times builds support systems for herself by doing things such as sharing a house with roommates Poison Ivy and Catwoman,[85] joining a roller derby team,[86] and working at a nursing home.[87] Despite the involuntary and sometimes adversarial nature of her association with the Suicide Squad, she connects with some of its members as well.[88] Despite his grim presentation, Batman can be caring and sensitive, and he has shown that side of himself to Harley before. So it isn't far-fetched to consider that he would somehow reach out to her biological family in an attempt to help her, as she is one of the only members of Batman's rogues' gallery known to have an ongoing relationship with her family. Supported by a Wayne Enterprises grant, the whole family could begin family therapy.

Ecosystemic structural family therapy (ESFT) follows the assumption that family structure and functioning influence its members' mental health and adaptive responses, and that an understanding of these will help therapists identify clients' needs, strengths, and social supports.[89] So in order to estimate Harley's chances of recovery, healing, and redemption (that is, assess the *prognosis*), we look at her family system.

When she goes home to celebrate the holidays with her family, readers first learn how Harley relates to her immediate relatives:[90] Her mother Sharon Quinzel shows concern for both of her grown children. Mama Sharon is supportive of her children, doing things such as allowing her son Barry to stay there where she can watch him and her grandchildren. Her argument with Harley is not that she is a criminal, but rather that she is not a hero like Superman, Wonder Woman, or Star Girl. Sharon and Harley know brother Barry is lazy. Despite his belief that he's going to be a rock star, he has wasted much money that Harley has given him. Barry's children's look up to their aunt. Harley continues to stay in contact with her father, Nick, who is a con artist in that version of their family story. Though she knows he cannot be trusted, Harley tells him, "Now that I've been a criminal myself, I think I understand some of the choices you had to make." In the alternate universe depicted in the *Injustice* stories, Harley's family also includes sister Delia who cares for Lucy, Harley's daughter by the Joker. Harley has frequent contact with both Delia and Lucy, who sees her as an eccentric aunt without knowing Harley is her mother.[91]

Optimally, ESFT would call for Harley to get help from those who care the most about her, which would be her mother Sharon and her friend-with-benefits Pamela Isley, a.k.a. Poison Ivy. Because of Ivy's criminal record, Sharon may be leery and might not want to work with her, but Poison Ivy has proved time and again that she will support Harley and her healing.[92] Harley Quinn has the ability to rely on her family to feel supported and to trust them to help her in mental health treatment. If her family members accompany her to treatment, as opposed to just individual treatment, Harley may finally begin to identify them as full supports and utilize them to help her move past the anger and loathing that she has for the Joker to stronger and healthier relationships.

Brilliant Conclusion
Travis Langley

"Y'know, I'm a sick man, mister vigilante. I'm really not responsible for what I do. With the proper therapy, I'm sure I could be cured."
—The Joker to the Punisher[93]

> *"No pill can instill empathy, no vaccine can prevent murder in cold blood, and no amount of talk therapy can change an uncaring mind."*
> —journalist and scientist Ross Pomeroy[94]

As you can see, our treatment team members are pessimistic, to say the least, about whether any psychotherapy can help the Joker become a well-balanced, mentally sound member of society. Other types of treatment would have been worthy of inclusion here. For example, *dialectical behavior therapy* (DBT) was originally developed to treat people with chaotic personalities or self-destructive tendencies, and has been used to help abuse survivors.[95] It should not be difficult to imagine its relevance for either the Joker or Harley. Even so, there's a limit to how many ways one chapter should repeat the same basic point: Treating him is a waste of time at best and a risk to many lives at worst, but working with her may be worth a try *if* she's open to the idea, motivated to change, and committed to the ongoing process.

One or two professionals I've met say confidently that they could cure the Joker. Sorry, but in my experience, that ranks up there with saying, "Let's start a treatment group with Jeffrey Dahmer, John Wayne Gacy, Elizabeth Báthory, Charles Manson, and Attila the Hun so I can fix them all." Overwhelmingly, therapists we heard from reached a bleak consensus. "His prognosis is very poor," says Popcorn Psychology podcast's Ben Stover, a therapist and clinical director who notes that the Joker has no interest in changing and "likely would find it funny to make you think you are close to him and to a solution before turning on you."[96] One therapist who wrote for *Supernatural Psychology: Roads Less Traveled* remarks, "He doesn't want to get better, so he won't. We aren't magicians."[97] With so much agreement that therapy will not work on the Joker, does the typical expectation that counseling can cure the killer clown derive from optimism, naïveté, or conceit? "In my experience: mostly optimism," suggests forensic psychologist Colt Blunt. "It's difficult to be a therapist and not believe everyone has some capacity for positive change. However, I think they're wrong and this thinking can be dangerous in the wrong setting."[98]

Consider the world's most heinous serial offenders, the ones who knew exactly what they were doing, who never grew a conscience, and who hurt more people when given the chance. Some of them fooled more than a few therapists, journalists, and, oddly enough, fans. Even therapists who see some signs for hope should proceed with extreme caution. As prominent psychopathy expert Robert Hare warns, "Most therapy programs do little more than provide psychopaths with new excuses and rationalizations for their behavior and new insights into human vulnerability. They may learn new and better ways of manipulating other people."[99] Therapy might teach them new tricks as they learn more about what others want to hear and see from them.

Our contributors show greater, albeit cautious, optimism for Dr. Harleen Quinzel. As Harley Quinn, she has been sidekick, villain, victim, hero, and antihero. Given her history, leaving her unsupervised might be unwise because she has vacillated from bad to good and back to bad more than once. During times of stress, she might backslide and abruptly return to full villainy—*spontaneous recovery* of behavior seemingly extinguished. The risk is especially great considering signs of addictive behavior in her reactions to the Joker. How often has she furiously sworn him off forever one moment but then yearned for him adoringly in the next?[100] It's not all about him, though. Harley likes to misbehave. "The old days were so funnn!" she tells her mother. "It's just . . . things were so simple back when I was a crook," she adds. "Sometimes I just feel overwhelmed and hopeless. I mean, what if I can't hack real life?" These are warning signs.[101] Her mother is right to stay close and offer support. Too often, Harley either gets locked up without receiving adequate mental health services or is allowed to run free without appropriate and supportive supervision—one extreme or another, neither of which includes a realistic (if any) treatment plan.

The therapies for Harley all call for her to be open to help. Her thoughts on counseling are complicated, though. "I don't believe in trauma," she asserts during a confessional session, then mocks her past clients from her own time as a psychiatrist.[102] Her bluster, though, soon breaks down into tears. She appears to be rationalizing, contextualizing therapy in terms of her own past failures. Resistance to therapy is common, and past defenses sometimes have to break down before the person can open up. Her sheer attempt to enter therapy does show that she will try to accept help anyway.

The fact that Harley acts heroically at times, helping others out of genuine sympathy and concern, means there is great hope for her. If the Joker embodies a dangerous distillation of every part of the dark tetrad, maybe Harleen Quinzel can represent the possibility that, no matter what they've done, a criminal can reform. Maybe, just maybe, she can live up to Batman's dream that rehabilitation efforts will succeed, his belief that people can become better, and his faith that most of us want to do right by one another.

"Sometimes people deserve to have their faith rewarded."
—Batman [103]

NOTES

1. *Batman: The Killing Joke* (1988).
2. *Batman: The Killing Joke* (1988).
3. Langley, R. M. (2019, March 10). Personal communication.
4. e.g., *Batman* #638 (2005).
5. Fennell (1992); Morris et al. (2006); Tajjudin & Goodwin (2016).
6. *Batman* #258 (1974).
7. Dunlop & Pinals (2016); Marshall et al. (2005).
8. *Batman: White Knight* #1 (2017). Note, though, that the story, with its exploration of the Batman/Joker dynamic is not canon and therefore depicts a Joker, Jack Napier, who is essentially a different character.
9. *Batman: Cacophony* #3 (2009).
10. *JLA* #15 (1998); *Batman: Legends of the Dark Knight* #145 (2001); *The Spectre* #51 (1997).
11. *The Spectre* #51 (1997).
12. Paraphrased from Langley (2012), p. 138.
13. Fard et al. (2011); Haslam-Hopwood (2003); Yank et al. (1994).
14. *Punisher/Batman* (1994).
15. Salekin (2002). Bassil-Morozow, H. (2004).
16. Langley (2012); Goodwin & Tajjudin (2016); Zullo (2018).
17. Hare & Neumann (2008); Patrick et al. (2009).
18. Carich et al. (2001).
19. Day et al. (2000); Gery et al. (2009); Hanson & Scott (1995).
20. Carich et al. (2003).
21. Hare (2003).
22. Robinson & Rogers (2015).
23. Olver (2018).
24. *The Batman Adventures: Mad Love* (1993); *Batman: Harley Quinn* #1 (1999).
25. Mann & Barnett (in press).
26. *Batman: The Killing Joke* (1988).
27. Heidegger (1962), cited by Spinelli (2005).
28. Spinelli (2005), p. 105.
29. Barnett & Madison (2012), p. 2.
30. Craig (2012), p. 7.
31. Craig (2012), p. 9.
32. Spinelli (2005).
33. *The Dark Knight* (2008 motion picture).
34. *Batman: The Killing Joke* (1988).
35. *Suicide Squad* (2016 motion picture).
36. *Batman and Robin* #14 (2010).
37. Spinelli (2005).
38. *Gotham City Sirens* #24 (2011).
39. Barnett & Madison (2012).
40. Craig (2012).
41. Schreiber (1973).
42. Thigpen & Cleckley (1957).
43. Vall et al. (2015).
44. Oka & Whiting (2011), p. 483.
45. Wendt et al. (2018).
46. O'Leary (2008).
47. *Batman: The Animated Series*, episode 1–11, "Be a Clown" (September 15, 1992).
48. *The Lego Batman Movie* (2017 motion picture).
49. e.g., *Infinite Crisis* #7 (2006).
50. Some of us are betting against any probability of it.—Editor
51. White (2007), p. 9.
52. White (2007).
53. *The Batman Adventures: Mad Love* (1994).
54. White (2007).
55. *The Batman Adventures: Mad Love* (1994); *Suicide Squad* #14–15 (2012–2013).
56. White (2007).
57. *Batman: The Animated Series*, episode 1–56, "Harley and Ivy" (January 18, 1993).

58. *Batman: The Animated Series*, episode 1–33, "The Laughing Fish" (January 10, 1993). The last time she expresses her disdain of fish, he acts concerned for a second, but on the other occasions, he either ignores her objections or shoves a spoonful of fish into her mouth anyway.

59. *Batman: Harley Quinn* (2000).

60. Hayes et al. (2006).

61. McKay et al. (2012).

62. *The Batman Adventures: Mad Love* (1994).

63. *Batman: White Knight* #2 (2017).

64. Beginning in *Harley Quinn* #3 (2014).

65. *Batman: The Animated Series*, episode 1–56, "Harley and Ivy" (January 18, 1993).

66. Ghosh & Giboa (2014); Piaget (1923/1926).

67. Siegler et al. (2003).

68. Young et al. (2006).

69. A cognitive interpretation of behaviorist John Watson's (1920) Little Albert study.

70. *Secret Origins* #4 (2014).

71. Young & First (2003).

72. Young et al. (2006).

73. Enns (2004).

74. Kahn (2010).

75. Conlin (2017).

76. *Harley Quinn* #1 (2014).

77. *Suicide Squad* #6 (2011).

78. *Batman: The Killing Joke* (2012).

79. Mejia (2005).

80. *Batman: Harley Quinn* (1999).

81. Mejia (2005).

82. Conlin (2017).

83. Enns (2004).

84. *Batman: Harley Quinn* (1999).

85. *Gotham City Sirens* #1 (2009).

86. *Harley Quinn* #1 (2014).

87. *Harley Quinn* #3 (2014).

88. *Suicide Squad* #1 (2011).

89. Hyatt-Burkhart (2017); Jones & Lindblad-Goldberg (2002).

90. *Gotham City Sirens* #7 (2010).

91. *Injustice 2* #17 (2018).

92. Robinson (2017).

93. *Punisher/Batman* (1994).

94. Pomeroy (2014).

95. Decker & Naugle (2008); Linehan et al. (1991, 1999)—a topic suggested by Billy San Juan and Esteban Gonzales. This whole chapter evolved in response to Dr. San Juan's DBT idea.

96. Stover (2019).

97. Dickson (2019), who co-authored Kus et al. (2017).

98. Blunt (2019).

99. Hare (1993/1999), pp. 196-197.

100. e.g., *Gotham City Sirens* #1 (2009); *The Batman Adventures: Mad Love* (1994).

101. *Harley Quinn* #51 (2019).

102. *Heroes in Crisis* #1 (2019).

103. *The Dark Knight* (2008 motion picture).

CASE REPORT V CURRENT RECOMMENDATION: RISK MANAGEMENT ASSESSMENT FOR THE SADIST

Summary

Patient "Joker" was referred for risk assessment as part of routine review. Actuarial assessment reveals a significantly elevated static (historical, unchanging) risk for future violence. Of forensic patients with similar scores, 69% were reported to recidivate within 12 years of opportunity. Further, it is important to note that patient's static risk may indeed be elevated beyond predictions as limited information is known about his early history. Further evaluation utilizing a structured professional judgment measure revealed several additional static factors of concern. Patient has a clear history of diagnosis of personality disorders, most notably including antisocial and narcissistic personality disorders. He has a limited history of gainful employment, instead supporting himself through criminal endeavors. He reported being widowed and having a generally positive relationship with his wife until the time of her death, a report he has at times contradicted;[1] regardless of which, his subsequent romantic relationship has been significant for conflict, including domestic violence and attempted murder. He has frequently endorsed attitudes supportive of violence toward others, and, indeed, records suggest that he has presented as deriving pleasure from the pain of others, indicative of a significant degree of sadism. He has consistently been resistant to meaningful participation in treatment, and has utilized such treatment for his own gain, including to manipulate staff and seek methods of escape. Of questionable significance is his mental health history, as records have provided varying and conflicting accounts of his psychiatric diagnoses; as such, it is currently unclear if patient has ever experienced a *bona fide* psychotic disorder, or if his presentation is instead wholly explained by his personality pathology.[2]

As previously noted, utilization of the PCL-R revealed a score indicative of significant traits of psychopathy, which exceed the established cutoff to be labeled as a psychopath. Patient presents with a number of notable traits and features of psychopathy, including glibness/superfi-

cial charm, grandiose sense of self-worth, need for stimulation/prone-
ness to boredom, pathological lying, conning/manipulation, lack of
remorse or guilt, callousness/lack of empathy, parasitic lifestyle, poor
behavioral controls, lack of realistic long-term goals, irresponsibility,
revocation of conditional release, criminal versatility, and, to a lesser
degree, shallow affect. Patient's score was significantly elevated in
comparison to the typical male forensic patient in North America.

Patient's risk is further elevated past baseline by multiple dynamic
(present-focused, changeable) factors. Patient continues to present
with ongoing violent ideation and intent, often expressing his desire
to inflict significant harm or death on those people whom he has perceived as wronging him in the past. Insight is difficult to ascertain;
though patient presents as recognizing—and indeed embracing—the
risk he poses to others, he simultaneously endorses no desire to make
efforts to manage this. He continues to fail to achieve even min-
imum treatment expectations, and consistently violates facility rules.
He presents with ongoing behavioral and affective instability, as evidenced by his volatile nature and propensity for violence, which is difficult to forecast. Predicting his future behavior, absent the structure
of Arkham, is based primarily on his past forays into the community;
that is, should he be released to the community, it is highly likely
he would disregard any and all treatment and management requirements, fail to obtain necessary services, and would almost assuredly
continue his criminal endeavors, both violent and nonviolent.

Conclusions/Recommendations

Based on the totality of available information, it is the opinion of
the undersigned that the patient's risk for future violence is high.
As such, the undersigned offers the following recommendations for
ongoing management of his risk for violence:

- Based on the patient's history of significant violence,
  including multiple homicides, in combination with the
  results of the current assessment, it is the opinion of
  the undersigned that ongoing detention within Arkham

is necessary to manage patient's risk of violence to the public.

- The patient's personality configuration, which is specifically notable for a high degree of psychopathy and sadism, suggests that conventional treatment modalities for violent offenders would be contraindicated. Specifically, treatments focused on victim empathy are unlikely to result in positive changes to personality, and indeed are more likely to result in patient developing further methods of preying on others. Further, the very act of learning about the terror he inflicts on his victims may be pleasurable for him.

- Interventions should focus on behavior management, offering clearly delineated expectations and consequences. Failure to engage in appropriate behaviors should be dealt with according to established facility procedures, including potential loss of liberty, restriction of property, and transfer to more restrictive housing.

- Physical security will be paramount in managing patient's risk. Staff should be diligent in maintaining direct observation of patient's actions and conduct frequent and random searches of his room and property. Any communications should be closely monitored.

- Given the patient's risk of elopement, risk to the public, and risk to Arkham patients and staff, it is highly recommended he not be allowed any independent privileges; that is, he should be kept in restraints and accompanied by staff at all times when not secured in his room. Staff should be rotated frequently to avoid fatigue, and no less than two staff should be assigned to monitor him at any given time. Administration

should prioritize assignment of staff who are seasoned
and have demonstrated resistance to manipulation
attempts.

The undersigned's review of the patient is complete with the submission of this report.

Regards,

Forensic Examiner

Notes
1. *Batman: The Killing Joke* (1988).
2. American Psychiatric Association
   (2000—DSM-IV-R, 2013—DSM-5).

Last Laugh:
Hahahahahahahahahahahahahaha!

TRAVIS LANGLEY

"Some men aren't looking for anything logical, like money.
They can't be bought, bullied, reasoned, or negotiated with.
Some men just want to watch the world burn."
—Alfred Pennyworth[1]

WE COULDN'T LET this end without that bit of insight from Bruce Wayne's butler and father figure, could we? After Alfred tries to make a point about how desperate mobsters "turned to a man they didn't fully understand," Bruce lumps the Joker in with other criminals, saying they're not complicated. So Alfred tries harder to caution him that "perhaps this is a man *you* don't fully understand either" and tells him about the bandit who stole rubies for sport, then threw them away. It's the kind of cautionary note that therapists, investigators, correctional officers, probation officers, and anybody else dealing with manipulative criminals might take to heart: No matter how many suspects and felons fall into recognizable patterns, never assume you can anticipate them all. Force yourself to think outside the box of your own essential humanity when you have to deal with some who show less humanity.

The Joker is a quixotic, chaotic, flexible character, adaptable enough to fit an array of stories that range from those suitable for small children to those that might unnerve the steadiest of adults. He changes to suit the kind of story. More specifically, he changes to suit the kind of Batman in the story at hand. So many people ask who my favorite Joker is, but they're not interchangeable. Jack Nicholson was perfect for the

1989 movie, but that's not the Joker *The Dark Knight* needed—and Heath Ledger's Joker absolutely does not belong in the Adam West show. Much as we'll joke about the Cesar Romero depiction, his was the right Joker for the stories being told. The character adapts in ways that not every villain can. A silly Dracula is just a silly Dracula, possibly parody. Still, I would not be surprised if Mark Hamill could have adjusted his performance to fit any of those depictions, in his own special way.

Delving into the Joker's mind can be unsettling, to say the least. I've enjoyed writing this book, but it's probably good to take a break from exploring a perspective so disturbed. At least two of the actors who played the role reported great difficulty sleeping.[2] When I mentioned this once, Adam West said, "Cesar never had trouble sleeping."[3] Ledger had a history of struggling with his sleeping even before he played this character, so be careful about reading too much into that.[4] We are here to look at human nature but through the filter of fiction. Despite real-world examples along the way, we're analyzing characters to help us talk about human nature. We are not generally analyzing living people or even the recently deceased. Bonnie and Clyde aren't around to care what we have to say about them, nor are the friends and family who knew them. And in case any readers had expected us to analyze the guy who introduced himself as the Joker to witnesses at the movie theater he shot up and to the officers who arrested him, I have to point something out: He never said that. He did *not* say he was the Joker. It was an erroneous report that has bloated into myth.[5] And even that bit of mythbusting, made necessary only because of people's expectations, is all the attention we're giving him here—more consideration than he deserves.

The first book on the psychology of a specific superhero had to look at Batman.[6] The Dark Knight has issues, psychology defines him, and his enemies fill their own asylum. The first book on the psychology of a specific supervillain, in turn, has to look at the so-called king of that asylum. He embodies so many types of human evil and yet he infuses his bedlam with fun.

Just try not to cross paths with that clown in the middle of the night. Probably not in broad daylight, either, come to think of it. So sit back from the comfort of your home or a movie theater here on Earth-Prime, and let yourself enjoy the show.

Robin (Jason Todd): "You caught the Joker . . . saved their lives. That's something."

Batman: "No, Robin, that's everything."[7]

NOTES

1. *The Dark Knight* (2008 motion picture).
2. Lyall (2007); Mehta (2017).
3. Rosenberg et al. (2009).
4. White (2017).
5. Meyer (2015/2016).
6. Langley (2012). Everyone who has ever told me they saw a previous such book has incorrectly cited books (often excellent books, at that) that looked at philosophy, culture, or media—e.g., *Batman Unmasked: Analyzing a Cultural Icon*, by Will Brooker (2001).
7. *Detective Comics* #570 (1987).

About the Editor

Travis Langley, PhD, Distinguished Professor of Psychology, teaches courses on crime, media, and social behavior at Henderson State University. He received his bachelor's from Hendrix College and graduate degrees from Tulane University in New Orleans. His first book, *Batman and Psychology: A Dark and Stormy Knight*, has ranked as one of the top works in comics studies for years, and its audio edition has been one of the best-selling audiobooks of any kind. Dr. Langley is the series editor and lead writer for his Popular Culture Psychology books on *The Walking Dead*, *Game of Thrones*, *Star Wars*, *Star Trek*, *Doctor Who*, *Supernatural*, and many superheroes., and many superheroes. *The Joker Psychology: Evil Clowns and the Women Who Love Them* is his 13th book.

Documentaries such as *AMC Visionaries: Robert Kirkman's Secret History of Comics*, Morgan Spurlock's *Superheroes Decoded*, and *Necessary Evil: Super-Villains of DC Comics* have featured him as an expert interviewee; *Legends of the Knight* spotlighted how he uses stories such as Batman's to teach real psychology; and *Batman & Bill* on Hulu presented him among those who helped see Bill Finger recognized as Batman's co-creator. Travis regularly speaks on media and heroism at universities, conferences, and conventions throughout the world.

Clowns still make him smile—with certain exceptions, of course.

Follow Travis Langley as **@Superherologist** on Twitter, where he ranks among the 10 most popular psychologists. Join him as he investigates the best and worst in human nature through his *Psychology Today* blog, "Beyond Heroes and Villains," and through the Batman and Psychology fan page at **Facebook.com/BatmanBelfry**.

Special Contributors

Jack C. Harris was a senior at the Philadelphia College of Art when he suggested locating H. P. Lovecraft's Arkham Sanitarium in Gotham City to house Two-Face and the Joker. Dennis O'Neil, who wrote the first stories in which Arkham appeared, credit Harris as the asylum's creator. Jack Harris subsequently wrote comic book stories starring Batgirl, Supergirl, Wonder Woman, Spider-Man, the Hulk, and many more, along with the graphic novel *Batman: Castle of the Bat*. He edited numerous comic book titles and taught for the BFA cartooning program at the School of Visual Arts in New York City.

Steve Englehart earned his psychology degree from Wesleyan College before writing comic books. His run in *Detective Comics* with artists Marshall Rogers and Terry Austin has been called the definitive depiction of Batman. It includes the story often cited as the ultimate proof that the Joker really is insane, "The Laughing Fish!" Steve has written nearly every major superhero, as well as novels, children's books, television shows, video games, and more. His creation Star-Lord of *Guardians of the Galaxy* fame is just one example of his many contributions to popular culture.

Michael Uslan, JD, PhD hon., Doctor of Comic Books, is a comic book historian, author, educator, and filmmaker experienced in taking on one Goliath after another. After teaching the first accredited university course on comics folklore, he went on to write comic book adventures of some of our most enduring heroes (The Shadow, Batman, Archie). Michael is best known for bringing Batman to the big screen as executive producer of every Batman movie since the 1980s—originally another giant battle because studio executives had trouble believing audiences could take Batman seriously.

Contributors

Apryl Alexander, PsyD, is a clinical assistant professor at the Graduate School of Professional Psychology at the University of Denver, where she teaches forensic psychology. Dr. Alexander serves as director of the Forensic Institute of Research, Service, and Teaching (FIRST) Outpatient Competency Restoration program and co-director of the University of Denver Prison Arts Initiative (DU PAI). Her research focuses broadly on violence and victimization, forensic assessment, and trauma- and culturally-informed practice. She previously wrote for *Black Panther Psychology: Hidden Kingdoms.*

Eric Bailey, MA, teaches the history of writing and storytelling at Henderson State University. He looks at the connections between ancient mythic figures such as Gilgamesh and modern superheroes and villains such as Iron Man and the Joker, including how they help people face the challenges of life today. He and Travis have been discussing stories for centuries.

Colt J. Blunt, PsyD, LP, has worked as a forensic examiner throughout his career and serves as a guest lecturer and trainer for a number of organizations and educational institutions. He additionally directs a postdoctoral fellowship for aspiring forensic psychologists. His academic interests include the intersection of psychology and law, including the study of criminal behavior. He previously contributed to *The Walking Dead Psychology: Psych of the Living Dead; Star Wars Psychology: Dark Side of the Mind; Game of Thrones Psychology: The Mind is Dark and Full of Terrors; Star Trek Psychology: The Mental Frontier; Supernatural Psychology: Roads Less Traveled;* and *Daredevil Psychology: The Devil You Know.*

Jenna Busch is the founder of Legion of Leia, now at VitalThrills.com. She co-hosted *Cocktails with Stan* with the legendary Stan Lee and hosted *Most Craved.* Busch has co-authored chapters and features in every book in this Popular Culture Psychology series from *Star Wars Psychology: Dark Side of the Mind* onward. She can be reached on Twitter @JennaBusch.

Shelly Clevenger, PhD, is a criminologist who studies sexual assault and intimate-partner violence. She has published numerous peer-reviewed journal articles and books in this area. She has presented her original research on these topics to the UN Women and on Capitol Hill at a congressional briefing. She often uses comic books in her courses to examine interpersonal violence, rape, and gender. She first fell in love with the world of Batman as a child when she read *Detective Comics* #40 and met Basil Karlo, also known as Clayface. While the Joker is cool, Clayface is, in her opinion, the absolute best villain, as he can be anyone. She is also the (self-proclaimed) biggest Incredible Hulk comic book fan in the world. She collects all things Hulk.

 **Erin Currie, PhD, LP,** is an instructor, therapist, and consultant by day. Driven to use her psychology superpowers for good, she founded the consulting practice MyPsychgeek, LLC, to help people develop their own superpowers through professional and team development. By night she gives her inner geek free rein to write about the psychological factors that influence her favorite characters. She also wrote for *Game of Thrones Psychology, Doctor Who Psychology, Wonder Woman Psychology,* and *Supernatural Psychology.*

Sibe Doosje, PhD, teaches clinical and health psychology at Utrecht University, Netherlands. Emphasizing humor in relation to health, he researches instrument development, gender differences in sense of humor, and healthcare clowning. His Humor Lab gives him a voice for popularizing science. Internationally recognized, he lectures and gives workshops on the science of humor.

 Larisa A. Garski, MA, LMFT, is a psychotherapist and supervisor at Empowered Therapy in Chicago, IL. She specializes in working with women, families, and young adults who identify as outside the mainstream—such as those in the geek and LGBTQIA communities. She regularly appears at pop culture conventions, speaking on panels related to mental health and geek wellness. Her work as a clinical writer and researcher whose work has appears in a variety of books including but not limited to *Supernatural Psychology: Roads Less Traveled, Daredevil Psychology: The Devil You Know,* and *Westworld Psychology: Violent Delights.*

Wind Goodfriend, PhD, is a professor of psychology, director of the trauma advocacy program, and assistant dean of graduate programs at Buena Vista University in Storm Lake, Iowa. She earned her bachelor's degree at Buena Vista University, then her master's and PhD in social psychology from Purdue University. Dr. Goodfriend has won the "Faculty of the Year" award at BVU several times and has won the Wythe Award for Excellence in Teaching. She is also the principal investigator for the Institute for the Prevention of Relationship Violence and has authored three psychology textbooks with SAGE Publications.

As a child, **Ryan Harder** bought his first Batman comics in a multipack from a rural Iowa hardware store. He has since dedicated a disproportionate amount of his free time to critical study and analysis of the Dark Knight's world. Ryan is the web development manager at Buena Vista University, where he has ruined many important meetings by making Batman references. He lives in Storm Lake, Iowa, with his wife, two exceptionally bright sons, and a pair of reasonably behaved cats.

Jeffrey Henderson has lectured and taught courses on storyboarding/visual storytelling/film direction at the Art Center College of Design in Pasadena, CA, and The Savannah College of Art & Design/SCAD. His original work includes *Star Wars: The Sable Corsair* (Lucasfilm's Audience Choice award-winner). He has worked as a storyboard/concept artist for *The Dark Knight, Fargo,* Sam Raimi's Spider-Man films, *Destiny, Injustice 2,* and the *Dishonored* series. Find him at PlanetHenderson.com, his Threadless shop at PlanetHenderson.Threadless.com, and @PlanetHenderson on his Twitter and Instagram.

Vanessa Hicks, PsyD, is a licensed clinical psychologist in Wisconsin. She earned her doctorate in psychology from The Chicago School of Professional Psychology in 2016. Dr. Hicks has served on several convention panels focused on critical discussions of the manifestations of psychological concepts in various aspects of American popular culture. She is an active proponent of multicultural counseling and theory, and works dynamically with clients in therapy to understand how individuals make meaning of the world within their various cultural contexts. When clinically beneficial, Dr. Hicks incorporates elements of popular culture into treatment (i.e., "Geek Therapy").

Asher Johnson, MA, is completing his PhD in clinical psychology, emphasizing in forensics and crime. He has spoken on various geek psychology panels at fan conventions to discuss his application of superhero redemption therapy to inmates and parolees. He spent two years providing mental health services to state prisoners and three years working with federal and county probationers. He provides specialized treatment to registered sexual offenders who are on parole

J. Scott Jordan, PhD, is a cognitive psychologist who studies the roots of cooperative behavior. He often uses popular culture in his classes to illustrate the relevance of social-cognitive psychology to daily life. He has contributed chapters to *Captain American vs. Iron Man: Freedom, Security, Psychology*; *Wonder Woman Psychology: Lassoing the Truth*; *Star Trek Psychology: The Mental Frontier*; *Supernatural Psychology: Roads Less Traveled*; *Daredevil Psychology: The Devil You Know*; *Westworld Psychology: Violent Delights*; and *Black Panther Psychology: Hidden Kingdoms*. He is extremely proud of his international comic book collection.

Kathleen La Forgia, MS, MFT, is a practicing family therapist, specializing in working with military personnel and their families. She is producer and host of the Geek Therapy Network podcasts *Geek Family Therapy* and the Steven Universe-focused *Here Comes a Thought*. Find her on Twitter @ KatMFT.

Martin Lloyd, PhD, LP, received his doctorate in clinical psychology from the University of Minnesota. He has worked in various prisons and high-security hospitals, including the US Medical Center for Federal Prisoners and Patton State Hospital. He currently practices as a forensic psychologist in Minnesota and occasionally teaches forensic psychology at Gustavus Adolphus College. His chapter in this volume, his seventh contribution to this series, is an extension of the first conversation he ever had with Dr. Travis Langley at the Wizard World Chicago Comic Con convention.

Justine Mastin, MA, LMFT, of Blue Box Counseling in Minneapolis, specializes in working in clients who self-identify as outside the mainstream such as those in geek, scular, and LGBTQIA communities. She leads YogaQuest, a yoga organization that blends geek narratives with yoga. Justine appears at popular culture conventions and has contributed to numerous books in this Popular Culture Psychology series. Find her at blueboxcounseling.com or Twitter @mindbodyfandom.

Leandra Parris, PhD, is an assistant professor of psychology at Illinois State University. A school psychologist by training, Leandra specializes in peer relationships, trauma-informed care, social justice, and school climate. A devotee of popular culture, Leandra often uses narrative therapy and media in her work as a researcher and educator. Outside of work, Leandra strives to pass on her love of science fiction/fantasy, Pink Floyd, and storytelling to her children. *Batman: The Killing Joke* was the first story that converted her to a regular comics reader as a teenager.

Benjamin Radford, MEd, is a folklorist and award-winning author of a dozen books, including *Bad Clowns* (University of New Mexico Press).

Aaron Sagers is an entertainment journalist who travels the nation discussing popular culture at fan conventions. He was host and co-executive producer on Travel Channel's *Paranormal Paparazzi* and authored *Paranormal Pop Culture*. For *Doctor Who Psychology: A Madman with a Box*, he interviewed several *Doctor Who* stars. Find him geeking out on Twitter @AaronSagers and Instagram.

Billy San Juan, PsyD, received a doctorate in clinical psychology from Alliant International University. He is a contributor to several of the Popular Culture Psychology series of books, a fiction writer with publications in various anthologies, and has contributed flavor text to the *Magic: The Gathering* card game. He has spoken on panels at various conventions, including San Diego Comic-Con, WonderCon, and LA Comic Con.

William Sharp is a certified psychoanalyst who teaches at Northeastern University with a private practice in Brookline MA. His textbook, *Talking Helps,* is one of the few addressing the "impossible profession" of psychoanalytically informed counseling. He enjoys using popular media to explain complex psychoanalytic topics in his psychology courses. You can follow him @DrWilliamSharp for tweets on personality theories, psychoanalysis, psychology, and of course, all things Who.

Yoni Sobin, PsyD, the "Nerd Therapist," is a clinical psychologist who practices acceptance-based cognitive-behavioral therapy by integrating movies and comics into therapy. He runs support groups, provides consultation, and speaks on the integration of mental health and popular culture. He has worked in rehabilitative psychiatric hospitals (unlike Arkham) and runs an independent practice (sobinpsychology.com).

Amanda Vicary, PhD, is an associate professor of psychology at Illinois Wesleyan University. She has been a guest on several crime podcasts, as well as on ID TV's *Married with Secrets* (as a crime expert, not as the one with secrets). She studies romantic relationships and crime, and especially likes it when those two intersect. When not at work, she can be found watching *The Bachelor* or *Dateline*'s "Saturday Night Mystery"—for work, of course.

Eric D. Wesselmann, PhD, is an associate professor of psychology at Illinois State University. He publishes research on various topics, such as social exclusion, stigma, and religion/spirituality. When not at work, he and his spouse train their four little superheroes at home to be the best heroes they can be. His first *Batman* comics were prizes that came with the *Batman* (1988) breakfast cereal. He has contributed to the majority of volumes in the Popular Culture Psychology series.

References

Comic Book References

Stories with titles in brackets [ ] originally appeared untitled. The titles listed for them were assigned in reprint collections, and different collections sometimes assign different titles to the same story.

52 #27 (2007). "The Past Best Hope." Script: G. Johns, G. Morrison, G. Rucka, & M. Waid. Art: K. Giffen, J. Bennett, R. José, N. De Castro, M. Benes, R. Ramos, & P. Rollins.

52 #39 (2007). "Powers & Abilities." Script: G. Johns, G. Morrison, G. Rucka, & M. Waid. Art: K. Giffen, A. Smith, & R. Snyder.

Action Comics #13 (1939). "Superman vs. the Cab Protective League." Script: J. Siegel. Art: J. Shuster & P. Cassidy.

Adventure Comics #462 (1979). "Only Legends Live Forever (Part 2)." Script: P. Levitz. Art: J. Staten & D. Giordano.

Arkham Asylum: A Serious House on Serious Earth (1989). Script: G. Morrison. Art: D. McKean.

Arkham Asylum: A Serious House on Serious Earth. Fifteenth Anniversary Edition (1989/2004). Script: G. Morrison. Art: D. McKean.

Arkham Asylum: Madness (2010). Script/Art: S. Kieth. *Batgirl* #1 (2011). "Shattered." Script: G. Simone. Art: A. Syaf & V. Cifuentes.

Batgirl #14 (2013). "Collision, Part One: A Courtship of Razors." Script: G. Simone. Art: E. Benes, D. Sampere, V. Cifuentes, & M. Irwin.

Batgirl #28 (2014). "Silver." Script: Gail Simone. Art: F. Pasarin & J. Glapion.

Batman #1 (1940a). ["The Joker" or "Batman vs. the Joker" in different reprint collections.] Story: J. Robinson & B. Finger. Script: B. Finger. Art: B. Kane & J. Robinson.

Batman #1 (1940b). ["The Giants of Hugo Strange."] Script: B. Finger. Art: B. Kane & J. Robinson.

Batman #1 (1940c). ["The Cat."] Script: B. Finger. Art: B. Kane & J. Robinson.

Batman #1 (1940d). "The Joker Returns." Script: B. Finger. Art: B. Kane & J. Robinson.

Batman #2 (1940). ["The Joker Meets the Cat-Woman."] Script: B. Finger. Art: B. Kane, J. Robinson, & G. Roussos.

Batman #3 (1940). "The Batman vs. the Cat-Woman." Script: B. Finger. Art: B. Kane, J. Robinson, & G. Roussos.

Batman #4 (1941). "The Case of the Joker's Crime Circus." Script: B. Finger. Art: B. Kane & J. Robinson.

Batman #5 (1941). "The Riddle of the Missing Card." Script: B. Finger. Art: B. Kane, J. Robinson, & G. Roussos.

Batman #7 (1941). [Indexed as "The Joker's Practical Jokes" or "Wanted: Practical Jokers" in different reprint collections.] Script: B. Finger. Art: B. Kane, G. Russos, & J. Robinson.

Batman #8 (1941). "The Cross Country Crimes." Script: B. Finger. Art: B. Kane, J. Robinson, & G. Roussos.

Batman #9 (1942). "The Case of the Lucky Law-Breakers!" Script: B. Finger. Art: B. Kane, J. Robinson, & G. Roussos.

Batman #10 (1942). "The Princess of Plunder!" Script: J. Schiff. Art: J. Robinson, F. Ray, & G. Roussos.

Batman #11 (1942). ["The Joker's Advertising Campaign."] Script: B. Finger. Art: B. Kane, J. Robinson, & G. Roussos.

Batman #12 (1942). "The Wizard of Words." Script: B. Finger. Art: B. Kane & J. Robinson.

Batman #16 (1943). "The Joker Reforms!" Script: D. Cameron. Art: B. Kane, J. Robinson, & G. Roussos.

Batman #28 (1945). "Shadow City." Script: D. Cameron. Art: J. Burnley & J. Robinson.

Batman #44 (1947–1948). "Gamble with Doom!" Script: Unknown. Art: J. Mooney.

Batman #47 (1948). "The Origin of the Batman!" Script: B. Finger. Art: B. Kane & C. Paris.

Batman #57 (1950). "The Funny Man Crimes!" Script: B. Kane, L. S. Schwartz, & C. Paris.

Batman #63 (1951). "The Joker's Crime Costumes!" Script: B. Finger. Art: D. Sprang & C. Paris.

Batman #66 (1951). "The Joker's Comedy of Errors!" Script: B. Finger. Art: B. Kane, L. S. Schwartz, & C. Paris.

Batman #73 (1952). "The Joker's Utility Belt!" Script: D.V. Reed. Art: D. Sprang & C. Paris.

Batman #74 (1952–1953). "The Crazy Crime Clown!" Script: A. Schwartz. Art: D. Sprang & C. Paris.

Batman #80 (1953). "The Joker's Movie Crimes!" Script: B. Finger. Art: D. Sprang & C. Paris.

Batman #128 (1959). "The Interplanetary Batman!" Script: B. Finger. Art: S. Moldoff.

Batman #130 (1960). "The Case of the Crazy Crimes." Script: B. Finger. Art: S. Moldoff & C. Paris.

Batman #147 (1962). "Batman Becomes Bat-Baby." Script: B. Finger. Art: S. Moldoff & C. Paris.

Batman #169 (1965). "Letters to the Batcave." [Editor J. Schwartz's response to reader L. Brown.]

Batman #189 (1967). "Fright of the Scarecrow!" Story: G. Fox. Art: I. Novick & J. Giella.

Batman #210 (1969). "Letters to the Batcave." [Letter by reader M. Evanier.]

Batman #251 (1973). "The Joker's Five-Way Revenge!" Script: D. O'Neil. Art: N. Adams.

Batman #258 (1974). "Threat of the Two-Headed Coin!" Script: Dennis O'Neil. Art: Irv Novick & Dick Giordano.

Batman #307 (1979). "Dark Messenger of Mercy." Script: L. Wein. Art: J. Calnan & D. Giordano.

Batman #321 (1980). "Dreadful Birthday, Dear Joker . . . !" Script: L. Wein. Art: W. Simonson & D. Giordano.

Batman #326 (1980). "This Way Lies Madness." Script: L. Wein. Art: I. Novik & F. McLaughlin.

Batman #357 (1983). "Squid." Script: G. Conway. Art: D. Newton & A. Alcala.

Batman #400 (1986). "Resurrection Night!" Script: D. Moench. Artists: Various.

Batman #408 (1987). "Did Robin Die Tonight?" Script: M. A. Collins. Art: C. Warner & M. DeCarlo.

Batman #420 (1988). "Ten Nights of the Beast, Part 4." Script: J. Starlin. Art: J. Aparo & M. DeCarlo.

Batman #426–429 (1988–1989). "A Death in the Family." Script: J. Starlin. Art: J. Aparo & M. DeCarlo.

Batman #439 (1989). "Batman Year III, Chapter Four: Resolutions." Script: M. Wolfman. Art: P. Broderick & M. Bair.

Batman #440 (1989). "A Lonely Place of Dying, Chapter One: Suspects." Script: M. Wolfman & G. Pérez. Art: J. Aparo & M. DeCarlo.

Batman #441 (1989). "A Lonely Place of Dying, Chapter Three: Parallel Lines." Script: M. Wolfman. Art: J. Aparo & M. DeCarlo.

Batman #484 (1992). "Warpaint." Script: D. Moench. Art: T. Grindberg & T. Scott.

Batman #485 (1992). "Faces of Death." Script: D. Moench. Art: T. Grindberg & T. Scott.

Batman #486 (1992). "Heavy Metalhead." Script: D. Moench. Art: J. Aparo.

Batman #487 (1992). "Box of Blood." Script: D. Moench. Art: J. Aparo.

Batman #491 (1993). "The Freedom of Madness." Script: D. Moench. Art: J. Aparo.

Batman #493 (1993). "Red Slash." Script: D. Moench. Art: N. Breyfogle.

Batman #494 (1993). "Night Terrors." Script: D. Moench. Art: J. Aparo & T. Mandrake.

Batman #495 (1993). "Stranger Deadfellows." Script: D. Moench. Art: J. Aparo & B. Wiacek.

Batman #496 (1993). "Die Laughing." Script: D. Moench. Art: J. Aparo & J. Rubinstein.

Batman #497 (1993). "The Broken Bat." Script: D. Moench. Art: J. Aparo & D. Giordano.

Batman #608–619 (2002–2003). "Hush." Script: J. Loeb. Art: J. Lee & S. Williams.

Batman #633 (2004). "War Games, Act 3, Part 8: No Going Back." Script: B. Willingham. Art: K. Loh, A. Sowd, R. Ramos, & A. DeKraker.

Batman #638 (2005). "Under the Hood, Part 4: Bidding War." Script: J. Winick. Art: D. Mahnke & T. Nguyen.

Batman #639–642 (2005). "Family Reunion." Script: J. Winick. Art: D. Mahnke, P. Lee, T. Nguyen, & C. Smith.

Batman #643 (2005). "War Games, Part 2: Minor Discrepancies." Script: B. Willingham. Art: G. Gamuncoli & S. Hope.

Batman #644 (2005). "War Games, Part 4: Judgment at Gotham." Script: B. Willingham. Art: G. Gamuncoli & S. Hope.

Batman #648–650 (2006). "All They Do Is Watch Us Kill." Script: J. Winick. Art: D. Mahnke, T. Nguyen, E. Battle, & R. Ramos.

Batman #655 (2006). "Batman & Son, Part 1: Building a Better Batmobile." Script: G. Morrison. Art: A. Kubert.

Batman #663 (2007). "The Clown at Midnight." Script: G. Morison. Art: J. Van Fleet.

Batman #681 (2008). "Batman R.I.P., The Conclusion—Hearts in Darkness." Script: G. Morrison. Art: T. Daniel & S. Florea.

Batman #1 (2011). "The Court of Owls, Part One: Knife Trick." Script: S. Snyder. Art: G. Capullo & J. Glapion.

Batman #13 (2012a). "Knock Knock." Script: S. Snyder. Art: G. Capullo & J. Glapion.

Batman #13 (2012b). "Tease." Script: S. Snyder & J. Tynion IV. Art: Jock.

Batman #14 (2013). "Funny Bones." Script: S. Snyder. Art: G. Capullo & J. Glapion.

Batman #15 (2013). "But Here's the Kicker." Script: S. Snyder. Art: G. Capullo & J. Glapion.

Batman #16 (2013a). "Castle of Cards." Script: S. Snyder. Art: G. Capullo & J. Glapion.

Batman #16 (2013b). "Judgment." Script: S. Snyder & J. Tynion IV. Art: Jock.

Batman #17 (2013). "The Punchline." Script: S. Snyder. Art: G. Capullo & J. Glapion.

Batman #39 (2015). "Endgame, Part Five." Script: S. Snyder. Art: G. Capullo & D. Miki.

Batman #48 (2018). "The Best Man, Part 1." Script: T. King. Art: M. Janín.

Batman & Robin Eternal #3 (2015). "Seeing Red." Script: T. Seeley, J. Tynion IV, & S. Snyder. Art: P. Pelletier, S. Eaton, T. Kordos, M. Deering, & W. Faucher.

Batman and Robin #13 (2010). "Batman and Robin Must Die, Part One: The Garden Death." Script: G. Morrison. Art: F. Irving.

Batman and Robin #14 (2010). "Batman and Robin Must Die, Part Two: The Triumph of Death." Script: G. Morrison. Art: F. Irving & P. Brosseau.

Batman and the Outsiders #14 (1984). "Two by Two . . ." Script: Mike W. Barr. Art: B. Willingham & B. Anderson.

Batman Annual #8 (1982). "The Messiah of the Crimson Sun." Script: M. W. Barr. Art: T. von Eeden.

Batman Annual #11 (1987). "Love Bird." Script: M. A. Collins. Art: N. Breyfogle & A. DeGuzman.

Batman Annual #14 (1990). "The Eye of the Beholder." Script: A. Helfer. Art: C. Sprouse & S. Mitchell.

Batman Annual #1 (2017). "The Not So Silent Night of the Harley Quinn." Script: P. Dini. Art: N. Adams.

Batman Chronicles #6 (1996). "Choices." Script: M. Nevins. Art: J. Delperdang & R. McCarthy.

Batman Kellogg's Special (1966). "The Joker's Happy Victims!" Script: E. N. Bridwell. Art: C. Infantino & M. Anderson.

Batman Secret Files #1 (2018). "One." Script: C. L. Eaton. Art: E. Casagrande.

Batman: Arkham Knight Genesis #3 (2015). [Untitled]. Script: P. Tomasi. Art: D. Soy.

Batman: Arkham Reborn (2010). Script: D. Hine. Art: J. Haun.

Batman: Cacophony #1–3 (2008–2009). Script: K. Smith. Art: W. Flanagan & S. Hope.

Batman: Dark Victory #13 (2000). "Peace." Script: J. Loeb. Art: T. Sale.

Batman: Earth One (2012). Script: G. Johns. Art: G. Frank & J. Sibal.

Batman: Harley Quinn (1999). Script: P. Dini. Art: Y. Guichet & A. Sowd.

Batman: Legends of the Dark Knight #65 (1994). "Going Sane, Part One: Into the Rushing River." Script: J. M. DeMatteis. Art: J. Staten & S. Mitchell.

Batman: Legends of the Dark Knight #66 (1994). "Going Sane, Part Two: Swimming Lessons." Script: J. M. DeMatteis. Art: J. Staten & S. Mitchell.

Batman: Legends of the Dark Knight #68 (1995). "Going Sane, Part Four: The Deluge." Script: J. M. DeMatteis. Art: J. Staten & S. Mitchell.

Batman: Legends of the Dark Knight #145 (2001). "The Demon Laughs, Part Four: Mad about You." Script: C. Dixon. Art: J. Aparo & J. Cebollero.

Batman: Legends of the Dark Knight #206 (2006). "The Madman of Gotham, Part Three." Script: J. Gray. Art: S. Cummings.

Batman: Shadow of the Bat #3 (1992). "The Last Arkham (Part III of IV)." Script: A. Grant. Art: N. Breyfogle.

Batman: Shadow of the Bat #37 (1995). "The Joker (Part I)—The King of Comedy." Script: A. Grant. Art: B. Kitson & J. Stokes.

Batman: The Dark Knight #1–4 (1986). Script: F. Miller. Art: F. Miller & K. Janson.

Batman: The Dark Knight Returns—trade paperback collection, the popular name for *Batman: The Dark Knight* #1–4 (1986).

Batman: The Killing Joke (1988). Script: A. Moore. Art: B. Bolland.

Batman: The Long Halloween #4 (1997). "New Year's Eve." Script: J. Loeb. Art: T. Sale.

Batman: The Long Halloween #13 (1997). "Punishment." Script: J. Loeb. Art: T. Sale.

Batman: The Man Who Laughs (2005). Script: E. Brubaker. Art: D. Mahnke.

Batman: Three Jokers (2019). Script: G. Johns. Art: J. Fabok.

Batman: Two-Face #1 (1995). "Crime and Punishment." Script: J. M. DeMatteis. Art: S. McDaniel.

Batman: Vengeance of Bane #1 (1993). "Vengeance of Bane." Script: C. Dixon. Art: G. Nolan & E. Barreto.

Batman: White Knight #1–8 (2017–2018). Script/Art: S. Murphy.

Birds of Prey #8 (1999). "On Wings." Script: C. Dixon. Art: G. Land & D. Geraci.

Birds of Prey #16 (2000). "The Joker's Tale." Script: C. Dixon. Art: J. Guice.

Birds of Prey #60 (2003). "Feeding the Game." Script: G. Simone. Art: E. Benes, A. Lei, & R. Lea.

Black Canary/Oracle: Birds of Prey #1 (1996). "One Man's Hell." Script: C. Dixon. Art: G. Frank & J. Dell.

Catwoman #12–16 (2002–2003). "Relentless." Script: E. Brubaker. Art: C. Stewart.

Countdown #31 (2007). "The Origin of the Joker." Script: M. Waid. Art: B. Bolland.

Crime Patrol #15 (1949–1950). "Return from the Grave!" Script/Art: A. Feldstein. New York, NY: EC Comics.

Crisis on Infinite Earths #1 (1985). "The Summoning." Script: M. Wolfman. Art: G. Pérez & J. Ordway.

Crisis on Infinite Earths #11 (1986). "Aftershock." Script: M. Wolfman. Art: G. Pérez & J. Ordway.

Crisis on Infinite Earths #12 (1986). "Final Crisis." Script: M. Wolfman. Art: G. Pérez & J. Ordway.

DC Comics Bombshells #1 (2015). "Enlisted." Script: M. Bennett. Art: M. Sauvage.

DC Nation #0 (2018). "The Joker: Your Big Day." Script: T. King. Art: C. Mann.

DC Rebirth #1 (2016). "Lost." Script: G. Johns. Art: E. Van Sciver & G. Frank.

Deadpool: Pulp #1–4 (2010). Script: A. Glass & M. Benson. Art: L. Campbell. New York, NY: Marvel Comics.

Detective Comics #27 (1939). "The Case of the Chemical Syndicate." Script: B. Finger. Art: B. Kane.

Detective Comics #29 (1939). "The Batman Meets Doctor Death." Script: G. Fox. Art: B. Kane.

Detective Comics #31 (1939). "Batman versus the Vampire, Part 1." Script: G. Fox. Art: B. Kane & S. Moldoff.

Detective Comics #33 (1939). "The Legend of the Batman—Who He Is and How He Came to Be." Script: B. Finger. Art: B. Kane.

Detective Comics #38 (1940). "Robin the Boy Wonder." Script: B. Finger. Art: B. Kane & J. Robinson.

Detective Comics #45 (1940). "The Case of the Laughing Death." Script: B. Finger. Art: B. Kane, J. Robinson, & G. Roussos.

Detective Comics #58 (1941) ["One of the Most Perfect Frame-Ups."] Script: B. Finger. Art: B. Kane, J. Robinson, & G. Roussos.

Detective Comics #60 (1942). "The Case of the Costume-Clad Killers." Script: J. Schiff. Art: B. Kane, J. Robinson, & G. Roussos.

Detective Comics #62 (1942). "Laugh, Town, Laugh!" Script: B. Finger. Art: B. Kane, J. Robinson, & G. Roussos.

Detective Comics #64 (1942). "The Joker Walks the Last Mile!" Script: B. Finger. Art: B. Kane, J. Robinson, & G. Roussos.

Detective Comics #66 (1941). "The Crimes of Two-Face!" Script: B. Finger. Art: B. Kane, J. Robinson, & G. Roussos.

Detective Comics #140 (1948). "The Riddler!" Script: B. Finger. Art: D. Sprang & C. Paris.

Detective Comics #168 (1951). "The Man behind the Red Hood." Script: Uncredited in Gold (1988); credited to B. Finger in Wildman (2014) and according to Bob Kane; unspecified subsequent writer according to Jerry Robinson (2009 interview—see Explaining the Joke 2–1 in this book—probably B. Finger. Art: S. Moldoff & G. Roussos, according to Gold (1988); L. S. Schwartz & G. Roussos, according to Wildman (2014)—probably L. S. Schwartz & G. Roussos.

Detective Comics #193 (1953). "The Joker's Journal." Script: D. V. Reed. Art: B. Kane, L. S. Schwartz, & C. Paris.

Detective Comics #332 (1964). "The Joker's Last Laugh!" Script: J. Broome. Art: S. Moldoff & J. Giella.

Detective Comics #388 (1969). "Public Luna-Tic Number One!" Script: J. Broome. Art: B. Brown & J. Giella.

Detective Comics #457 (1976). "There is No Hope in Crime Alley!" Script: D. O'Neil. Art: D. Giordano & T. Austin.

Detective Comics #475 (1978). "The Laughing Fish!" Script: S. Englehart. Art: M. Rogers & T. Austin.

Detective Comics #476 (1978). "Sign of the Joker!" Script: S. Englehart. Art: M. Rogers & T. Austin.

Detective Comics #483 (1979). "The Curse of Crime Alley." Script: D. O'Neil. Art: D. Newton & D. Adkins.

Detective Comics #526 (1983). "All My Enemies Against Me!" Script: G. Conway. Art: D. Newton & A. Alcala.

Detective Comics #570 (1987). "The Last Laugh!" Script: M. W. Barr. Art: A. Davis & P. Neary.

Detective Comics #606 (1989). "The Mud Pack, Part Three: Killer Clay!" Script: A. Grant. Art: N. Breyfogle & S. Mitchell.

Detective Comics #611 (1990). "Snow and Ice, Part Two: Bird of Ill Omen." Script: A. Grant. Art: N. Breyfogle & S. Mitchell.

Detective Comics #660 (1993). "Crocodile Tears." Script: C. Dixon. Art: J. Balent & S. Hanna.

Detective Comics #726 (1998). "Fool's Errand." Script: C. Dixon. Art: B. Stelfreeze.

Detective Comics #737 (1999). "The Code, Part 2." Script: B. Carlton. Art: T. Morgan.

Detective Comics #741 (2000). "Endgame, Part 3: Sleep in Heavenly Peace." Script: G. Rucka & D. Grayson. Art: D. Scott & D. Eaglesham.

Detective Comics #741 (2000). "Endgame, Part Three: . . . Sleep in Heavenly Peace." Script: D. Grayson & D. Rucka. Art: D. Eaglesham, D. Scott, S. Buscema, S. Parsons, & R. Hunter.

Detective Comics #809 (2005). "War Crimes, Part 1: To the Victor Go the Spoils." Script: A. Gabrych. Art: P. Woods & BIT.

Detective Comics #810 (2005). "War Crimes, Part 3.: A Consequence of the Truth." Script: A. Gabrych. Art: P. Woods & BIT.

Detective Comics #831 (2007). "Kind of Like Family." Script: P. Dini. Art: D. Kramer & W. Faucher.

Detective Comics #837 (2007). "Honor Among Thieves." Script: P. Dini. Art: D. Kramer & W. Faucher.

Detective Comics #1 (2011). "Detective Comics." Script: T. S. Daniel. Art: T. S. Daniel & R. Winn.

Detective Comics #23.2 (2013). "Harley Lives." Script: M. Kindt. Art: N. Googe.

Doomsday Clock #1 (2018). "The Annihilated Place." Script: G. Johns. Art: G. Frank.

Fantastic Four #1 (1961). "The Fantastic Four." Script: S. Lee. Art: J. Kirby, G. Klein, & C. Rule. New York, NY: Marvel Comics.

Flashpoint #1 (2011). "Chapter One of Five." Script: G. Johns. Art: A. Kubert & S. Hope.

Giant-Size X-Men #1 (1975). "Second Genesis!" Script: L. Wein. Art: D. Cockrum & P. Iro. New York, NY: Marvel Comics.

Gotham Central #15 (2004). "Soft Targets, Part Four of Four." Script: E. Brubaker & G. Rucka. Art: M. Lark & S. Gaudiano.

Gotham City Sirens #1 (2009). "Union." Script: P. Dini. Art: G. March.

Gotham City Sirens #6 (2010). "The Last Gag." Script: P. Dini. Art: G. March.

Gotham City Sirens #7 (2010). "Holiday Story." Script: P. Dini. Art: D. Lopez & A. Lopez.

Green Lantern #33 (1964). "Wizard of the Light-Wave Weapons!" Script: G. Fox. Art: G. Kane & S. Greene.

Green Lantern #85 (1971). "Snowbirds Don't Fly." Script: D. O'Neil. Art: N. Adams.

Green Lantern #54 (1994). "Forced Entry." Script: R. Marz. Art: S. Carr, D. Aucoin, D. Banks, & R. Tanghal.

Harley Quinn #5 (2001). "Larger Than Life." Script: K. Kesel. Art: T. Dodson & R. Dodson.

Harley Quinn #7 (2001). "Be Cruel 2 Your School." Script: K. Kesel. Art: P. Woods & M. Lipka.

Harley Quinn #25 (2002). "Once More, With Feeling!" Script: K. Kesel. Art: C. Rousseau & D. Davis.

Harley Quinn #29 (2003). "Vengeance Unlimited, Part Four." Script: A. J. Lieberman. Art: M. Huddleston & T. Nixey.

Harley Quinn #2 (2014). "Helter Shelter." Script: A. Conner & J. Palmiotti. Art: C. Hardin & S. Roux.

Harley Quinn #3 (2014). "Love Stinks!" Script: A. Conner & J. Palmiotti. Art: C. Hardin.

Harley Quinn #1 (2014). "Hot in the City." Script: A. Conner & J. Palmiotti. Art: C. Hardin.

Harley Quinn #51 (2018). "Triumph, Part One." Script: S. Humphries. Art: S. Basri.

Harley Quinn and Power Girl #1 (2015). "Extrastellar Exploitations." Script: A. Conner, J. Palmiotti, & J. Gray. Art: S. Roux.

Harley Quinn and Power Girl #6 (2016). "They Part." Script: J. Gray, A. Conner, & J. Palmiotti. Art: S. Roux, Moritat, E. Fernandez, & Flaviano.

Harley's Little Black Book #1 (2015). "Little Black Book." Script: J. Palmiotti & A. Conner. Art: A. Conner, J. Timms, & D. Johnson.

Heroes in Crisis #1 (2018). "I'm Just Warming Up." Script: T. King. Art: C. Mann.

Heroes in Crisis #2 (2018). "Then I Become Superman." Script: T. King. Art: C. Mann & T. Moore.

Heroes in Crisis #3 (2019). "Master of the Lagoon." Script: T. King. Art: C. Mann & L. Weeks.

Heroes in Crisis #4 (2019). "$%@# This." Script: T. King. Art: C. Mann.

Heroes in Crisis #5 (2019). "Blood in the Way." Script: T. King. Art: C. Mann & T. Moore.

Heroes in Crisis #6 (2019). "Who Is Saved?" Script: T. King. Art: C. Mann & M. Gerads.

House of Secrets #92 (1971). "Swamp Thing." Script: L. Wein. Art: B. Wrightson.

Infinite Crisis #1 (2005). "Infinite Crisis." Script: G. Johns. Art: P. Jimenez & A. Lanning.

Infinite Crisis #4 (2006). "Homecoming." Script: G. Johns. Art: P. Jimenez, G. Pérez, I. Reis, O. Albert, M. Campos, D. Geraci, A. Lanning, J. Palmiotti, & L. Stucker.

Infinite Crisis #5 (2006). "Faith." Script: G. Johns. Art: P. Jimenez, J. Ordway, I. Reis, A. Lanning, & A. Thibert.

Infinite Crisis #6 (2006). "Touchdown." Script: G. Johns. Art: Art: P. Jimenez, G. Pérez, I. Reis, J. Bennett, A. Lanning, J. Ordway, S. Parsons, & A. Thibert.

Infinite Crisis #7 (2006). "Finale." Script: G. Johns. Art: Various.

Infinity Gauntlet #1–6 (1991). Script: S. Starlin. Art: G. Peréz, R. Lim, J. Rubenstein, & T. Christopher. New York, NY: Marvel Comics.

Injustice: Gods Among Us #2 (2013). "Part Two." Script: T. Taylor. Art: M. S. Miller & B. Redondo.

JLA #15 (1998). "Rock of Ages, Part Six: Stone of Destiny." Script: G. Morrison. Art: G. Frank, H. Porter, G. Land, J. Dell, & B. McLeod.

Joker's Asylum: The Joker #1 (2008). "The Joker's Mild!" Script: A. Nelson. Art: A. Sanchez.

Justice 2 #17 (2018). "Save the World." Script: T. Taylor. Art: B. Redondo & J. Albarran.

Justice League #48 (2016). "Darkseid War, Act Three: Gods of Justice—Chapter 2, Crime Pays." Script: G. Johns. Art: J. Fabok.

Justice League #50 (2016). "Darkseid War, Conclusion, Death and Rebirth." Script: G. Johns. Art: J. Fabok.

Justice League of America #21 (1963). "Crisis on Earth-One!" Script: G. Fox. Art: M. Sekwosky & B. Sachs.

Justice League of America #77 (1969). "Snapper Carr—Super-Traitor!" Script: D. O'Neil. Art: D. Dillin & J. Giella.

Justice League: Cry for Justice #5 (2010). "The Lie." Script: J. Robinson. Art: M. Cascioli & S. Clark.

Legends of the Dark Knight 100-Page Super Spectacular #1 (2014). "Dr. Quinn's Diagnosis." Script: J. Zubkavich. Art: N. Googe.

Luke Cage Noir #1 (2009). "Moon over Harlem." Script: M. Benson & A. Glass. Art: S. Martinbrough. New York, NY: Marvel Comics.

Luke Cage Noir #4 (2010). "A Harlem Sunset." Script: A. Glass & M. Benson. Art: S. Martinbrough. New York, NY: Marvel Comics.

New Adventures of Superboy #22 (1981). "Map of Smallville." Script/Art: Uncredited.

Plastic Man #64 (1956). [Six comic book stories.] New York, NY: Quality Comics.

Punisher/Batman (1994). "Deadly Knights." Script: C. Dixon. Art: J. Romita, Jr., & K. Janson. New York, NY: Marvel Comics.

Real Fact Comics #5 (1946). "The True Story of Batman and Robin!" Script: Unknown, perhaps editor J. Schiff. Art: W. Mortimer.

Robin #13 (1995). "Wings over Gotham." Script: C. Dixon. Art: J. Cleary, P. Jimenez, & R. Kryssing.

Robin #130 (2004). "The Only Light in Gotham." Script: B. Willingham. Art: J. Proctor, R. Campanella, & R. Ramos.

Salvation Run #2 (2007). "Take This World and Shove It!" Script: B. Willingham. Art: S. Chen & W. Wong.

Secret Origins #4 (2014). "Harley Quinn." Script: J. Palmiotti & A. Conner. Art: S. Roux.

Secret Origins of the World's Greatest Superheroes (1989). "The Man Who Falls." Script: D. O'Neil. Art: D. Giordano.

Sensation Comics #1 (1942). "This is the Story of Wildcat." Script: B. Finger. Art: I. Hasen.

Spectre #51 (1997). "A Savage Innocence." Script: J. Ostrander. Art: T. Mandrake.

Squadron Supreme #1 (2015). Script: J. Robinson. Art: L. Kirk & P. Neary.

Suicide Squad #1 (1987). "Trial by Blood." Script: J. Ostrander. Art: L. McDonnell & K. Kesel.

Suicide Squad #48 (1990). "In Control." Script: J. Ostrander & K. Yale. Art: G. Isherwood.

Suicide Squad #49 (1991). "Out of Control." Script: J. Ostrander & K. Yale. Art: L. McDonnell & G. Isherwood.

Suicide Squad #1 (2011). "Kicked in the Teeth." Script: A. Glass. Art: F. Dallocchio, S. Hanna, & R. Getty.

Suicide Squad #10 (2012). "Judas Rising." Script: A. Glass. Art: F. Dagnino.

Suicide Squad #14–15 (2013). "Running with the Devil." Script: A. Glass. Art: F. Dagnino.

Suicide Squad #19 (2013). "Red Rain." Script: A. Glass. Art: C. Richards.

Suicide Squad #6–7 (2012). "The Hunt for Harley Quinn." Script: A. Glass. Art: C. Henry, I. Guara, & S. Hanna.

Swamp Thing #53 (1986). "The Garden of Earthly Delights." Script: A. Moore. Art: J. Totleben.

Tales of the Teen Titans #44 (1984). "The Judas Contract, Book Three: There Shall Come a Titan!" Script: M. Wolfman. Art: G. Pérez & D. Giordano.

The Amazing Spider-Man #121 (1973). "The Night Gwen Stacy Died." Script: G. Conway. Art: G. Kane, J. Romita, & T. Mortellaro. New York, NY: Marvel Comics.

The Amazing Spider-Man #129 (1974). "The Punisher Strikes Twice!" Script: G. Conway. Art: R. Andru, F. Giacola, & D. Hunt. New York, NY: Marvel Comics.

The Batman Adventures #12 (1992). "Batgirl: Day One." Script: K. Puckett. Art: M. Parobeck.

The Batman Adventures Holiday Special #1 (1995). "The Harley and the Ivy." Story: P. Dini & R. Del Carmen. Art: R. Del Carmen.

The Batman Adventures: Mad Love (1994). Script: P. Dini & B. Timm. Art: B. Timm.

The Best of DC #10 (1981). "The Origin of the Penguin!" Script: M. Fleischer. Art: R. Tanghal & T. Blaisdell.

The Brave and the Bold #31 (2010). "Small Problems." Script: J. M. Straczynski. Art: C. Hardin & W. Wong.

The Dark Knight Returns—see *Batman: The Dark Knight* #1–4 (1986).

The Flash #123 (1961). "Flash of Two Worlds." Script: G. Fox. Art: C. Infantino & J. Giella.

The Hood #1–6 (2002). "Blood from Stones." Script: B. K. Vaughn. Art: K. Holtz & E. Powell. New York, NY: Marvel Comics.

The Incredible Hulk #180 (1974). "And the Wind Howls . . . Wendigo!" Script: L. Wein. Art: H. Trimpe & J. Abel. New York, NY: Marvel.

The Incredible Hulk #181 (1974). "And Now . . . the Wolverine!" Script: L. Wein. Art: H. Trimpe & J. Abel. New York, NY: Marvel.

The Joker #1 (1975). "The Joker's Double Jeopardy!" Script: D. O'Neil. Art: I. Novick & D. Giordano.

The Joker #5 (1976). "The Joker Goes Wilde!" Script: M. Pasko. Art: I. Novick & T. Blaisdell.

The Joker #7 (1976). "Luthor—You're Driving Me Sane!" Script: E. S! Maggin. Art: I. Novick & F. McLaughlin.

The Killing Joke—see *Batman: The Killing Joke* (1988).

The Marvel Family #84 (1954). "Then There Were None." Script: Unknown. Art: K. Schaffenberger. Robbinsdale, MN: Fawcett Publications.

The Untold Legend of the Batman #1 (1980). "In the Beginning." Script: L. Wein. Art: J. Byrne & J. Aparo.

Ultimatum #3 (2009). "Death Becomes Her." Script: J. Loe. Art: D. Finch & D. Miki. New York, NY: Marvel Comics.

Underworld Unleashed #1 (1995). "Underworld Unleashed." Script: M. Wait. Art: H. Porter & D. Green.

Watchmen #1–12 (1986–1986). Script: A. Moore. Art: D. Gibbons.

World's Finest Comics #3 (1941). [Indexed as "Riddle of the Human Scarecrow" or "The Scarecrow!"] Script: B. Finger. Art: B. Kane, J. Robinson, & G. Roussos.

World's Finest Comics #48 (1950). "Song of Crime!" Script: B. Finger. Art: B. Kane, L. S. Schwartz, & S. Barry.

World's Finest Comics #177 (1968). "Duel of the Crime Kings! The Traitor, the Liar, and the Genius." Script: J. Shooter. Art: C. Swan & M. Esposito.

Year One: Batman/Scarecrow #1 (2005). Script: B. Jones. Art: S. Murphy.

Zero Hour #4 (1994). "Zero Hour (Part I)." Script: D. Jurgens. Art: D. Jurgens & J. Ordway.

Other References

Abagnale & Associates (n.d.). *About Frank*. Frank W. Abagnale: https://www.abagnale.com/about-frank.htm.

Abagnale, F., Jr., & Redding, S. (1980). *Catch me if you can*. New York, NY: Grosset & Dunlap.

Ainsworth, S. E., & Maner, J. K. (2014). Assailing the competition: Sexual selection, proximate mating motives, and aggressive behavior in men. *Personality & Social Psychology Bulletin, 40*(12), 1648–1658.

Akalin, O. (2011, June 3). *Frank Sinatra and Tommy Dorsey Band*. Frank Sinatra: http://www.thefranksinatra.com/articles/frank-sinatra-and-tommy-dorsey-band.

Algoe, S. B., & Haidt, J. (2009). Witnessing excellence in action: the 'other-praising' emotions of elevation, gratitude, and admiration. *Journal of Positive Psychology, 4*(2), 105–127.

Allnutt, S., Samuels, A., & O'Driscoll, C. (2007). The insanity defence: From wild beasts to M'Naghten. *Australian Psychiatry, 15*(4), 292–298.

Alonsagay, A. I. (2018, February 18). *15 bad things the Joker has done to Harley Quinn*. ScreenRant: https://screenrant.com/joker-bad-things-done-harley-quinn/.

American Law Institute (1985). *Model penal code: Official draft and explanatory notes: Complete text of model penal code as adopted at the 1962 annual meeting of the American Law Institute at Washington, D.C., May 24, 1962*. Philadelphia, PA: The Institute.

American Psychiatric Association (1952). *Diagnostic and statistical manual of mental disorders* (1st ed.) (DSM-I). Washington, DC: American Psychiatric Association.

American Psychiatric Association (1968). *Diagnostic and statistical manual of mental disorders* (2nd ed.) (DSM-II). Washington, DC: American Psychiatric Association.

American Psychiatric Association (1980). *Diagnostic and statistical manual of mental disorders* (3rd ed.) (DSM-III). Washington, DC: American Psychiatric Association.

American Psychiatric Association (1987). *Diagnostic and statistical manual of mental disorders* (3rd ed., rev.) (DSM-III-R). Washington, DC: American Psychiatric Association.

American Psychiatric Association (2000). *Diagnostic and statistical manual of mental disorders* (4th ed., revised) (DSM-IV-TR). Washington, DC: American Psychiatric Association.

American Psychiatric Association (2013). *Diagnostic and statistical manual of mental disorders* (5th ed.) (DSM-5). Washington, DC: American Psychiatric Association.

American Psychological Association (2003, June 1; revised 2017, January 1). *Ethical principles of psychologists and code of conduct*. American Psychological Association, Ethics Office: https://www.apa.org/ethics/code.

Anderson, S. (2016, August 31). *Feeling depressed after reaching a big goal? Here's why*. Deseret News: https://www.deseretnews.com/article/865661356/Feeling-depressed-after-reaching-a-big-goal-Heres-why.html.

Anderson, S. W., Bechara, A., Damasio, H., Tranel, D., & Damasio, A. R. (1999). Impairment of social and moral behavior related to early damage in human prefrontal cortex. *Nature Neuroscience, 2*(11), 1032–1037.

Andrae, T. (1989). Origins of the Dark Knight: A conversation with artists Bob Kane and Jerry Robinson. In R. M. Overstreet (Ed.), *Official Overstreet price guide*, (19), A-72–A-93.

Andrae, T. (2011). *Creators of the superheroes*. Neshannock, PA: Hermes.

Andrae, T. (2015, June). Personal communication.

Apter, M. J. (2007). *Reversal theory: The dynamics of motivation, emotion, and personality* (2nd ed.). Oxford, UK: Oneworld.

Arriaga, X. B. (2002). Joking violence among highly committed individuals. *Journal of Interpersonal Violence, 17*(6), 591–610.

Arriaga, X. B., & Capezza, N. M. (2005). Targets of partner violence: The importance of understanding coping trajectories. *Journal of Interpersonal Violence, 20*(1), 89–99.

Arriaga, X. B., Capezza N. M., & Daly C. A. (2016). Personal standards for judging aggression by a relationship partner: How much aggression is too much? *Journal of Personality & Social Psychology, 110*(1), 36–54.

Arya, U. (2015). Linguistic creativity construction in newspaper headlines: A content analysis of five Indian dailies. *Amity Journal of Media & Communication Studies, 4*(1–2), 149–167.

Attardo, S., Attardo, D. H., Baltes, P., & Petray, M. J. (1994). The linear organization of jokes: Analysis of two thousand texts. *Humor: International Journal of Humor Research, 7*(1), 27–54.

Ayres, J. (2016, February 20). *When were superheroes grim and gritty?* Los Angeles Review of Books: https://lareviewofbooks.org/article/when-were-superheroes-grim-and-gritty/.

Bailey, G. (2018, April 5). *Jack Nicholson's Joker voted best comic book movie villain of all time.* Independent: https://www.independent.co.uk/arts-entertainment/films/news/comic-book-movies-best-villain-jack-nicholson-heath-ledger-danny-devito-batman-joker-superman-a8289711.html.

Bails, J. (1965). If the truth be known or "A Finger in every plot!" *CAPA-Alpha,* (12), unnumbered pages.

Baker, D. (n.d.). *Bob Kane was a liar enamel pin.* Hey Dave Baker: http://www.heydavebaker.com/store-1/bob-kane-was-a-liar-enamel-pin.

Baraban, E.V. (2004). The motive for murder in "The Cask of Amontillado" by Edgar Allan Poe. *Rocky Mountain Review of Language & Literature, 58*(2), 47–62.

Barden, J., Rucker, D. D., & Petty, R. E. (2005). "Saying one thing and doing another": Examining the impact of event order on hypocrisy judgments of others. *Personality & Social Psychology Bulletin, 31*(11), 1463–1474.

Barker, C., & Jones, S. (1997). *Clive Barker's A–Z of horror.* New York, NY: Harper Prism.

Barnett, L., & Madison, G. (Eds.). (2012). *Existential therapy: Legacy, vibrancy, and dialogue.* New York, NY: Routledge.

Bartels, D. M., & Pizarro, D. A. (2011). The mismeasure of morals: Antisocial personality traits predict utilitarian responses to moral dilemmas. *Cognition, 121*(1), 154–161.

Barrett, L. (2018). *How emotions are made.* Boston, MA: Mariner.

Bassett, M., Sperlinger, D., & Freeman, D. (2009). Fear of madness and persecutory delusions: Preliminary investigation of a new scale. *Psychosis, 1*(1), 39–50.

Bassil-Morozow, H. (2004). Gothic archetypes in Hollywood: The Trickster and the Shadow in *Batman* and *The Mask. Anglophonia: French Journal of English Studies, 15*, 199–208.

Batson, C. D., Duncan, B. D., Ackerman, P., Buckley, T., & Birch, K. (1981). Is empathic emotion a source of altruistic motivation? *Journal of Personality & Social Psychology, 40*(2), 290–302.

Baumeister, R. F. (1991). *Meanings of life.* New York, NY: Guilford.

Baumeister, R. F. (2010). Social psychologists and thinking about people. In R. F. Baumeister & E. J. Finkel (Eds.), *Advanced social psychology: The state of the science* (pp. 5–24). New York, NY: Oxford University Press.

Beaussart, M. L., Kaufman, S. B., & Kaufman, J. C. (2012). Creative activity, personality, mental illness, and short-term mating success. *Journal of Creative Behavior, 46*(3), 151–167.

Bender, H. E., Kambam, P., & Pozios, V. K. (2011, September 20). *Putting the Caped Crusader on the couch.* New York Times: https://www.nytimes.com/2011/09/21/opinion/putting-the-caped-crusader-on-the-couch.html.

Bender, H. E., Kambam, P., Pozios, V. K., & Safarik, M. E. (2012, March 16). *Detecting deviants in the dark: Profiling Gotham's serial killers.* Panel presented at WonderCon, Anaheim, CA.

Bentley, H. (2009, January 7). *Hans Zimmer and James Newton Howard.* KCRW: https://www.kcrw.com/music/shows/morning-becomes-eclectic/hans-zimmer-and-james-newton-howard.

Berendt, J., & Uhrich, S. (2016). Enemies with benefits: The dual role of rivalry in shaping sports fans' identity. *European Sport Management Quarterly, 16*(5), 613–634.

Berlin, J. S. (2007). *The joker and the thief: Persistent malingering as a specific type of therapeutic impasse.* Psychiatric Times: https://www.psychiatrictimes.com/joker-and-thief-persistent-malingering-specific-type-therapeutic-impasse.

Besl, A. (n.d.). *How 3 dark personality traits can affect job performance.* Select International: http://www.selectinternational.com/blog/how-3-dark-personality-traits-can-affect-job-performance.

Besner, L. (2012, October 15). *Who are you? Amnesia in popular culture.* Hazlitt: https://hazlitt.net/feature/who-are-you-amnesia-popular-culture.

Bill Finger Award (n.d.). *Bill Finger Award.* Comic-Con International: https://www.comic-con.org/awards/bill-finger-award-node.

Bjørkly, S. (1997). Clinical assessment of dangerousness in psychotic patients: Some risk indicators and pitfalls. *Aggression & Violent Behavior, 2*(2), 167–178.

Black, M. C., Basile, K. C., Briedling, M. J., Smith, S. G., Walters, M. L., Merrick, M. T., Chen, J., & Stevens, R. (2011). *The National intimate partner and sexual violence survey (NISVIS): 2010 summary report.* Atlanta, GA: National Center for Injury Prevention and Control, Centers for Disease Control and Prevention.

Blair, T. & Frith, U. (2000). Neurocognitive explanations of the antisocial personality disorders. *Criminal Behaviour & Mental Health, 10*(S1), S66–S81.

Bleske, A. L., & Shackelford, T. K. (2001). Poaching, promiscuity, and deceit: Combatting mating rivalry in same-sex friendships. *Personal Relationships, 8*(4), 407–424.

Bloch, R. (1960/1995). The clown at midnight. In R. M. Matheson & R. Mainhardt (Eds.), *Robert Bloch: Appreciations of the master.* New York, NY: Tor.

Blunt, C. (2019, March 25). [Social media comment]. Re: https://www.facebook.com/drtravislangley/posts/2322003834500162.

Boers, F., & Lindstromberg, S. (2005). Finding ways to make phrase-learning feasible: The mnemonic effect of alliteration. *System, 33*(2), 225–238.

Boers, F., Lindstromberg, S., & Eyckmans, J. (2014). Is alliteration mnemonic without awareness-raising? *Language Awareness, 23*(4), 291–303.

Boers, F., & Stengers, H. (2008). Adding sound to the picture: An exercise in motivating the lexical composition of metaphorical idioms in English, Spanish and Dutch." In L. Cameron, M. Zanotto, & M. Cavalcanti (Eds.), *Confronting metaphor in use: An applied linguistic approach* (pp. 63–78). Amsterdam, Netherlands: John Benjamins.

Bonaduce, D. (2001). *Random acts of badness: My story.* New York, NY: Hyperion.

Book, A. S., Visser, B. A., Blais, J., Hosker-Field, A., Methot-Jones, T., Gauthier, N. Y., Volk, A., Holden, R. R., & D'Agata, M. T. (2016). Unpacking more "evil": What is at the core of the dark tetrad? *Personality & Individual Differences, 90*, 269–272.

Bordini, G. S., & Sperb, T. M. (2013). Sexual double standard: A review of the literature between 2001 and 2010. *Sexuality & Culture, 17*(4), 686–704.

Botzung, A., Rubin, D. C., Miles, A., Cabeza, R., & LaBar, K. S. (2010). Mental hoop diaries: Emotional memories of a college basketball game in rival fans. *Journal of Neuroscience, 30*(6), 2130–2137.

Bradbury, R. (1970). The meadow. In R. Bradbury (Author), *The golden apples of the sun* (pp. 119–134). New York, NY: Bantam.

Brewer G., & Abell, L. (2015). Machiavellianism in long-term relationships: Competition, mate retention, and sexual coercion. *Scandinavian Journal of Psychology, 56*(3), 357–362.

Bridwell, E. N. (1986). Comics pioneers [letter to the editor]. *David Anthony Kraft's Comics Interview* (38), 66.

Brioux, B. (2008). *Truth and rumors: The reality behind TV's most famous myths.* Westport, CT: Praeger.

Broadview Pictures (2014, January 27). *Heath Ledger's Joker diary—too young to die—Heath Ledger.* BroadviewPictures: https://www.youtube.com/watch?v=kJMoKMieNn8.

Brock, S., Nickerson, A., Reeves, M., Conolly, C., Jimerson, S., Pesce, R., & Lazzaro, B. (2016). *School crisis prevention and intervention: The PREPaRE model*. Bethesda, MD: National Association of School Psychologists.

Brooker, W. (2001). *Batman unmasked: Analyzing a cultural icon*. New York, NY: Continuum.

Brown, P. J., Recupero, P. R., & Stout, R. (1995). PTSD substance abuse comorbidity and treatment utilization. *Addictive Behaviors, 20*(2), 251–254.

Burlingame, R. (2013, August 3). *Wolverine creator Wein made more money from The Dark Knight trilogy than X-Men movies*. Comic Book: https://comicbook.com/blog/2013/08/03/wolverine-creator-wein-made-more-money-from-the-dark-knight-trilogy-than-x-men-movies/. Quoted from original source, now missing: http://herocomplex.latimes.com/comics/wolverine-len-wein-on-hugh-jackman-comic-book-movies-getting-paid/#/0.

Bushman, B. J. (2002). Does venting anger feed or extinguish the flame? Catharsis, rumination, distraction, anger, and aggressive responding. *Personality & Social Psychology Bulletin, 28*(6), 724–731.

Buss, D. M. (1994). *The evolution of desire: Strategies of human mating*. New York, NY: Basic.

Buss, D. M., & Schmitt, D. P. (1993). Sexual strategies theory: An evolutionary perspective on human mating. *Psychological Review, 100*(2), 204–232.

Cajun, R., (2016, August 27). *The DCEU three Joker theory*. Amino Comics: https://aminoapps.com/c/comics/page/blog/the-dceu-three-joker-theory/oJid_uBGngZa2YQw3G5DqJVpq4X3ng.

Callahan, L. A., McGreevy, M. A., Cirincione, C., & Steadman, H. J. (1992). Measuring the effects of the guilty but mentally ill (GBMI) verdict: Georgia's 1982 GBMI reform. *Law & Human Behavior, 16*(4), 447–462.

Campbell, J. (1949/2008). *The hero with a thousand faces* (3rd ed.). Novato, CA: New World Library.

Canfield, J. (2017, January 18). *The 15 most WTF things the Joker did to Harley Quinn*. ScreenRant: https://screenrant.com/worst-most-wtf-things-the-joker-did-to-harley-quinn/.

Cantor, C., & Price, J. (2007). Traumatic entrapment, appeasement and complex post-traumatic stress disorder: Evolutionary perspectives of hostage reactions, domestic abuse and the Stockholm syndrome. *Australian & New Zealand Journal of Psychiatry, 41*(5), 377–384.

Carich, M. S., Kassel, M., & Stone, M. (2001). Enhancing social interest in sex offenders. *Journal of Individual Psychology, 57*(1), 18–25.

Carich, M. S., Metzger, C. K., Baig, M. S. A., & Harper, J. J. (2003). Enhancing victim empathy for sex offenders. *Journal of Child Sexual Abuse, 12*(3–4), 255–276.

Carlsson, A., Waters, N., & Carlsson, M. L. (1999). Neurotransmitter interactions in schizophrenia—therapeutic implications. *Biological Psychiatry, 46*(10), 1388–1395.

Carroll, N. (2014). *Humour: A very short introduction*. Oxford, UK: Oxford University Press.

Carveth, D. L. (2012). Concordant and complementary counter-transference: A clarification. *Canadian Journal of Psychoanalysis, 20*(1), 70–84.

Chabrol, H., Van Leeuwen, N., Rodgers, R., & Sejourne, N. (2009). Contributions of psychopathic, narcissistic, Machiavellian, and sadistic personality traits to juvenile delinquency. *Personality & Individual Differences, 47*(7), 734–739.

Chamizo, S. (2015, July 17). *Tarot Tuesday: The meaning of the Fool*. House of Intuition: https://houseofintuitionla.com/blogs/news/tarot-tuesday-the-meaning-of-the-fool.

Chapais, B. (2015). Competence and the evolutionary origins of status and power in humans. *Human Nature, 26*(2), 161–183.

Charney, M. (1978). *Comedy high and low: An introduction to the experience of comedy*. Oxford, UK: Oxford University Press.

Chester, D. (2016). *The fantasy fiction formula*. Manchester, UK: Manchester University Press.

Christensen, D., & Wallman, B. (2018, March 28). *Crazed girls flood Parkland school shooter Nikolas Cruz with fan mail*. Sun Sentinel: https://www.sun-sentinel.com/local/broward/parkland/florida-school-shooting/fl-reg-nikolas-cruz-prison-love-letters-20180327-story.html.

Christie, R., & Geis, F. L. (1970). *Studies in Machiavellianism.* New York, NY: Academic Press.

Cialdini, R. B. (2007). *Influence: The psychology of persuasion.* New York, NY: HarperCollins.

Cleckley, H. M. (1941/1976). *The mask of sanity: An attempt to clarify some issues about the so-called psychopathic personality.* Maryland Heights, MO: Mosby.

Cleman, J. (2001). Irresistible impulses: Edgar Allan Poe and the insanity defense. In H. Bloom (Ed.), *Bloom's biocritiques: Edgar Allan Poe* (pp. 66–67). Philadelphia, PA: Chelsea House.

Clevenger, S. (2019). *Sexual assault and intimate partner violence survivors research in Illinois 2013–2018.* (Unpublished manuscript). Illinois State University, Normal, IL.

Clevenger, S., Navarro, J. N., Marcum, C. D., & Higgins, G. E. (2018). *Understanding victimology: An active learning approach.* Abingdon-on-Thames, UK: Routledge.

Cloer, R. (2018, February 1). *When should the Copper Age start and end?* Comics Price Guide: http://blog.comicspriceguide.com/2018/02/01/when-should-the-copper-age-start-and-end/.

Collard, J. J., Cummins, R. A., & Fuller-Tyskiewicz, M. (2016). Measurement of positive irrational beliefs (positive cognitive illusions). *Journal of Happiness Studies, 17*(3), 1069–1088.

Comic-Con International (n.d.). *Bill Finger Award.* Comic-Con International: https://www.comic-con.org/awards/bill-finger-award-node.

Commons, D., Greenwood, K. M., & Anderson, R. A. (2016). A preliminary investigation into worry about mental health: Development of the Mental Health Anxiety Inventory. *Behavioural & Cognitive Psychotherapy, 44*(3), 347–360.

Conley, N. (2017, February 26). *15 wildly different origin stories for the Joker.* ScreenRant: https://screenrant.com/batman-joker-craziest-origin-stories/.

Conlin, S. E. (2017). Feminist therapy: A brief integrative review of theory, empirical support, and call for new directions. *Women's Studies International Forum, 62,* 78–82.

Connell, R. (1971). *Gender and power.* Stanford, CA: Stanford University Press.

Conroy, K. (2019, March 29). Personal communication.

Conroy, K., & Langley, T. (2017, October). *Kevin Conroy Q&A.* Wizard World Oklahoma City Comic Con, Oklahoma City, OK. Part 1: https://www.youtube.com/watch?v=VPgCw0m0H-ME&t=2s. Part 2: https://www.youtube.com/watch?v=-joLtI39pSE.

Corrigan, P. W., River, L. P., Lundind, R. K., Wasowski, K. U., Campion, J., Mathisen, J., Goldstein, H., Bergman, M., Gagnon, C., & Kubiak, M. A. (2000). Stigmatizing attributions about mental illness. *Journal of Community Psychology, 28*(1), 91–102.

Costa, P. T., & McCrae, R. R. (1991). Facet scales for agreeableness and conscientiousness: A revision of the NEO personality inventory. *Personality & Individual Differences, 12*(9), 887–898.

Craig, E. (2012). Existential psychotherapy, discipline, and démarche: Remembering essential horizons. In Barnett, L., & Madison, G. (Eds.). (2012). *Existential therapy: Legacy, vibrancy, and dialogue.* New York, NY: Routledge.

CrashLanden (2011, May 11). *The comic book greats Bob Kane Stan Lee part 2.* CrashLanden: https://www.youtube.com/watch?v=Cbivgi9ZZpY.

Craun, S. W., & Bourke, M. L. (2014). The use of humor to cope with secondary traumatic stress. *Journal of Child Sexual Abuse, 23*(7), 840–852.

Craun, S. W., & Bourke, M. L. (2015). Is laughing at the expense of victims and offenders a red flag? Humor and secondary traumatic stress. *Journal of Child Sexual Abuse, 24*(5), 592–602.

Cronin, B. (2005, October 27). *Comic book urban legends revealed #22!* Comic Book Resource: https://www.cbr.com/comic-book-urban-legends-revealed-22/.

Cronin, B. (2008). *Comic book urban legends revealed #174.* Comic Book Resources: https://www.cbr.com/comic-book-urban-legends-revealed-174/.

Cronin, B. (2015, August 2). *75 greatest Joker stories master list.* Comic Book Resource: https://www.cbr.com/75-greatest-joker-stories-master-list/.

Curran, T., Hill, A. P., Appleton, P. R., Vallerand, R. J., & Standage, M. (2015). The psychology of passion: A meta-analytical review of a decade of research on intrapersonal outcomes. *Motivation & Emotion, 39*(5), 631–655.

Czerner, T. G. (2002). *What makes you tick: The brain in plain English*. New York, NY: Wiley.

Dahl, M., & Beavers, E. (2017). *Bedtime for Batman*. North Mankato, MN: Capstone.

Damasio, A. (1979). The frontal lobes. In K. M. Hellman & E. Valenstein (Eds.), *Clinical neuropsychology* (pp. 310–412). New York, NY: Oxford University Press.

Daniels, L. (1999). *Batman: The complete history*. New York, NY: Chronicle.

Davies, C. (1990). *Ethnic humor around the world: A comparative analysis*. Bloomington, IN: Indiana University Press.

Davis, K. L., Buchsbaum, M. S., Shihabuddin, L., Spiegel-Cohen, J., Metzger, M., Frecska, E., Keefe, R. S., & Powchik, P. (1998). Ventricular enlargement in poor-outcome schizophrenia. *Biological Psychiatry, 43*(11), 783–793.

Davis, M., & Whalen, P. J. (2001). The amygdala: Vigilance and emotion. *Molecular Psychiatry, 6*(1), 13–34.

Day, A., Casey, S., & Gerace, A. (2010). Interventions to improve empathy awareness in sexual and violent offenders: Conceptual, empirical, and clinical issues. *Aggression & Violent Behavior, 15*(3), 201–208.

Decker, S. E., & Naugle, A. E. (2008). DBT for sexual abuse survivors: Current status and future directions. *Journal of Behavior Analysis of Offender & Victim: Treatment & Prevention, 1*(4), 52–69.

DeKeseredy, W. S., Dragiewicz, M., & Schwartz, M. D. (2018). *Abusive Endings: Separation and divorce violence against women*. Berkeley, CA: University of California Press.

DePaulo & Kashy (1998). Everyday lies in close and casual relationships. *Journal of Personality & Social Psychology, 74*(1), 63–79.

Descartes, R. (1647/1993). *Meditations on first philosophy*. Indianapolis, IN: Hackett.

Dickens, C. (1836). *The posthumous papers of the Pickwick Club*, a.k.a. *The Pickwick papers*. London, UK: Chapman & Hall.

Dickinson, E. (1862/1998). *Letters from Dickinson to Mary Bowles, Spring 1862*. Dickinson Electronic Archives: http://archive.emilydickinson.org/correspondence/mbowles/l262.html

Dickson, C. (2019, March 25). [Social media comment]. Re: https://www.facebook.com/drtravis-langley/posts/2322003834500162.

Dini, P., & Cadigan, P. (2018). *Harley Quinn: Mad love* [novelization]. London, UK: Titan.

Dooley, F. P. (1900). *Mr. Dooley's philosophy*. New York, NY: R. H. Russell.

Dorkly Staff (2013, February 19). *The 25 greatest comic book villains of all-time*. Dorkly: http://www.dorkly.com/post/50525/the-25-greatest-comic-book-villains-of-all-time/page:5.

Dougherty, M. R. P. (2001). Integration of the ecological and error models of overconfidence using a multiple-trace memory model. *Journal of Experimental Psychology: General, 130*(4), 579–599.

Douglas, J. E. (2007). *Inside the mind of BTK: The true story behind thirty years of hunting for the Wichita serial killer*. San Francisco, CA: Jossey Bass, Wiley.

Dovidio, J. F., Piliavin, J. A., Schroeder, D. A., & Penner, L. A. (2006). *The social psychology of prosocial behavior*. Mahwah, NJ: Erlbaum.

Ducharte, P. (1929). *The Italian comedy*. London, UK: Harrap.

Duignan, B. (n.d.). *What's the difference between a psychopath and a sociopath? And how do both differ for narcissists?* Encyclopaedia Britannica: https://www.britannica.com/story/whats-the-difference-between-a-psychopath-and-a-sociopath-and-how-do-both-differ-from-narcissists.

Duncan, M. (2016, June 8). *The quintessential portrayal of Batman was a cartoon*. AV Club: https://news.avclub.com/the-quintessential-portrayal-of-batman-was-a-cartoon-1798248101.

Dunlap, E., Golub, A., Johnson, B. D., & Wesley, D. (2002). Intergenerational transmission of conduct norms for drugs, sexual exploitation and violence: A case study. *British Journal of Criminology, 42*(1), 1–20.

Dunlop, J., & Pinals, D. A. (2016). Criteria for increasing involuntary medication dosage for a committed insanity acquittee. *Journal of the American Academy of Psychiatry & the Law, 44*(4), 501–503.

Dunning, D. Leuenberger, A., & Sherman, D. A. (1995). A new look at motivational interference: Are self-serving theories of success a product of motivational forces? *Journal of Personality & Social Psychology, 69*(1), 58–68.

Durham v. United States (1954). 214 F.2d 862 (D.C. Cir.).

Dutton, D. G., & Painter, S. (1993). Emotional attachments in abusive relationships: A test of traumatic bonding theory. *Violence & Victims, 8*(2), 105–120.

Elliott, F. (1978). Neurological aspects of antisocial behavior. In W. H. Reid (Ed.), *The psychopath: A comprehensive study of antisocial disorders and behaviors* (pp. 146–189). New York, NY: Bruner/Mazel.

Ellison, H. (1965/2016). "Repent, Harlequin," said the Ticktockman. In A. Vandermeer & J. Vandermeer (Eds.), *The big book of science fiction* (pp. 491–499). New York, NY: Vintage.

Englehart (2012, personal communication).

Enns, C. Z. (2004). *Feminist theories and feminist psychotherapies: Origins, themes, and diversity*. Binghampton, NY: Haworth.

Eury, M., & Kronenberg, M. (2009). *The Batcave companion*. Raleigh, NC: TwoMorrows.

Evans, W., & Davis, B. (2018). Exploring the relationships between sense and coherence and historical trauma among American Indian youth. *American Indian & Alaska Native Mental Health Research, 25*(3), 1–25.

Ewing, C. P., & McCann, J. T. (2006). *Minds on trial: Great cases in law and psychology*. Oxford, UK: Oxford University Press.

Fansplainer (2018a, October 18). *Real-life Joker: How to spot a psychopath*. Fansplainer: https://www.youtube.com/watch?v=hnCmdu-Rl_c&list=PLo07e6rCi3jVaWMQYv9D_9naXl9YEUROM&index=9.

Fansplainer (2018b, December 14). *Real-life Joker: Nature vs. nurture in psychopathy*. Fansplainer: https://www.youtube.com/watch?v=hASSo2fav9U&index=10&list=PLo07e6rCi3jVaWMQYv9D_9naXl9YEUROM.

Farber, B. A., & Doolin, E. M. (2011). Positive regard. *Psychotherapy, 48*(1), 58–64.

Fard, V. O, Mehrabi, T., & Fanian, N. (2011). Psychiatric team's experience of working in psychiatric wards. *Iranian Journal of Nursing & Midwifery Research, 16*(1), 20–25.

Fazel, S. & Danesh, J. (2002). Serious mental disorder in 23,000 prisoners: A systematic review of 62 surveys. *The Lancet, 359*(9306), 545–550.

Feddes, E. J. (2017, June 27). *The summer of Batman '66—part two*. Spunky Bean: http://www.spunky-bean.com/comic-books/the-summer-of-batman-66-part-two/.

Feldberg, I. (2016, February 11). *Stephen King revisits a horror story that belongs to history*. Boston Globe: https://www.bostonglobe.com/arts/2016/02/10/stephen-king-revisits-horror-story-that-belongs-history/UNGcmBdNHvxnGzvTPpqvgM/story.html.

Fennell, P. (1992). The Criminal Procedure Act (Insanity and Unfitness to Plead) Act 1991. *Modern Law Review, 55*(4), 547–555.

Festinger, L. (1957). *A theory of cognitive dissonance*. Stanford, CA: Stanford University Press.

Fingeroth, D. (2004). *Superman on the couch: What superheroes really tell us about ourselves and our society*. New York, NY: Continuum.

Finger, A., Langley, T., Bailey, E., Coogan, P., & Fingeroth, D. (2014a, April). *1939: The year that changed everything*. Wizard World St. Louis Comic Con. St. Louis, MO.

Finger, A., Cruz, B., Langley, T., Andrae, T., Evanier, M., Meriwether, L., Nobleman, M. T., Robinson, J., Uslan, M., & O'Neil, D. (2014b, July). *Spotlight on Bill Finger, the co-creator of Batman*. San Diego Comic-Con International, San Diego, CA.

Fleming, A. (2009). *Portrait of the artist: Malcolm McLaren, musician.* The Guardian: https://www.theguardian.com/culture/2009/aug/10/malcolm-mclaren-musician.

Ford, C.V. (1996). *Lies! Lies! Lies! The psychology of deceit.* Washington, DC: American Psychiatric Press.

Forensic Behavior Services (n.d.). *Mark Safarik.* FBS: https://fbsinternational.com/associates/mark-safarik/.

Franco, A., Malhotra, N., & Simonovits, G. (2016). Underreporting in psychology experiments: Evidence from a study registry. *Social Psychological & Personality Science, 7*(1), 8–12.

Frank, J. B. (1990). Clowning around: Serious business at Clown College. *Tampa Bay, 5*(1) 31–34.

Franklin, K. (2012, May 2). *Homicidal triad: Predictor of violence or urban myth?* Psychology Today: https://www.psychologytoday.com/us/blog/witness/201205/homicidal-triad-predictor-violence-or-urban-myth.

Frederick, E. (2016, July 30). *Experts still disagree on role of Tower shooter's brain tumor.* The Daily Texan: http://www.dailytexanonline.com/2016/07/30/experts-still-disagree-on-role-of-tower-shooters-brain-tumor.

Freud, S. (1905/1960). *Der Witz und seine Beziehung zum Unbewußten* [Jokes and their relation to the unconscious] (J. Stachey, Trans.). New York, NY: Norton.

Freud, S. (1928). Humor. *International Journal of Psychoanalysis, 9*(1), 1–6.

Fuller, K. (2019, February 27). *The difference between psychopath versus sociopath.* Thrive Global: https://thriveglobal.com/stories/the-difference-between-psychopath-verus-sociopath/.

Gans, H. J. (1975). *Popular culture and high culture: An analysis and evaluation of taste.* New York, NY: Basic.

Gao, Y., & Raine, A. (2010). Successful and unsuccessful psychopaths: A neurobiological model. *Behavioral Sciences & the Law, 28*(2), 194–210.

Gery, I., Miljkovitch, R., Berthoz, S., & Soussignan, R. (2009). Empathy and recognition of facial expressions of emotion in sex offenders, non-sex offenders and normal controls. *Psychiatry Research, 165*(3), 252–262.

Ghosh, V. E. & Gilboa, A. (2014). What is a memory schema? A historical perspective on current neuroscience literature. *Neuropsychologia, 53,* 104–114.

Giammarco, E. (2013). Edgar Allan Poe: A psychological profile. *Personality & Individual Differences, 54*(1), 3–6.

Gilbert, H. (2016, July 31). *5 Joker comics better than 'The Killing Joke.'* Fandom: https://www.fandom.com/articles/5-joker-comics-better-killing-joke.

Glahn, D. C., Bearden, C. E., Cakir, S., Barrett, J. A., Najt, P., Monkul, E. S., Maples, N., Velligan, D. I., & Soares, J. C. (2006). Differential working memory impairment in bipolar disorder and schizophrenia: Effects of lifetime history of psychosis. *Bipolar Disorders, 8*(2), 117–123.

Glenn, A. L. (2011). The other allele: Exploring the long allele of the serotonin transporter gene as a potential risk factor for psychopathy: A review of the parallels in findings. *Neuroscience & Biobehavioral Reviews, 35*(3), 612–620.

Gobin, R. L., & Freyd, J. J. (2014). The impact of betrayal trauma on the tendency to trust. *Psychological Trauma: Theory, Research, Practice, & Policy, 6*(5), 505–511.

Gold, M. (Ed.) (1988). *The greatest Joker stories ever told.* New York, NY: DC Comics. [Not to be confused with Joy, B. (Ed.) (2008). *The Joker: The greatest stories ever told.* New York, NY: DC Comics.]

Goldberg, E. (2001). *The executive brain: Frontal lobes and the civilized mind.* Oxford, UK: Oxford University Press.

Goleman, D. J. (1989). What is negative about positive illusions? When benefits for the individual harm the collective. *Journal of Social & Clinical Psychology, 8*(2), 190–197.

Goodfriend, W. (2016, July 30). *Mad love: Personality disorders in Harley Quinn & the Joker.* Psychology Today: https://www.psychologytoday.com/us/blog/psychologist-the-movies/201607/mad-love-personality-disorders-in-harley-quinn-the-joker.

Goodfriend, W., & Arriaga, X. B. (2018). Cognitive reframing of intimate partner aggression: Social and contextual influences. *International Journal of Environmental Research & Public Health, 15*(11), 2464. https://doi.org/10.3390/ijerph15112464.

Goodwin, J., & Tajjudin, I. (2016). "What do you think I am? Crazy?" The Joker and stigmatizing representations of mental ill-health. *Journal of Popular Culture, 49*(2), 385–402.

Gordon, S. (2012). Introduction. In P. Kane & M. O'Regan (Eds.), *The mammoth book of body horror* (unnumbered pages). Philadelphia, PA: Running Press.

Gorenstein, E. E. (1982). Frontal lobe functions in psychopaths. *Journal of Abnormal Psychology, 91*(5), 368–379.

Gould, J. (2015, June 8). *Joker who? The inspiration behind each actor's portrayal.* Geek & Sundry: https://geekandsundry.com/joker-who-the-inspiration-behind-each-actors-portrayal/.

Graham, D. L. R., & Rawlings, E. I. (1998). Bonding with abusive dating partners: Dynamics of Stockholm syndrome. In B. Levy (Ed.), *Dating violence: Young women in danger* (pp. 119–135). Seattle, WA: Seal Press.

Graham, D. L. R., Rawlings, E. I., Ihms, K., Latimer, D., Foliano, J., Thompson, A., Suttman, K., Farrington, M., & Hacker, R. (1995). A scale for identifying "Stockholm syndrome" reactions in young dating women: Factor structure, reliability, and validity. *Violence & Victims, 10*(1), 3–22.

Graham, D. L. R., with Rawlings, E. I., & Rigsby, R. K. (1994). *Loving to survive: Sexual terror, men's violence, and women's lives.* New York, NY: New York University Press.

Grand, H. G. (1959). The fear of becoming insane. *American Journal of Psychotherapy, 13*(1), 51–54.

Grant, B. G., Chou, S. P., Goldstein, R. B., Huang, B., Stinson, F. S., Saha, T. D., Smith, S. M., Dawson, D. A., Pullay, A. J., Pickering, R. P., & Ruan, W. J. (2008). Prevalence, correlates, disability, and comorbidity of DSM-IV borderline personality disorder: Results from the Wave 2 National Epidemiological Survey on Alcohol and Related Conditions. *Journal of Clinical Psychiatry, 69*(4), 533–545.

Gray, R. (2011). Lies, liars, and lie detection. *Federal Probation, 75*(3), 31–36.

Grohol, J. N. (2018, July 8). *Difference between a psychopath vs sociopath.* PsychCentral: https://psychcentral.com/blog/differences-between-a-psychopath-vs-sociopath/.

Gustines, G. G. (2010, October 4). *The Joker in the deck: Birth of a supervillain.* New York Times: https://www.nytimes.com/2010/10/05/books/05robinson.html.

Haidt, J., Rozin, P., McCauley, C., & Imada, S. (1997). Body, psyche, and culture: The relationship between disgust and morality. *Psychology & Developing Societies, 9*(1), 107–131.

Halberstam, J. (1995). *Skin shows: Gothic horror and the technology of monsters.* Raleigh, NC: Duke University Press.

Hamm, S. (2019, March 10). [Untitled tweet]. Twitter: https://twitter.com/SamuelHamm/status/1104841873842032640.

Hampson, M. E., Hicks, R. E., & Watt, B. D. (2017). Beliefs about employment of people living with psychosis. *Australian Journal of Psychology.* Advance online publication: https://onlinelibrary.wiley.com/doi/full/10.1111/ajpy.12172.

Hanley, T. (2017). *The many lives of the Catwoman: The felonious history of a feline fatale.* Chicago, IL: Chicago Review Press.

Hanson, K., & Scott, H. (1995). Assessing perspective taking among sexual offenders, nonsexual criminals, and nonoffenders. *Sexual Abuse: A Journal of Research & Treatment, 7*, 259–277.

Hansson, P., Juslin, P., & Winman, A. (2008). The role of short-term memory capacity and task experience for overconfidence in judgment under uncertainty. *Journal of Experimental Psychology: Learning, Memory, & Cognition, 34*(5), 1027–1042.

Hare, R. D. (1978). Psychopathy and electrodermal responses to nonsignal stimulation. *Biological Psychology, 6*(4), 237–246.

Hare, R. D. (1980). A research scale for the assessment of psychopathy in criminal populations. *Personality & Individual Differences, 1*(2), 111–119.

Hare, R. D. (1984). Performance of psychopaths on cognitive tasks related to frontal lobe function. *Journal of Abnormal Psychology, 93*(2), 133–140.

Hare, R. D. (1993/1999). *Without conscience: The disturbing world of the psychopaths among us.* New York, NY: Guilford.

Hare, R. D. (1996). Psychopathy: A clinical construct whose time has come. *Criminal Justice & Behavior, 23*(1), 25–54.

Hare, R. D. (2003). *The Hare psychopathy checklist—revised* (2nd ed.). Toronto: Multi-Health Systems.

Hare, R. D., & Neumann, C. S. (2008). Psychopathy as a clinical and empirical construct. *Annual Review of Clinical Psychology, 4,* 217–246.

Harenski, C. L., Thornton, D. M., Harenski, K. A., Decety, J., & Kiehl, K. A. (2012). Increased frontotemporal activation during pain observation in sexual sadism. *Archives of General Psychiatry, 69*(3), 283–292.

Haslam-Hopwood, G. T. G. (2003). The role of the primary clinician in the multidisciplinary team. *Bulletin of the Menninger Clinic, 67*(1), 5–17.

Haugen, P. T., Evces, M., & Weiss, D. S. (2012). Treating posttraumatic stress disorder in first responders: A systematic review. *Clinical Psychology Review, 32*(5), 370–380.

Hayes, R. A., & Slater, A. (2008). Three-month-olds' detection of alliteration in syllables. *Infant Behavior & Development, 31*(1), 153–156.

Hayes, S. C., Luoma, J. B., Bond, F. W., Masuda, A., & Lillis, J. (2006). Acceptance and commitment therapy: Model, processes and outcomes. *Behaviour Research & Therapy, 44*(1), 1–25.

Heckers, S., Barch, D. M., Bustillo, J., Gaebel, W., Gur, R., Malaspina, D., Owen, M. J., Schultz, S., Tandon, R., Tsuang, M., Van Os, J., & Carpenter, W. (2013). Structure of the psychotic disorders classification in DSM-5. *Schizophrenia Research, 150*(1), 11–14.

Heidegger, M. (1962). *Being and time.* New York, NY: Harper & Row.

Helle, C. (2016, July 25). *Harley Quinn and the Joker are not #RelationshipGoals.* Odyssey: https://www.theodysseyonline.com/harley-quinn-joker-relationshipgoals.

Henderson, J. (1964). Ancient myths and modern man. In C. G. Jung (Ed.), *Man and his symbols* (pp. 95–156). New York, NY: Dell.

Henrich, J., & Gil-White, F. J. (2001). The evolution of prestige: Freely conferred deference as a mechanism for enhancing the benefits of cultural transmission. *Evolution & Human Behavior, 22*(3), 165–196.

Hight, B. (2001, November 11; posted online 2016, September 3). *UT tower shooter claims one more life.* Statesman: https://www.statesman.com/NEWS/20160903/UT-Tower-shooting-claims-one-more-life.

Hilton, D., Régner, I., Cabantous's, L, Charalambride, L., & Vautier, S. (2011). Do positive illusions predict overconfidence in judgment? A test using interval production and probability evaluation measures of miscalibration. *Journal of Behavioral Decision Making, 24*(2), 117–139.

Hollenitsch, N. (2016, December 14). *The trickster, the drag queen, and the goddess: Exploring gender and sexuality through an archetypal lens.* Pacifica Post: https://www.pacificapost.com/the-trickster-the-drag-queen-and-the-goddess-exploring-gender-and-sexuality-through-an-archetypal-lens.

Hood, B. M. (2009). *Supersense: Why we believe in the unbelievable.* San Francisco, CA: HarperOne.

Hoogland, C. E., Ryan Schultz, D., Cooper, C. M., Combs, D. J. Y., Brown, E. G., & Smith, R. H. (2015). The joy of pain and the pain of joy: In-group identification predicts schadenfreude and gluckschmerz following rival groups' fortunes. *Motivation & Emotion, 39*(3), 260–281.

Hooten, C. (2015, August 10). *A look inside Heath Ledger's sinister "Joker journal" for The Dark Knight.* Independent: https://www.independent.co.uk/arts-entertainment/films/news/a-look-inside-heath-ledger-s-sinister-joker-journal-10448048.html.

Hoppenbrouwers, S., & Bulten, B. (2016). Parsing fear: A reassessment of the evidence for fear deficits in psychopathy. *Psychological Bulletin, 142*(6), 573–600.

Hornberger, R. H. (1959). The differential reduction of aggressive responses as a function of interpolated activities. *American Psychologist, 14*(7), 354.

Howes, R. (2016, October 26). *Why people lie to their therapists.* Psychology Today: https://www.psychologytoday.com/us/blog/in-therapy/201610/why-people-lie-their-therapists.

Hudnall, A. (2015, September 6). *Archetypes: Jester.* Ariel Hudnall: https://arielhudnall.com/2015/09/06/archetypes-jester/.

Hyatt-Burkhart, D. (2017). Ecosystemic structural family therapy. In J. Carlson & S. B. Dermer (Eds.), *The SAGE encyclopedia of marriage, family, and couples counseling* (p. 506). Thousand Oaks, CA: SAGE.

Hyde, L. (1999). *Trickster makes this world: Mischief, myth, and art.* New York, NY: North Point Press.

Ide, W. (2017, February 12). *The Lego Batman Movie review—sporadically hilarious spin-off.* The Observer: https://www.theguardian.com/film/2017/feb/12/lego-batman-movie-spin-off-review.

IGN (2009). *Top 100 comic book villains.* IGN: https://www.ign.com/lists/top-100-comic-book-villains/100.

Infinite Midlives (2014, July 26). *SDCC 2014: Jim Steranko vs. Bob Kane.* Infinite Midlives: https://www.youtube.com/watch?v=fadzZwx85e0.

Irving, W. (1807). *The Salmagundi papers.* New York, NY: Longworth.

Jackson, M. (2013, July 10). *The time Jim Steranko slapped Bob Kane at San Diego Comic-Con.* SyFy Wire: https://www.syfy.com/syfywire/time-jim-steranko-slapped-bob-kane-san-diego-comic-con.

Jakobwitz, S., & Egan, V. (2006). The "dark triad" and normal personality traits. *Personality and Individual Differences, 40*(2), 331–339.

Jauk, E., Neubauer, A. C., Mairunterregger, T., Pemp, S., Sieer, K. P., & Rauthmann, J. F. (2016). How alluring are dark personalities? The dark triad and attractiveness in speed dating. *European Journal of Personality, 30*(2), 125–138.

Jewell, T. (2018, January 11). *Sociopath.* Healthline: https://www.healthline.com/health/mental-health/sociopath.

Johnson, A. (2017, October 30). *The best horror films of the 21st century.* The Young Folks: https://www.theyoungfolks.com/film/111419/the-best-horror-films-of-the-21st-century/.

Johnson, J. G., Cohen, P., Chen, H., Kasen, S., & Brooks, J. S. (2006). Parenting behaviors associated with risk for offspring personality disorder during adulthood. *Archives of General Psychiatry, 63*(5), 579–587.

Johnson, M. K., & Raye, C. L. (1981). Reality monitoring. *Psychological Review, 88*(1), 67–85.

Johnson, M. P. (1995). Patriarchal terrorism and common couple violence: Two forms of violence against women. *Journal of Marriage & the Family, 57*(2), 283–294.

Johnson, M. P. (2007). Domestic violence: The intersection of gender and control. In L. L. O'Toole, J. R. Schiffman, & M. L. K. Edwards (Eds.), *Gender violence: Interdisciplinary perspectives* (2nd ed.; pp. 257–268). New York, NY: New York University Press.

Jonason, P. K., Koenig, B. L., & Tost, J. (2010). Living a fast life. *Human Nature, 21*(4), 428–442.

Jonason, P. K., Lyons, M., Baughman, H. M., & Vernon, P. A. (2014). What a tangled web we weave: The Dark Triad traits and deception. *Personality & Individual Differences, 70*, 117–119.

Jonason, P. K., Webster, G. D., Schmitt, D. P., Li, N. P., & Crysel, L. (2012). The antihero in popular culture: Life history theory and the dark triad personality traits. *Review of General Psychology, 16*(2), 192–199.

Jones, C. W., & Lindblad-Goldberg, M. (2002). Ecosystemic structural family therapy. In F. W. Kaslow (Ed.), *Comprehensive handbook of psychotherapy: Interpersonal/humanistic/existential* (vol. 3, pp. 3–33). Hoboken, NJ: Wiley.

Jones, D. N., & Paulhus, D. L. (2010). Differentiating the dark triad within the interpersonal circumplex. In L. M. Horowitz & S. N. Strack (Eds.), *Handbook of interpersonal theory and research* (pp. 249–267). New York, NY: Guilford.

Jones, D. N., & Paulhus, D. L. (2017). Duplicity among the dark triad: Three faces of deceit. *Journal of Personality & Social Psychology, 113*(2), 329–342.

Jones, J. (2015, October 7). *The mystery of Edgar Allan Poe's death: 19 theories on what caused Poe's demise.* Open Culture: http://www.openculture.com/2015/10/the-mystery-of-edgar-allan-poes-death-19-theories-on-what-caused-the-poets-demise-166-years-ago-today.html.

Jung, C. G. (1933). *Modern man in search of a soul.* Oxford, UK: Harcourt, Brace.

Jung, C. G. (1964). Approaching the unconscious. In C. G. Jung (Ed.), *Man and his symbols* (pp. 1–94). New York, NY: Dell.

Jung, C. G. (1968/1991). *The archetypes and the collective unconscious.* CW9 pt. 1 (2nd ed.). Princeton, NJ: Princeton University Press.

Jusczyk, P. W., Goodman, M. B., & Baumann, A. (1999). Nine-month-olds' attention to sound similarities in syllables. *Journal of Memory & Language, 40*(1), 62–82.

Kahn, J. S. (2010) Feminist therapy for men: Challenging assumptions and moving forward. *Women & Therapy, 34*(1), 59–76.

Kaiser, W. (n.d.). *Wisdom of the fool.* Encyclopedia of Ideas: https://sites.google.com/site/encyclopediaofideas/human-nature/wisdom-of-the-fool.

Kane, B. (1967). An open letter to all "Batmanians" everywhere (dated September 14, 1965). *Batmania* (17), a.k.a. *The Batmania Annual* (1).

Kane, B., with Andrae, T. (1989). *Batman and me.* Forestville, CA: Eclipse.

Kane, B., with Andrae, T. (1989/1996). *Batman and me: The saga continues . . .* Van Nuys, CA: Zanart. [Andrae is credited in this updated edition's interior but not on the cover.]

kaptainkristian (2016, July 7). *Batman—evolving the legend.* kaptainkristian: https://www.youtube.com/watch?v=u5Cdguyut8s.

Karbank, O. (2017, December 13). *The 15 worst things the Joker has done to Harley Quinn.* Comic Book Resources: https://www.cbr.com/worst-things-joker-harley-quinn/.

Karlin, S. (2014, July 21). *Who created Batman? A DC comics historian weighs in on the controversy.* Fast Company: https://www.fastcompany.com/3033002/who-really-created-batman-a-dc-comics-historian-weighs-in.

Karson, M. (2016, March 14). *Working with involuntary therapy patients.* Psychology Today: https://www.psychologytoday.com/us/blog/feeling-our-way/201603/working-involuntary-therapy-patients.

Kaufhold, J. A. (2008). *The neuroses of Edgar Allan Poe: A fever called living.* New York, NY: iUniverse.

Kaufman, M., Goetz, T., Lipnevich, A. A., & Pekrun, M. (2018). Do positive illusions of control foster happiness? *Emotion.* Advance online publication: http://dx.doi.org/10.1037/emo0000499.

Kaufman, S. B., Kozbelt, A., Silvia, P., Kaufman, J. C., Ramesh, S., & Feist, G. J. (2016). Who finds Bill Gates sexy? Creative mate preferences as a function of cognitive ability, personality, and creative achievement. *Journal of Creative Behavior, 50*(4), 294–307.

Kelly, N. (2014). Women therapists and resistance to erotic countertransference. *Modern Psychoanalysis, 39*(2), 135–165.

Kenreck, T. (2015, August 3). *Why the Joker is the best villain of all time.* Forbes: https://www.forbes.com/sites/toddkenreck/2015/08/03/why-the-joker-is-the-best-villain-of-all-time.

Kenrick, D. T., & Funder, D. C. (1988). Profiting from controversy: Lessons from the person-situation debate. *American Psychologist, 43*(1), 23–34.

Ker, J. (1993). *A most dangerous method: The story of Jung, Freud, and Sabina Spielrein.* New York, NY: Vintage.

Kiehl, K. A. (2006). A cognitive neuroscience perspective on psychopathy: Evidence for paralimbic system dysfunction. *Psychiatry Research, 142*(2–3), 107–128.

Kiehl, K. A. (2014). *The psychopath whisperer: The science of those without conscience.* New York, NY: Broadway.

Kiehl, K. A., Bates, A. T., Laurens, K. R., Hare, R. D., & Liddle, P. F. (2006). Brain potentials implicate temporal lobe abnormalities in criminal psychopaths. *Journal of Abnormal Psychology, 115*(3), 443–453.

Kihlstrom, J. F. (2013). The person-situation interaction. In D. Carlston (Ed.), *Oxford handbook of social cognition* (pp. 786–805). New York, NY: Oxford University Press.

Kilpatrick, D. G., Resnick, H. S., Milanak, M. E., Miller, M. W., Keyes, K. M., & Friedman, M. J. (2013). National estimates of exposure to traumatic events and PTSD prevalence using DSM-IV and DSM-5 criteria. *Journal of Traumatic Stress, 26*(5), 537–547.

King, B. (2006). *The lying ape: An honest guide to a world of deception.* Cambridge, UK: Icon.

King, S. (1981/1983). *Danse macabre.* New York, NY: Berkley.

King, S. (1986). *It.* New York, NY: Viking.

Kistler, A. (2019, April 2). *Why Batman stopped killing people in 1940—and why that's been his default for eight decades.* Polygon: https://www.polygon.com/2019/4/2/18292128/batman-no-killing-rule-zack-snyder.

Kleiman, K. (2013, February 1). *Lying in therapy.* Psychology Today: https://www.psychologytoday.com/us/blog/isnt-what-i-expected/201302/lying-in-therapy.

Klock, G. (2002). *How to read superhero comics and why.* New York, NY: Continuum.

Kluger, J. (2013a, April 23). The brain of a bomber: Did damage caused by boxing play a role in the Boston bombings? Time: http://healthland.time.com/2013/04/23/cte/.

Kluger, J. (2013b, May 3). The evil brain: What lurks inside a killer's mind. Time: http://science.time.com/2013/05/03/evil-brain/.

Knight, J. R. (2004). *Bonnie and Clyde: A twenty-first-century update.* Burnet, TX: Eakin.

Koenigs, M., Kruepke, M., Zeier, J., & Newman, J. P. (2012). Utilitarian moral judgment in psychopathy. *Social, Cognitive, & Affective Neuroscience, 7*(6), 708–714.

Koenigs, M., Young, L., Adolphs, R., Tranel, D., Cushman, F., Hauser, M., & Damsio, A. (2007). Damage to the prefrontal cortex increased utilitarian moral judgments. *Nature, 446*(7138), 908–911.

Kolvachik, K. (2014, August 13). *Is it a bald-faced or bold-faced lie?* Mental Floss: http://mentalfloss.com/article/57985/it-bald-faced-or-bold-faced-lie.

Koster-Hale, J., & Saxe, R. (2013). Functional neuroimaging of theory of mind. In S. Baron-Cohen, H. Tager-Flusberg, & M. V. Lombardo, *Understanding other minds: Perspectives from developmental social neuroscience* (3rd ed., pp. 132–163). Oxford, UK: Oxford University Press.

Kottler, J. A. (2010). *The lust for blood: Why we are fascinated by death, murder, horror, and violence.* Amherst, NY: Prometheus.

Kram, M, Jr. (2001). *Ghosts of Manila: The fateful blood feud between Muhammad Ali and Joe Frazier.* New York, NY: Harper.

Kreager, D. A., & Staff, J. (2009). The sexual double standard and adolescent peer acceptance. *Social Psychology Quarterly, 72*(2), 143–164.

Kress, N. (2005). *Characters, emotion, & viewpoint: Techniques and exercises for crafting dynamic characters and effective viewpoints.* Cincinnati, OH: Writer's Digest Books.

Kroc, R. (1977). *Grinding it out: The making of McDonald's.* Raleigh, NC: Contemporary.

Krutch, J. W. (1926). *Edgar Allan Poe: A study in genius.* New York, NY: Knopf.

Kuiper, N. A., & Leite, C. (2010). Personality impressions associated with four distinct humor styles. *Scandinavian Journal of Psychology, 51*(2), 115–122.

Kus, E., Dickson, C., & Scarlet, J. (2017). Family by choice or by blood. In T. Langley (Ed.), *Supernatural psychology: Roads less traveled* (pp. 31–39). New York, NY: Sterling.

Lange, J., & Boecker, L. (2018). Schadenfreude as social-functional dominance regulator. *Emotion.* Advance online publication. https://psycnet.apa.org/doiLanding?doi=10.1037%2Femo0000454.

Langley, R. M. (2019, March 10). Personal communication.

Langley, T. (2012). *Batman and psychology: A dark and stormy knight.* Hoboken, NJ: Wiley.

Langley, T. (2014a, May 6). *DC "all good with Finger and his family"—his family responds.* NerdSpan: http://www.nerdspan.com/dc-all-good-with-finger-and-his-family-his-family-responds/.

Langley, T., Finger, A., Capullo, G., O'Nale, R., Fingeroth, D., & Coogan, P. (2014a, April). *Batman at 75.* Wizard World St. Louis Comic Con. St. Louis, MO.

Langley, T., Finger, A., Mayer, C., Nodell, J., & Wheeler-Nicholson, N. (2014b, October). *Granddaughters of the comic book revolution: The Golden Age lives!* Comics Scholars Forum, New York Comic Con, New York, NY.

Langley, T., Fingeroth, D., O'Nale, R., Finger, A., & Coogan, P. (2014c, April). *Bill Finger at 100: Who really created Batman?* Wizard World St. Louis Comic Con, St. Louis, MO.

Langley, T., Rosenberg, R., Uslan, M., Wein, L., Englehart, S., & Meriwether, L. (2012, July). *The Dark Knight Rises: Is Batman broken?* Panel presented at the Comics Arts Conference, San Diego Comic-Con International, San Diego, CA.

Large, M. M., Ryan, C. J., Nielssen, O. B., & Hayes, R. A. (2008). The danger of dangerousness: Why we must remove the dangerousness criterion from our mental health acts. *Journal of Medical Ethics, 34*(2), 877–881.

Laurent, S. M., Clark, B. A. M., Walker, S., & Wiseman, K. D. (2014). Punishing hypocrisy: The roles of hypocrisy and moral emotions in deciding culpability and punishment of criminal and civil moral transgressors. *Cognition & Emotion, 28*(1), 59–83.

Lavergne, G. M. (1997). *A sniper in the tower.* Denton, TX: University of North Texas Press.

Laverty, C. D. (1951). *Science and pseudo-science in the writings of Edgar Allan Poe* (doctoral dissertation). Durham, NC: Duke University.

Lea, R. B., Rapp, D. N., Elfenbein, A., Mitchel, A. D., & Romine, R. S. (2008). Sweet silent thought: Alliteration and resonance in poetry comprehension. *Psychological Science, 19*(7), 709–716.

Lee, S. (2016). Foreword: The head! The heart! The heroes! In T. Langley (Ed.), *Captain America vs. Iron Man: Freedom, security, psychology* (pp. xii–xv). New York, NY: Sterling.

Lee, S. (2018). Foreword: The devil you know. In T. Langley (Ed.), *Daredevil psychology: The devil you know* (pp. xii–xiii). New York, NY: Sterling.

Leistedt, S. J., & Linkowski, P. (2014). Psychopathy and the cinema: fact or fiction? *Journal of Forensic Sciences, 59*(1), 167–174.

Lenzi, G. A. (1966). Tentative requiem for the M'Naghten Rule. *Crime & Delinquency, 12*(2), 170–178.

Letamendi, A., Rosenberg, R., Langley, T., & Wein, L. (2011, July). *The superhero battlefield.* Panel presented at San Diego Comic-Con International, San Diego, CA.

Levine, J. (2014, January 17). *Nothing romantic about Harley Quinn & Joker.* Arousing Grammar: https:// arousinggrammar.com/2014/01/17/nothing-romantic-about-harley-quinn-joker/.

Levine, L. J., & Burgess, S. L. (1997). Beyond general arousal: Effects of specific emotions on memory. *Social Cognition, 15*(3), 157–181.

Levy, D. A. (1997). *Tools of critical thinking: Metathoughts for psychology.* Needham Heights, MA: Allyn & Bacon.

Levy, D. M. (2010). *Studies in sibling rivalry.* New York, NY: Kessinger.

Levy, N., Harmon-Jones, C., & Harmon-Jones, E. (2018). Dissonance and discomfort: Does a simple cognitive inconsistency evoke a negative affective state? *Motivation Science, 4*(2), 95–108.

Lieberman, M. D. (2013). *Social: Why our brains are wired to connect.* New York, NY: Crown.

Likalaruku (2009, January 10). *Joker: The very definition of a sociopath.* Comic Vine: https://comicvine. gamespot.com/profile/likalaruku/blog/joker-the-very-definition-of-a-sociopath/38841/.

Lindstromberg, S., & Boers, F. (2008). The mnemonic effect of noticing alliteration in lexical chunks. *Applied Linguistics, 29*(2), 200–222.

Linehan, M. (2014). *DBT skills training manual* (2nd ed.). New York, NY: Guilford.

Linehan, M. M., Armstrong, H. E., Suarez, A., Allmon, D., & Heard, H. L. (1991). Cognitive-behavioral treatment of chronically parasuicidal borderline patients. *Archives of General Psychiatry, 48*(12), 1060–1062.

Linehan, M. M., Schmidt, H., III, Dimeff, L. A., Craft, J. C., Kanter, J., & Comtois, K. A. (1999). Dialectical behavior therapy for patients with borderline personality disorder and drug-dependence. *American Journal on Addictions, 8,* 279–292.

Lissek, S., Bass, J. M. P., Pine, D. S., Orme, K., Dvir, S., Rosenberger, E., & Grillon, C. (2005). Sensation seeking and the aversive motivational system. *Emotion, 5*(4), 396–407.

Little, B. (2017, September 13). *A brief history of creepy clowns.* History: https://www.history.com/news/a-brief-history-of-creepy-clowns.

Lloyd, M. (2017). Psychology on trial: The other legacy of William Moulton Marston. In T. Langley & M. Wood (Eds.), *Wonder Woman psychology: Lassoing the truth.* (pp. 15-25). New York, NY: Sterling.

Locke, J. (1693/2006). *Some thoughts concerning education and of the conduct of the understanding.* Indianapolis, IN: Hackett.

Lopez, L. (2016, August 30). *Harley Quinn and the Joker romanticize domestic abuse.* Sonoma State Star: http://www.sonomastatestar.com/artsandentertainment/2016/8/30/harley-quinn-and-the-joker-romanticize-domestic-abuse.

Louhelainen, J. (2019). Forensic investigation of a shawl linked to the "Jack the Ripper" murders. *Journal of Forensic Science.* Advance online publication: https://onlinelibrary.wiley.com/doi/abs/10.1111/1556-4029.14038.

Lovecraft, H. P. (1919/1965). Letter to Reinhardt Kleiner, September 14, 1919. In A. Derleth & D. Wandrel (Eds.), *H. P. Lovecraft Selected Letters, I* (pp. 86–88). Sauk City, WI: Arkham House.

Lovecraft, H. P. (1921/1965). Letter to the Gallomo (to Galpin, Lovecraft, Moe), October 6, 1921. In A. Derleth & D. Wandrel (Eds.), *H. P. Lovecraft Selected Letters, I* (pp. 155–156). Sauk City, WI: Arkham House.

Lovecraft, H. P. (1927/2008). *Supernatural horror in literature & other literary essays.* Cabin John, MD: Wildside Press.

Lovecraft, H. P. (1930/1971). Letter to Maurice W. Moe, September 4, 1930. In A. Derleth & D. Wandrel (Eds.), *H. P. Lovecraft Selected Letters, III* (p. 167). Sauk City, WI: Arkham House.

Lovecraft, H. P. (1932/1976). Letter to Robert E. Howard, June 8, 1932. In A. Eerleth & J. Turner (Eds.), *H. P. Lovecraft selected letters, IV* (pp. 43–45). Sauk City, WI: Arkham House.

Lovecraft, H. P. (1937). The thing on the doorstep. *Weird Tales, 29*(1), 52–70.

Lupoff, R. A. (1960, April). Re-birth. *Comic Art, 1*(1).

Lyall, S. (2007, November 4). *In Stetson or wig, he's hard to pin down.* New York Times: https://www.nytimes.com/2007/11/04/movies/moviesspecial/04lyal.html.

Lynley (2016, May 1). *The Trickster archetype in storytelling.* Slap Happy Harry: http://www.slaphappy-larry.com/trickster-magician-archetype/.

M'Naghten's Case, 10 CL & F. 200, 8 Eng. Rep. 718 (1843).

Macdonald, J. M. (1963). The threat to kill. *American Journal of Psychiatry, 120*(2), 125–130.

Machiavelli, N. (1532/1903). *The prince.* London, UK: Grant Richards.

Maddrey, J. (2004). *Nightmares in red, white, and blue: The evolution of the American horror film.* Jefferson, NC: McFarland.

Mahoney, D., & Markel, B. (2016). An integrative approach to conceptualizing and treating complex trauma. *Psychoanalytic Social Work, 23*(1), 1–22.

Makridakis, S., & Moleskis, A. (2015). The costs and benefits of positive illusions. *Frontiers in Psychology, 6*, ArtID 859.

Mallett, X. (2015, July 27). *Psychopaths versus sociopaths: What is the difference?* The Conversation: http://theconversation.com/psychopaths-versus-sociopaths-what-is-the-difference-45047.

Mann, R. E., & Barnett, G. D. (2013). Victim empathy intervention with sexual offenders: Rehabilitation, punishment, or correctional quackery? *Sexual Abuse: A Journal of Research & Treatment, 25*(3), 282–301.

Manning-Jones, S., de Terte, I., & Stephens, C. (2016). Secondary traumatic stress, vicarious posttraumatic growth, and coping among health professionals: A comparison study. *New Zealand Journal of Psychology, 45*(1), 20–29.

Marmar, C. R., McCaslin, S. E., Metzler, T. J., Best, S., Weiss, D. S., Fagan, J., Liberman, A., Pole, N., Otte, C., Yehuda, R., Mohr, D., & Neylan, T. (2006). Predictors of posttraumatic stress in police and other first responders. *Annals of the New York Academy of Sciences, 1071*(1), 1–18.

Marshall, M., Lewis, S., Lockwood, A., Drake, R., Jones, P., & Croudace, T. (2005). Association between duration of untreated psychosis and outcome in cohorts of first-episode patients. *Archives of General Psychiatry, 62*, 975–983.

Marston, G. (2018, November 9). *10 best Batman and Joker stories of all time.* Newsarama: https://www.newsarama.com/22735-10-best-batman-and-joker-stories-of-all-time.html#s2.

Marston, W. M. (1917). Systolic blood pressure symptoms of deception. *Journal of Experimental Psychology, 2*(2), 117–163.

Marston, W. M. (1928). *Emotions of normal people.* Torquay, UK: Devonshire Press.

Martens, W. H. J. (2004). Therapeutic use of humor in antisocial personalities. *Journal of Contemporary Psychology, 34*(4), 351–361.

Martin, R. A., & Ford, T. (2018). *The psychology of humor: An integrative approach* (2nd ed.). London, UK: Academic Press.

Masip, J., Sporer, S. L., Garrido, E., & Herro, C. (2005). The detection of deception with the reality monitoring approach: A review of the empirical evidence. *Psychology, Crime, & Law, 11*(1), 99–122.

McClelland, D. C. (1975). *Power: The inner experience.* New York, NY: Irvington-Wiley.

McCrea, S. (2005). *The case for Shakespeare: The end of the authorship question.* Westport, CT: Greenwood.

McDonald, M. M., Donnellan, M. B., & Navarrete, C. D. (2012). A life history approach to understanding the Dark Triad. *Personality & Individual Differences, 52*(5), 601–605.

McGrath, A. (2017). Dealing with dissonance: A review of cognitive dissonance reduction. *Social & Personality Psychology Compass, 11*(12), 1–17.

McGraw, P., & Warner, J. (2014). *The humor code: A global search for what makes things funny.* New York, NY: Simon & Schuster.

McGraw, S. L., & Foley, L. A. (2000). Perceptions of insanity based on occupation of defendant and seriousness of crime. *Psychological Reports, 86*(1), 163–174.

McKay, M., Lev, A., & Skeen, M. (2012). *Acceptance and commitment therapy for interpersonal problems: Using mindfulness, acceptance, and schema awareness to change interpersonal behaviors.* Oakland, CA: New Harbinger.

McKenzie, S. (2006). Queering gender: Anima/Animus and the paradigm of emergence. *Journal of Analytical Psychology, 51*(3), 401–421.

McPhee, R. (2013, August 31). *Real Bonnie & Clyde: Has history been too harsh on her role in the infamous killer couple?* Mirror: https://www.mirror.co.uk/news/real-life-stories/real-bonnie-clyde-history-been-2239712.

Međedović, J., & Petrović, B. (2015). The Dark Tetrad: Structural properties and location in the personality space. *Journal of Individual Differences, 36*(4), 228–236.

Mehr, B. (2016). *Trouble boys: The true story of the Replacements.* Philadelphia, PA: Da Capo.

Mehta, M. (2017, April 7). *"Menacing, mercurial, droll, and diabolic"—Heath Ledger's Joker.* Medium: https://medium.com/five-guys-facts/menacing-mercurial-droll-and-diabolic-heath-ledgers-joker-3bacd80e195c.

Meier, B. P., & Dionne, S. (2009). Downright sexy: Verticality, implicit power, and perceived physical attractiveness. *Social Cognition, 27*(6), 883–892.

Mejia, X. E. (2005). Gender matters: Working with adult male survivors of trauma. *Journal of Counseling Development, 83*(1), 29–40.

Melton, G. B., Petrila, J., Poythress, N. G., Slobogin, C., Otto, R. K., Mossman, D., & Condie, L. O. (2018). *Psychological evaluations for the courts: A handbook for mental health professionals and lawyers* (4th ed.). New York, NY: Guilford.

Mental Health America (2013, October 31). *Mind over pop culture: The short stories of Edgar Allan Poe.* Mental Health America: http://www.mentalhealthamerica.net/blog/mind-over-pop-culture-short-stories-edgar-allan-poe.

Meyer, J. P. (2015, September 18; updated 2016, April 21). *Meyer: The James Holmes "Joker" rumor.* Denver Post: https://www.denverpost.com/2015/09/18/meyer-the-james-holmes-joker-rumor/.

Meyers, J. (1992). *Edgar Allan Poe: His life and legacy.* New York, NY: Cooper Square.

Meyers, P. (2010). *Liespotting: Proven techniques to detect deception.* New York, NY: St. Martin's.

Millican, J. (2016, March 26). *The top 10 horror comedies of the 21st century.* Horrorfreak News: https://horrorfreaknews.com/top-10-horror-comedies-21st-century/2596.

Molay, J. (2012, May 20). *A transgender psychology 4: The Animus and the Anima.* Crossdreamers: http://www.crossdreamers.com/2012/05/transgender-psychology-4-animus-and.html.

Molay, J. (2017, February 11). *Waking up the Anima—Jung applied to transgender women.* Crossdreamers: http://www.crossdreamers.com/2017/02/waking-up-anima-jung-applied-to.html.

Monts, J. K., Zurcher, L. A., & Nydegger, R. V. (1977). Interpersonal self-deception and personality correlates. *Journal of Social Psychology, 103*(1), 91–99.

Morreall, J. (1982). A new theory of laughter. *Philosophical Studies, 42*(2), 243–254.

Morris, A. J., Elcock, S., Hardie, T., & Mackay, R. D. (2006) Changes to (un)fitness to plead and insanity proceedings. *Journal of Forensic Psychiatry & Psychology, 17*(4), 603–610.

Morris, S. (2012, February 5). *Clowning around: Charles Dickens, Joseph Grimaldi, and Shakespeare.* The Shakespeare Blog: http://theshakespeareblog.com/2012/02/clowing-around-charles-dickens-joseph-grimaldi-and-shakespeare/.

Mougin, L. (1989). "Writer: Steve Englehart." *David Anthony Kraft's Comics Interview Super Special: Batman*, 53–63.

Müller, J. L., Gänsbauer, S., Sommer, M., Döhnel, K., Weber, T., Schmidt-Wilcke, T., & Hajak, G. (2008). Gray matter changes in right superior temporal gyrus in criminal psychopaths. Evidence from voxel-based morphometry. *Psychiatry Research, 163*(3), 213–222.

Muszalski, A. (2009, March 25). *The original inspiration for Batman's Joker, German actor Conrad Veidt.* Laughing Squid: https://laughingsquid.com/the-original-inspiration-for-batmans-joker-german-actor-conrad-veidt/.

Nairne, J. S., Thompson, S. R., & Pandeirada, J. N. (2007). Adaptive memory: Survival processing enhances retention. *Journal of Experimental Psychology: Learning, Memory, & Cognition, 33*(2), 263–273.

Namnyak, M., Tufton, N., Szekely, R., Toal, M., Worboys, S., & Sampson, E. L. (2008). "Stockholm syndrome": Psychiatric diagnosis or urban myth? *Acta Psychiatrica Scandinavica, 117*(1), 4–11.

Nasar, S. (1998). *A beautiful mind.* New York, NY: Simon & Schuster.

National Coalition Against Domestic Violence. (2017). http://www.ncadv.org.

National Domestic Violence Hotline. (2019). Get the facts and figures. NDVH: https://www.thehotline.org/resources/statistics/.

National Voice of Domestic Violence. (2018). Eliminate that seven times statistic. NDVH: https://www.thehotline.org/2013/06/10/50-obstacles-to-leaving-1-10/.

Navarro, J. N., Clevenger, S., & Marcum, C. D. (2016) (Eds). *The virtual enemy: The intersection between intimate partner abuse, technology, and cybercrime.* Durham, NC: Carolina Academic Press.

Nichols, S. (1980). *Jung and Tarot: An archetypal journey.* York Beach, ME: Weiser.

Nichols, S. (2019). *Tarot and the archetypal journey: The Jungian path from darkness to light.* Newburyport, MA: Weiser.

Nobleman, M. T. (2008, June 26). *Another Batman mystery.* Nobleman: https://www.noblemania.com/2008/06/another-batman-mystery.html.

Nobleman, M. T. (2012). *Bill the boy wonder: The secret co-creator of Batman.* Waterton, MA: Charlesbridge.

Nobleman, M. T. (2013a, January 8). *Bob Kane's niece.* Noblemania: https://www.noblemania.com/2013/01/bob-kanes-niece.html.

Nobleman, M. T. (2013b, August 11). *Carmine Infantino previously unpublished interview 6/9/06.* Noblemania: https://www.noblemania.com/2013/08/carmine-infantino-previously.html.

Nobleman, M. T. (2014, March 30). *Interview with co-author of Bob Kane's autobiography.* Noblemania: https://www.noblemania.com/2014/03/interview-with-co-author-of-bob-kanes.html.

Nutton, J., & Fast, E. (2015). Historical trauma, substance use, and indigenous peoples: Seven generations of harm from a "Big Event." *Substance Use & Misuse, 50*(7), 839–847.

Nyberg, A. K. (1998). *Seal of approval: History of the Comics Code.* Jackson, MS: University Press of Mississippi.

O'Boyle, E. H., Forsyth, D. R., Banks, G. C., & McDaniel, M. A. (2012). A meta-analysis of the Dark Triad and work behavior: A social exchange perspective. *Journal of Applied Psychology, 97*(3), 557–579.

O'Callaghan, L. (2015, October 6). *Exclusive: Jared Leto asked Grant Morrison for advice on the Joker.* Games Radar: https://www.gamesradar.com/exclusive-jared-leto-asked-grant-morrison-advice-joker/.

O'Leary, K. D. (2008). Couple therapy and physical aggression. In A. S. Gurman (Ed.). *Clinical handbook of couple therapy* (4th ed.) (pp. 478–498). New York, NY: Guilford.

O'Neil, D. (2010). Introduction. In N. C. C. Couch (Author), *Jerry Robinson: Ambassador of comics* (pp. 11–13). New York, NY: Abrams.

O'Neil, D. (2018, October 27). Personal communication.

Ogle, J. A., & Bushnell, J. A. (2014). The appeal of emotional intelligence. *Medical Education, 48*(5), 458–460.

Ogloff, J. R. P. (1991). A comparison of insanity defense standards on juror decision making. *Law & Human Behavior, 15*(5), 509–531.

Oka, M. & Whiting, J. B. (2011) Contemporary MFT theories and intimate partner violence: A review of systemic treatments. *Journal of Couple & Relationship Therapy, 10*(1), 34–52.

Olver, M. E. (2018). Can psychopathy be treated? What the research tells us. In E. L. Jelic & C. Calkins (Eds.), *New Frontiers in Offender Treatment* (pp. 287–306). New York, NY: Springer.

Opie, I., & Opie, P. (1951/1997). *The Oxford dictionary of nursery rhymes* (2nd ed.). Oxford, UK: Oxford University Press.

Orwell, G. (1949/2007). *Nineteen eighty-four.* Langhorne, PA: Chelsea House.

Otto, B. K. (2001). *Fools are everywhere: The court jester around the world.* Chicago, IL: University of Chicago Press.

Overstreet, R. M. (2005). *Overstreet comic book price guide* (35th ed.). New York, NY: Gemstone, House of Collectibles.

Ozer, E. J., Best, S. R., Lipsey, T. L., & Weiss, D. S. (2003). Predictors of posttraumatic stress disorder and symptoms in adults: A meta-analysis. *Psychological Bulletin, 129*(1), 52–73.

Pandey, M. K. (2009). *Analytical reasoning* (3rd ed.). New Delhi, Delhi, India: BSC.

Paskind, H. A. (1931). A study of phobias. *Journal of Neurology & Psychopathology, 12*(45), 40–46.

Patrick, C. J., Fowles, D. C., & Krueger, R. F. (2009). Triarchic conceptualization of psychopathy: Developmental origins of disinhibition, boldness, and meanness. *Development & Psychopathology, 21*(3), 913–938.

Paulhus, D. L. (2014). Toward a taxonomy of dark personalities. *Current Directions in Psychological Science, 23*(6), 421–426.

Paulhus, D. L., & Williams, J. M. (2002). The dark triad of personality: Narcissism, Machiavellianism, and psychopathy. *Journal of Research in Personality, 36*(6), 556–563.

Pemment, J. (2013). Psychopathy versus sociopathy: Why the distinction has become crucial. *Aggression & Violent Behavior, 18*(5), 458–461.

Peterson, T. J. (n.d.). *Sociopath definition: Extremely antisocial, no conscience*. Healthy Place: https://www. healthyplace.com/personality-disorders/sociopath/sociopath-definition-extremely-antisocial-no-conscience.

Petri, H. L. (1996). *Motivation: Theory, research, and applications* (4th ed.). Pacific Grove, CA: Brooks/Cole.

Phillips, K. R. (2005). *Projected fears: Horror films and American culture*. Westport, CT: Praeger.

Piaget, J. (1923/1926). *The language and thought of the child*. London, UK: Routledge & Kegan Paul.

Pickhardt, C. E. (2015, May 5). *Adolescence and honoring agreements*. Psychology Today: https://www.psychologytoday.com/us/blog/surviving-your-childs-adolescence/201505/adolescence-and-honoring-agreements.

Pierson, D. S. (1999). Natural killers—turning the tide of battle. *Military Review, 79*(2), 60–65.

Pink, D. H. (2009). *Drive: The surprising truth about what motivates us*. New York, NY: Riverhead.

Poca, M. A., Sahuquillo, J., Mataró, M., Benejam, B., Arikan, F., & Báguena, M. (2005). Ventricular enlargement after moderate or severe head injury: A frequent and neglected problem. *Journal of Neurotrauma, 22*(11), 1303–1310.

Poe, E. A. (1835/1981). Morella. In A. Perry, (Ed.), *The complete Edgar Allan Poe* (pp. 14–17). New York, NY: Crown.

Poe, E. A. (1838/1981). Ligeia. In A. Perry (Ed.), *The complete Edgar Allan Poe* (pp. 115–125). New York, NY: Crown.

Poe, E. A. (1843/1981a). The black cat. In A. Perry (Ed.), *The complete Edgar Allan Poe* (pp. 381–387). New York, NY: Crown.

Poe, E. A. (1843/1981b). The pit and the pendulum. In A. Perry (Ed.), *The complete Edgar Allan Poe* (pp. 344–354). New York, NY: Crown.

Poe, E. A. (1845/1981a). The Imp of the Perverse. In A. Perry (Ed.), *The complete Edgar Allan Poe* (pp. 516–520). New York, NY: Crown.

Poe, E. A. (1845/1981b). The system of Dr. Tarr and Prof. Fether. In A. Perry (Ed.), *The complete Edgar Allan Poe* (pp. 527–538). New York, NY: Crown.

Poe, E. A. (1846/1981). The cask of Amontillado. In A. Perry (Ed.), *The complete Edgar Allan Poe* (pp. 542–546). New York, NY: Crown.

Poe, E. A. (1846/1984). The philosophy of composition. In *Edgar Allan Poe: Essays and reviews* (pp. 569–577). New York, NY: Library of America.

Poe, E. A. (1848/2009). *Letter to George W. Eveleth, January 4, 1848*. Edgar Allen Poe Society of Baltimore: https://www.eapoe.org/works/letters/p4801040.htm.

Poe, E. A. (1849/1981). Hop-Frog. In A. Perry (Ed.), *The complete Edgar Allan Poe* (pp. 565–571). New York, NY: Crown.

Pomeroy, R. (2014, July 10). *Can psychopaths be cured?* Real Clear Science: https://www.realclearscience.com/blog/2014/07/can_psychopaths_be_cured.html.

Porfirio, R. (1972/2011). Bill Finger interview. In T. Andrae (Ed.), *Creators of the superheroes* (pp. 85–89). Neshannock, PA: Hermes.

Porter, A J. (2008). The dubious origins of the Batman. In D. O'Neil (Ed.), *Batman unauthorizied* (pp. 85–98). Dallas, TX: BenBella.

Poulson, R. L., Wuensch, K. L., Brown, M. B., & Braithwaite, R. L. (1997). Mock jurors' evaluations of insanity defense verdict selection: The role of death penalty attitudes. *Journal of Social Behavior & Personality, 12*(4), 1065–1078.

Powell, C. A., & Smith, R. H. (2013). Schadenfreude caused by the exposure of hypocrisy in others. *Self & Identity, 12*(4), 413–431.

Powers, B. (n.d.). *Character building: Psychopath vs. sociopath*. Bill Powers: https://authorbillpowers.com/2018/04/03/character-building-psychopath-vs-sociopath/.

Prokosch, M. D., Coss, R. G., Scheib, J. E., & Blozis, S. A. (2009). Intelligence and mate choice: Intelligent men are always appealing. *Evolution and Human Behavior, 30*(1), 11–20.

Proulx, T., & Heine, S. J. (2006). Death and black diamonds: Meaning, mortality, and the meaning maintenance model. *Psychological Inquiry, 17*(4), 309–318.

Purse, M. (2018, November 13). *How sociopaths are different from psychopaths: Both are forms of antisocial personality disorder.* Very Well Mind: https://www.verywellmind.com/what-is-a-sociopath-380184.

Quora (n.d.). *Is the Joker a psychopath or a sociopath?* Quora: https://www.quora.com/Is-the-Joker-a-psychopath-or-a-sociopath.

Quote Investigator (2013, February 10). *I rob banks because that's where the money is.* Quote Investigator: https://quoteinvestigator.com/2013/02/10/where-money-is.

Rachman, S. (2012). Health anxiety disorders: A cognitive construal. *Behaviour Research & Therapy, 50*(7–8), 502–512.

Radford, B. (2016). *Bad clowns.* Albuquerque, NM: University of New Mexico Press.

Radish, C. (2013, May 14). *Grant Morrison talks DC Comics, being a rock star in the comics world, and his take on Batman, Superman, Wonder Woman, and Multiversity.* The Collider: http://collider.com/grant-morrison-dc-comics-batman-superman-interview/.

Ranker Community (n.d.). *The greatest movie villains of all time.* Accessed April 1, 2019 from Ranker: https://www.ranker.com/crowdranked-list/the-best-movie-villains-of-all-time.

Reed, P. A. (2014, August 25). *The pen is mightier than the sword: Screenwriter Sam Hamm talks Batman '89.* Comics Alliance: https://comicsalliance.com/sam-hamm-interview-batman-89-tim-burton/.

Reed, R. (n.d.). *Secret origins of the Batman, chapter two of three: Partners of peril!* Dial B for Blog: http://www.dialbforblog.com/archives/390/.

Reichert, D. (2004). *Chasing the devil: My twenty-year quest to capture the Green River Killer.* New York, NY: Little, Brown.

Reif, A., Rösler, M., Freitag, C. M., Schneider, M., Eujen, A., Kissling, C., Wenzler, D., Jacob, C. P., Retz-Junginger, P., Thome, J., L., Lesch, K.-P., & Retz, W. (2007). Nature and nurture predispose to violent behavior: Serotonergic genes and adverse childhood environment. *Neuropsychopharmacology, 32*(11), 2375–2383.

Ressler, R. K., Burgess, A. W., & Douglas, J. E. (1988). *Sexual homicide patterns and motives.* New York, NY: Simon & Schuster.

Reveley, A. M., Reveley, M. A., & Murray, R. M. (1984). Cerebral ventricular enlargement in non-genetic schizophrenia: A controlled twin study. *British Journal of Psychiatry, 144*(1), 89–93.

Reyes, M. (2017, September 8). *Master of horror Stephen King revealed his personal feelings on clowns.* Business Insider: https://www.businessinsider.com/stephen-king-thinks-clowns-are-scary-2017-9.

Ringgenberg, S. (1988/2012, November 28). *Jerry Robinson interview, 1988.* Barry's Pearls of Comic Book Wisdom: http://forbushman.blogspot.com/2012/11/jerry-robinson-interview-1988.html.

Roberts, W. W., & Nagel, J. (1996). First-order projections activated by stimulation of hypothalamic sites eliciting attack and flight in rats. *Behavioral Neuroscience, 10*(3), 509–527.

Robinson, A. V. (2017, September 21). *Harley Quinn and Poison Ivy: The greatest partnership.* DC Comics: https://www.dccomics.com/blog/2017/09/21/harley-quinn-and-poison-ivy-the-greatest-partnership.

Robinson, E. V., & Rogers, R. (2015). Empathy faking in psychopathic offenders: The vulnerability of empathy measures. *Journal of Psychopathology & Behavioral Assessment, 37*, 545–552.

Robinson, J. (1974/2011). *The comics: An illustrated history of comic strip art.* Milwaukie, OR: Dark Horse.

Robinson, J. (2009, July). Personal communication.

Robinson, J. (2010, September). Personal communication.

Robinson, J. (2011, July). Personal communication.

Robinson, J. (2017). *Jerry and the Joker: Adventures and comic art.* Milwaukie, OR: Dark Horse.

Robinson, K. M. (n.d.). *Sociopath vs. psychopath: What's the difference?* WebMD: https://www.webmd.com/mental-health/features/sociopath-psychopath-difference#1.

Rodriguez, D. N., & Strange, D. (2015). False memories for dissonance-inducing events. *Memory, 23*(2), 203–212.

Rogers, C. (1956). Client-centered theory. *Journal of Counseling Psychology, 3*(2), 115–120.

Rogers, R. (2008). *Clinical assessment of malingering and deception* (3rd ed.) New York, NY: Guilford.

Ronson, J. (2011). *The psychopath test: A journey through the madness industry.* New York, NY: Riverhead.

Rose, L. E., & Campbell, J. (2000). The role of social support and family relationships in women's responses to battering. *Health Care for Women International, 21*(1), 27–39.

Rosenberg, R., Langley, T., Robinson, J., Englehart, S., Uslan, M., & West, A. (2009, July). *Is the Joker a psychopath? You decide!* Comics Arts Conference, San Diego Comic-Con International, San Diego, CA.

Ross, L. (1977). The intuitive psychologist and his shortcomings: Distortions in the attribution process. In L. Berkowitz (Ed.), *Advances in experimental social psychology* (pp. 173–220). New York, NY: Academic Press.

Rozin, P., Haidt, J., and McCauley, C. R. (1999). Disgust: The body and soul emotion. In T. Dalgleish & M. J. Power (Eds.), *Handbook of cognition and emotion* (pp. 429–445). Hoboken, NJ: Wiley.

Rozin, P., Lowery, L., & Ebert, R. (1994). Varieties of disgust faces and the structure of disgust. *Journal of Personality & Social Psychology, 66*(5), 870–881.

Rule, A. (1980). *The stranger beside me.* New York, NY: Penguin.

Salekin, R. T. (2002). Psychopathy and therapeutic pessimism: Clinical lore or clinical reality? *Clinical Psychology Review, 22*(1), 79–112.

Salisbury, M. (2000). *Artists on comic art.* London, UK: Titan.

Sapolsky, R. (1994). *Why zebras don't get ulcers: The acclaimed guide to stress, stress-related diseases, and coping* (3rd ed.). New York, NY: Holt.

Sasser, M., & Sasser, C. W. (2014). *Fire cops: On the case with America's arson investigators.* New York, NY: Gallery.

Saxe, R., & Kanwisher, N. (2003). People thinking about thinking people: The role of the temporo-parietal junction in "theory of mind." *Neuroimage, 19*(4), 1835–1842.

Schalling, D. (1978). Psychopathy-related personality variables and the psychophysiology of socialization. In R. D. Hare & D. Schalling (Eds.), *Psychopathic behavior: Approaches to research* (pp. 85–106). Chichester, UK: Wiley.

Schindler, I., Zink, V., Windrich, J., & Menninghaus, W. (2013). Admiration and adoration: Their different ways of showing and shaping who we are. *Cognition & Emotion, 27*(1), 85–118.

Schlender, S. (2014, October 1). *No joke: US professor unlocks humor code.* VOA: https://www.voanews.com/a/it-is-no-joke-as-us-professor-unlocks-humor-code/2469440.html.

Schmidt, N. B., & Joiner, T. E. (2002). Structure of the Anxiety Sensitivity Index psychometrics and factor structure in a community sample. *Journal of Anxiety Disorders, 16*(1), 33–49.

Schreiber, C. (1973). *Sybil.* Washington, DC: Regnery.

Schultz, D. P., & Schultz, S. E. (2012). *A history of modern psychology* (10th ed.). Belmont, CA: Wadsworth.

Schulze, L., Dziobek, I., Vater, A., Heekeren, H. R., Bajbouj, M., Renneberg, B., Heuser, I., & Roepke, S. (2013). Gray matter abnormalities in patients with narcissistic personality disorder. *Journal of Psychiatric Research, 47*(10), 1363–1369.

Seifert, B. (2014, August 14). *The Bob Kane files: What Kane's personal copies of the earliest Batman comics tells us about one of comics history's most enigmatic creators.* Bleeding Cool: https://www.bleeding-cool.com/2014/08/14/the-bob-kane-files-what-kanes-personal-copies-of-the-earliest-batman-comics-tells-us-about-one-of-comics-historys-most-enigmatic-creators/.

Selle, K., Brown, A. A., El-Alayli, A., & Ewert, S. (2017). Grandiose narcissists' public versus private attributions for a collaborative success. *Current Psychology.* Advance online publication: https://link.springer.com/article/10.1007/s12144-017-9628-2.

Senelick, L. (1995). Harlequin. In M. Banham (Ed.), *The Cambridge guide to the theatre* (new ed., p. 472). Cambridge, MA: Cambridge University Press.

Serafino, J. (2013, September 8). *The 25 greatest comic book villains of all time.* Complex: https://www.complex.com/pop-culture/2013/09/greatest-comic-book-villains.

Shakespeare, W. (1623/1982a). *King Lear.* In *The illustrated Stratford Shakespeare* (pp. 832–862). London, UK: Chancellor.

Shakespeare, W. (1623/1982b). *Twelfth night: or, what you will.* In *The illustrated Stratford Shakespeare* (pp. 289–311). London, UK: Chancellor.

Sharrett, C. (1991). Batman and the twilight of the idols: An interview with Frank Miller. In R. E. Pearson & W. Uricchio (Eds.), *The many lives of the Batman* (pp. 33–46). New York, NY: Routledge.

Shpancer, N. (2017, August 18). *Confused about successful jerks? Get to know the dark triad.* Psychology Today: https://www.psychologytoday.com/us/blog/insight-therapy/201708/confused-about-successful-jerks-get-know-the-dark-triad.

Siegel, A. (2005). *The neurobiology of aggression and rage.* Boca Raton, FL: CRC Press.

Siegel, A., Bhatt, S., Bhatt, R., & Zalcman, S. S. (2007). The neurobiological bases for development of pharmacological treatments of aggressive disorders. *Current Neuropharmacology, 5*(2), 135–147.

Siegler, R. S., DeLoache, J. S., & Eisenberg, N. (2003). *How children develop.* New York, NY: Worth.

Simone, G. (1999). *Front page.* Women in Refrigerators: https://www.lby3.com/wir/.

Sims, C. (2013, September 13). *Ask Chris #164: Bob Kane is just the worst.* Comics Alliance: https://comicsalliance.com/ask-chris-164-bob-kane-is-just-the-worst/.

Sinfield, A. (2004). *On sexuality and power.* New York, NY: Columbia University Press.

Singer, S. D., & Hensley, C. (2004). Learning theory to childhood and adolescent firesetting: Can it lead to serial murder? *International Journal of Offender Therapy & Comparative Criminology, 48*(4), 461–476.

Skibba, R. (2016, November 3). *Psychologists argue about whether smiling makes cartoons funnier.* Nature: https://www.nature.com/news/psychologists-argue-about-whether-smiling-makes-cartoons-funnier-1.20929#/b1.

Skinner, B. F. (1939). The alliteration in Shakespeare's sonnets: A study in literary behavior. *Psychological Record, 3*(16), 186–192.

Skodol, A. E., et al. (2011). Personality disorder types proposed for DSM-5. *Journal of Personality Disorders, 25*(2), 136–169.

Skrapec, C., & Ryan, K. (2016). *The Macdonald triad: Persistence of an urban legend.* Paper presented at the annual meeting of the American Society of Criminology, San Francisco CA.

Sliter, M., Kale, A., & Yuan, Z. (2014). Is humor the best medicine? The buffering effect of coping humor on traumatic stressors in firefighters. *Journal of Organizational Behavior, 35*(2), 257–272.

Smári, J., Erlendsdóttir, G., Björgvinsdóttir, A., & Ágústsdóttir, V. R. (2003). Anxiety sensitivity and trait-symptom measures of anxiety and depression. *Anxiety, Stress, & Coping, 16*(4), 375–386.

Śmieja, M., & Stolarski, M. (2016). Assortative mating for emotional intelligence. *Current Psychology, 37*(1), 180–187.

Smith, M. K., & Montgomery, M. B. (1989). The semantics of winning and losing. *Language in Society, 18*(1), 31–57.

Smith, R. A. (2001). *Challenging your preconceptions: Thinking critically about psychology* (2nd ed.). Belmont, CA: Wadsworth.

Sociopath World (2011, July 24). *The Joker.* Sociopath World: http://www.sociopathworld.com/2011/07/joker.html.

Sonne, J. L., & Jochai, D. (2014). The "vicissitudes of love" between therapist and patient: A review of the research on romantic and sexual feelings, thoughts, and behaviors in psychotherapy. *Journal of Clinical Psychology, 70*(2), 182–195.

Sparr, L. F. (2009). Personality disorder and criminal law: An international perspective. *Journal of the American Academy of Psychiatry & the Law, 37*(2), 168–181.

Speaight, G. (1980). *The book of clowns.* London, UK: Sidgwick & Jackson.

Spencer, N. (2012, April 16). *Machiavelli's The Prince, part four: Benevolence to complement brutality.* The Guardian: https://www.theguardian.com/commentisfree/2012/apr/16/machiavelli-the-prince-benevolence.

Spinelli, E. (2005). *The interpreted world: An introduction to phenomenological psychology* (2nd ed.). Thousand Oaks, CA: Sage.

Staley, B. (2018, February 18). *A history of Marvel's incredible, cannibalistic Hulk.* Comic Book Resources: https://www.cbr.com/incredible-hulk-cannibal-history/.

State v. Shank (1988). 322 N.C. 243, 367 S.E.2d 639.

Stefana, A. (2017). Erotic transference. *British Journal of Psychotherapy, 33*(4), 505–513.

Stein, S. (2014, June 23). *The vestigial clown.* Paris Review: https://www.theparisreview.org/blog/2014/06/23/the-vestigial-clown/.

Steranko, J. (1970). *The Steranko history of comics* (title page), a.k.a. *History of comics—volume one* (indicia). Reading, PA: Supergraphics.

Stern, A. (1938). Psychoanalytic investigation of and therapy in the borderline group of neuroses. *Psychoanalytic Quarterly, 7*(4), 467–489.

Stevens, D. (2008, July 17). *No joke.* Slate: https://slate.com/culture/2008/07/the-dark-knight-reviewed.html.

Stone, E. A. (2017). Do women compete for mates when men are scarce? Sex ratio imbalances and women's mate competition cross-culturally. In M. L. Fisher (Ed.), *The Oxford handbook of women and competition* (pp. 249–264). New York, NY: Oxford University Press.

Stover, B. (2019, March 25). [Social media comment]. Re: https://www.facebook.com/drtravislangley/posts/2322003834500162.

Strack, F., Martin, L. L., & Stepper, D. (1988). Inhibiting and facilitating conditions of the human smile: A nonobtrusive test of the facial feedback hypothesis. *Journal of Personality & Social Psychology, 54*(5), 768–777.

Strube, M. J., & Barbour, L. S. (1984). Factors related to the decision to leave an abusive relationship. *Journal of Marriage and the Family, 46*(4), 837–844.

Substance Abuse and Mental Health Service Administration. (2014). *SAMHSA's concept of trauma and guidance for a trauma-informed approach.* HHS Publication No. (SMA) 14-4884. Rockville, MD: Substance Abuse & Mental Health Services Administration.

Sullivan, E. A., & Kosson, D. S. (2006). Ethnic and cultural variations in psychopathy. In C. J. Patrick (Ed.), *Handbook of psychopathy* (pp. 437–458). New York, NY: Guilford.

Swann, W. B., Jr. (1997). The trouble with change: Self-verification and allegiance to the self. *Psychological Science, 8*(3), 177–183.

Swartz, H. A., Cyranowski, J. M., Cheng, Y., & Amole, M. (2018). Moderators and mediators of a maternal depression treatment study: Impact of maternal trauma and parenting on child outcomes. *Comprehensive Psychiatry, 86*, 123–130.

Sweetman, J., Spears, R., Livingstone, A. G., & Manstead, A. S. (2013). Admiration regulates social hierarchy: Antecedents, dispositions, and effects on intergroup behavior. *Journal of Experimental Social Psychology, 49*(3), 534–542.

Tajjudin, I., & Goodwin, J. (2016, May 24). *The Joker: Mental status examination.* PsychCentral: https://pro.psychcentral.com/the-joker-mental-status-examination/.

Tapley, K. (2008, August 11). *Ledger drew inspiration from the work of Grant Morrison.* In Contention: http://www.incontention.com/2008/08/11/ledger-drew-inspiration-from-the-work-of-grant-morrison/.

Taylor, S. E. (1989). *Positive illusions: Creative self-deception and the healthy mind.* New York, NY: Basic.

Taylor, S., Koch, W. J., Woody, S., & McLean, P. (1996). Anxiety sensitivity and depression: How are they related? *Journal of Abnormal Psychology, 105*(3), 474–479.

Tedeschi, R. G., & Calhoun, L. G. (2004). Posttraumatic growth: Conceptual foundations and empirical evidence. *Psychological Inquiry, 15*(1), 1–18.

thatguitarrguy (2012, October 4). *It takes me back . . . (analysis of "The Cask of Amontillado" by Edgar Allan Poe).* thatguitarrguy: https://thatguitarrguy.wordpress.com/2012/10/04/it-takes-me-back-analysis-of-the-cask-of-amontillado-by-edgar-allan-poe/.

Thigpen, C. H., & Cleckley, H. M. (1957). *The three faces of Eve.* New York, NY: McGraw-Hill.

Thill, S. (2009, December 22). *Who's the best Batman of all time?* Wired: https://www.wired.com/2009/12/best-batman/.

Thomas, M. E. (2013). *How to spot a sociopath.* Psychology Today: https://www.psychologytoday.com/us/articles/201305/how-spot-sociopath.

Thorne, N. (2014, April 5). *Perfect chaos: Why the Joker is the greatest comic-book villain.* Sequart: http://sequart.org/magazine/40157/perfect-chaos-why-the-joker-is-the-greatest-comic-book-villain/.

Thorson, J. A. (1985). A funny thing happened on the way to the morgue: Some thoughts on humor and death, and a taxonomy of the humor associated with death. *Death Studies, 9*(3–4), 201–216.

Tilley, C. L. (2012). Seducing the innocent: Fredric Wertham and the falsifications that helped condemn comics. *Information & Culture: A Journal of History, 47*(4), 383–413.

Tollin, A. (1975). Profile on Jerry Robinson—creator of the Joker. *The Amazing World of DC Comics, 2*(4), 2–7.

Tracy, N. (n.d.). *Psychopath vs. sociopath: What's the difference?* Healthy Place: https://www.healthyplace.com/personality-disorders/psychopath/psychopath-vs-sociopath-what-s-the-difference.

Tracy, S. J., Myers, K. K., & Scott, C. W. (2006). Cracking jokes and crafting selves: Sensemaking and identity management among human service workers. *Communication Monographs, 73*(3), 283–308.

Treger, S., Sprecher, S., & Erber, R. (2013). Laughing and liking: Exploring the interpersonal effects of humor use in initial social interactions. *European Journal of Social Psychology, 43*(6), 532–543.

Triezenberg, K. (2004). Humor enhancers in the study of humorous literature. *Humor: International Journal of Humor Research, 17*(4), 411–418.

Twelftree, B. (2015, July 14). *Batman and the Joker: An iconic comic book bromance.* Fernby Films: https://www.fernbyfilms.com/2015/07/14/batman-and-the-joker-an-iconic-comic-book-bromance/.

Twine, F. W. (2013). *Girls with guns: Firearms, feminism and militarism.* London, UK: Routledge.

United States v. Brawner, 471 F.2d 9696 (D.C. Cir. 1972).

Uslan, M. (2011). *The boy who loved Batman: A memoir.* San Francisco, CA: Chronicle.

Uslan, M. (February 3, 2019). Personal communication.

USLegal (n.d.). *The insanity defense among the states.* USLegal: https://criminallaw.uslegal.com/defense-of-insanity/the-insanity-defense-among-the-states/.

Vaillant, G. E. (1977/1998). *Adaptation to life.* Cambridge, MA: Harvard University Press.

Vall, B., Seikkula, J., Laitila, A., & Holma, J. (2015). Dominance and dialogue in couple therapy for psychological intimate partner violence. *Contemporary Family Therapy, 38*(2), 223–232.

Van der Kolk, B. (2014). *The body keeps the score: Brain, mind, and body in the healing of trauma.* New York, NY: Penguin.

Verbeke, W. J. M. I., Rietdijk, W. J. R., van den Berg, W. E., Dietvorst, R. C., Worm, L., & Bagozzi, R. P. (2011). The making of a Machiavellian brain: A structural MRI analysis. *Journal of Neuroscience, Psychology, & Economics, 4*(4), 205–216.

Veselka, L, Schermer, J. A., Martin, R. A., & Vernon, P. A. (2010). Relations between humor styles and the Dark Triad traits of personality. *Personality & Individual Differences, 48*(6), 772–774.

Vess, M., Routledge, C., Landau, M. J., & Arndt, J. (2009). The dynamics of death and meaning: The effects of death-relevant cognitions and personal need for structure on perceptions of meaning in life. *Journal of Personality & Social Psychology, 97*(4), 728–744.

Vicary, A. M. (2011). *An investigation into the potential romantic appeal of convicted killers* (Unpublished doctoral dissertation). University of Illinois at Urbana-Champaign, Champaign, IL.

Vicary, A. M., & Fraley, R. C. (2010). Captured by true crime: Why are women drawn to tales of rape, murder, and serial killers? *Social Psychological & Personality Science, 1*(1), 81–86.

Vineyard, J. (2008, August 4). *Arkham Asylum scribe Grant Morrison opens up about Heath Ledger's Joker diary.* MTV: http://www.mtv.com/news/movies//2008/08/04/arkham-asylum-scribe-grant-morrison-opens-up-heath-ledgers-joker-diary/. [Not online as of this writing. See Tapley (2008) for summary and excerpt.]

Voger, M. (2006). *The Dark Age: Grim, great & gimmicky post-modern comics.* Raleigh, NC: TwoMorrows.

Wade, T. J., & Fowler, K. (2006). Sex differences in response to sexual and emotional infidelity: Considerations of rival attractiveness and financial status. *Journal of Cultural & Evolutionary Psychology, 4*(1), 37–50.

Wallace, D. (2011). *The Joker.* New York, NY: Universe.

Wagenmakers, T. B., Beek, T., Dijkhoff, G., & Zwaan, R. A. (2016). Registered replication report: Strack, Martin, & Stepper (1988). *Perspectives on Psychological Science, 11*(6), 917–928.

Walen, S. R. (1982). Phrenophobia. *Cognitive Therapy & Research, 6*(4), 399–408.

Walker, L. (1979). *The battered woman.* New York, NY: Harper & Row.

Walker, L. E. (1984). *Battered woman syndrome.* New York, NY: Springer.

Walters, S. B. (2000). *The truth about lying: How to spot a lie and protect yourself from deception.* Naperville, IL: Sourcebooks.

Warren, C., & McGraw, A. P. (2016). Differentiating what is humorous from what is not. *Journal of Personality & Social Psychology, 110*(3), 407–430.

Watson, J. B. (1920). Conditioned emotional reactions. *Journal of Experimental Psychology, 3*(1), 1–14.

Webb, C. T., & Levinson, D. F. (1993). Schizotypal and paranoid personality disorder in the relatives of patients with schizophrenia and affective disorders: A review. *Schizophrenia Research, 11*(1), 81–92.

Weems, S. (2014). *Ha! The science of when we laugh and why.* New York, NY: Basic.

Wein, L. (2015, September 11). Personal communication.

Weinberger, D. R., Bigelow, L. B., Kleinman, J. E., Klein, S. T., Rosenblatt, J. E., & Wyatt, R. J. (1980). Cerebral ventricular enlargement in chronic schizophrenia: An association with poor response to treatment. *Archives of General Psychiatry, 37*(1), 11–13.

Weiner, B. (2006). *Social motivation, justice, and the moral emotions.* Mahwah, NJ: Erlbaum.

Weiner, B. A. (1985). The insanity defense: Historical development and present status. *Behavioral Sciences & the Law, 3*(1), 3–35.

Weiner, B., Perry, R. P., & Magnusson, J. (1988). An attribution analysis of reactions to stigmas. *Journal of Personality & Social Psychology, 55*(5), 738–748.

Weiner, R. G., & Peaslee, R. M. (2015). Introduction. In R. M. Peaslee & R. G. Weiner (Eds.), *The Joker: A serious study of the Clown Prince of Crime.* Jackson, MS: University Press of Mississippi.

Weiner, R., Peaslee, R., Langley, T., Means-Shannon, H., Wein, L., & Litsey, R. (2016, July). *The Joker: Serious study of the clown prince of crime.* Panel presented at the Comics Arts Conference, San Diego Comic-Con International, San Diego, CA.

Weiss, T. C. (2013, November 13; rev. 2017, March 19). *Sociopaths: Symptom and traits.* Disabled World: https://www.disabled-world.com/disability/types/psychological/sociopaths.php.

Weldon, G. (2016). *The caped crusade: Batman and the rise of nerd culture.* New York, NY: Simon & Schuster.

Wendt, S., Buchanan, F., Dolman, C., & Moss, D. (2018). Engagement: Narrative ways of working with men when domestic violence is noticed in couple counselling. *Journal of Social Work.* https://doi.org/10.1177/1468017318794253.

Wenger, J. L., & Brown, R. O. (2014). Sport fans: Evaluating the consistency between implicit and explicit attitudes toward favorite and rival teams. *Psychological Reports, 114*(2), 572–584.

Werth, K. (1979). *Noodles, nitwits, and numbskulls.* New York, NY: Dell.

Wertham, F. (1954/2004). *Seduction of the innocent.* New York, NY: Rinehart.

Wertheimer, M. (2000). *A brief history of psychology* (4th ed.). Fort Worth, TX: Harcourt.

White, A. (2017, April 24). *Heath Ledger's fatal overdose wasn't a result of Joker role, claims sister.* The Telegraph: https://www.telegraph.co.uk/films/0/heath-ledgers-fatal-overdose-wasnt-result-joker-role-claims/.

White, E. B. (1941/1980). Some remarks on humor. In E. B. White & K. S. White (Eds.), *A subtreasury of American humor* (pp. xi–xxii). New York, NY: Coward McCann.

White, M. D. (2008). Why doesn't Batman kill the Joker? In M. D. White & R. Arp (Eds.), *Batman and philosophy: The dark knight of the soul* (pp. 5–16). Hoboken, NJ: Wiley.

White, M. K. (2007). *Maps of narrative practice.* New York, NY: Norton.

Whitenton, L. (2015, October 9). *Montrestor the OJ (original Joker)? "The Cask of Amontillado" by Edgar Allan Poe.* Whitenton World: https://whitentonworld.weebly.com/blog/montresor-the-oj-original-joker-the-cask-of-amontillado-by-edgar-allan-poe.

Whitman, C. (1966, July 31). [Letter].

Whitson, J. A., & Galinsky, A. D. (2008). Lacking control increases illusory pattern perception. *Science, 322*(5898), 115–117.

Wiener, J. L., & Mowen, J. C. (1986). Source credibility: On the independent effects of trust and expertise. In R. J. Lutz (Ed.), *Advances in Consumer Research*, vol. 13 (pp. 306–310). Provo, UT: Association for Consumer Research.

Wilding, M. (2016, August 22). *Why reaching your goals can surprisingly make you less happy.* Forbes: https://www.forbes.com/sites/melodywilding/2016/08/22/why-reaching-your-goals-can-surprisingly-make-you-less-happy/#296871bfb880.

Wildman, R. (Ed.) (1974). *The Joker: A celebration of 75 years.* New York, NY: DC Comics.

Williams, O. (2016, October 5). *Empire's greatest villains—The top 50.* Empire: https://www.empireonline.com/movies/features/greatest-villains/.

Williams-Washington, K. N., & Mills, C. P. (2018). African American historical trauma: Creating an inclusive measure. *Journal of Multicultural Counseling & Development, 46*(4), 246–263.

Wisnieski, A. (2012, December 26). *Clinton in comic strips depicted two eras of life in Gotham City.* Riverdale Press: https://riverdalepress.com/stories/Clinton-comic-strips-depicted-two-eras-of-life-in-Gotham-City,51587.

Wizard Staff (2006). 100 greatest villains of all time. *Wizard, 1*(177), 84–95.

Wolf, B. (2016, February 24). *The Joker—sociopath or psychopath.* Amino: https://aminoapps.com/c/comics/page/blog/the-joker-sociopath-or-psycopath/aai0_unnYaY1lJNZMkj1VZZWP2JQjd.

Wolfe, R. (2014, April 22). Psychology professor: It's all in your head. *Arkansas Democrat-Gazette.* Online archive: https://www.arkansasonline.com/news/2014/apr/22/psychology-professor-its-all-your-head-20140422.

World Health Organization (1992). *The ICD-10 classification of mental and behavioural disorders: Clinical descriptions and diagnostic guidelines.* Geneva, Switzerland: World Health Organization.

World Health Organization (2018, December). *ICD-11 for mortality and morbidity statistics.* World Health Organization: https://icd.who.int/browse11/l-m/en.

Wyer, R. S., & Collins, J. E. (1992). A theory of humor elicitation. *Psychological Review, 99*(4), 663–688.

Yahoo Answers (n.d.). *Is the Joker a sociopath or a psychopath (Batman's Joker)?* Yahoo Answers: https://answers.yahoo.com/question/index?qid=20130612222646AAS5wPP.

Yang, Y. & Raine, A. (2009). Prefrontal structural and functional brain imaging findings in antisocial, violent, and psychopathic individuals: A meta-analysis. *Psychiatry Research: Neuroimaging, 174*(2), 81–88.

Yank, G. R., Barber, J. W., & Spradlin, W. W. (1994). Mental health treatment teams and leadership: A systems model. *Behavioral Science, 39*(4), 293–310.

Young, H. E. (1994). *Been there. Done that. Now what?* Nashville, TN: Broadman & Holman.

Young, J. E., Klosko, J. S., & Weishaar, M. E. (2006). *Schema therapy: A practitioner's guide.* New York, NY: Guilford.

Young, J., & First, M. (2003). *Schema mode listing.* Schema Therapy: http://schematherapy.com/id72.htm.

Young, L., Camprodon, J. A., Hauser, M., Pascual-Leone, A., & Saxe, R. (2010). Disruption of the right temporoparietal junction with transcranial magnetic stimulation reduces the role of beliefs in moral judgments. *Proceedings of the National Academy of Science, 107*(15), 6753–6758.

Zambrano, M. (2018, March 8). *15 times the Joker proved that he secretly loves Batman.* Screen Rant: https://screenrant.com/batman-moments-prove-joker-love/.

Zehr, E. P. (2011). *Becoming Batman: The possibility of a superhero.* Baltimore, MD: Johns Hopkins University Press.

Zeigler-Hill, V., & Besser, A. (2011). Humor style mediates the association between pathological narcissism and self-esteem. *Personality & Individual Differences, 50*(8), 1196–1201.

Zimmerman, D. J. (1986/1989a). Bob Kane. *David Anthony Kraft's Comics Interview Super Special: Batman,* 10–20. Reprint from *David Anthony Kraft's Comic Interview,* (31).

Zimmerman, D. J. (1986/1989b). Fred Finger. *David Anthony Kraft's Comics Interview Super Special: Batman,* 21–29. Reprint from *David Anthony Kraft's Comic Interview,* (31).

Zuckerman, M. (1979). *Sensation seeking: Beyond the optimal level of arousal.* Hillsdale, NJ: Erlbaum.

Zuckerman, M. (1994). *Behavioral expressions and biosocial bases of sensation seeking.* New York, NY: Cambridge University Press.

Zullo, V. L. (2018). What's diagnosis got to do with it? Psychiatry, comics, and Batman: The Killing Joke. *Inks: The Journal of the Comics Studies Society, 2*(2), 194–214.

Index